ROMAN CAMPS

DATE DUE

MY 12			

936.204
We   Welfare, Humphrey
     Roman camps in England: the field archaeology.
By Humphrey Welfare and Vivien Swan. London,
HMSO, c.1995.
     xii,196p. illus.

ISBN:0-11-300039-1

1.Excavations (Archaeology)—England. 2.Camps,
(Military)—England. 3.Romans—England. 4.Eng-
land—Antiquities, Roman. I.Swan, Vivien. II.Title.

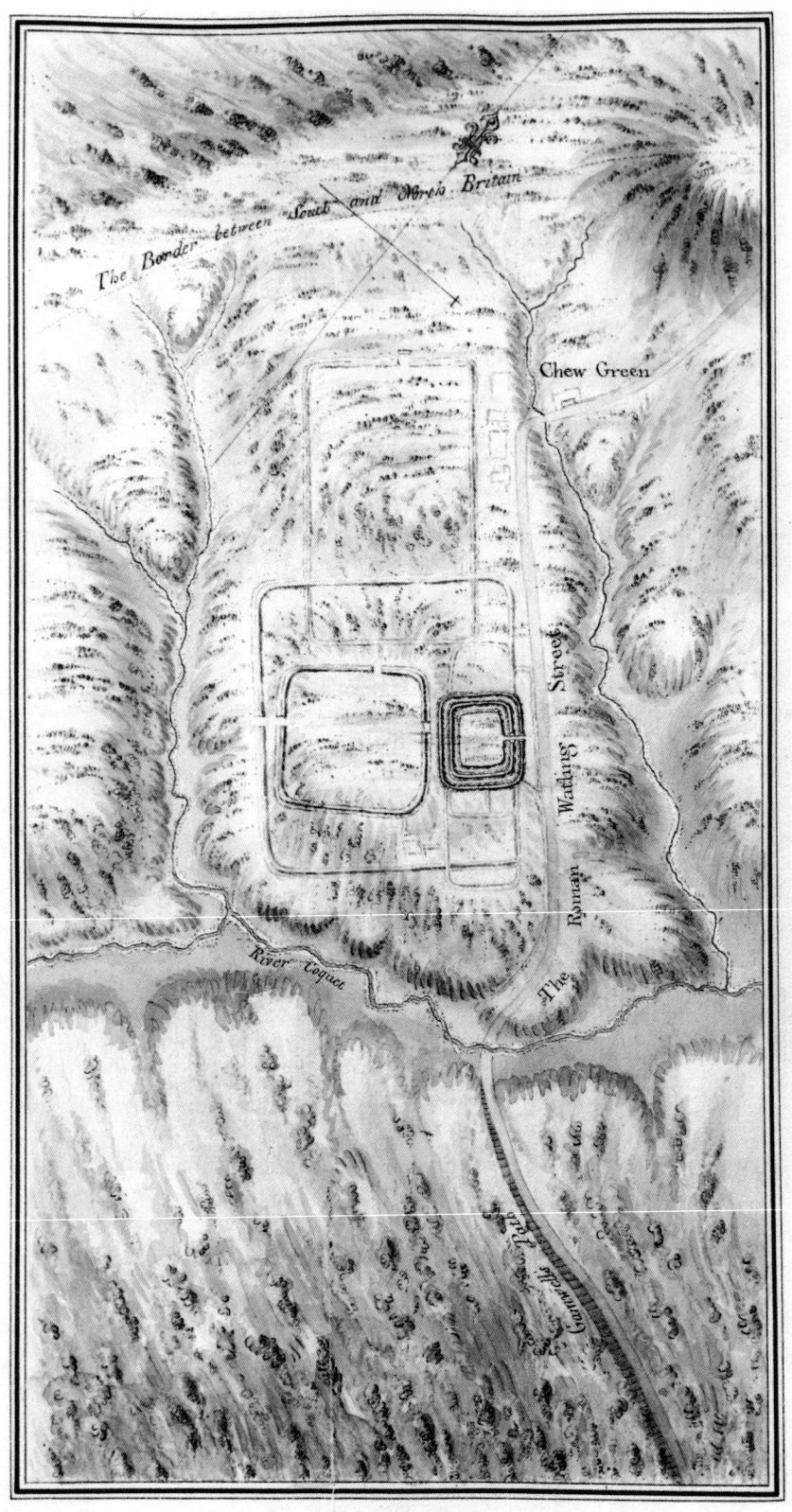

Frontispiece *The earthworks at Chew Green in Northumberland, surveyed by William Roy in 1774. The large square plan of camp I and the more elongated camp III, to the N, are clearly visible, along with the later fort and the multiple defences of the roadside fortlet. A slightly less accurate version of this survey was reproduced in Roy's posthumous* Military Antiquities of the Romans in North Britain *(1793). (Society of Antiquaries of London MS)*

ROMAN CAMPS IN ENGLAND

The Field Archaeology

Humphrey Welfare and Vivien Swan

LONDON: HMSO

© Crown copyright 1995
First published 1995

ISBN 0 11 300039 1

British Library Cataloguing in Publication Data
A CIP catalogue record for this book is available
from the British Library

Front cover photograph: RCHME, © Crown copyright. (NMR 12397/04)
Back cover photograph: Tim Gates 7/6/93. Copyright reserved. (TMG 14747/06)

Published by HMSO and available from:

HMSO Publications Centre
(Mail, fax and telephone orders only)
PO Box 276, London SW8 5DT
Telephone orders 0171 873 9090
General enquiries 0171 873 0011
(queuing system in operation for both numbers)
Fax orders 0171 873 8200

HMSO Bookshops
49 High Holborn, London WC1V 6HB
(counter service only)
0171 873 0011 Fax 0171 831 1326
68–69 Bull Street, Birmingham B4 6AD
0121 236 9696 Fax 0121 236 9699
33 Wine Street, Bristol BS1 2BQ
0117 9264306 Fax 0117 9294515
9–21 Princess Street, Manchester M60 8AS
0161 834 7201 Fax 0161 833 0634
16 Arthur Street, Belfast BT1 4GD
01232 238451 Fax 01232 235401
71 Lothian Road, Edinburgh EH3 9AZ
0131 228 4181 Fax 0131 229 2734
The HMSO Oriel Bookshop
The Friary, Cardiff CF1 4AA
01222 395548 Fax 01222 384347

The HMSO's Accredited Agents
(see Yellow Pages)

and through good booksellers

Printed in the United Kingdom for HMSO
Dd 295263 6/95 C8

Contents

List of Illustrations	vi
List of Commissioners	viii
Chairman's Foreword	ix
Acknowledgements	x
Editorial Notes	xi
Abbreviations	xii
Introduction	1
An Inventory of Roman Camps in England	29
Addenda	181
References	182
Index	186

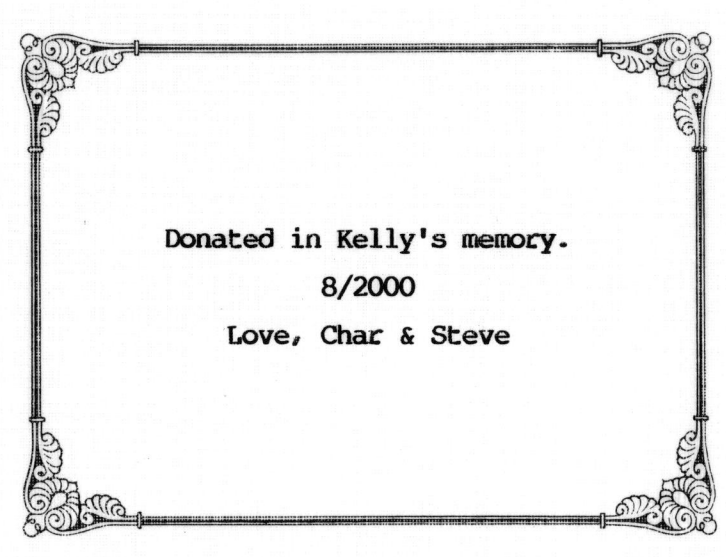

Illustrations

Frontispiece The earthworks at Chew Green in Northumberland surveyed in 1774.
Figure 1 Nowtler Hill, Cumbria, as published in *Magna Britannia* (1816).
Figure 2 Distribution of Roman camps in England.
Figure 3 Distribution of Roman camps in the vicinity of Hadrian's Wall.
Figure 4 Camps and other Roman military sites in the central section of Hadrian's Wall.
Figure 5 Rey Cross, County Durham.
Figure 6 Diagram of comparative plans.
Figure 7 Greenlee Lough, Northumberland.
Figure 8 Swine Hill 1 and 2, Northumberland.
Figure 9 Cawthorn C, North Yorkshire.
Figure 10 Plumpton Head, Cumbria.
Figure 11 Chapel Rigg, Northumberland.
Figure 12 Birdhope 1, 2 and 3, Northumberland.
Figure 13 Fell End, Northumberland.
Figure 14 North Yardhope, Northumberland.
Figure 15 Barrockside, Cumbria.
Figure 16 Barrockside, Cumbria.
Figure 17 Beaumont, Cumbria.
Figure 18 Boomby Lane 1 and 2, Cumbria.
Figure 19 Brackenrigg 1 and 2, Cumbria.
Figure 20 Brackenrigg, Cumbria.
Figure 21 Brougham, Cumbria.
Figure 22 Brougham, Cumbria.
Figure 23 Crackenthorpe, Cumbria.
Figure 24 Galley Gill and Knowe Farm, Cumbria, with Old Penrith fort to the S.
Figure 25 Golden Fleece, Cumbria.
Figure 26 Golden Fleece, Cumbria.
Figure 27 Kirkby Thore 1, 2 and 3, Cumbria.
Figure 28 Knockcross, Cumbria.
Figure 29 Knockcross, Cumbria.
Figure 30 Knowe Farm, Cumbria.
Figure 31 Langwathby Moor, Cumbria.
Figure 32 Moss Side 1 and 2, Cumbria.
Figure 33 Nowtler Hill 1 and 2, Cumbria.
Figure 34 Plumpton Head, Cumbria.
Figure 35 Troutbeck, Cumbria. Location plan of the fort and camps 1, 2 and 3.
Figure 36 Troutbeck 1, Cumbria.
Figure 37 Troutbeck 2, Cumbria.
Figure 38 Troutbeck 3, Cumbria.
Figure 39 Troutbeck 1 and 3, Cumbria.
Figure 40 Warcop, Cumbria.
Figure 41 Warcop, Cumbria.
Figure 42 Watchclose, Cumbria.
Figure 43 Willowford, Cumbria.
Figure 44 Higher Kingdon, Devon.
Figure 45 Higher Kingdon, Devon.
Figure 46 North Tawton, Devon.
Figure 47 Bowes Moor, County Durham.
Figure 48 Rey Cross, County Durham.
Figure 49 Sandforth Moor, County Durham.
Figure 50 Brampton Bryan, Hereford and Worcester.
Figure 51 Camps and other military sites in Hereford and Worcester and in southern Shropshire.
Figure 52 Buckton Park, Hereford and Worcester.
Figure 53 Shurnock, Hereford and Worcester.
Figure 54 Shurnock, Hereford and Worcester.
Figure 55 Walford, Hereford and Worcester.
Figure 56 Ancaster, Lincolnshire.
Figure 57 Newton on Trent 1 and 2, Lincolnshire.
Figure 58 Horstead, Norfolk.
Figure 59 Bagraw, Northumberland.
Figure 60 Bean Burn 1 and 2, Northumberland.
Figure 61 Bellshiel, Northumberland.
Figure 62 Birdhope 1, 2 and 3, Northumberland.
Figure 63 Brown Dikes, Northumberland.
Figure 64 Burnhead, Northumberland.
Figure 65 Carham, Northumberland.
Figure 66 Cawfields, Northumberland.
Figure 67 Cawfields, Northumberland.

Figure 68	Chapel Rigg, Northumberland.	*Figure 108*	Swine Hill 1 and 2, Northumberland.
Figure 69	Chesters Pike, Northumberland.	*Figure 109*	Twice Brewed, Northumberland.
Figure 70	Chew Green I and III, Northumberland, with fort IV and fortlet V.	*Figure 110*	Walwick Fell, Northumberland.
Figure 71	Chew Green, Northumberland.	*Figure 111*	West Woodburn, Northumberland.
Figure 72	Coesike West 1 and 2 and Coesike East, Northumberland.	*Figure 112*	Bootham Stray 1 and 2, North Yorkshire.
Figure 73	Coesike West 1 and 2 and Coesike East, Northumberland.	*Figure 113*	Breckenbrough, North Yorkshire.
Figure 74	Crooks, Northumberland.	*Figure 114*	Catterick Bridge, North Yorkshire.
Figure 75	Crooks, Northumberland.	*Figure 115*	Cawthorn C, North Yorkshire.
Figure 76	Dargues, Northumberland.	*Figure 116*	Cawthorn C, North Yorkshire.
Figure 77	Dargues, Northumberland, *c* 1850.	*Figure 117*	Cawthorn C, North Yorkshire.
Figure 78	East Learmouth, Northumberland.	*Figure 118*	Cawthorn C, North Yorkshire.
Figure 79	Farnley 1, 2 and 3, Northumberland.	*Figure 119*	Malham, North Yorkshire.
Figure 80	Featherwood East, Northumberland.	*Figure 120*	Malham, North Yorkshire.
Figure 81	Featherwood West, Northumberland.	*Figure 121*	Wath, North Yorkshire.
Figure 82	Fell End, Northumberland.	*Figure 122*	Calverton 1 and 2, Nottinghamshire.
Figure 83	Glenwhelt Leazes, Northumberland.	*Figure 123*	Farnsfield, Nottinghamshire.
Figure 84	Glenwhelt Leazes, Northumberland.	*Figure 124*	Gleadthorpe Plantation, Nottinghamshire.
Figure 85	Greenlee Lough, Northumberland.	*Figure 125*	Holme, Nottinghamshire.
Figure 86	Grindon Hill, Northumberland.	*Figure 126*	Camps and other military sites in the vicinity of Wroxeter, Shropshire.
Figure 87	Grindon School, Northumberland.	*Figure 127*	Attingham Park and Ismore Coppice, Shropshire.
Figure 88	Haltwhistle Burn 1, 2, 3 and 4, Northumberland, with the fortlet, within its outwork.	*Figure 128*	Bromfield, Shropshire.
Figure 89	Haltwhistle Burn 1, 2, 3 and 4 and Markham Cottage 1 and 2, Northumberland.	*Figure 129*	Bromfield, Shropshire.
Figure 90	Lees Hall, Northumberland.	*Figure 130*	Brompton 1 and 2, Shropshire.
Figure 91	Limestone Corner, Northumberland.	*Figure 131*	Burlington 1 and 2, Shropshire.
Figure 92	Limestone Corner, Northumberland.	*Figure 132*	Burlington 1 and 2, Shropshire.
Figure 93	Markham Cottage 1 and 2, Northumberland.	*Figure 133*	Cound Hall, Shropshire.
Figure 94	Markham Cottage 1 and 2, Northumberland.	*Figure 134*	Norton 1 and 2, Shropshire.
Figure 95	Milestone House, Northumberland.	*Figure 135*	Quatt, Shropshire.
Figure 96	Norham, Northumberland.	*Figure 136*	Stretford Bridge 1 and 2, Shropshire.
Figure 97	Norham, Northumberland.	*Figure 137*	Uffington, Shropshire.
Figure 98	North Yardhope, Northumberland.	*Figure 138*	Upper Affcot, Shropshire.
Figure 99	Seatsides 1, Northumberland.	*Figure 139*	Whittington, Shropshire.
Figure 100	Seatsides 2, Northumberland.	*Figure 140*	Norton Fitzwarren, Somerset.
Figure 101	Seatsides 2 and Twice Brewed, Northumberland.	*Figure 141*	Greensforge 4 and 5, Staffordshire.
Figure 102	Silloans, Northumberland.	*Figure 142*	Greensforge 1, 2 and 3, Staffordshire.
Figure 103	Sills Burn North and South, Northumberland.	*Figure 143*	Greensforge, Staffordshire.
Figure 104	Sunny Rigg 1, Northumberland.	*Figure 144*	Swindon, Staffordshire.
Figure 105	Sunny Rigg 1, Northumberland.	*Figure 145*	Wall 1 and 2, Staffordshire.
Figure 106	Sunny Rigg 2, Northumberland.	*Figure 146*	Water Eaton 1, 2, 3, 4 and 5, Staffordshire, with the vexillation fortress, the settlement of *Pennocrucium* and two forts.
Figure 107	Sunny Rigg 3, Northumberland.	*Figure 147*	Water Eaton 1, Staffordshire.

Commissioners

Chairman
The Right Honourable Lord Faringdon

Vice Chairman
Antony Charles Thomas CBE DL

Malcolm Airs
Amanda Arrowsmith
Martin Biddle
Richard Bradley
Michael Fulford
Richard David Harvey Gem
Derek John Keene
Trevor Reginald Mortensen Longman
Gwyn Idris Meirion-Jones
Marilyn Palmer
Anne Clare Riches
Robert Anthony Yorke

Secretary
Tom Grafton Hassall

Chairman's Foreword

Only in a few places within the bounds of the former Roman Empire do the remains of its military might still exist in such profusion and complexity, and in such a relatively good state of preservation, as in the former province of Britannia. Yet, despite their international importance and notwithstanding the considerable amount of scholarly work on them, no complete inventory of these remains has been made.

The Royal Commission on the Historical Monuments of England has long been aware of the lack of detailed information within the National Monuments Record with respect to Roman military remains. In the last ten years, many Roman forts and fortlets, aqueducts, civil settlements, signal stations, temples and cemeteries have been recorded and the whole series of monuments that comprise Hadrian's Wall have been resurveyed. In particular, all of the temporary military camps have been examined, whether their remains survive as upstanding earthworks or are revealed by cropmarks in arable land.

In publishing this book, the intention is to emphasise the importance of analytical field archaeology in relation to Roman studies. In addition, however, we wish to draw attention to the very fragile nature of this type of site and, despite the legal protection afforded to most examples, the irreversible damage and destruction that have taken place and continue to take place to Roman camps in England.

The Royal Commission has not attempted to place the camps in their historical setting nor in their military context in relation to the conquest or subjugation of the province of Britannia. This is not the primary task for the Royal Commission, and such detailed chronological and functional information is rarely forthcoming about Roman camps. Rather, as the national body of archaeological record, the Royal Commission seeks to offer an objective and accurate statement of the form and nature of these remains, which relate to the time when Britain lay within the orbit of a wider imperial world.

The Commissioners wish to express their special thanks to the landowners who have allowed access to the monuments in their charge. Without their help and co-operation the project would not have been possible. They also desire to record their appreciation of the good work accomplished by their executive staff in the production of this volume and of the archive that lies behind it. In particular they wish to acknowledge the contribution of the late Mr R A H Farrar who worked on the project until his retirement.

The complete archive of material relating to the camps is available to the public and may be consulted at the National Monuments Record Centre, Kemble Drive, Swindon SN2 2GZ.

FARINGDON

Acknowledgements

Several members of staff of the Royal Commission have contributed to the preparation of this inventory. Many of the initial surveys of the surviving earthworks were the work of the late Mr R A H Farrar. Additional ground surveys and all the descriptive accounts of the earthworks were undertaken by Humphrey Welfare, Keith Blood, Iain Sainsbury, Peter Topping, Mark Bowden, Donnie Mackay, Robert Wilson-North, Christopher Dunn, and Vivien Swan. Vivien Swan prepared the final inventory accounts of the sites represented only by cropmarks. The transcription of sites from aerial photographs has been made by Grahame Soffe and Victoria Fenner, with additional contributions from Robert Bewley, Simon Crutchley, Damian Grady, Peter Horne, David Macleod, Fiona Small and Helen Winton. The introduction has been written by Humphrey Welfare. All the line-drawings were prepared by Philip Sinton. Stephanie Taylor was responsible for all the initial editorial work, while Robin Taylor, assisted by Susan Whimster, saw the book through production; Peter Gunn prepared the index. Other members of staff involved were Mark Barratt, Moira Hegerty, Joanne Hodgson, Brian Hopper, Clare King, Richard Mead, Anthony Perry, Jonathan Prosser, Bernard Thomason, Davina Turner and Jane Waite. Genevieve Ryan and Adam Welfare assisted with some of the surveys during short-term contracts. The overall supervision of the project in its later stages was by Christopher Taylor. The Royal Commission is particularly grateful for the help and advice given by Gordon Maxwell of the Royal Commission on the Ancient and Historical Monuments of Scotland, who read and commented on the text, and to David Wilson of the Cambridge University Committee for Aerial Photography.

In addition to the Royal Commission's own national library of air photographs, within the National Monuments Record, the following provided air photographs used in the survey: Ministry of Defence (Air), Cambridge University Committee for Aerial Photography, Cumbria County Council, Professor Barri Jones, Professor Dennis Harding, Derrick Riley, Tim Gates, Raymond Selkirk, Derek Edwards and Frances Griffith. The Frontispiece is reproduced by permission of the Society of Antiquaries of London, Figure 1 is reproduced by permission of the British Library, Figures 16 and 30 are reproduced by permission of Cumbria County Council and Figures 29 and 41 are © Crown copyright/ MOD. The air photographs supplied by the Cambridge University Committee for Aerial Photography are Cambridge University Collection: copyright reserved. The map backgrounds to all illustrations of transcribed air photographic evidence are based on the Ordnance Survey 1:10 000 scale maps with the permission of the Controller of Her Majesty's Stationery Office, © Crown copyright.

Editorial Notes

The inventory includes all Roman temporary camps known in England up to March 1994, with addenda for Cheshire, Northumberland and Oxfordshire to November 1994. Not all sites previously regarded as camps have been included because in some cases re-examination of the evidence has failed to confirm their identification. Entries in the inventory are ordered first by county and then alphabetically by the name of the site. Post-1974 county boundaries and names have been adopted. Where a camp has been referred to in the past by a name other than that by which it is currently known and listed in this inventory, that former name is given in brackets.

The National Grid Reference for the centre of each camp is included at the beginning of the inventory account; its unique National Archaeological Record (NAR) number and the name of the civil parish in which it is located appear at the end of each entry. Heights above sea level are given in metres above Ordnance Datum (OD), the mean level of the sea at Newlyn in Cornwall.

New surveys were made of all the surviving earthworks at scales of 1:1 250 or 1:1 000 and they are reproduced at 1:2 500. Those sites which rely on air photographic evidence were transcribed at 1:2 500 and are here reproduced at 1:5 000. While this may not be convenient for direct comparative purposes, the scales have been chosen deliberately to reflect the inherent difference in metrical accuracy between the ground survey of the surviving earthworks of a ditch and the less direct record of such a ditch as a cropmark recorded by an aerial camera. In the illustrations in the inventory this air photographic evidence is shown in black and the topographical background, including earthworks, is screened grey. The numbers along the margins of the plans of these air photographic sites are the coordinates to the National Grid; in each case those shown are 100 m apart. Only a small number of the air photographs which exist for each site are referred to in the inventory. The remainder can be retrieved by means of the computerised record in the Air Photographs section of the National Monuments Record. Details of the location and source, the date, and the negative numbers of those photographs reproduced in this book are given in the captions.

Abbreviations

CBA	Council for British Archaeology
CUCAP	Cambridge University Committee for Aerial Photography
NAR	National Archaeological Record (a constituent part of the National Monuments Record)
NMR	National Monuments Record
NMR AP	National Monuments Record, Aerial Photographs
NRO	Northumberland Record Office
OS	Ordnance Survey
RAF	Royal Air Force
RCHME	Royal Commission on the Historical Monuments of England

Introduction

> Roman remains of several kinds, as well as several not Roman, are popularly known as 'Roman Camps'; but it is best to restrict the name to Roman works for the temporary accommodation of troops.
>
> R G Collingwood *The Archaeology of Roman Britain* (1930)

This book sets out the archaeological evidence for Roman military camps in England, concentrating on the remains that are still visible as earthworks and on the evidence that aerial photography has revealed about those that have been levelled by the plough.

By their nature, the temporary camps of any period leave relatively few remains, and as earthworks they are rarely spectacular. A Roman camp was a lightly built but effective defensive enclosure constructed to accommodate highly mobile troops 'under canvas' or, more accurately, in tents made of leather (van Driel-Murray 1990). The standard form for a camp was a rectangle with rounded angles, the familiar 'playing-card' shape, defined almost invariably by a single bank broken only by the simplest of gates. On some sites the bank was constructed wholly or partly of turf, but if soil or rubble was used this was provided from an external ditch.

Despite the apparent simplicity of the remains, the study of Roman camps is not entirely straightforward. The difficulties encountered stem from the evidence itself and from the ways in which it has been interpreted in the past. The very term 'Roman camp' has, at times, been a catch-all, used by non-specialists to encompass almost any type of archaeological earthwork. These enthusiastic misidentifications were lampooned as early as 1816 by Walter Scott in *The Antiquary*, in which Jonathan Oldbuck attempts to convince anyone who will listen that he has discovered a 'Roman camp' on the Kaim of Kinprunes. For all the familiarity of the term, however, comparatively little has been written about the particular archaeological category — temporary military defences — to which the label 'Roman camp' is properly applied. The study of Roman camps has been consistently overshadowed by and confused with the greater complexities and depths of information offered by the more permanent examples of the Roman military science of castrametation, the forts. The ruins and earthworks of the forts were easily identified by the early antiquaries who were slow to spot the more modest remains of the camps. In the early 18th century, John Horsley, the great pioneer in the study of Hadrian's Wall, noted only two, Brown Dikes in Northumberland and Watchclose in Cumbria, in an area now known to have a particularly dense concentration of camps that still survive as earthworks.

Greater clarity, and a wider consciousness, was first achieved by William Roy, an early exponent of archaeological field survey in Britain, who began to record Roman remains in Scotland in the 1750s; his posthumous publication (Roy 1793) made the earthworks of many of the surviving camps familiar to antiquaries. In England he surveyed only a few camps: Crackenthorpe in Cumbria, Rey Cross in County Durham, Chew Green in Northumberland (Frontispiece), and Cawthorn in North Yorkshire. Later publications, such as those of Daniel and Samuel Lysons (1816) and Henry MacLauchlan (1852a, 1852b; 1857; 1858), included further surveys of camps (Figs 1 and 77); in some cases the records made were of sites that were subsequently levelled by cultivation and which are now known only from cropmarks.

The phrase 'Roman temporary camp' has often been used to classify these sites. It does, however, beg the question as to how temporary any one defensive enclosure may have been. Without the most extensive and painstaking excavations, archaeology is unlikely to be able to distinguish earthworks constructed for an overnight stop or for a seasonal campaign from those sites which were regularly reoccupied, perhaps on an annual basis, in due season.

Several different Latin terms are used in the contemporary literary sources to describe various kinds of military enclosures, without there being any clear guidance to tie each term to the surviving remains or to the various

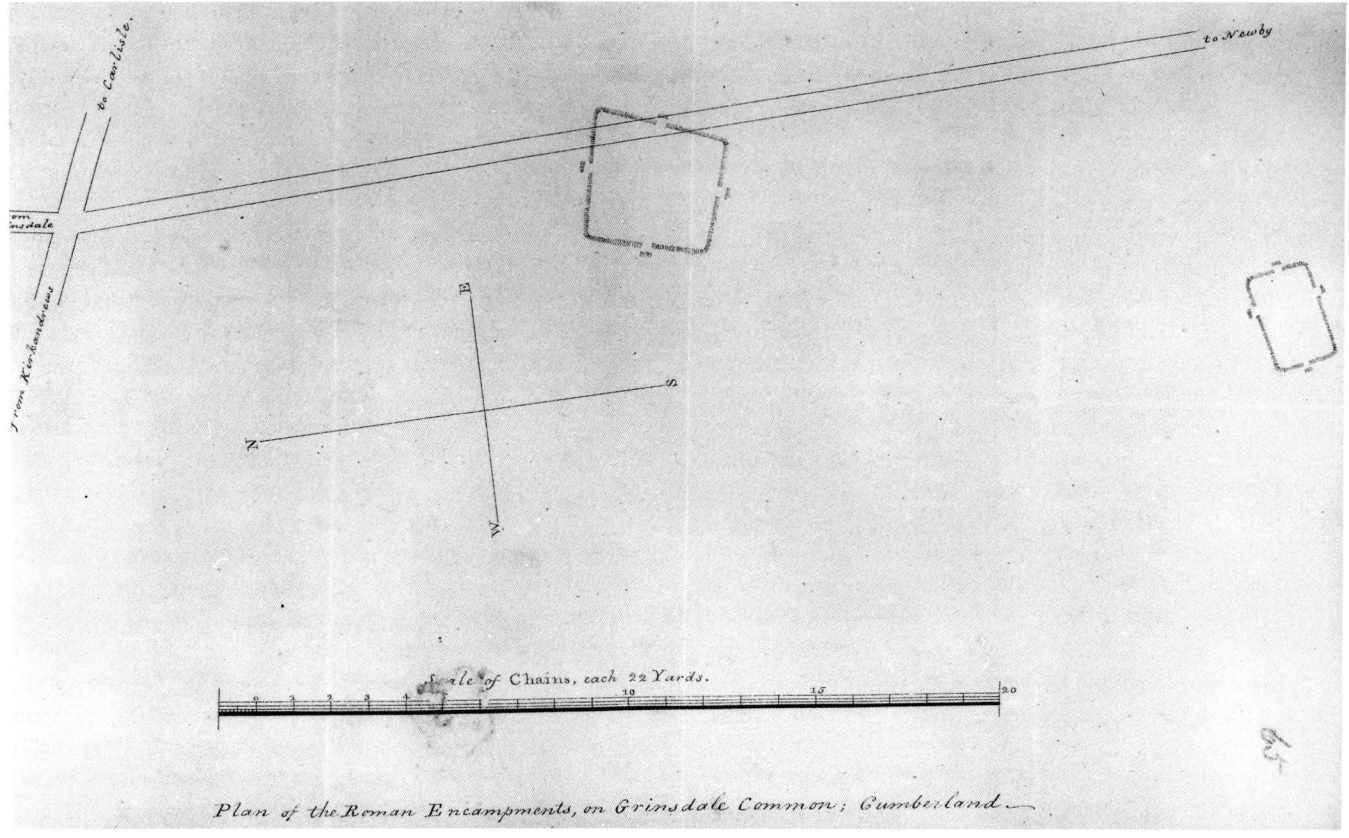

Figure 1 *Nowtler Hill, Cumbria, as published by Daniel and Samuel Lysons in* Magna Britannia *(1816). The camps were then within the area of Grinsdale Common and survived as earthworks. Subsequent cultivation has levelled the sites, and the camps are now visible only as cropmarks.* (BM Add MS 9462 fol 65)

archaeological classifications now applied to them. This problem is not confined to camps. The so-called vexillation fortresses, all apparently pre-Flavian in date, seem to have been temporary or semi-permanent; as with some of the camps, it is still unclear whether these fortresses were constructed as winter quarters or as the bases from which the army campaigned in summer (Bishop and Freeman 1993, 171–5). Neither is there complete agreement about the English terms that should be used to describe the sites treated in this book (cf Lepper and Frere 1988, 260–1). Here the simplest term of all, 'Roman camp', has been adopted, approaching the problem from the field archaeology, rather than from etymology. This generic term encompasses the various functional categories that have been assigned, usually with little concrete evidence, to some sites in the past: 'marching camps', 'labour camps' and 'practice camps' (*see* Function, *below*).

It seems that by the end of the 1st century AD, when much of Britain had been conquered by the Roman army, the form of the camp was well established and familiar; so much so, perhaps, that it was rarely described in contemporary military commentaries. A few Roman literary sources do describe the building of camps in some detail, and even purport to be military manuals. However, as will become clear in this analysis of the evidence, these idealised designs and procedures are only partly reflected in the actual structures revealed and recorded by field archaeology. The most relevant sources are *De munitionibus castrorum*, a somewhat theoretical work (Lenoir 1979) attributed to Hyginus Gromaticus, written either in the 1st century or in the 3rd century, and *Epitoma Rei Militaris* compiled from earlier sources at the end of the 4th century by Vegetius (Milner 1993). Interesting sidelights are provided by other authors, such as Josephus who wrote about the Jewish revolt against Rome in AD 66–70, and Sallust who described the Jugurthine wars in Numidia at the end of the 2nd century BC. The reliefs on Trajan's Column, in Rome, provide some contemporary illustrations (Lepper and Frere 1988, 260–6).

No attempt is made here to analyse the literary texts in detail, although occasional reference is made to them where they confirm the archaeological evidence. This emphasis on the information retrievable by field archaeology is deliberate, and is particularly appropriate when dealing with military traditions and practice of which there is now only limited knowledge. Whatever his training, and whatever the contemporary textbooks may have said, the day-to-day decisions as to where a camp should be built, and how it should be designed and constructed, were always taken by the soldier on the ground. Factors which had to be taken into account would have included the proximity of the enemy, the topography, vegetation and ground conditions, the fitness and morale of the troops, the weather, and the time until sunset. Countering these infinite variations, the traditions of the particular unit would have imposed a powerful framework within which action would be taken. The results, whether the troops were on peacetime manoeuvres or were on campaign, would always have been a compromise.

Comparatively little archaeological excavation has been carried out on the camps, and what has been done has yielded relatively little information. In particular, there is sparse evidence for the dates at which any specific Roman camp in England was constructed. The occupation of Britain lasted for more than three centuries, from the initial conquest in AD 43 to the early years of the 5th century when Rome decided that it could no longer support a garrison. The island was never fully conquered and the tension that this must have caused, especially in the North and West, ensured that a military presence was always necessary. It is safe to assume that the first of the camps were thrown up in the earliest days of the invasion, but it is not known when the practice died out. Vegetius, writing at the end of the 4th century, regrets that the traditions of camp construction had been lost, but it is possible that this was not in fact so in the remote and rather vulnerable province of Britannia. The uncertainties of the information available — the secondhand nature of most of the literary sources, the expediency demanded of soldiers in the field, and the paucity of conventional excavated evidence — somewhat obscure the study of Roman camps. This has been compounded in the 20th century when large numbers of camps have been identified as earthworks or as cropmarks. Perhaps because of their unspectacular form, scholarly attention has not been focused on objective archaeological description. Rather it has turned towards theoretical considerations, including the equations that attempt to link the sizes of camps and the details of their design to the progress of campaigns in the late 1st and the early 3rd centuries. These theories are not pursued here.

In this book it is the information available from field archaeology in England that is set out; no attempt has been made at a wider synthesis, a task which would have had to consider scattered information from the rest of the Empire, evidence which varies greatly both in its completeness and in its quality.

The Inventory of sites set out below is not likely to be an exhaustive catalogue. 'Roman camps' have been identified with bewildering frequency, and variable accuracy, by antiquaries and archaeologists since the late 16th century. There may be genuine examples, extant or destroyed, that have been missed, and the discovery of further examples is likely to continue, particularly by the recognition of cropmarks through the medium of aerial photography. Some sites have been omitted from the Inventory because the balance of the evidence did not confirm the classification, despite the fact that they may have been identified and published as camps, or even partly excavated as such, comparatively recently. The earliest 'camp' yet known in England — the invasion bridgehead of AD 43 at Richborough in Kent (Cunliffe 1968, 232–4) — is also omitted here for it would seem to be functionally and morphologically atypical.

In the following Inventory the records of over 130 camps are published. In the case of 76 of them, information as to their form is derived from the transcription of aerial photographs, supplemented by checks on the ground to establish the detailed topography. Surviving earthworks were identified for a further 56 camps; the plans published here are based, in each case, on a detailed examination and interpretation of the extant remains and a metrically accurate survey.

Survival and distribution

The known distribution of Roman camps in England is evidently incomplete (Figs 2 and 3). Their fragile remains have survived best in the marginal lands of the North and West although even here, as elsewhere, some earthworks will have been masked by the growth of peat, or by later human activity: by cultivation, by the construction of Roman forts and medieval castles, and by the growth of farms and villages. There is little doubt that those that may have existed in the arable heartlands of the South and East of England will have succumbed in a similar way, under more intensive cultivation and a denser pattern of settlement.

The problem of reconstructing the original distribution of camps is further compounded by at least three factors, each of which is hard to quantify. There is the possibility that in some camps the ditch was of small scale, and the bank — however it was constructed — represented the main defence. If a bank was built entirely of turf, no ditch would have been necessary, although one was provided nevertheless at Cawthorn (Fig 9). The subsurface remains of such camps would not produce a cropmark in arable land, and thus the site would not normally be readily identifiable by archaeological prospection. In addition, excavation has occasionally suggested that the defences examined were deliberately slighted when the troops left, and that the ditch was back-filled (*see below*); if so, a cropmark might not form above it. Finally, the diverse plans of the surviving earthworks make it likely that the cropmarks of some genuine camps may not have been recognised from the air. Any one of these factors would lessen the likelihood that camps would be detected in the lowlands.

In the upland pastures around the central section of Hadrian's Wall, there has been a long history of pastoral activity — the ideal agricultural regime for the survival of earthworks; this, combined with a great deal of antiquarian

Figure 2 *Distribution of Roman camps in England.*

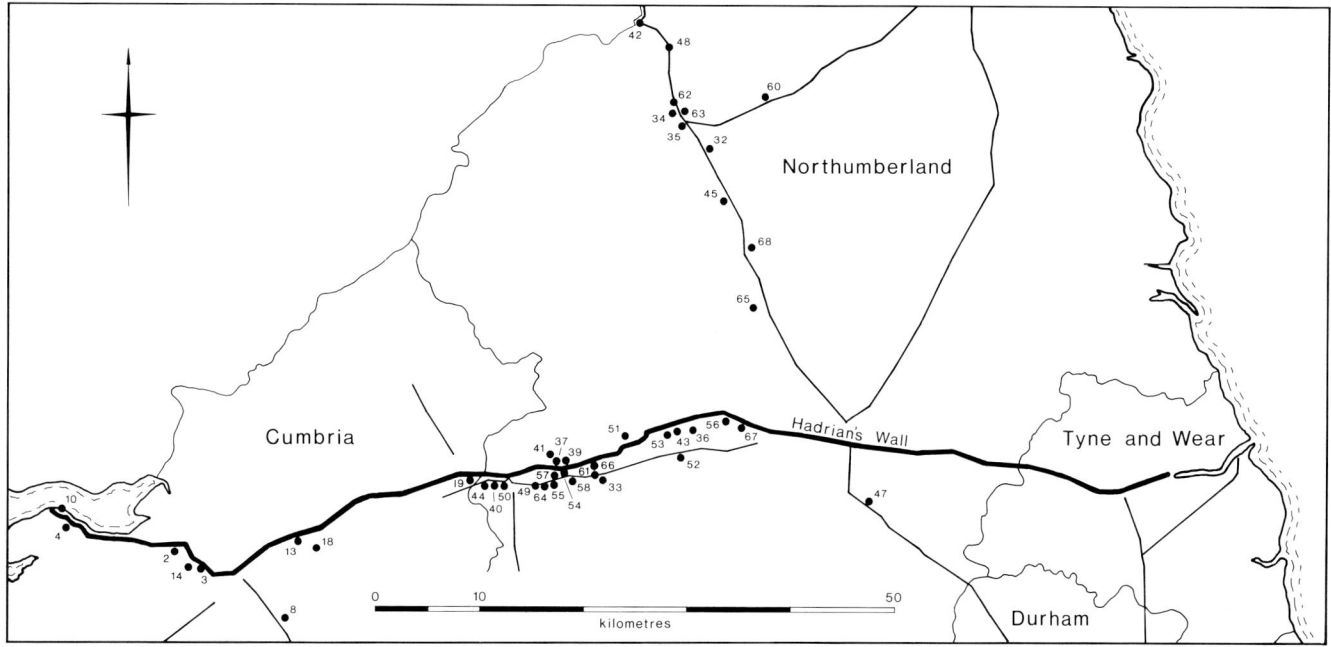

Figure 3 *Distribution of Roman camps in the vicinity of Hadrian's Wall.*

Key to Figs 2, 3, 4 and 6

Cumbria

1 Barrockside
2 Beaumont
3 Boomby Lane 1,2
4 Brackenrigg 1,2
5 Brougham
6 Crackenthorpe
7 Galley Gill
8 Golden Fleece
9 Kirkby Thore 1,2,3
10 Knockcross
11 Knowe Farm
12 Langwathby Moor
13 Moss Side 1,2
14 Nowtler Hill 1,2
15 Plumpton Head
16 Troutbeck 1,2,3
17 Warcop
18 Watchclose
19 Willowford

Devon

20 Higher Kingdon
21 North Tawton

County Durham

22 Bowes Moor
23 Rey Cross
24 Sandforth Moor

Hereford and Worcester

25 Brampton Bryan
26 Buckton Park
27 Shurnock
28 Walford

Lincolnshire

29 Ancaster
30 Newton on Trent 1,2

Norfolk

31 Horstead

Northumberland

32 Bagraw
33 Bean Burn 1,2
34 Bellshiel
35 Birdhope 1,2,3
36 Brown Dikes
37 Burnhead
38 Carham
39 Cawfields
40 Chapel Rigg
41 Chesters Pike
42 Chew Green I,III
43 Coesike West 1,2 and Coesike East
44 Crooks
45 Dargues
46 East Learmouth

Northumberland cont.

47 Farnley 1,2,3
48 Featherwood East and West
49 Fell End
50 Glenwhelt Leazes
51 Greenlee Lough
52 Grindon Hill
53 Grindon School
54 Haltwhistle Burn 1,2,3,4
55 Lees Hall
56 Limestone Corner
57 Markham Cottage 1,2
58 Milestone House
59 Norham
60 North Yardhope
61 Seatsides 1,2
62 Silloans
63 Sills Burn North and South
64 Sunny Rigg 1,2,3
65 Swine Hill 1,2
66 Twice Brewed
67 Walwick Fell
68 West Woodburn

North Yorkshire

69 Bootham Stray 1,2
70 Breckenbrough
71 Catterick Bridge
72 Cawthorn C
73 Malham
74 Wath

Nottinghamshire

75 Calverton 1,2
76 Farnsfield
77 Gleadthorpe Plantation
78 Holme

Shropshire

79 Attingham Park
80 Bromfield
81 Brompton 1,2
82 Burlington 1,2
83 Cound Hall
84 Ismore Coppice
85 Norton 1,2
86 Quatt
87 Stretford Bridge 1,2
88 Uffington
89 Upper Affcot
90 Whittington

Somerset

91 Norton Fitzwarren

Staffordshire

92 Greensforge 1,2,3,4,5
93 Swindon
94 Wall 1,2
95 Water Eaton 1,2,3,4,5

Roman Camps in England

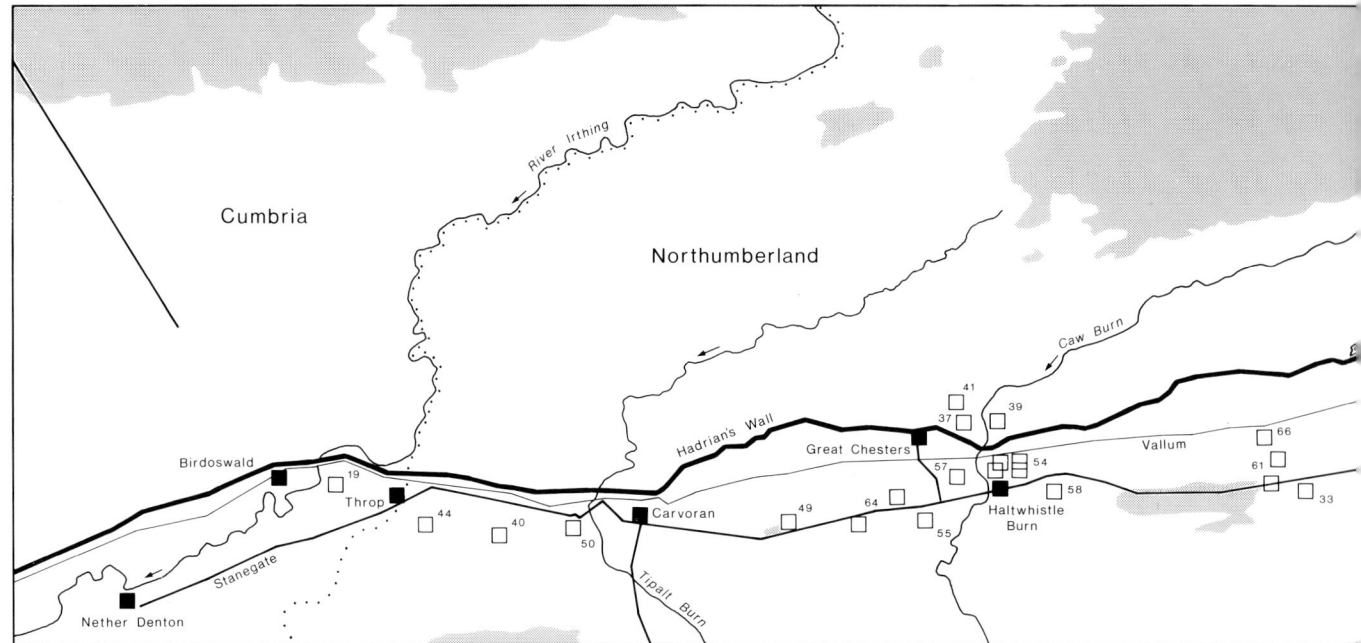

Figure 4 *Camps and other Roman military sites in the central section of Hadrian's Wall. The numbers refer to the list of sites set below Fig 3.*

and archaeological fieldwork, has revealed a dense concentration of camps (Fig 4) which is likely to be close to the original number thrown up by the Roman army in this area. For most of England, however, the distribution plotted on Figures 2 and 3 indicates survival, and the success of fieldwork, rather than the true geographical incidence of construction. The camps identified along the line of Dere Street, the major Roman road that ran from York into eastern Scotland, may be taken as an example. In the uplands of Northumberland many camps have survived as earthworks, but farther south, on the arable lowlands of Northumberland, Durham, and North Yorkshire, the distribution is sparse. This is despite the fact that the same troops who built the camps in the uplands would have required several overnight stops, probably about 30 km apart, on their journey to or from York. In the Vale of York itself, camps are still virtually unknown.

In some parts of the Midlands the known distribution of camps is slightly denser, despite the prevalence of modern arable, but it is not clear how far the factors affecting the survival and retrieval of archaeological information have determined the clusters of camps which have been recorded as cropmarks in Shropshire and Staffordshire, and in Nottinghamshire. These clusters must be due, at least in part, to the intensive aerial reconnaissance carried out in these areas by Arnold Baker and Derrick Riley respectively. In the national perspective, the immense contribution to aerial archaeology made by Kenneth St Joseph stemmed from his keen focus on Roman military remains, particularly the camps.

In the gradual progress of the conquest and in the spread of military occupation, many more camps must have existed than are known today. Although there may be reasonable confidence that most of the sites that survive as earthworks have been identified in the uplands, yet there is no certainty that the clusters known in the lowlands are representative of the numbers that may also have been constructed in the rest of England. Strategies of archaeological prospection may have influenced the apparent geographical distribution of camps, most notably the former tendency to seek cropmarks along or adjacent to the course of Roman roads; however, with the increase in aerial photography, the distortion that this factor would cause is probably less marked than once it was. The discovery of camps in Devon, Norfolk and Oxfordshire is particularly encouraging. In those areas, such as the Thames Valley, where there has been a prodigious amount of aerial photography, it seems likely that relatively few camps were constructed.

Leaving aside the effects of later landscape change and of archaeological fieldwork, the clusters of camps that have been identified must have come about through the action of several contributory factors. These probably included tactical considerations on successive campaigns, the needs of troops on manoeuvres, or the provision of camps for soldiers employed in civil engineering. All of these would have affected and determined the choice of the general area in which to camp or the selection of a particular site.

The choice of a site

The selection of a suitable site for a camp was a process that demanded some skill. Roman literary sources make it clear

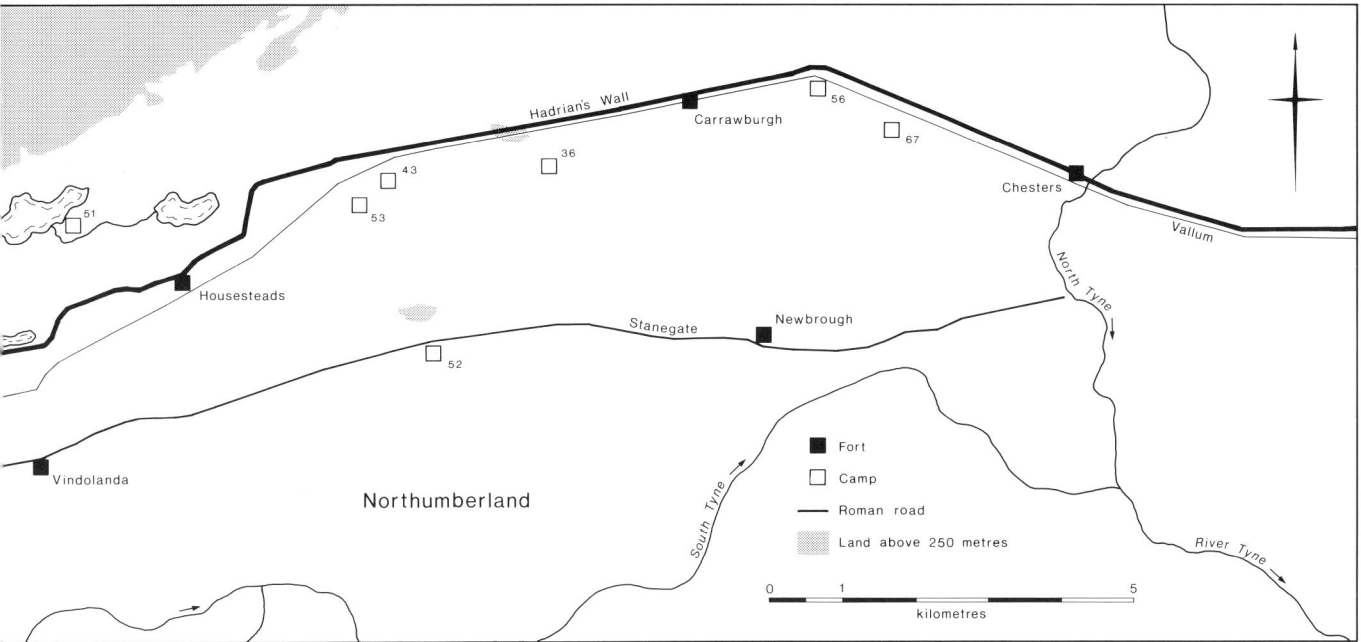

that this role fell to an advance party of surveyors (Vegetius II, 7); they had to choose the best land available on the route and had to lay out an area corresponding to the size of the unit to be accommodated (Vegetius III, 8). The reality of dealing quickly with these matters when troops were on manoeuvres or on campaign, and especially when moving in hostile territory, undoubtedly posed more testing problems than the bland military textbooks imply. The texts make it clear, however, that ideally the camp should have been on a slight rise, with the main gate facing the enemy or the line of advance; the rear gate should have been set on the highest point, in order to provide an uninterrupted view over the surrounding countryside. Firewood, fodder and a good water-supply had to be readily available, and any risk of flooding had to be avoided. If a gentle slope was not available, the next preference was to lay out the camp on level ground, or on a hill or a mountain; failing all these, the surveyors had to make the best choice they could in an awkward topography ('*necessaria castra*'). Sites overlooked by high ground, or those close to a steep valley which might provide 'dead ground' for a covert approach by an enemy, were to be avoided. The enemy might also hide their advance by coming through a forest, so a site adjacent to standing woodland was not recommended (Hyginus chapter 57). This last factor, probably so commonly encountered but so difficult to trace in the archaeological record, may partly explain the siting of a few camps which, on topographical grounds alone, appears to be less than ideal.

In some areas, the number of appropriate sites available at the end of a day's march may have been very limited. At Chew Green in Northumberland, close to the modern border with Scotland, a series of camps and other military sites overlap one another on the only place in the vicinity that offered relatively level ground. Wherever they were, the advance party of surveyors may have had very little time in which to make their decision, and some local tactical strength in the choice of the site for the camp might be the best that they could have hoped for. Although it was essentially a defensive structure, a camp, especially one established as a temporary halt along a road, was not seen as a place from which to fight but was the base from which a more active and mobile form of self-defence would be conducted. A dominant position, such as those occupied by hillforts, was therefore not necessary.

In most instances, nevertheless, great emphasis was evidently placed upon securing a position that had the benefit of some natural defence. The field archaeology confirms the recommendations of the literary sources in this respect. There was a strong preference for the slopes of a gentle spur or ridge, and one rampart of the camp, usually that to the rear, is most often found on a crest, a position that ensured good visibility. Examples of the latter, a common characteristic, include Greensforge 5 in Staffordshire and, along Hadrian's Wall, the camps at Burnhead, Lees Hall and Markham Cottage 2 in Northumberland, and at Willowford in Cumbria. At Burnhead this meant that the camp faced away from Hadrian's Wall, only 60 m to the south-west. The relationship between this camp and the Wall is unknown, but the orientation of the camp may have ensured that it faced the enemy.

The preference for this topographical position, with the rear defences on a crest, is so frequently found that in some cases, as for example at Buckton Park in Hereford and Worcester, its occurrence has been enough to influence the classification as camps of sites with few other diagnostic features. It also provides other clues. In Northumberland, Seatsides 1 seems to be an example of a camp which was redesigned: in a secondary phase a rampart may have run along the crest of a ridge, the preferred design, but in the first phase a much larger camp seems to have straddled the ridge. At Higher Kingdon in Devon, and at Boomby Lane in Cumbria, the sites of the camps also crossed a ridge. Such a hilltop situation provided good external views, but at the expense of the visibility of the whole perimeter or of all of the interior. At Fell End in Northumberland, a camp, later crossed by the Stanegate, just to the south of Hadrian's Wall, occupies a hilltop and the slopes on either flank but still uses the natural crest lines to advantage in its perimeter. More rarely, as at Wath in North Yorkshire, the camp was set on a level summit where steep slopes to the west provided good natural defences. Elsewhere, as at Brougham, Cumbria, and Shurnock, Hereford and Worcester, the steep tip of a spur was utilised in a similar way. At the camp known as the Golden Fleece, near Carleton in Cumbria, it is the forward rampart that is aligned along the crest of the hill. No doubt this was dictated by expediency but the exact reason for the choice is unclear.

The utilisation of a cliff or steep scarp to provide natural defence along which the forward side of the camp could be laid out, presumably facing the enemy, provides more obvious advantages. Examples of this are seen at Norham in Northumberland, where the site is on the lip of the scarp, 7 m high, above the flood plain of the Tweed, and at Knockcross on the northern coast of Cumbria. Milestone House, Northumberland, a camp with a most unusual, almost triangular, plan, uses the crest of a ridge for its long southern side. This is conventional enough, but much less so was the decision to utilise the next ridge to the north which, although approximately parallel to the southern side, affords a considerably shorter stretch of natural defences. This comparatively tiny northern flank lies along the top of a vertical crag, 8 m high, which is so steep that no bank was considered necessary. A tactical advantage had, however, been gained. The position chosen ensured that the soldiers on watch had a clear view of the low ground immediately to the north, at the foot of the crag. This is a good example of an instance in which expediency and common sense over-ruled the usual dictats of the military manuals.

More conventionally rectangular is the great camp at Rey Cross, on the summit of Stainmore in County Durham, which was laid out with natural defences very much in mind (Fig 5). The western rampart is on the crest, looking down towards the Eden valley, and the southern defences stand on the rock spine forming the lip of the valley of the River Greta. To the north and east the ground is more level but in one part of the northern side no bank seems to be provided, as at Milestone House. This may possibly have been because the blanket bog visible today was already encroaching on this side and formed enough of an obstacle in itself.

Despite the recommendation of Hyginus (chapter 57) that ravines may provide unwelcome cover for the enemy, the steep slopes that they afford were utilised to good effect at Dargues and at Swine Hill, Northumberland. At Chapel Rigg, to the south of Hadrian's Wall and in the same county, however, a small outwork apparently had to be provided in order to cover the dead ground within the ravine immediately to the south-west.

Poorly drained ground in the lowlands, as at Whittington in Shropshire, may have provided some defence, although the reconstruction of water-levels contemporary with any camp is hazardous from the evidence of fieldwork alone. At Holme, in Nottinghamshire, the camp stood on a slight rise in low-lying land and may have been close to a point at which the Trent could be crossed. At such river-crossings, troops were always vulnerable (cf Vegetius III, 7) and this may have been the determining factor in the position chosen. On a more positive note, access to drinking-water was always important, especially for the greater number of men accommodated in the larger camps. Ease of access to water may have determined the sites of Galley Gill and Kirkby Thore, in Cumbria, and those of the camps along the Sills Burn in Northumberland. The very unusual earthworks at Lees Hall, also in Northumberland, which may have been established at a time when hostility was still expected, actually enclose the upper reaches of a stream; the defences round the camps at Crackenthorpe, in Cumbria, and at Sills Burn South, in Northumberland, must have been interrupted for the stream that crosses each of them. At Chesters Pike, Northumberland, a site with no other apparent natural advantages, the camp appears to be almost too close to the water's edge. Such convenience could not always be achieved: at sites such as Fell End, in Northumberland, or the smaller ones nearby at Sunny Rigg, all the water must have been carried several hundred metres.

In some cases it is not at all clear why a site was chosen: at Crooks, in Northumberland, there is dead ground within 100 m of the camp; Malham, North Yorkshire, is overlooked by higher ground, and at Calverton, Nottinghamshire, the north-eastern side of camp 1 apparently lay at the foot of a slope on the edge of marshland. These choices may have been governed by factors beyond archaeological interpretation. The siting of camps 4 and 5 at Water Eaton in Staffordshire and the surprising location of Cawthorn C in North Yorkshire presumably made perfect sense at the time at which they were chosen. In these particular instances it may have been that the most advantageous sites in the immediate vicinity were already occupied. If so, the fact that, in any emergency, there would have been other Roman troops close at hand, must have made the choice of the site for a camp less critical.

When camps were constructed by troops on the march,

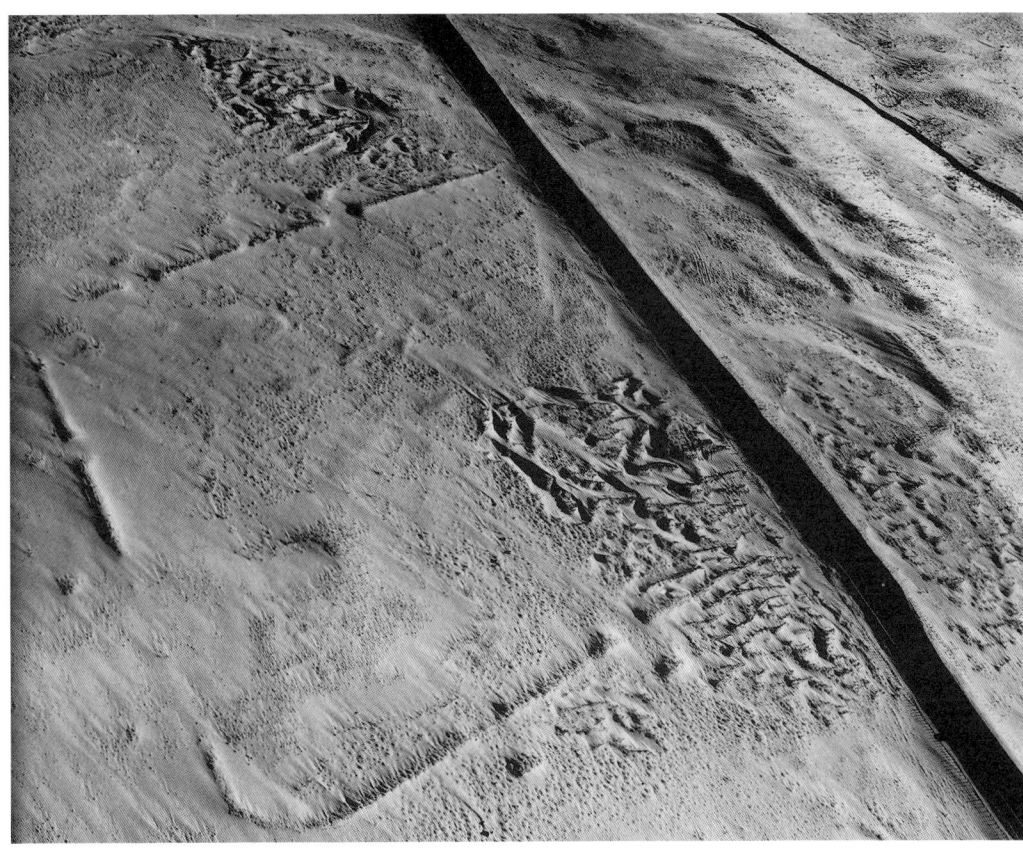

Figure 5 *Rey Cross, County Durham, from the NW under a light covering of snow; the valley of the River Greta lies upper right. The traverses are clearly visible, as is the later quarrying across the SW quadrant. Since this photograph was taken the A66 has been made into a dual carriageway.* (22.1.73, CUCAP BLM 85)

whether on manoeuvre or on a campaign, the choice of a site must inevitably have been influenced by the course of the road or of the route that they were following. From the position of their earthworks relative to the road, some camps seem to be earlier than the local road system, in so far as it can retrieved today. Unless the choice of site was so circumscribed as to make it inevitable that a road would have to cross the camp, this seems to have been avoided; such a choice would have weakened the defences and disrupted the internal layout. In most cases, therefore, wherever a road cuts across a camp it is likely that the camp was constructed on a route along which a road was later built, and that the camp is not contemporary with the road itself. Examples of these putative earlier camps may be seen at Troutbeck 1 and 2 in Cumbria, Fell End, Markham Cottage 1, Seatsides 1 and Silloans in Northumberland, Stretford Bridge 1 in Shropshire, and at Greensforge 3 in Staffordshire. In the latter two examples the camps may still postdate the establishment of the adjacent fort, each of which controls a river-crossing. The road at Rey Cross in County Durham, conventionally dated in its original form to the late 1st century, changes alignment where it crosses the eastern rampart of the camp. It is therefore likely that the camp here preceded the construction of the road. At Brompton 1, in Shropshire, excavation revealed that the ditch of the camp was earlier than the construction of the road leading to the adjacent fort of Pentrehyling.

From fieldwork evidence, however, the alignment or lack of alignment with a road is a poor clue to the relative chronological position of a camp, for topographical considerations may have been a much stronger factor in the choice of site, as at Burlington 1 in Shropshire. Nevertheless, if the camp faces away from the road, the camp is, in all probability, earlier, as seems to have been the case at Farnley 3 in Northumberland. Despite these uncertainties, it is clear that in the normal course of events camps were built alongside roads wherever there was a suitable site, with the camp facing on to the road, as for example at Dargues and Sills Burn North, in Northumberland. The topography sometimes imposed other restrictions on the space available, and the military surveyors therefore had to squeeze the camp into the site selected without encroaching on the road, as at Crackenthorpe, in Cumbria, and at Featherwood West, in Northumberland. Occasionally there were exceptions. Camp III at Chew Green lies axially along the road but seems to face the fort to the south; at Sills Burn South, also in Northumberland, the narrow space between the road and the burn constricted the design and the camp is oriented to the south along the road — presumably the direction of advance. These aspects will be explored further below.

The distribution of the camps, as far as it is known, must reflect in some fragmentary way the patterns of troop movements on campaign or on manoeuvre. In many cases circumstances dictated that camps were built in close proximity to one another, as for example at various points in Redesdale in Northumberland, along Hadrian's Wall (Fig 4), around the road junction and close to the vexillation fortress at Water Eaton in Staffordshire, at Stretford Bridge in Shropshire, and at Kirkby Thore in Cumbria. Eighteenth-century references suggest there may have been as many as eight camps on Bootham Stray, just outside the fortress at York, but their function is uncertain. The individual camps within each of these clusters were not necessarily constructed to the same design or at the same time. The simple geographical proximity of camps reveals very little except that a series of suitable sites was available along a given route.

Whether the troops were on campaign or on manoeuvre, they had been trained to construct a camp quickly and efficiently; it may have been just as easy for them to build new defences from scratch, rather than to reoccupy, adapt and refurbish existing ones. Similarly, the proximity of other Roman military sites such as forts and fortresses — for example those at Wall, Water Eaton, and Greensforge in Staffordshire, North Tawton in Devon, Buckton in Hereford and Worcester, Cawthorn in North Yorkshire, and at Brompton, Stretford Bridge and around Wroxeter in Shropshire — may not be particularly informative since the relative chronologies are usually uncertain and the exact functions of the camps are unknown. Where, however, the fort or fortress occupies the prime site, as in the case of Chew Green IV in Northumberland, Cawthorn D in North Yorkshire, and the vexillation fortress at Newton on Trent in Lincolnshire, the adjacent camp is likely to have been a secondary one.

It is clear that a few camps were constructed over earlier sites. In most cases this seems to have been due to coincident criteria, such as topographical advantages and good drinking-water, governing the choice of site. Assuming that the site suited the Roman military need, the presence of prehistoric barrows or cairns, as at Brompton and Bromfield in Shropshire, and at Bellshiel in Northumberland, would have caused only a minor disruption to the internal layout. Earlier field-systems, as at Greenlee Lough, Haltwhistle Burn and Swine Hill, or the trackways at Glenwhelt Leazes and Fell End, all in Northumberland, would have posed no problem, nor would the slight remains of timber houses beside the fields within the camp at Swine Hill. On the other hand, the putative stone circle within the camp at Rey Cross, County Durham, would certainly have disrupted the pattern of the tent-lines, as might the sizeable enclosure — perhaps another prehistoric ceremonial monument — within Stretford Bridge 1 in Shropshire. Elsewhere, as at Horstead in Norfolk, the relative chronologies of the cropmarks recorded remain uncertain.

Design and construction

Proportions and size (Fig 6)

Having chosen their site, the surveyors would tailor the design of the camp to suit the size of the unit. The whole of this process is outlined in some detail by Vegetius (III, 8), but it would have to be done rapidly and was evidently achieved with varying degrees of accuracy and under differing operational and topographical constraints. No doubt the precise approach varied somewhat from unit to unit.

The defensive perimeter was usually laid out on a rectangular plan; Vegetius (III, 8) recommended that 'appearance should not prejudice utility, although those camps of which the length is one-third longer than the width are deemed more attractive'; this ideal can be seen in Northumberland at Silloans and, in a less regular form, at Featherwood West. In practice, several variations are found: a ratio of approximately 3:2 between the length and breadth of the camp is commonly encountered, as at Swindon in Staffordshire, and in Northumberland at Bellshiel, Dargues, Lees Hall, Seatsides 2, Sunny Rigg 1 and, less accurately, at Burnhead and Chew Green III. A square plan, as seen at North Yardhope, was also often adopted by those building the smaller camps; examples of this include Bean Burn, Brown Dikes, Coesike, Grindon School, and Walwick Fell. Where this type of plan occurs in the larger camps it seems to be stratigraphically early, for example at Chew Green I, Haltwhistle Burn 2 and at Swine Hill, probably dating to the late 1st century. Apart from Swindon, all the camps mentioned here are in Northumberland. The many departures from the rectangular plan will be mentioned below.

The surveyors had to apply an equation which ensured that the area enclosed conformed to the size of the unit — however that might be constituted — but the equation itself is not entirely clear (Hanson 1978, 142–3; Maxwell 1982; Pitts and St Joseph 1985, 232–44). At best it was an ideal to be strived for; there can be no doubt that practical considerations (*see below*) came forcefully into play. Richmond and McIntyre (1934) used the area within the well-preserved earthworks at the camp at Rey Cross, on Stainmore in County Durham, in their attempt to understand the internal arrangement and strength of the garrison there. As it turns out, the attempt was probably flawed by their failure to take into account, and to subtract from their calculations, those areas which would not have been readily habitable, even temporarily. It is not known how accurate the Romans themselves were in making such allowances.

In the present study the enclosed areas of the camps have been carefully measured, taking each irregularity of the plan into account, wherever adequate survival of the perimeter has made this practicable. For cropmark sites, the area within the ditch, rather than that within the bank, has been recorded. In a few cases, where necessary, as at Brompton, Shropshire, topographical constraints have made an estimate

Introduction

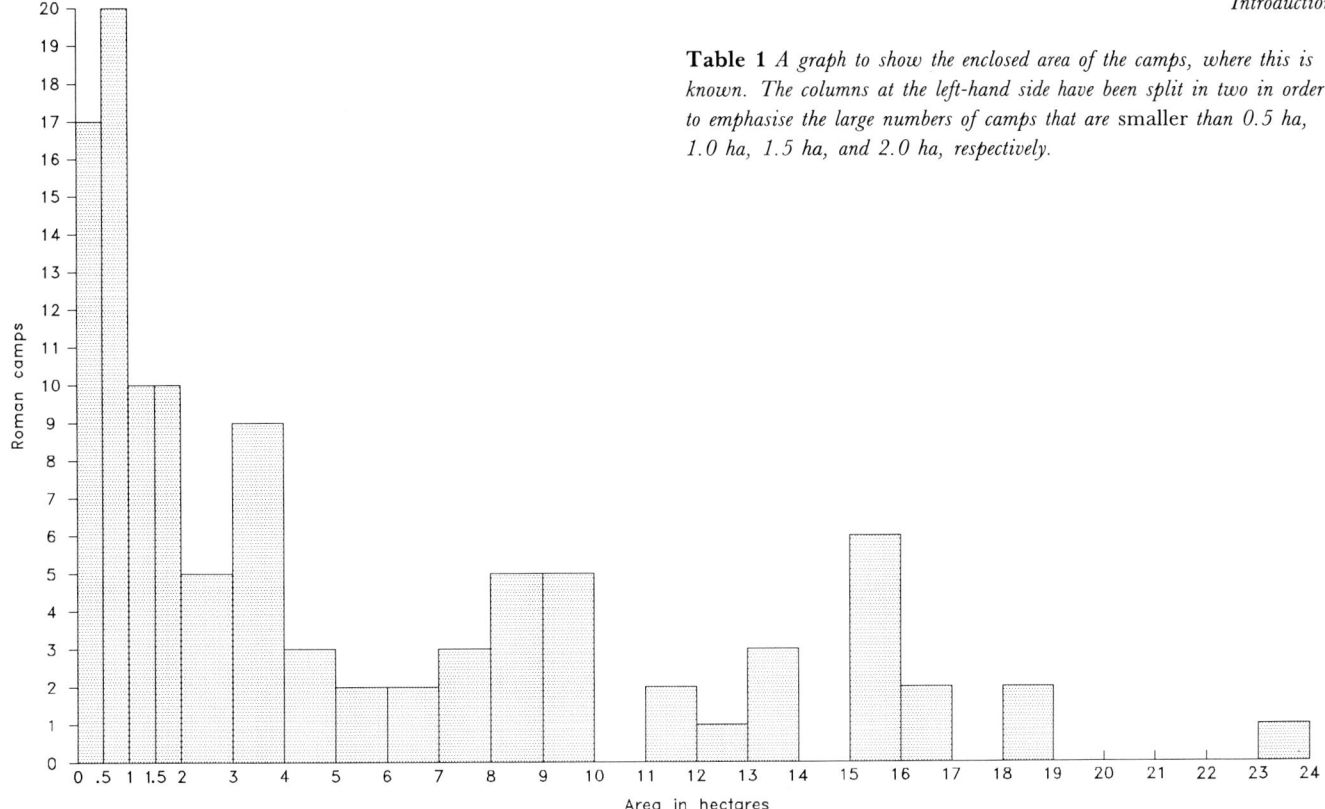

Table 1 *A graph to show the enclosed area of the camps, where this is known. The columns at the left-hand side have been split in two in order to emphasise the large numbers of camps that are smaller than 0.5 ha, 1.0 ha, 1.5 ha, and 2.0 ha, respectively.*

possible even though the defences are not complete. The area of 106 of the camps can be measured with some certainty (Table 1). Nearly half of them are very small; 17 enclosed an area of less than 0.5 ha (1.2 acres), and a further 20 were less than 1.0 ha (2.4 acres). Another 20 covered between 1.0 ha and 1.9 ha (4.7 acres) inclusive. Thereafter, in the larger size ranges, some marked bunching is evident (not shown in detail on Table 1). This occurs between 3.1 ha and 4.0 ha (7.6–9.9 acres: 10 sites), between 7.7 ha and 9.7 ha (19.0–24.0 acres: 11 sites), and from 15.0 ha to 16.8 ha (37.0–41.5 acres: 7 sites).

These groupings, which are based on size ranges that approximately double each time, must relate to the strength of the units most commonly on manoeuvre or in action. Whatever the exact nature of that relationship, there does not seem to be any clear correlation between the groupings and their geographical distribution in England. The largest camps, of which the perimeters are sufficiently complete, are those at Uffington in Shropshire (about 18 ha at its largest extent), Silloans in Northumberland (18.4 ha), and Brampton Bryan in Hereford and Worcester (23 ha). Inevitably, however, the larger the size enclosed the less likely it is that evidence for the whole perimeter has survived intact; in the upper range, therefore, the list is certainly incomplete. The very small camps, which are present in large numbers, have often been interpreted as practice works (*see below*); however, they may also be evidence that small detachments of troops were on the move around the country in the course of their normal duties. One of the writing-tablets found at Vindolanda in Northumberland, written about AD 90, contains part of a report on the current strength of the First Cohort of Tungrians stationed in the fort (Bowman and Thomas 1991). This shows that, at the time that the report was written, there were seven detachments on duty at other places, some of the detachments being of less than a dozen men.

Orientation (*Fig 6*)

According to the military manuals, the alignment and orientation of the camp was determined by the direction of travel, the position of the enemy or the main source of danger (Hyginus chapter 56; Vegetius I, 23), none of which is directly detectable archaeologically. It is clear, however, that topographical features or artificial constraints were equally influential. The two separate camps at Kirkby Thore in Cumbria, and many of those around the Haltwhistle Burn in Northumberland, share a common orientation; at Markham Cottage, Burnhead, and Cawfields this seems to have been deliberate, and not wholly dictated by the topography, but the reason behind it is unclear. Elsewhere,

Figure 6 *(overleaf) Diagram of comparative plans, to a common orientation and scale (1:10 000), of those camps of which the perimeter is known or can be inferred. The numbers refer to the list of sites set below Fig 3.*

Roman Camps in England

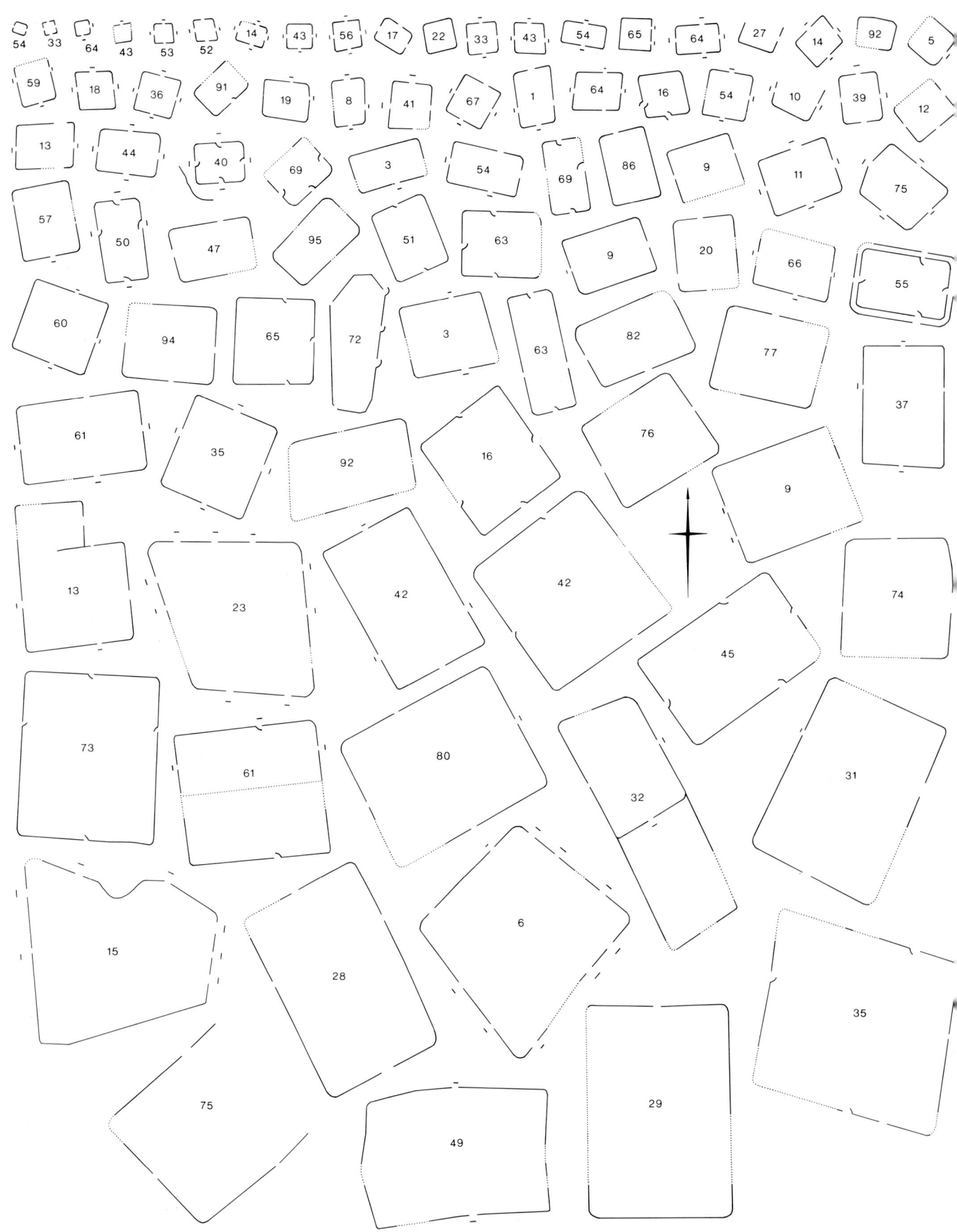

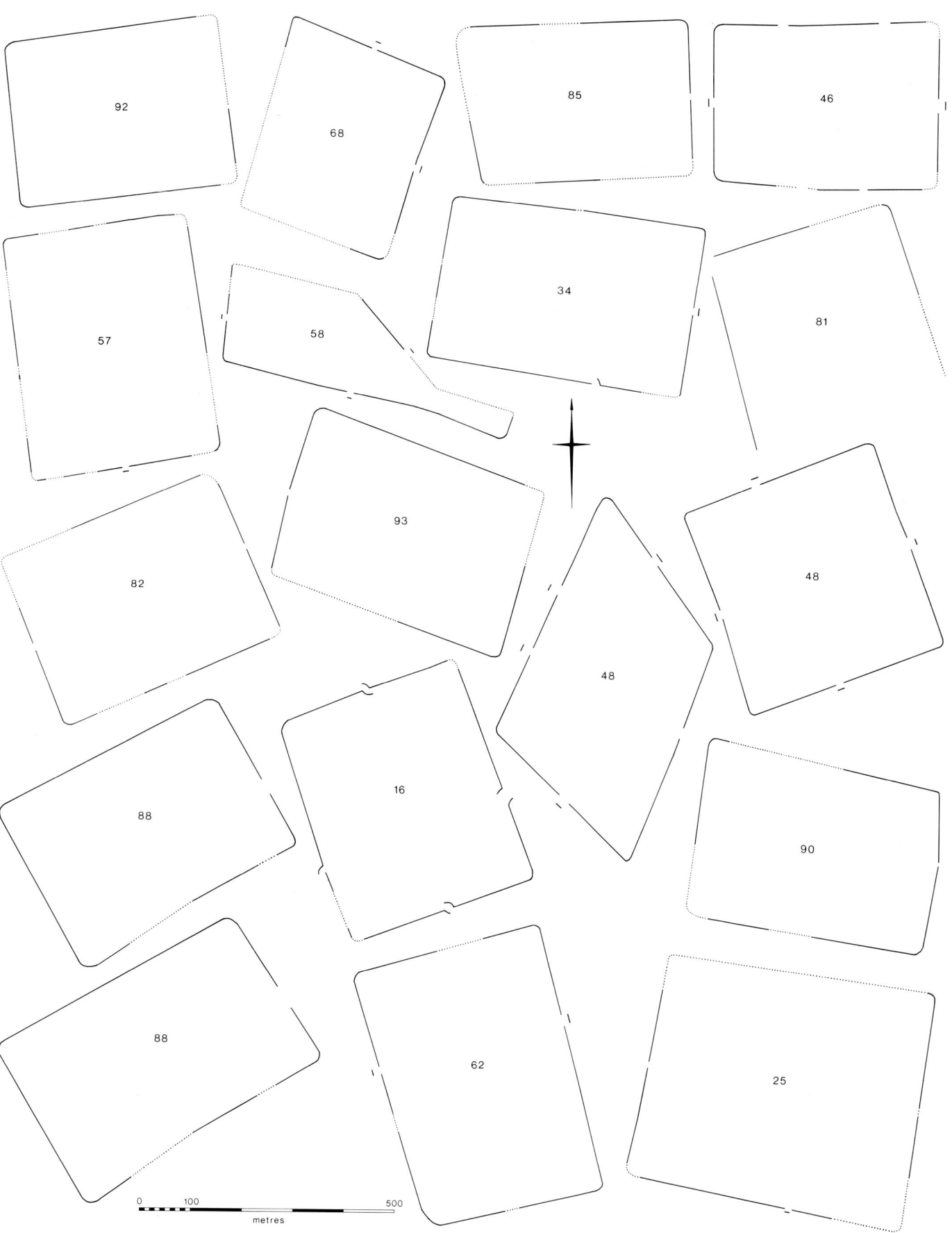

as on Bootham Stray in North Yorkshire or at Farnley in Northumberland, the orientations vary widely and for no apparent reason. Most commonly, the orientation is determined by an existing road, whether the camp is aligned along it, as at Sills Burn South, Northumberland, or is set with its axis at right angles, as was the case at Dargues, also in Northumberland.

It is frequently possible to suggest in which direction the camp was designed to face, for the lateral gates — those in the longer sides — may be offset towards the end in which the main gate was positioned. Internally, this allowed the headquarters to front on to the T-junction of roads thus formed, and to look down towards the main gate. Evidence of the particular direction in which the camp faced seems to survive at Barrockside, Golden Fleece, and Troutbeck 2 in Cumbria, at Featherwood East, Glenwhelt Leazes, Haltwhistle Burn 1, Seatsides 1 and 2, Sills Burn North and South, Sunny Rigg 1, Birdhope 2, Burnhead, Dargues, Lees Hall, Norham, North Yardhope and Swine Hill 1 in Northumberland, and at Malham in North Yorkshire. Sometimes the orientation of the camp probably indicates the direction in which the troops were travelling, as at Sills Burn South, North Yardhope and Sunny Rigg. On other occasions it seems clear that the camp has been laid out to face the main source of danger, for instance at Norham, Northumberland, and Knockcross, Cumbria. That said, wherever the enemy was thought to be, and whatever the intended direction of travel, topographical convenience and a basic level of tactical strength still seem to have been the most potent factors in the choice of a site and of its orientation. A good example of this may be the camp at Greenlee Lough, Northumberland, isolated in the scarplands to the north of Hadrian's Wall, where an orientation down a gentle south-facing dip slope and a ready supply of water provided all the necessary advantages (Fig 7).

The provision and position of gates is a good guide to the direction in which a camp faced, but this evidence must be used with caution; Featherwood West camp, in Northumberland, evidently fronted on to Dere Street, despite the fact that an extra gate was provided on the left flank, something which might otherwise suggest an orientation almost at right angles to the road. Indeed, it is only possible to identify the direction in which a camp was designed to face if the defences are more or less regular in their overall layout; where they are not, as in the case of Milestone House in Northumberland, the intended orientation cannot usually be determined from field survey alone, and would be difficult to prove even by excavation.

Figure 7 *Greenlee Lough, Northumberland, from the SE. The waters of the Lough lie to the N, at the foot of the steep escarpment. The extensive prehistoric cord-rig cultivation which underlies the camp is clearly visible on the gentle dip slope, as is the later post-medieval narrow ridge-and-furrow which overlies part of the NW side of the camp. (4.2.71, CUCAP BEW 61)*

Atypical plans (*Fig 6*)

A recurrent feature in the design of camps was the realignment of the perimeter at the point where the defences were broken for a gate. This often resulted in a radical departure from the playing-card shape. In some instances the realignments follow the folds of the local topography. Examples of this in Northumberland include East Learmouth, where only the western side is straight, and Fell End, where each of the four major sides is effectively composed of two parts, articulated at the gates. More rarely, the reason is quite unclear, as at Calverton in Nottinghamshire: there is a radical realignment at the north-western gate of camp 2 there, and the sides of camp 1 bow outwards and then inwards. Sometimes a central gate was selected, for instance on the western side at Swindon in Staffordshire, but elsewhere it appears that the position of the gate itself has been shifted away from the central point on that flank in order to comply with a realignment prompted by the topography.

In the large sites, such as Whittington in Shropshire, Troutbeck 2 in Cumbria, Walford in Hereford and Worcester, and Bellshiel, Fell End and West Woodburn in Northumberland, the defences were so long that setting them out must have taxed the most competent of Roman military surveyors. It must be significant that at East Learmouth only the western side is straight; along each of the other three sides the visibility is obstructed by the topography. Realignments at gates are, however, also to be found in the plans of some of the small sites, such as Watchclose and Willowford in Cumbria where intervisibility would not have been a problem.

Surveying

The common practice of realignment of the defences may provide clues as to some of the ways in which the surveyors set about their work with their *gromae*: simple cross-staffs that provided right angles. Any lack of visibility along the full intended length of a side seems to have dictated that another survey station had to be set up at each intervening crest. These stations, additional to any normal scheme (*see below*), might result in realignments of the defences, whether deliberately, or by accident — as was apparently the case on the northern side of Bellshiel in Northumberland. Similarly, any change to the area enclosed by an existing earthwork, as perhaps at Bagraw in Northumberland, might also produce a slight misalignment.

The layout of the two camps at Featherwood, Northumberland, may be instructive: at the gates of the western camp there are realignments, but three of these coincide with local crests which were thus good surveying points. On the eastern flank of Featherwood East the position of the gate is again significant, even though in this instance the realignments are on either side of the gate — at the two points where the perimeter crosses the horizon lines as seen *from* that gate. Perhaps more surprising is that the northern and southern sides of the camp at Featherwood East are not intervisible and yet are parallel. At Higher Kingdon, in Devon, where the site straddles the summit, again creating severe problems for the surveyor, a regular plan was also achieved. Similarly, the northern and southern sides at Seatsides 1 in Northumberland each lie 11 m below the crest of the ridge there, but are nevertheless parallel. The only conclusion can be that the lines of the defences were set out from survey stations along the ridge itself.

Elsewhere, the reconstruction of the method of setting-out is more complex and more speculative. The right angles provided by the *groma* could be used in at least two ways. In the normal scheme the surveyor would set up his instrument in the traditional place at the junction (*gromae locus*) of the long and short axis of the intended camp, immediately in front of the position to be occupied by the headquarters tent; from there he could use the sighting-lines of the *groma* to project outwards for predetermined distances to the four main gates. From two or more of these he could then observe and measure to the angles of the camp. This is the method recommended by Hyginus (chapter 12). However, the field evidence suggests that where the topography was awkward a slightly more laborious alternative may have been used. A measured line could be ranged on one side of the site and, at right angles to it, the position of the road across the short axis could be marked off; further right angles and measurements from the three points first established would produce the positions of the other two corners, of the main gates and of the centre of the camp. In either method the *groma* had to be set up on any intervening crest that restricted full visibility.

In practice, the larger the military unit, indicated by the size of the camp, the more likely it must have been that the force included a fully competent surveyor. In these larger sites, well-controlled allowances were evidently made for variations in the topography; in a few of the smaller sites, however, less care seems to have been taken. Thus, at Sunny Rigg 3, Grindon Hill, and Limestone Corner (22 m, 40 m, and less than 50 m across respectively), all in Northumberland, the plan is not rectangular, and therefore a *groma* is unlikely to have been used. This is also true of the secondary camps at Swine Hill in Northumberland (Fig 8) and at Burlington in Shropshire, which lie within the angles of their predecessors.

Where the general plan of a camp was rectangular, the corners of the enclosure were usually quarter-circles and were rarely right angles. In some cases, such as at Kirkby Thore 2 in Cumbria, Buckton Park in Hereford and Worcester, and at Brown Dikes, Silloans, and Walwick Fell in Northumberland, the radius of the arc was very small. The reason for this is unclear, although at Whittington, in Shropshire, it may have been determined by the topography. Elsewhere, the arcs have a much larger radius than normal; the camps at Brougham and Warcop in Cumbria, only about 23 km apart in the Eden valley on the road from Carlisle to the Stainmore Pass, share this characteristic,

Figure 8 *Swine Hill 1 and 2, Northumberland, from the W. The small camp 2 occupies the NW quarter of its predecessor. The internal* claviculae *of the larger camp are clearly visible. The modern road in the background follows the course of the Roman road, Dere Street.* (16.5.88, CUCAP AQO 84)

which may indicate that they are broadly contemporary or even associated with one another.

The effects of topography, and other modifications

As might be expected, the greatest external influence upon the design of a camp was the topography. Thus at sites such as Rey Cross in County Durham, Walford in Hereford and Worcester, and Troutbeck 2 in Cumbria, the positions of two of the sides were determined by the desire to make good use of pronounced natural scarps. The other two sides of each camp were then laid out in such a way as to achieve the size of enclosure required. Although there was on occasion a significant departure from the normal rectangular plan, it is evident that great care was taken to set out the defences accurately. The large camp at Crackenthorpe, in Cumbria, was squeezed in between the road and a ridge to the southwest, despite an intervening valley, and the layout on the unpromising site at Plumpton Head, also in Cumbria, was fixed by setting out the western rampart along a ridge.

Whatever the deficiencies of a site, and whatever compromises of design became necessary, the aim was still to produce a regular layout. On the high ground of the Cheviots, in Northumberland, the summit of Foulplay Head was occupied by a camp now known as Featherwood West. Here, the angle between Dere Street and the steep slopes down to the Cottonshope Burn was much less than a right angle; accepting this, the surveyors therefore laid the camp out as a regular diamond, a simple orderly design and one which ensured that there was adequate room for the troops to be accommodated. Elsewhere, minor changes in the alignment of the defences were sometimes deemed necessary in order to avoid a hollow, as at Whittington in Shropshire, or poorly drained areas which would have been quite unsuitable for the erection of tents. Examples of this are apparent at Boomby Lane and Plumpton Head in Cumbria, Rey Cross in County Durham, Silloans in Northumberland, and at Holme in Nottinghamshire.

Very occasionally the design of a camp is so aberrant and so dependent upon the topography that there is a strong impression that those in command were having to bow to expediency rather than follow theoretical precepts. The most obvious example of this is the camp at Milestone House in Northumberland. Here the southern side is set along a ridge, in familiar fashion, but a natural crag is used in place of part of the northern rampart, the rest of which slews diagonally across towards the southern ridge. The internal arrangements of this camp must have been anything but typical, and it is unlikely that it was occupied for more than a minimal length of time. Special factors may also have been taken into account in other instances, although quite what these factors were is no longer apparent. Thus there seems to be no obvious topographical reason for the asymmetry of the camp at Barrockside in Cumbria, and the extremely unusual design of Cawthorn C in North Yorkshire must have been determined in some way by the contemporary use of the rest of the site.

Additional features were evidently considered necessary on occasion. Two of the most exceptional of these are the outworks provided at Chapel Rigg and Lees Hall in Northumberland. In the case of Chapel Rigg the addition seems to have been the result of anxiety, perhaps arising from a miscalculation about the extent of the dead ground caused by the steep-sided gully immediately to the south-west. At Lees Hall a second bank, with no associated ditch, lies beyond the usual rampart and ditch, and yet seems to have been a primary feature. The camp at Milestone House, just across the valley, is likely to have been a hurried product, only temporarily occupied, whereas the unusually strong defences at Lees Hall, also suggesting a hostile contemporary countryside, may indicate a rather longer period of occupation. In almost every camp a single bank and a ditch were normally considered sufficient protection; however, at Troutbeck 2 and 3 in Cumbria, at Cawthorn C in North Yorkshire, and at Fell End in Northumberland, an outer bank was provided. It is unclear whether this provision was deliberate or whether it simply resulted from the deposition of excess spoil. If it was indeed intentional then a parallel at Oakwood, in Ettrick and Lauderdale in Scotland, may indicate that this was a relatively early characteristic, perhaps dating to the Flavian period. This extra bank may be more common than the surveys suggest; on the western side of Chew Green I, Northumberland, a slight, low external glacis mound, beyond the ditch and not apparent on the surface, was only revealed by excavation.

In two cases, Sills Burn North in Northumberland and Moss Side in Cumbria, an annexe seems to have been provided (cf Frere and St Joseph 1982, 27–9; Maxwell 1989, 63–5); without excavation, the chronological relationship between camp and annexe, and the function of the latter, cannot be readily determined. Similarly, the relative chronology of the two major elements of the earthworks at Bagraw, in Northumberland, is as yet unclear.

The defences: materials, form and construction

There are few literary references to illuminate the details of the construction of the bank and the ditch that normally formed the perimeter of a camp. Thus the three main sources of evidence are the form of the surviving earthworks and, to a lesser extent, the cropmarks of levelled sites, together with the results of the relatively small number of excavations that have investigated the defences of camps.

In theory, almost every man in a unit could be allotted a short section of the defences to construct, so that the perimeter could be thrown up very quickly (Josephus III, 84). A wide range of tools was used, including spades, shovels, mattocks, rakes and baskets (Vegetius I, 24; II, 25), all of which would have been utilised in the rapid construction of the earthworks. Of the two principal elements of the defences of a temporary camp it seems that the bank was considered more important than the ditch. Vegetius (III, 8) described how it might be constructed:

> The raised turves are laid out in line, forming a rampart. Above it, *valli*, ie stakes or wooden spars, are ranged along its length. The turf is cut round with iron tools, retaining the earth in its grass roots, ½ ft high, 1 ft wide and 1½ ft long. When the earth is too loose for it to be possible to cut out the earth like a brick, the fosse [ie the ditch] is dug in 'temporary style', 5 ft wide, 3 ft deep, with the rampart rising on the inside. Thus the army is enabled to rest secure and without fear.

(trans N P Milner 1993)

From surface indications alone the width of the defences varies greatly — from 6.4 m across at Rey Cross in County Durham, down to 1.9 m across in the minimal bank at Bowes Moor nearby. Even without excavation it is apparent that the material for the bank — turf, stones and earth — was often scraped up from a broad swathe. At Rey Cross the ditch is barely apparent on the surface, despite the massiveness of the banks, while at Bellshiel in Northumberland, and perhaps at Limestone Corner also, the full perimeter of the ditch was evidently not completed because the underlying rock was too close to the surface.

Occasionally some stone is visible in the make-up of the rampart, as at Rey Cross, and at West Woodburn in Northumberland, but the preferred construction material was definitely turf. It seems to have constituted all of the rampart at Cawthorn C in North Yorkshire (Fig 9), at Bowes Moor in County Durham, and at Sunny Rigg 1 and Birdhope 2 in Northumberland. Elsewhere, probably in response to the materials naturally available, turf revetments or kerbs formed only the face of the rampart, as at Troutbeck 1 in Cumbria, and at Chew Green III, Haltwhistle Burn 1, and Greenlee Lough in Northumberland. Sometimes, however, there was a revetment to the rear also, as for instance at Sills Burn South in Northumberland. At Haltwhistle Burn 1 turf also formed the foundation of the bank.

Earthen ramparts alone were not considered sufficient protection. Troops on the march were expected to carry stakes which could be driven into the rampart in order to strengthen the defences (Polybius XVIII, 18.8: Livy 57). Evidence of stakes along the forward face of the bank has been tentatively identified in excavation at Galley Gill in Cumbria, but at Bromfield in Shropshire the stakes that were found had been burnt *in situ* at the bottom of the ditch. Between the bank and the external ditch a level berm has occasionally been identified, as at Farnsfield, Nottinghamshire, at Troutbeck 1 in Cumbria, and in Northumberland at Greenlee Lough, and possibly Haltwhistle Burn 1; the berm is usually narrow, no more than about 0.35 m across, but in the massive defences of Rey Cross, County Durham, it attains a width of 1.0 m.

The external ditch of a camp, which gives rise to the cropmarks by which sites have been identified from the air, evidently varied greatly in its dimensions. At Rey Cross, and at Sunny Rigg and Haltwhistle Burn 2 in Northumberland, the excavators observed that the material in the bank was greater than that which could have been supplied from the ditch; a thin layer had evidently been scraped off a much wider area in order to provide upcast material. The ditch was thus a secondary source rather than an imperative necessity. The profile of the ditch might vary, even within one site, as at Bromfield, from a broad U-shape to a much

Figure 9 *Cawthorn C, North Yorkshire. A section excavated through the NW defences on 4 September 1924, illustrating the original proportions of the external ditch, and the layers of turf that made up the bank.* (F G Simpson: NMR BB78/10254)

crisper V. The ditches sectioned at Farnsfield in Nottinghamshire, Galley Gill in Cumbria, Greenlee Lough in Northumberland, at Whittington, Brompton, and Burlington in Shropshire, and at Swindon in Staffordshire, were all described by their excavators as V-shaped. However, given the wide variations recorded in the excavated profiles of ditches surrounding camps, this V-shape cannot be regarded as an immutable and exclusively Roman trait. It certainly cannot be taken as diagnostic of date without corroborative evidence. The proportions of ditches recorded in excavation vary, but a width of about 1.8 m and a depth of about 0.8 m below the modern plough-soil are not atypical. These shallow dimensions compare closely with those recommended by Vegetius. Only rarely does the ditch seem to have been an obstacle in itself, for instance at Farnsfield, Nottinghamshire, where the ditch was recorded as being 2.8 m wide and a full 1.8 m deep.

Another feature which, like the V-shaped profile, has often been cited as a Roman characteristic, has been found but rarely. This is the 'ankle-breaker' or 'cleaning slot', an abrupt axial channel cut out along the bottom of the ditch. This has been recorded at Cawthorn C in North Yorkshire, at Farnsfield in Nottinghamshire and at Upper Affcot in Shropshire, but it is evident that it was not considered essential and that ditches with shallow, sagging proportions were at least as common. Depending on the subsoil, a cleaning slot is the normal product of the digging of a ditch for its own sake, especially if the site is reoccupied and the existing ditch is cleaned out (*see below*).

In striking camp, the stakes in the rampart would presumably be removed, and it seems that the earthworks might also be slighted if their existence might possibly afford some advantage to the enemy (cf Josephus III, 90). Excavation has provided some evidence for the back-filling of the ditch at Brackenrigg and at Galley Gill in Cumbria, and at Bromfield in Shropshire; however the comparatively good state of preservation of many surviving earthworks demonstrates that these precautionary measures were rarely thought to be necessary.

Gates

The gates provided through the perimeter of a camp were very simple. There was no imposing gatehouse, no guard-chambers, nor even simple doors, but rather a defensible causeway across the external ditch and a break in the line of the rampart. Although in the ideal arrangement there would be four such gates, one in each side, the actual number varies from at least twelve at Crackenthorpe in Cumbria, to a single one in the smaller examples such as Sunny Rigg 3 and Haltwhistle Burn 4 in Northumberland.

The arrangement of these gates around the perimeter, and thus the internal layout of the camp (*see below*), might be affected by the topography or by the need to face a road, or by the position of the enemy, but an attempt at regularity was usually made. In the short sides of a camp there would normally be a single central gate, but in the long sides the provision varied. The side gates were often offset in a ratio of 1:2, either accurately or approximately, down the long axis. Sites where this can be seen include Boomby Lane, Moss Side 2, Nowtler Hill 2, and Troutbeck 2, all in Cumbria, Walford in Hereford and Worcester, Horstead in Norfolk, and Dargues, Haltwhistle Burn 1, Norham, and Sills Burn South, in Northumberland. A ratio of 2:3 is found at Barrockside and Golden Fleece in Cumbria, Brampton Bryan in Hereford and Worcester, Seatsides 1 in Northumberland, and Bromfield in Shropshire. Whether, as seems likely, these differences were due to the particular needs and traditions of the units that constructed these camps, is not known. Elsewhere, the gates are centrally placed, even, as at Cawfields, Chapel Rigg and Crooks (all in Northumberland), where the camp is not square.

Topography certainly had its effect on the choice of site for a gate; the surveyor may have been well content when he could contrive, as in the case of the western gate of Chew Green I, Northumberland, to place a central gate exactly on a natural crest. When multiple gates were required, careful measurements must have been taken to ensure that the gates were regularly spaced; this care is evident round part of the perimeter at Crackenthorpe in Cumbria and at Cawthorn C in North Yorkshire, although in the latter, an exceptionally unusual design, the gates are provided only along one side of the camp. Problems of intervisibility, probably compounded by simple errors of measurement, led to the provision of opposing gates which were not quite opposite to one another. This seems to have been true at Featherwood East in Northumberland, Boomby Lane in Cumbria, and at Walford in Hereford and Worcester. For those gates defended by *claviculae* (*see below*), an offset position would be a natural consequence, in order to compensate for their dog-leg design. Even so, at some sites, like Lees Hall in Northumberland, the offset is such as to prevent a straight internal road or gap between the tent-lines; thus within each gate an abrupt bend in the internal road must have been necessary.

In the rear rampart, the gate might be omitted altogether, particularly in the smaller camps such as Watchclose in Cumbria, and at Coesike West in Northumberland, but also at slightly larger ones such as North Yardhope. This economy is readily comprehensible where the topography made the provision of a gate unnecessary or impractical, as at Willowford in Cumbria. More surprising, perhaps, are the cases in which a gate was provided despite the topography: on the northern sides of Fell End and North Yardhope, in Northumberland, where the steep slopes meant that the traverse had to be set so close to the perimeter that each gate must have been of limited practical use.

A note of caution should be sounded on the interpretation of the disposition of the gates in sites now known only from cropmarks. Later drainage schemes or natural scouring may have cut through the causeway of the gate, and the cropmark of the ditch may then appear continuous, as at Plumpton Head in Cumbria. Gates affected in this way will only be located if their additional defences (*claviculae* or traverses) can be identified. Elsewhere, the former existence of a gate may be postulated where a modern road crosses the defences, as for example at Haltwhistle Burn 1, and possibly at Twice Brewed, both in Northumberland. The reason for this is readily apparent: a routeway across an upstanding earthwork will naturally develop in such a way as to link those points where it is easiest to cross the artificial scarps, that is from gate to gate.

Camps were rapidly constructed and thus their design, which had to be kept simple, varied comparatively little. This is particularly true of the gates, which were little more than guarded gaps with defences that usually took one of two basic forms (*see below*). The break forming a gate through the line of the bank is usually difficult to measure with any accuracy, for the rampart-terminals have often been abraded or disturbed; nevertheless, the break normally seems to have been about 7 m to 12 m wide. At a small number of sites this seems to have been greatly exceeded, as for example at Plumpton Head in Cumbria where some of the breaks in the cropmark of the ditch appear to be as much as 18 m to 20 m across (Fig 10).

Few gates have been excavated in England in modern times. However at Farnsfield in Nottinghamshire the bank was found to extend just under 1 m beyond the square terminals of the V-shaped ditch, reducing the effective width of the gate to about 5.7 m. There was no evidence for a timber tower, no pivots for wooden doors and no revetted end to the bank; this simplicity, reflected within the area excavated at Galley Gill in Cumbria, was almost certainly the norm. At North Yardhope in Northumberland and at Troutbeck 1 in Cumbria, stone was roughly laid in the

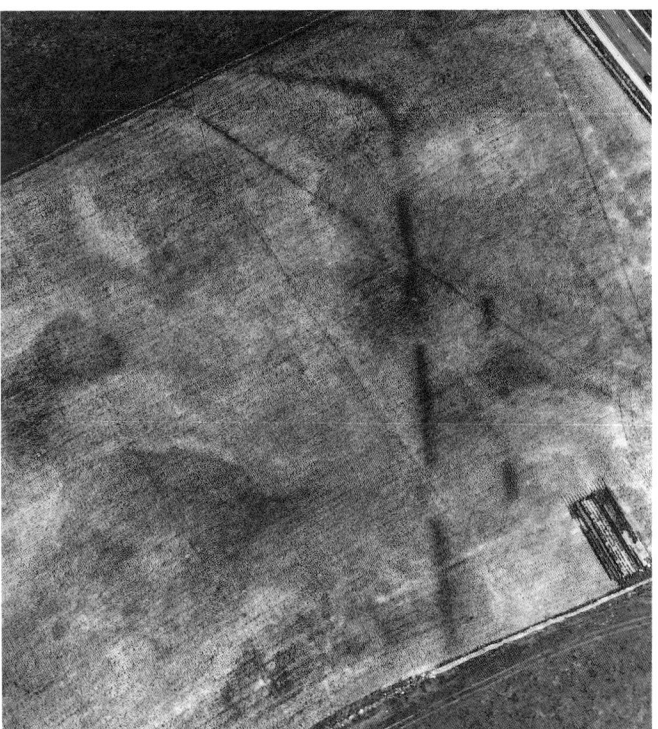

Figure 10 *Plumpton Head, Cumbria. The cropmarks of the SE side from the S. The wide causeways across the ditch were protected by traverses set unusually far forward.* (1.8.74, CUCAP BRC 7)

southern and south-eastern gates, respectively. This seems to have been crude paving to combat boggy conditions, and its presence presumably indicates that the troops were camped there for more than a single night.

Gate defences

In any defensive scheme a gate is always potentially a weak point. If, in the provision of gates to their camps, the Romans were economical about the details of construction, they certainly took great care to ensure that the overall layout of the gate afforded simple but effective protection. The limited range of designs that they chose is the single most distinctive diagnostic trait in the classification of Roman camps. In the forts of the late 1st century AD, which share many features of their designs with the camps, the break in the rampart was often strengthened by turning the bank inwards at right angles for a few metres in order to create a recessed entrance (cf Jones 1975, 118). Among the camps in England this feature has only been identified with any certainty at Rey Cross in County Durham. The camps at Burnhead and Cawfields in Northumberland also appear to share this type of gate; it is conceivable that the short inward turn simply provided access to the top of the bank by means of an *ascensus*, although, given the dimensions of the earthworks, this would have been barely necessary. At Limestone Corner in Northumberland the inturned ends of the bank may relate to the much later phase of reuse known there.

A much more common defensive design was the *clavicula*, a short continuation of the defences which curved in an arc within the camp (and, more rarely, externally) so as to impede any attackers who might try to rush the gate (cf Lenoir 1977). Unless the curving bank was also accompanied for its full length by a ditch, as was sometimes the case, gateways of this type may be difficult to identify on levelled sites known only from cropmarks. In its commonest form — the curving internal bank — the *clavicula* survives as an earthwork at Troutbeck 1 in Cumbria, at Bellshiel, Birdhope, Chew Green I, Dargues, Greenlee Lough, Lees Hall, Sills Burn and Swine Hill in Northumberland, and at Bootham Stray and Malham in North Yorkshire.

The radius of the arc varies somewhat, being particularly large at Dargues and, apparently, becoming angular at Bootham Stray; in most cases the earthworks are too abraded for the range of measurements to be considered statistically without excavation. The cropmarks at Norton Fitzwarren in Somerset and at Newton on Trent in Lincolnshire appear to show that in some cases the ditch was also carried round the arc of the internal *clavicula*. This has been difficult to identify on the ground. It was demonstrated by excavation at Troutbeck 1, but only at Dargues is the ditch still visible as a distinct earthwork. This paucity of information is no doubt due to the erosion and silting that would be particularly marked at any gateway. As might be expected, no ditch was found associated with the turf-built *claviculae* examined in 1936 at Chew Green I in Northumberland.

In North Yorkshire, camp C at Cawthorn, wholly unusual in its design, has well-preserved *claviculae*, although these project outwards from the defences and have no internal element. In another variation, at Troutbeck 2 and 3 in Cumbria, and at the fort and annexe known as Cawthorn B, the gate was defended by internal and external *claviculae* with, at Troutbeck, the outer ditch following the arc. Such distinctive designs are rare. The chances of identifying the course of campaigns would be greater if these designs — which must have been the deliberate choice of individual military surveyors, and which were recommended by Hyginus (chapter 55) — had been found in a string of sites suitably spaced along major routes. Knowledge is still too fragmentary to pursue this theory further. Similarly, the apparent absence from England of the complex 'Stracathro-type' gateways, which incorporate a *clavicula*, may further weaken the prospects of mapping campaigns in this way. Given the incidence of such gateways in Scotland (Maxwell 1981; 1989, 50–3, 56–9; Maxwell and Wilson 1987, 29–32), it is perhaps surprising that no examples have been identified on Dere Street, the main road to the north, or anywhere else in England.

Although *claviculae* are not uncommon, a greater number of examples have been found of gates defended with simple traverses — a detached length of bank and ditch set a short distance forward of the defences and parallel to them. The intention was the same: to check any hostile rush on the gate. Here the term traverse is used rather than the disputed Latin forms *tutulus* and *titulum*. The charming translation of these words for the traverse as 'Tommy Atkins' — a personification of the sentry guarding the gate — is not proven (Henderson and Keppie 1987).

The length of the traverse seems to have been governed by the width of the gate: an overlap with the ends of the main rampart was necessary, but no more. At Cawfields, Silloans and at both the camps at Featherwood, all in Northumberland, the traverses are elongated into bar-shapes as much as 18 m long, while at Rey Cross in County Durham, and probably at Crackenthorpe in Cumbria, they are round or oval. At Rey Cross no associated ditches are visible, although a wide and shallow scoop may have been dug out to provide the material, and in this respect the surface remains mirror those of the main perimeter. This similarity of construction between traverse and perimeter is only to be expected, a pattern confirmed in Northumberland at Haltwhistle Burn 1 where the bank of the traverse, like that of the rampart, was found to have a foundation and a forward revetment of turf, retaining material upcast from the ditch.

The distance that the traverse was set forward of the rampart varied considerably, even within the design of one camp, as for instance at Glenwhelt Leazes in Northumberland. At Plumpton Head in Cumbria, where the gates are extremely wide, the traverses were also set well forward, apparently about 18 m, approximately the distance recommended by Hyginus (chapter 49). In contrast, the northern gate at North Yardhope in Northumberland, perched more than 6 m above the burn, had its traverse only 1 m forward of the main ditch, compared to the more normal distance of about 5 m at the other gates. At Haltwhistle Burn 2, also in Northumberland, the access provided between the inner edge of the traverse bank and the outer edge of the main ditch is only about 1.5 m, a distance which is surprising because here the topography imposes no particular constraints.

The ditch of a traverse would often be so shallow and small that it may be difficult to detect as a cropmark; such an absence from the aerial photograph does not imply that the gate was not defended in this way. The evidence of the surviving earthworks suggests that only in the most exceptional circumstances would a traverse have been considered unnecessary. In England this seems to have occurred only at the southern gate of Chew Green III, in the Cheviot Hills of Northumberland, where the counterscarp bank of fort IV was only 8 m away and thus provided adequate protection for the gate; here this is an argument for seeing the two fortifications as contemporary.

Chronology of gates

The relative chronologies of camps defended by *claviculae* and camps defended by traverses have been much discussed (cf Lenoir 1977), but evidence of absolute dating is almost non-existent in England. Field archaeology provides some pointers but, without improvements in absolute dating (*see below*), it can hazard no conclusions. At Chapel Rigg and Glenwhelt Leazes, less than 1 km apart on the western border of Northumberland, the gates are defended by both *claviculae* and traverses, used in combination (Fig 11). These appear to be contemporary. Elsewhere in the county, at Bellshiel and in the northern half of Seatsides 1, both types of gate again appear, although this may be an indication of the reuse of each site, the traverses probably being secondary. This seems also to have happened in the fort (IV) at Chew Green. At Swine Hill the larger camp, its gates defended by *claviculae*, was succeeded by a smaller one where traverses were constructed, and thus the sequence is clear. In the fort known as Cawthorn A in North Yorkshire, however, the excavators demonstrated that traverses were replaced by *claviculae*, reversing the sequence visible at Swine Hill.

Hyginus advocates the use of *claviculae* although the date of the compilation of this text, and those of any primary sources used, make the chronological value of this uncertain. The chronological relationship of the two types of gate may be beyond the immediate reach of archaeology. Furthermore, there may not have been any straightforward or continuous evolutionary process. Personal whim, regimental tradition, or the particular function served by the camp may all have been potent factors in the choice as to which design should be used.

Internal structures

Some of the camps may have been occupied only very briefly, so it is not surprising that they have yielded little in the way of internal structures. Excavation within the interior has rarely been considered likely to bear fruit, and has been undertaken on only a few occasions. Field archaeology is almost entirely silent as to what the internal structures were. The assumption is that there was a central range within which stood the administrative headquarters, the tent of the commanding officer and others for key stores, while lines of

Figure 11 *Chapel Rigg, Northumberland from the E, a camp provided with traverses and internal* claviculae. *(4.2.71, CUCAP BEW 31)*

tented barracks, stores and mobile workshops occupied most of the forward and rearward portions within the defences. Lines of pits, for rubbish and latrines, cooking-places behind the ramparts, and possibly stake-holes where conditions proved favourable for their recognition, are all that the excavator could hope to find (cf Pitts and St Joseph 1985, 223–44). Indeed, the ready identification of internal features might suggest a semi-permanent occupation, rather than a temporary one (*see* Classification, *below*).

Following the precepts of authors such as Vegetius and Hyginus, archaeologists have tended to seek in temporary camps the internal regularity that is commonly seen in permanently established Roman forts. This was no doubt the model. The practice, however, highlighted by the disposition of the gates and thus the inferred positions of internal 'streets', seems to have been much more expedient and pragmatic, as might be expected from an encampment hastily designed and constructed. The arrangement of the tent-lines would, no doubt, have been sensibly marshalled but is unlikely to have been so ordered as that reconstructed for Rey Cross by Richmond and McIntyre (1934). If the disposition of the gates is anything to go by, the tent-lines frequently must have converged, as for example at Plumpton Head in Cumbria or at Featherwood West in Northumberland, and the maintenance of a regular grid must have been impossible. Neither was the camp filled with tents only; an unknown proportion of the internal area must have been given over to baggage animals and other impedimenta.

Earlier man-made features, such as the prehistoric barrows or cairns at Brompton and Bromfield in Shropshire and at Bellshiel in Northumberland, may also have been minor inconveniences. More serious disruptions must have been caused by natural features, such as the outcropping rock and blanket bog at Rey Cross in County Durham, and the streams at Lees Hall and Sills Burn South in Northumberland and at Crackenthorpe in Cumbria. No tents could have been pitched on the steeper slopes within Fell End and Milestone House, both in Northumberland, or on the scarps within the camp at Crackenthorpe; each of them would have lost almost a quarter of their habitable areas in this way. This factor alone would seriously weaken any equation that seeks, uncritically, to link the internal areas of camps with the numerical strength of a unit.

The internal structures at Cawthorn C in North Yorkshire, which have not been excavated and may not even be contemporary with the defences, are clearly exceptional; recent excavation within the interior of Rey Cross revealed little more than a few stake-holes, randomly distributed, and some 4th-century pottery, but at Bromfield in Shropshire, ovens were found, cut into the base of the rampart. At Galley Gill, in Cumbria, pits and post-holes have been excavated; one pit, however, lined with basketwork and perhaps filled with grain, has been dated to the 10th or 11th centuries. This paucity of evidence should not discourage excavation when the opportunity arises; only then will the information on dating and on the reuse of camps during the Roman period be improved.

The reuse of camps in the Roman period

Given that camps were frequently built beside roads, and were thus accessible, and the economy of effort that refurbishment and reuse may have offered over construction from scratch, it is almost inevitable that the most suitable positions, those that offered topographical and tactical advantages, should have been reoccupied, perhaps on a number of occasions. Where there were further constraints on the choice of a location in which to camp, it is not at all surprising that the best sites were reused time and again; the palimpsest of earthworks surviving at Chew Green in Northumberland is a particularly good example. The only check on this willingness to reoccupy might have been a reluctance to stop for the night in a camp too recently fouled (Vegetius III, 2; cf Hanson 1978, 142). That apart, troops on the move could readily reoccupy a camp, as found, or could economically construct a second, or third, camp within the original defences. This seems to have happened with some regularity, but the practice is probably still under-represented in the archaeological record. At Rey Cross in County Durham, excavation revealed 4th-century pottery, suggesting some reuse at that time. On a major route, such as the Stainmore Pass, reoccupation should probably be regarded as the norm rather than the exception, although only where it is clear that additional earthworks have been constructed (as was the case at Rey Cross) can reuse be demonstrated from fieldwork alone.

The construction of a camp within a larger predecessor was a natural response, for no wise commanding officer would seek to have a larger camp than was necessary (cf Josephus III, 84). Quite how the exact position of the smaller camp was chosen seems to have depended upon the details of the topography and the advantages that these might provide. Occasionally, as at Markham Cottage in Northumberland and at Brompton in Shropshire, only one rampart would be shared; elsewhere, and more commonly, one camp occupies the angle of the other, as for instance at Swine Hill in Northumberland, Kirkby Thore in Cumbria, Burlington in Shropshire, and probably at another Cumbrian site, Brackenrigg. Although it appears that in most cases the smaller camp was the later one, at some sites, such as Calverton in Nottinghamshire and Coesike West in Northumberland, the chronology is by no means so clear. At Birdhope in Northumberland, camp 2 has no defences in common with the much larger camp 1; camp 3, on the other hand, probably shares one side with camp 2 although, whatever the relative chronology of these two, a conscious decision seems to have been taken not to share a second side, something which could easily have been achieved (Fig 12).

If the surveyor or the advance party had decided to reoccupy a camp, but only to use half of its area, as at Haltwhistle Burn 2 and 3, and at Seatsides 1 in Northumberland, three sides could be retained, even though some refurbishment might be necessary. In some instances, circumstances had evidently changed between one occupation and the next, and a choice was made to use the site but not the earlier alignment. Thus at Boomby Lane and Moss Side in Cumbria, and at Chew Green in Northumberland, the later defensive schemes cross over their predecessors. One result of reuse was that the northern bank of Chew Green I was levelled for a short distance, presumably so as to minimise the disturbance to the internal arrangements of camp III.

It should be expected that, if existing earthworks were reused, some of the elements of the previous defensive scheme may have become redundant. At Rey Cross in County Durham, where the excavated pottery suggests some activity later than might have been expected, field survey was able to record some surface indications of reuse, in that some of the gates seem to have been blocked at one time or another. This is also apparent in Northumberland at Lees Hall and Brown Dikes. More subtle are the possible signs of refurbishment tentatively identified not far away at Fell End.

There are a few instances in which the area enclosed seems to have been changed and the camp has contracted or expanded. Well-preserved examples of this survive in Northumberland at Haltwhistle Burn 2 and 3, and apparently at Seatsides 1. The clearest instance of this as a cropmark is within a meander of the River Severn at Uffington in Shropshire. The attraction, of course, was the economy of effort that such reuse provided. The contraction or expansion of an existing camp also illustrates the care with which accurate provision was made for the number of troops to be accommodated: no military commander, of any period, would wish the perimeter of his camp to be so large that it would not be readily defensible, but neither should the interior be too cramped or inconvenient.

Function

It is clear from the classical sources, from the design of the defences, and from the choice of site, that the primary function of camps was defence. At a more specific level, the function of a camp is usually beyond the reach of archaeological methods of retrieval. Many, especially the larger ones constructed beside routes, were clearly for troops on the march. Elsewhere, speculation has suggested that some were labour camps, accommodating men involved in a particular construction project, or that others were practice camps, built by troops on manoeuvre. Labour camps would undoubtedly have been constructed but the identification of them is fraught with uncertainty. Simple proximity, as that of a camp close to a major civil-engineering project such as

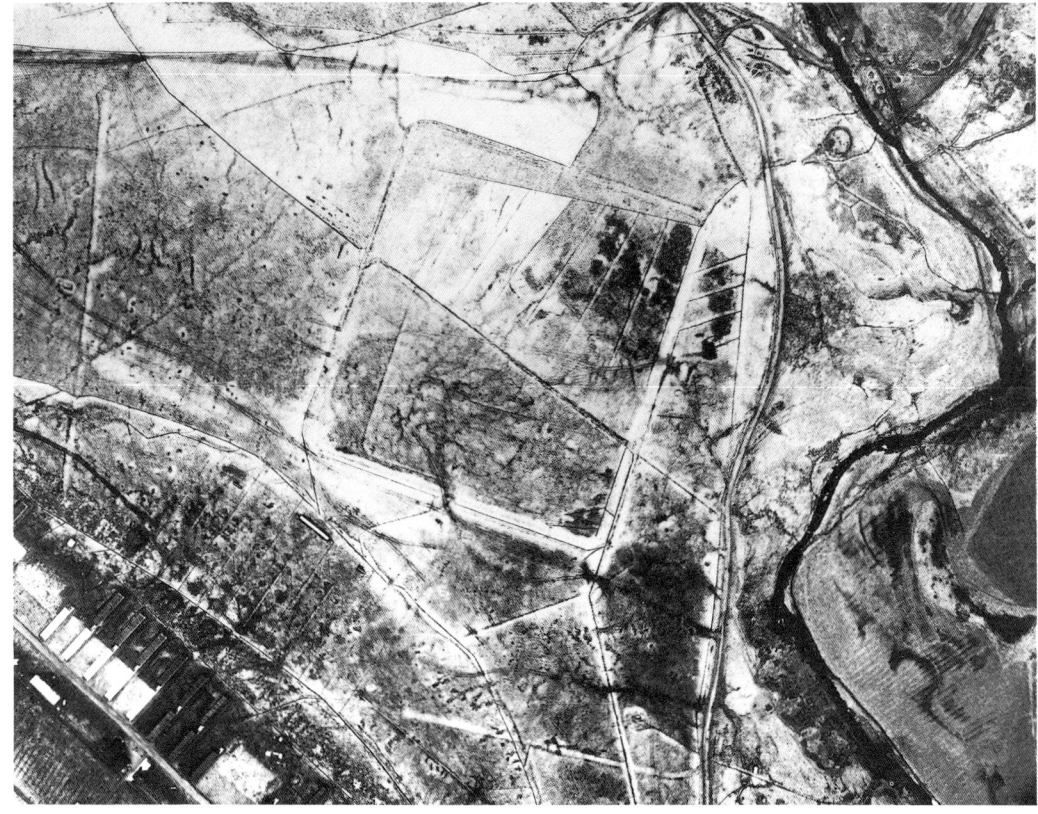

Figure 12 *Birdhope 1, 2 and 3, Northumberland, a vertical aerial photograph taken 11.4.37. The outline of camp 2 lies in the centre of the picture. The SE angle, the internal clavicula of the W gate and portions of the W and S sides of camp 1 are also visible. The SW angle and the W side of camp 3 are traceable within camp 2. The modern Redesdale Camp, visible in the lower left of the photograph, has been occupied by the British army since 1911.* (NMR AP NY 8298/1)

Hadrian's Wall, is, in itself, not an adequate demonstration of contemporaneity and association. Possible labour camps might include Bowes Moor in County Durham and perhaps Buckton Park in Hereford and Worcester, each of which is adjacent to Roman installations. Along the line of Hadrian's Wall some of those beside the Haltwhistle Burn in Northumberland, and the sites at Beaumont and Boomby Lane in Cumbria, may also have had this function. Those close to the Wall, but to the N of it — Burnhead, Cawfields and Chesters Pike in Northumberland — make the easy equation particularly hazardous. It has been suggested, without any particular justification, that the wholly atypical camp, Cawthorn C in North Yorkshire, might also have been a labour camp, accommodating troops engaged with the construction of one of the adjacent forts.

Although some camps may have been constructed just to keep an undisciplined army busy (Josephus III, 76, 84; Sallust 45), there were others, well attested in the literature, that seem to have been practice camps; these gave the troops experience of creating defences in the field (Vegetius I, 21, 25). There are examples, most demonstrably on Llandrindod Common in Wales (Daniels and Jones 1969), where the camps are so small and their gates so numerous as to make the enclosure itself nonsensical. This may, with caution, be a guide to identifying practice camps; the very smallest, those between about 25 m and 40 m square over the ramparts, which barely provided room to do much more than to pitch a tent, may fall into this category (cf Davies 1989, 138–9), although the remarks already made, about the small detachments of troops on the move, also have to be taken into consideration. Examples in England might include Sunny Rigg 3, Bean Burn 2, Haltwhistle Burn 4, Coesike, Grindon Hill and Grindon School, all in Northumberland. Some of these are not in good topographical positions, so some elements of the training — if such it was — seems to have been seriously awry. If the antiquarian references are correct, and there really were eight camps in relatively close proximity to one another on Bootham Stray, almost within sight of the fortress at York, then perhaps it may also be appropriate to classify the slightly larger examples surviving there as practice camps. Cawthorn C in North Yorkshire is so aberrant that it is not likely to have been a practice camp, as has been suggested in the past; neither is it safe to attribute this function to the camp at Chapel Rigg in Northumberland, just because it was provided with complex gates. No example of a camp built as a siegework, whether for practice (cf Jobey 1978) or in anger, has yet been identified in England.

Classification

The classification and identification of temporary camps in this study has been made more difficult by two things: the problem of disentangling some of the medium-sized examples from forts — with which they were bracketed by Roman surveyors and authors in the military science of castrametation — and the willingness of antiquaries to assign all manner of earthworks to this classification. Only in a few instances does it seem absolutely certain that a structure was a truly temporary one, defended for a minimal length of time, and therefore unequivocally a camp rather than a fort. Expediency of the kind that might typify a brief, overnight, stay may be clearly evident in the choice of an unusual site like Milestone House in Northumberland. A brief occupation may also be indicated by the fragility of the defensive steps taken at Bowes Moor in County Durham, whereas a slightly longer stay may be suggested by the provision of additional defences at Lees Hall in Northumberland. At Rey Cross in County Durham, however, the earthworks are massive, and it seems inherently unlikely that they were thrown up at the end of a day's march in order to defend a unit for a single night. This is despite the fact that the choice of topographical position and the design may point to no more than a comparatively short initial stay. Here, and elsewhere, there could have been some conscious intent to provide permanent defences that troops moving along a route could use, as required; speculation of this kind is, however, beyond the reach of field archaeology.

In a camp the most distinctive features are a rectangular plan, rounded angles, and the details of the gates, albeit that these characteristics are shared with some forts such as Cawthorn A, North Yorkshire, and Chew Green IV, Northumberland. A cropmark of a single rounded angle is not usually sufficient to suggest the presence of a camp, although there is a tendency to give these the benefit of the doubt when, as for instance at North Tawton in Devon, and around Wroxeter in Shropshire, they occur within a cluster of known Roman military sites. In earthworks, size and slightness of bulk cannot be used uncritically as a criterion as the massive bank of the camp at Rey Cross indicates. Similarly, at Featherwood West, in Northumberland, undoubtedly a camp, the scarp on the north-western side, set on a forward slope, reaches a height of 1.7 m. In distinguishing between camps and forts, therefore, the diagnostic features of a camp are negative ones: thus, the ditch is not likely to be massive, internal features such as roads would not normally be expected, and structural timberwork, found in excavation at Cawthorn A and B, would not be encountered. Nevertheless, a single distinctive gate-type, showing as a cropmark with a relatively narrow or shallow ditch, would usually be enough to include a site, however tentatively, within the corpus of camps: for instance Carham, Northumberland, and Newton on Trent in Lincolnshire.

Dating

Throughout this book the emphasis is upon the evidence provided by the surviving remains of the camps themselves; there is no attempt to link this archaeological information with historical events, known or deduced. This is inevitable and correct, not least because of the paucity of dating evidence available in England for these sites. As a result of their temporary nature, the camps have yielded few datable artefacts. Pottery excavated from the primary silt of the ditch at Galley Gill, in Cumbria, may be of the late 1st century, and a date no later than *c* AD 120 is usually suggested for the site at Cawthorn in North Yorkshire. Some samian dating to the first half of the 2nd century was found in the ditch of Brackenrigg 1, in Cumbria, and sherds of cooking-pot and mortarium came from Limestone Corner, Northumberland; the latter pottery, however, spanned the period from the early 2nd century to the late 3rd or 4th centuries and, as with the 4th-century pottery at Rey Cross in County Durham, does not provide unequivocal information about the camp's initial construction, or even about its reuse.

From their geographical position it may be reasonable to suppose that the camps identified in Norfolk, Oxfordshire, Devon and Somerset were probably constructed relatively early in the Roman conquest of Britain. In Shropshire, the military occupation of the fortress at Wroxeter seems to have ended before the close of the 1st century, probably *c* AD 87; it may be reasonable to infer, therefore, that the camps in the surrounding area were constructed up until that time. Nevertheless, troops presumably continued to move around all the civilian areas to the south of Hadrian's Wall long after the early 2nd century; they may have continued to build themselves a camp, if only out of military discipline and habit rather than an overriding need for defence. In most cases, however, because there is little other evidence to go on, the morphology of the camps has to be considered. The information gained at Cawthorn suggests that *claviculae* and traverses appear to overlap in time, the former being built well into the 2nd century; elsewhere it seems that a square plan may be characteristic of some of the earlier camps in England, and that the morphological similarity of the distinctive sites at Troutbeck 2 and 3 in Cumbria to those in Scotland suggests that they are contemporary, probably within the Flavian period.

There are a number of instances, all in Northumberland, that illustrate the importance of morphology and, sometimes, of siting as possible indicators of relative date. Burnhead and Cawfields, only 250 m apart and with some similarities in their gates, could have been laid out by the same military surveyors, even though the size and proportions of the two camps are quite different. The same may be true of Chapel Rigg and Glenwhelt Leazes. The two sites on either side of the summit at Featherwood are almost certainly directly contemporary; they both enclose the same area and perhaps accommodated two halves of the same force, for the western camp covers the dead ground invisible from the eastern one. These pointers are helpful, but more profitable clues to dating may be found in the examination of the relationships within the landscape and the approximate or relative dates that may, with caution, be deduced from this.

The camp at Red House, near Corbridge (*see* Addenda), apparently overlies part of the Agricolan vexillation fortress and, if so, must have been constructed after the fortress was abandoned in the late 1st century. The time interval between the two is unknown. Such a direct topographical relationship is rare; elsewhere less precise information has to be employed.

Despite the example at Rey Cross in County Durham, the relationship of a camp to a road is rarely clear (cf Silloans, in Northumberland), although excavation at Brompton, in Shropshire, showed that camp 1 is earlier than the road to the adjacent fort of Pentrehyling which was probably occupied from the early Flavian period until the reign of Hadrian. In a quite different way, the elongated camp at Sills Burn South, in Northumberland, squeezed in between Dere Street and the stream, evidently postdates the road.

Of itself, however, proximity may be of little assistance. The camps at Burnhead and Cawfields, mentioned above, share a particular design of gate and thus may be broadly contemporary. Their location next to Hadrian's Wall, however, provides no dating information. In contrast, at Limestone Corner and Haltwhistle Burn 4, camps which are just as close to the Wall, within Northumberland, it could be argued that the camps postdate the frontier defences, not because of any direct physical relationship but because the ridge on which the Wall was built severely restricts visibility immediately to the north.

In the same county, the provision of extra defences for the camp at Lees Hall, and the fact that the site appears to ignore the Stanegate, close by to the north, suggests that the camp precedes the road which was built in the late 1st century. Just across the modern road, the much larger site at Markham Cottage 1 is crossed by the Stanegate and the north-western corner of the camp was subsequently occupied by part of a Roman cemetery, presumably that for the fort at Great Chesters. It is therefore likely that this camp is earlier than the first half of the 2nd century, when the fort was established, and probably belongs in the late 1st century. In view of the Roman laws on burial, the camps at Birdhope, in Northumberland, probably also predate the scattered barrow cemetery that overlies the eastern side of the site. The dating evidence that this may provide is imprecise, for the fort at High Rochester, served by the cemetery, was occupied for a considerable period from the late 1st century onwards; this particular type of burial seems to have become established in the early 2nd century and continued in use into the 4th century. Even less certainty surrounds the dating of the putative camp 3 at Water Eaton, in Staffordshire, which seems to underlie the fort at Stretton Mill; the relationship between them could only be demonstrated by excavation.

How long camps continued to be constructed is not known. Vegetius, probably writing at the end of the 4th century, may have been exaggerating when he stated that the necessary knowledge had died out (Vegetius I, 21; Milner 1993, 22); the practice may well have continued into the 4th century. All in all, too little work has yet been done to enable a chronology to be constructed for the camps in England. Given the uncertainties of the sample, and with reuse being all too common, it is unwise to ascribe a date to any particular site without the benefits of extensive excavation and, preferably, the application of scientific dating methods.

Camps in the later landscape

The sites selected by the Roman army for its camps were chosen with great care for their topographical advantages, and it should therefore cause little surprise that subsequent generations recognised those advantages too. Inevitably, the range of secondary uses was very wide, as the following four examples from Northumberland may illustrate. A Norman chapel seems to have been built beside the road at Chew Green, within the fortlet overlying camp I; by 1249 the level ground around the site had become a trysting-place for the settlement of cross-Border criminal cases. Farther to the east, the Scots army may have camped on the site at Carham at the beginning of the Anglo-Scottish wars in 1296. Along Hadrian's Wall, at Limestone Corner and Brown Dikes, the camps seem to have been used as convenient sites for, respectively, a medieval farmstead and some shielings. At Galley Gill, in Cumbria, excavation has revealed medieval activity that could not have been detected by fieldwork alone.

Elsewhere, the abandoned earthworks of the camps must have obstructed later communications, for those who were crossing the countryside in the post-Roman period would have found such earthworks across their route. The natural reaction would have been to exploit the existing gaps in the defences, the gates. Thus, today, the positions of some of the gates are identifiable by the passage of later roads through them, as for instance at Haltwhistle Burn 1 in Northumberland, Brampton Bryan in Hereford and Worcester, Norton 1 in Shropshire, Cawthorn C in North Yorkshire, Horstead in Norfolk, and possibly at Twice Brewed in Northumberland. At Whittington, in Shropshire, a stretch of the bank itself seems to have been reused as a lane.

The defences of a camp have often been actively incorporated into the later landscape. Thus the ditch often forms part of the modern agricultural drainage system, as at

Figure 13 *Fell End, Northumberland, from the W. Although the remains of the camp are obvious, it is the effects of later land use that are most distinct in this photograph. The camp is bisected by hollow-ways following the line of the Stanegate as well as by extensive quarrying. Ridge-and-furrow cultivation and further quarrying interrupt the S perimeter. Towards the E end the camp is crossed from N to S by a modern colliery tramway, now abandoned. The steep slopes within the N half of the camp are clearly visible. (16.1.73, CUCAP BLL 31)*

Troutbeck 2 in Cumbria; if the camp has only been recorded as a cropmark this may make a gate difficult to identify unless the ditch of a traverse is visible. Most commonly of all, the defences have been utilised as portions of field boundaries — walls, hedges or upcast banks; examples of this can be seen at Willowford and Plumpton Head in Cumbria, and at Bellshiel, Swine Hill, Silloans, Seatsides 1, Markham Cottage, and Burnhead in Northumberland. The presence of a field boundary also may hamper the identification of gates, as for example at Sills Burn North, Northumberland, especially those gates that might have been blocked in a secondary phase of use in antiquity. At Brougham in Cumbria, Walford in Hereford and Worcester, and at Horstead in Norfolk, a distinct kink in an adjacent boundary suggests that the earthworks of the camp were still extant and had to be taken into consideration when these boundaries were laid out. At Upper Affcot in Shropshire the missing portion of the Roman perimeter appears to be largely preserved in the later hedgerows.

Occasionally, the earthworks of a camp are partly obscured by natural features. At Birdhope, in Northumberland, the northern defences are largely masked by peat, a phenomenon also identifiable at Chew Green III, Fell End and Silloans, all in the same county. Inevitably, however, it is normally the plough that has been responsible for levelling the earthworks; at Markham Cottage 1 in Northumberland, and at Troutbeck 2 in Cumbria, the defences of the camp have been incorporated into ridge-and-furrow. In some cases the date of this degradation is approximately known. At Uffington in Shropshire and Beaumont in Cumbria this probably happened in the medieval period, for in each case the camp was overlain by reversed-S ridge-and-furrow. In an arable landscape the levelling of the earthworks was almost inevitable. On its characteristic sloping site, and with its rear defences on the crest, a camp would be rapidly eroded by the plough and masked by hillwash. In the marginal lands of the North of England this process did not begin, in some cases, until the technological improvements of the 18th century. At Crackenthorpe in Cumbria the earthworks of the camp were ploughed after they were surveyed by Roy in 1769; at Watchclose, also in Cumbria, Horsley described the earthworks as 'very fair and visible' in the early 18th century, but by 1783 cultivation had begun and fifty years later the levelling was almost complete.

Within recent centuries, industrial activities have also disturbed and scarred the camps. Limestone quarries and 'sow kilns' (simple bonfire limekilns) are spread across the site at Milestone House in Northumberland. At Fell End (Fig 13) and Featherwood East, Northumberland, and at Rey Cross in County Durham, stone has been quarried, whilst at Bellshiel and Birdhope, both in Northumberland, small coal-pits have been dug. Agricultural drainage schemes have also severely damaged and disfigured the remains of a number of camps that had otherwise survived intact for nearly two millennia. North Yardhope in Northumberland is a particularly notable example of this (Fig 14).

Some of the most recent damage to the earthworks at Bellshiel and Birdhope in Northumberland is telling and ironic; in each case a trench has been dug by the British army into the evanescent ditch of the Roman camp. Even in the 20th century, therefore, the military mind is still looking at landscape through much the same eyes as it did in the 2nd and 3rd centuries AD, and is still exploiting topographical advantages in very much the same way.

Figure 14 *North Yardhope, Northumberland, from the NW, showing damage by modern land drains.* (28.6.76, CUCAP BYF 27)

An Inventory
of Roman Camps
in England

Cumbria

Barrockside *Figs 15 and 16*

NY 45434716

In 1984 a well-defined cropmark of a camp was photographed on the E side of the Petteril valley, some 520 m S of Barrockside Farm and just over 1 km NW of Low Hesket (NMR AP NY 4547/4–8). The Roman road from Old Penrith (*Voreda*) to Carlisle (*Luguvalium*) passes about 600 m to the E.

The camp, which has a N to S alignment, is positioned on almost level ground at 80 m above OD towards the end of a broad ridge which slopes very gently down to the NNE. A shallow gill with a stream, now mostly piped underground, runs for a short distance along the E side and then swings north-westwards immediately N of the camp, ultimately joining up with the Petteril valley. The views from the camp

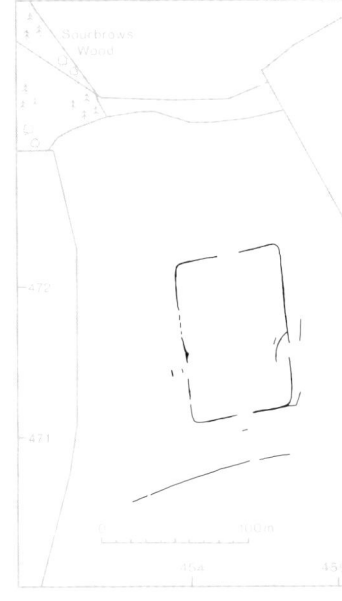

Figure 15 *Barrockside, Cumbria. The cropmarks of the E and W entrances are confused by possible geological features.*

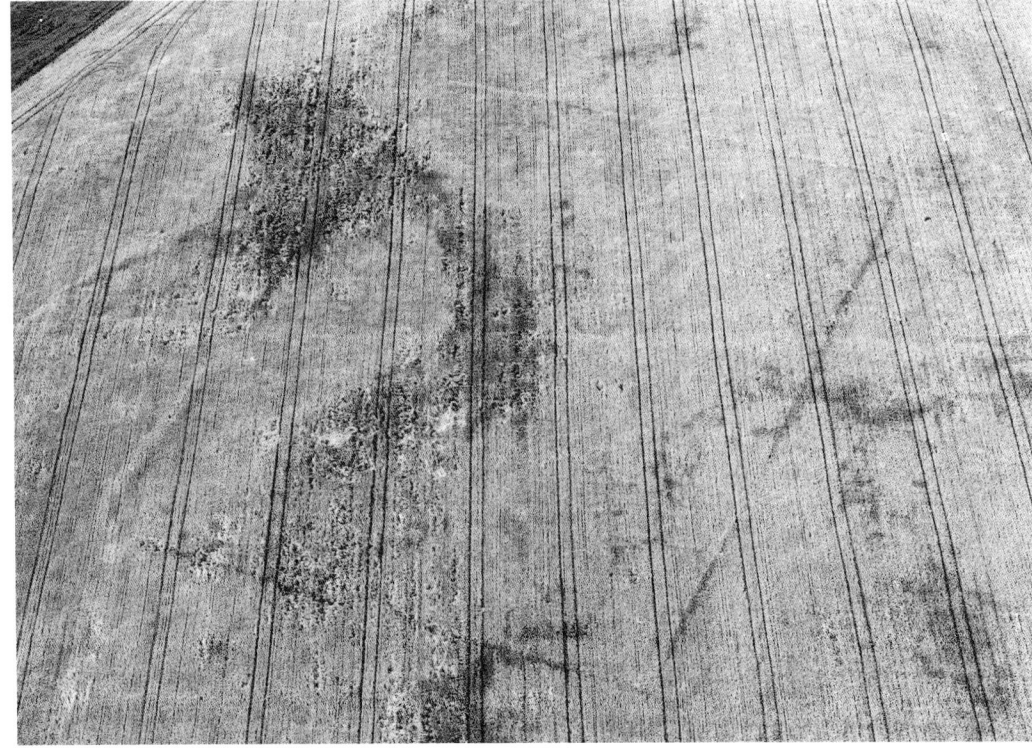

Figure 16 *Barrockside, Cumbria, from the SE.* (23.7.84, NMR AP NY 4547/8)

are extensive to the NW, W and SW along the valley of the Petteril, but to the N, NE and SE are restricted by distant ridges. To the S, however, a crest only 300 m away blocks the view.

The perimeter of the camp is irregular in its layout for its S side, which is approximately 73 m long, measures about 5 m less than the roughly parallel N side. This N side bows slightly inwards towards the entrance. The E and W sides, both about 107 m long, are not quite parallel, the NW and SE corners being obtuse and the NE and SW corners being acute. The W ditch is set back about 30 m from a steepening of the valley side, but there is no apparent topographical reason for the asymmetrical shape of the camp which encloses an area of about 0.8 ha (2.0 acres). All four sides appear to have opposing entrances. The positions of the E and W entrances, in a ratio of 2:3 along the E and W ditches, indicate that the camp faced S. Only the gate on the S side has a clear traverse, its ditch lying about 10 m beyond the causeway; another seems to have been provided at a similar distance outside the W gate, but possible indications outside the other entrances are too faint for certainty.

NY 44 NE 12   Hesket

Beaumont (Burgh-by-Sands) *Fig 17*

NY 33875910

The E segment of a camp has been recorded as cropmarks, 200 m WSW of Beaumont village between Milldykes Lane and a former canal and railway (St Joseph 1965, 78; CUCAP AGO 63–4). The Roman fort of Burgh-by-Sands (*Aballava*) lies only 1 km to the W and there is a marked concentration of military sites in the vicinity, although their character and relationships are not yet fully understood (Jones, G D B 1991, 102–3, 105; Maxwell and Wilson 1987, 13).

The camp, situated on the gently sloping S-facing side of a spur, less than 20 m above OD, overlooks the shallow valley of the Powburgh Beck, just E of its confluence with the Greathill Beck. The crest of the spur is occupied by the course of Hadrian's Wall and the site of Milecastle 71, less than 40 m to the N. In all other directions the views are far reaching.

Only the complete E side, about 160 m long, and parts of the N and S ditches, are visible. The cropmark of what may have been a traverse lies approximately at the midpoint of the E side, about 6 m out from the line of the ditch. The course of the ditch is unbroken as a cropmark, but a slight change in the alignment at this point adds some weight to the suggestion that there may have been a gate here. No indication of the W part of the perimeter survives and the topography does not hint at possible limits; all traces have been masked by surviving narrow ridge-and-furrow which, to judge from the reversed-S configuration of adjacent field boundaries, probably developed over earlier broad ridge-and-furrow.

NY 35 NW 24   Beaumont

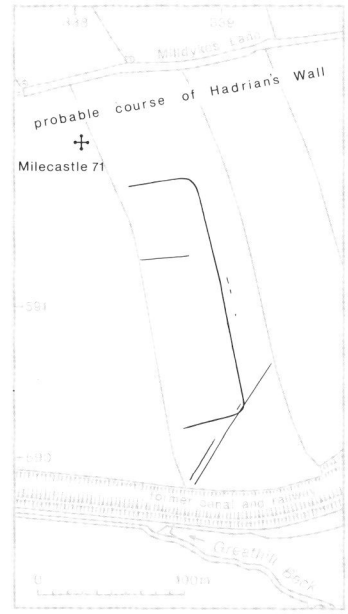

Figure 17 *Beaumont, Cumbria.*

Boomby Lane 1 and 2 (Grinsdale 3 and 4) *Fig 18*

1: NY 36875739   2: NY 36835740

Two superimposed camps, discovered from the air, are set on the summit and the S flank of a low hill, at about 50 m above OD and less than 100 m W of the left bank of the River Eden (St Joseph 1958, 87; Maxwell and Wilson 1987, 14). Their position, between Hadrian's Wall and the Vallum, commands wide-ranging views, especially across the lowlands to the N, and towards Annandale, Eskdale and Liddesdale.

Camp 1 is the larger, and is almost a parallelogram. It measures about 140 m from N to S by about 166 m transversely and occupies an area of approximately 2.3 ha (5.7 acres). It is less clearly defined on aerial photographs than camp 2 (NMR AP NY 3657/13–16). Its N and W sides utilise natural crest lines; to the S and E, where the ground falls gently away to the Eden, the perimeter avoids the largest of several poorly drained depressions which show on air photographs as dark cropmarks. Two visible gates, on the N and S sides, each guarded by a traverse set forward by about 10 m, are not quite opposite one another, the former being positioned on a ratio of 1:2 on the E to W axis, while the latter is in a slightly more central position. Thus,

Figure 18 *Boomby Lane 1 and 2, Cumbria.*

although no certain gate is visible on the E side, the camp appears to face ENE, towards Hadrian's Wall and the presumed course of the Military Way. The latter, however, has not yet been identified anywhere in this area.

Camp 2 measures approximately 72 m from N to S and 142 m from E to W and covers about 1.2 ha (2.9 acres). Its cropmarks are much more pronounced than those of camp 1 (CUCAP WE 60–2) and it overlaps the interior and W side of the latter; nothing more can be deduced of their relationship. Camp 2 straddles the summit of the hill, its W and S sides coinciding approximately with the crest lines. The topography of the hill, dipping gradually towards the ENE along the axis of the camp, may have determined its elongated shape. Just to the E of the central point of the S side, a traverse is clearly visible as a cropmark, but the equivalent point to the N is masked by the modern hedge line. The W side shows no evidence of a gate.

Other, mainly linear, cropmarks recorded on air photographs are of unknown date and function and appear to have no relationship to the camps.

NY 35 NE 22   Beaumont

Brackenrigg 1 and 2 *Figs 19 and 20*

NY 23346149

Parch marks, indicating the former existence of two camps immediately ENE of Brackenrigg, were discovered in 1984 (*Britannia*, 16 (1985), 274; Higham and Jones 1985, fig 40; Maxwell and Wilson 1987, 13; CUCAP CQN 88–93). The camps occupied the W half of a low ridge, at about 17 m above OD, and were apparently aligned along its axis from ENE to WSW. Despite its rather slight elevation, the site has extensive views over the lowlands of the S side of the Solway Firth. Hadrian's Wall is 800 m to the N, and Knockcross camp, on the coast, 1.3 km to the NNE. The ridge slopes away very gently to the SSW; views to the W are restricted, and to the SW they are blocked by Cocklakes Ridge only 300 m to 400 m away.

Each of the camps had a gate on the S and W protected by a traverse. Those of the inner camp, 2, are not precisely coaxial with the entrance of the outer camp, 1, and the relative position of a gap in the fragmentary cropmark of a N side suggests that this line of defence belonged to camp 2. The latter was, therefore, clearly the smaller overall, and measured approximately 93 m from NNW to SSE and at least 140 m from WSW to ENE. A slight diversion of the line of the N ditch of this camp, at the entrance gap, may suggest an external *clavicula*, but clarity is obscured by sowing lines and certainty is impossible (CUCAP CQN 88–93).

The marked lack of alignment of the S gates of the two camps, when taken together with the tendency for gates to be laid out in set proportion relative to the overall dimensions, may suggest that their E side was held in common, but its precise position is uncertain as a result of differential cropping. It clearly did not lie more than a further 60 m to the ENE, as no indications of it were visible in a potentially favourable crop beyond that point (NMR AP NY 2361/8; CUCAP CQN 92). If a standard proportion of 1:2, that is to say *praetentura*: *retentura*, prevailed in the overall dimensions of the camps, then their E side, or sides, probably lay about 10 m E of the present known limit of the cropmarks. Such a line is hinted at on some of the aerial photographs, but the indications are too tenuous to be plotted with any conviction (CUCAP CQN 88–9, 92). This overall disposition would mean that the camps faced ENE along the axis of the ridge.

Small-scale excavation in 1984 confirmed the position of the entrance gap in the WSW side of the larger camp (Jones and Maude 1985). Two sherds of samian ware from the primary fill of the N butt-end of the two-step V-shaped ditch suggested a date in the first half of the 2nd century (K Maude, pers comm). In another trench across the SSE side of the smaller camp, about 10 m ENE of its SW corner, there was evidence of a deliberate back-filling of the ditch. This was taken by the excavator to represent a levelling of camp 2 prior to the construction of camp 1; however, since no stratigraphic relationship was established between the two ditches, their sequence must remain open to question.

Two rectangular enclosures, incorporated into the SW and probable SE corners of the outer camp 1, are undated. Perhaps agricultural in function and post-Roman in date,

Figure 19 *Brackenrigg 1 and 2, Cumbria.*

Figure 20 *Brackenrigg, Cumbria, from the NE; a later enclosure is visible in the SW corner of camp 1.* (30.7.84, CUCAP CQN 90)

they seem to have been set out at a time when that camp's ditch, and perhaps its bank, were still apparent; this may reinforce the suggestion that camp 1 was the later of the two camps. Apart from the slight cropmarks of an irregular network of frost-wedges covering most of the site, the only other features are the parallel lines of modern drains, evident in the area just NE of the farm buildings, where they cut the WSW ditch of camp 1 and drain into the WSW ditch of camp 2.

NY 26 SW 34   Bowness

Brougham Figs 21 and 22

NY 54212918

The cropmarks of a small camp have been recorded 370 m ENE of the fort at Brougham (*Brocavum*), close to the confluence of the Rivers Eamont and Lowther, a position of great strategic importance where several natural routes meet (CUCAP CAL 11–13).

The camp, at about 120 m above OD, occupies the broad summit of a low WNW to ESE ridge, which slopes gently towards a steep escarpment bordering the River Eamont. The erosion of this scarp may have destroyed any NW side of the camp, but there is the barest hint of a turn in the SW ditch, suggesting the position of a W corner; the camp would

Figure 22 *Brougham, Cumbria, from the SW with the traverse clearly visible. The ditched enclosures to the SE of the camp may be fields, or burial plots associated with a Roman cemetery.* (22.7.76, CUCAP CAL 12)

thus have been about 73 m square and just over 0.5 ha (1.3 acres) may have been enclosed. The surviving corners seem to be of unusually large radius and the only certain entrance, positioned in the centre of the SE side, is protected by a relatively long traverse, set barely 5 m outside the ditch. The suggestion, on some aerial photographs, of a gap in the SW side is not substantiated by other photographs and seems to be the result of geological factors.

The camp was clearly positioned so that its rear rampart was on the crest overlooking the river. Although it seems to have faced SE, a local rise in the ridge meant that there would have been dead ground only 80 m to the ESE. The site chosen would have had extensive views over the site of the fort at Brougham and along the Eamont valley.

Cropmarks adjacent to the camp include some small ditched enclosures, perhaps fields or burial plots associated with a cemetery for the fort (*J Roman Stud* **57** (1967), 177, 204, 210).

NY 52 NW 7   Brougham

Figure 21 *Brougham, Cumbria.*

Crackenthorpe Fig 23

NY 65042378

The camp lies in undulating countryside 2 km SE of the camps and fort at Kirkby Thore (*Bravoniacum*) and alongside the Roman road leading down the Eden valley from the

Figure 23 *Crackenthorpe, Cumbria.*

Stainmore Pass. It is in an unusual position, being bisected by a steep-sided natural gully some 70 m wide and up to 7 m deep, drained by the former Gaylock Sike, now culverted. The outlook from the remainder of the camp is as good as can be obtained in a roadside position in this area, but the low ridge that runs southwards from about the midpoint of the SW defences limits the view from the S angle of the camp to only 100 m in a south-westerly direction.

It was evidently the topography that determined the positions of the NE and SW sides of the camp and thus the irregular layout of the defences as a whole. The NE side was intended to be parallel with the Roman road, the line of which, about 50 m away, gradually converges here with that of the line of the disused railway. The embankment of the latter now obstructs the forward lines of sight and reduces the impact of the defences which lay along a minor local crest overlooking the valley of the Trout Beck. The N angle of the perimeter is slightly obtuse, its position determined by another slight crest line which is followed by the NW rampart as far as the E lip of the gully. Similarly, the course of the SW defences was laid out along the rounded summit of a gently rolling spur although, as noted above, this diverges southwards from the ramparts. The camp encloses an area of 9.3 ha (23 acres). The deep gully of the Gaylock Sike covers 2.1 ha (5.2 acres) of the interior; thus a significant proportion would have been unsuitable for the erection of tents. Possibly in an attempt to compensate for this, the position of the S angle was pushed westwards in order to maximise the habitable area on the higher ground to the SW of the Sike. By contrast, the E angle of the camp, to the NE of Powis Cottage, was not conditioned by topographical considerations and is thus a right angle; the indications are, however, that the SE side was not straight but was realigned somewhere around its midpoint, although the reason for this is unclear. It seems that there was another slight change of direction in the SW side at the more northerly of its two known entrances.

When first recorded by Roy in 1769, the earthworks, except perhaps for the S angle, were in common land and were still in good condition; Roy compared the strength of the defences at Crackenthorpe to those at Burnswark in Annandale and Eskdale and to those at Rey Cross in County Durham (Jobey 1978, 80–2; Roy 1793, 73, pl XVII). Subsequent inclosure and cultivation have resulted in the earthworks having been almost entirely levelled. However, sections of the bank survive comparatively well in two places where a hedgerow crosses the Roman perimeter. At the E angle, on the S side of the lane to Long Marton, the fragment of the bank in the hedgerow stands 0.9 m high externally and 0.5 m high internally. Similarly, to the WSW of the N angle, in the hedge beside the A66, the bank is 0.6 m in height. Elsewhere, however, the defences are reduced to no more than a broad swelling which is 0.3 m high at most. When surveyed in 1975, the ditch could still be seen along the S half of the SW side and round the S angle, and also as a cropmark just to the W of the N angle. Its course was also observed in 1975 when the culvert for the Gaylock Sike was cut.

The gates of this camp, each defended by a traverse, are particularly noteworthy. The traverse mounds are now broad, low earthworks and none of them is more than about 0.2 m high. From Roy's observations, and from the RCHME survey in 1975, ten gates have been identified. On the NE, which was presumably the principal side of the camp, the gates were regularly spaced at intervals of about 60 m. This interval is repeated between the two gates in the E half of the SE side, but elsewhere the pattern varied. On the SW, the two gates are about 90 m apart but no third one has been identified to the N. A gate at the SW end of the SE side, close to the S angle and to the crest of the convex slopes into the gully, provided additional access to the habitable ground on the SW side; another entrance probably lay in an equivalent position on the NW side just to the NE of the W angle. The hedgerow on the W side of the A66 seems to have preserved the remains of another traverse as a very gentle and barely surveyable rise, up to 0.7 m high and at least 3 m wide; its position is now marked by a field gate. The mound is greatly spread and its centre lies about 12 m outside the foot of the rampart. The evidence for this traverse was unaccountably rejected by Richmond and McIntyre (1934, 58) in spite of Roy's explicit statement that one half of it survived beside the turnpike in 1769. Its position suggests that this was the only gate in the NW side to the E of the gully. Allowing for one extra gate to the S of Powis Cottage, there may originally have been at least twelve gates in the perimeter.

NY 62 SE 5   Crackenthorpe

Galley Gill (Old Penrith 2) *Fig 24*

NY 49083893

Parts of two sides and a curved angle of what appears to be a camp were revealed by aerial photography in 1949 on the E bank of the River Petteril, about 140 m N of Galley Gill Bridge (St Joseph 1951, 54; CUCAP DM 60; DO 53). These scant indications have since been supplemented by evidence from excavations in 1977 and 1979 (Poulter 1982). The main Roman road from Carlisle (*Luguvalium*) to the fort at Old Penrith (*Voreda*), which is situated less than 500 m to the SSE of the camp, passes barely 150 m to the E, while Knowe Farm camp lies a little over 300 m to the NNW.

The site chosen is the gently sloping SW-facing summit of a spur at about 122 m above OD, between the river and the Galley Gill. The promontory is protected by very steep slopes and there are good views all round, save to the NE. Immediately to the SE, the Galley Gill provides the only easy local access from the Roman road to the river. The

Figure 24 *Galley Gill and Knowe Farm, Cumbria, with Old Penrith fort to the S. The excavations at Galley Gill are marked 'a'.*

siting of the camp may, therefore, have been partly conditioned by the proximity of the river-crossing.

The NE and NW sides form an acute angle, and the NW ditch is interrupted for about 10 m by a causeway, presumably for an entrance. A narrower gap in the NE ditch is less well defined; this may be merely the result of recent agricultural activity or of natural drainage erosion down the slope, but a gate farther to the SE and not less than 4 m wide was located in the excavations (a on Fig 24). Other trenches to the SE suggested that the NE side continued for at least 70 m beyond the visible cropmark to a point not more than 20 m from the edge of the scarp of Galley Gill. If, as seems likely, the camp ditch turned near this scarp edge, then the excavated gate would have occupied a roughly central position in the NE side. If more or less central entrances may be assumed in both sides of the camp its dimensions would have been about 160 m from NW to SE by 100 m transversely and its area approximately 1.6 ha (3.9 acres). It is conceivable, however, that the natural defences of the spur were directly utilised, thus giving the camp a larger area and different proportions.

The excavated ditch was V-shaped, up to 2.2 m wide and at least 1.3 m deep; it had remained open for a short period before being back-filled. There was evidence that the rampart of clay, stones, rubble and turves had been fronted with a fence of stakes positioned immediately on the inner lip of the ditch; there was no berm apparent. Pottery from the primary silt, originally thought to date to the 2nd century only (Poulter 1982, fig 6, no. 5), could well be Flavian or Trajanic in the light of material from recent excavations at Old Penrith (Austen 1991, 156–8). Later pottery from the Galley Gill excavations may derive from activities centred on the *vicus*, of which cropmarks of tracks and enclosures can be seen NE and E of the fort.

Six post holes and five pits were identified during the limited excavations within the interior. The function and date of these are unclear, except for one pit, lined with basketwork and perhaps filled with grain, which was dated by radiocarbon to the 10th or 11th century AD.

NY 43 NE 4   Hesket

Golden Fleece (Carleton) *Figs 25 and 26*

NY 44175178

The site of a small camp lies 300 m ENE of the Golden Fleece (St Joseph 1951, 54; CUCAP DO 47–8) and 5 km SE of Carlisle (*Luguvalium*) at about 70 m above OD. It is situated on the gentle NW-facing slope of a broad NE to SW ridge, immediately overlooking the point at which an unnamed tributary joins the River Petteril. The most significant views seem to have been to the W and NW up the Petteril valley, since ridges obscure long-distance sight-lines in other directions. The Roman road from Carlisle to Old Penrith (*Voreda*), which passes about 450 m SW of the site, is also within view.

The enclosure covers an area of only about 0.5 ha (1.2 acres). Its sides are not exactly parallel, though there seems to be no particular topographical reason for this. Although the W corners are right angles, the S ditch is somewhat shorter than the N side. The camp apparently faced SSE; its forward rampart, 2.5 m higher than that of the N side, was positioned on the crest of the ridge, an exception to the norm. Four gates are apparent, three of which are guarded by traverses set about 8 m forward. The W entrance is obscured by the modern field boundary and a possible traverse here is only faintly detectable (CUCAP DO 47).

A herringbone pattern of modern drains, visible on aerial photographs, covers the field in which most of the camp lies.

NY 45 SW 14   St Cuthbert Without

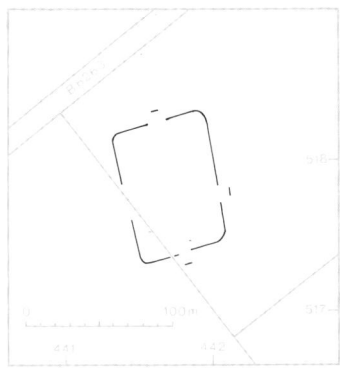

Figure 25 *Golden Fleece, Cumbria.*

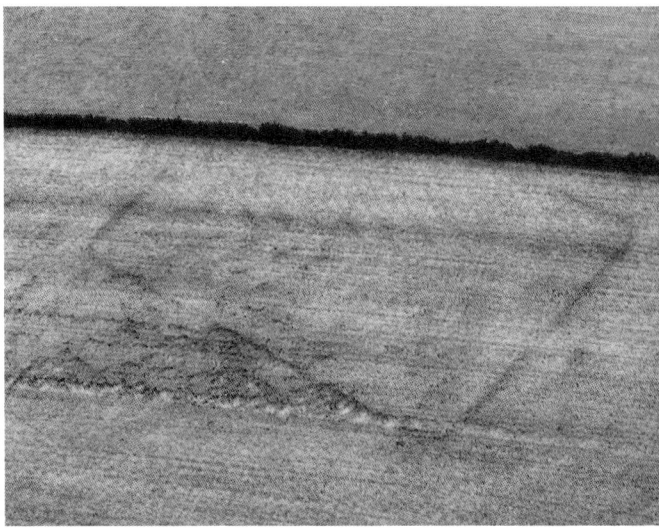

Figure 26 *Golden Fleece, Cumbria, from the SW.* (20.7.61, CUCAP ADZ 79)

Kirkby Thore 1, 2 and 3 *Fig 27*

1: NY 62642521   2: NY 62622516
3: NY 62442504

Three camps, about 1 km WSW of the Roman fort at Kirkby Thore (*Bravoniacum*), were visible as cropmarks in the summers of 1978 (*Britannia* 10 (1979), 283; NMR AP NY 6225/3–6) and 1984 (NMR AP NY 6225/2/151–3). They are situated on a gentle ENE-facing slope, at about 105 m to 110 m above OD, on the N bank of the River Eden, near a point where the river is fordable. There are extensive views in every direction and the main Roman road from York (*Eburacum*) to Carlisle (*Luguvalium*) is clearly visible 500 m to the N.

With the exception of its NE side, most of the perimeter of camp 1 is known. It is not quite rectangular and measures about 198 m from NNW to SSE, by at least 245 m transversely. The S and W angles are slightly over and a little less than ninety degrees respectively, and the overall area is at least 4.8 ha (almost 12 acres). One probable entrance has been identified just N of the central point of the SW side. It appears to have been defended by a traverse, though the crop indications are not entirely clear.

The location of this gate could have been one factor governing the size and shape of camp 2 which occupies the SW corner of camp 1 and shares parts of its SW and SE sides. Camp 2 measures approximately 158 m by 110 m and encloses about 1.7 ha (4.3 acres). The radius of the N angle appears unusually small and there are single central gates in the NE and SW sides.

The orientations of camps 1 and 2 seem to have been conditioned by the topography. The SW ditch, shared by both enclosures, is aligned on a local crest from which it is set back slightly, and the NE side of camp 2 coincides with a very slight rise. Although the precise position of the NE ditch of camp 1 cannot now be traced, it may not have lain much farther E than the recorded cropmarks. Its disappearance may be partly a result of erosion from a former channel of the River Eden, a portion of which survives as a gully, and which is still marked by the present parish boundary. If the line of this boundary E and S of camps 1 and 2 represents the course of the Eden in the Roman period, they may have been sited deliberately within a marked bend.

Camp 3 lies immediately SW of camps 1 and 2 on a similar alignment. It is approximately rectangular, measures about 115 m by 104 m and covers about 1.2 ha (3 acres). The very tenuous nature of the cropmarks makes it uncertain which of the apparent interruptions in the ditch represent gates. The SW side occupies the summit of a broad ridge and the camp may thus have faced NE.

1 and 2: NY 62 NW 27
3: NY 62 NW 41   Kirkby Thore

Figure 27 *Kirkby Thore 1, 2 and 3, Cumbria.*

Knockcross (Old Police House)
Figs 28 and 29

NY 23026272

A small camp on the S shore of the Solway Firth, known from cropmarks (St Joseph 1951, 55; Jones 1992; CUCAP DI 18–19), occupies level ground on the seaward edge of a low cliff at about 4 m above OD and 650 m E of the fort of Bowness-on-Solway (*Maia*). The course of Hadrian's Wall passes about 190 m to the SW of the camp.

The S side and parts of the E and W sides are known, but any NW angle may have been destroyed by erosion and the NW quadrant of the interior is largely overlain by the modern house called Grey Havens. The layout is not quite regular, for the SW angle is slightly obtuse. There is a hint on the aerial photographs, too faint for plotting, that the E side begins to turn a corner near the cliff edge, but the indications are largely obscured by the plough headland at this point. The E side therefore may have extended to about 74 m and the total area enclosed would have been at least 0.6 ha (1.5 acres). The single gates in the E and W sides are each guarded by a traverse, the ditches of which were set approximately 10 m out from the perimeter.

Grey Havens appears to have been built in the late 19th century on the site of a mound, perhaps a barrow (NAR NY 26 SW 5). There is now no trace of this, though a rise 0.8 m high on the edge of the cliff immediately N of the house may be part of the mound. To the W of the camp, cropmarks of ridge-and-furrow are visible.

NY 26 SW 4   Bowness

Knowe Farm (Old Penrith 3)
Figs 24 and 30

NY 48893932

Unusually distinct cropmarks of a camp have been recorded on a terrace above the River Petteril (St Joseph 1951, 54; NMR AP NY 4839/15). The Roman road from Carlisle (*Luguvalium*) to the fort at Old Penrith (*Voreda*), which lies only 850 m to the SSE, passes within about 200 m of the site. Galley Gill camp lies 300 m to the SSE.

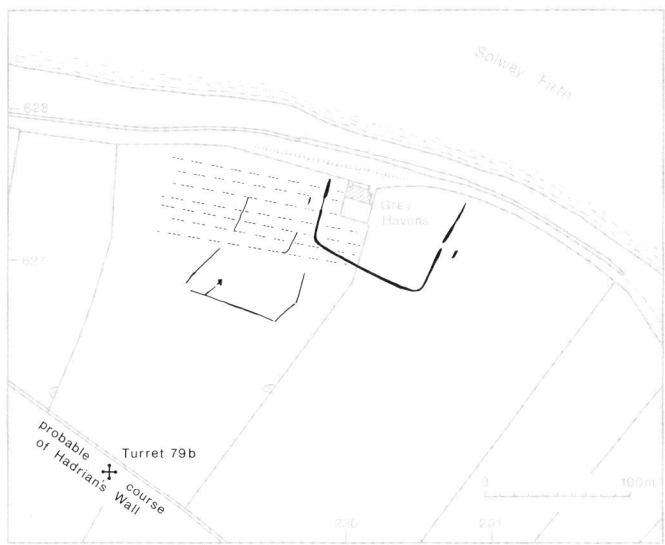

Figure 28 *Knockcross, Cumbria.*

Figure 29 *Knockcross, Cumbria, from the S.* (6.7.49, CUCAP DI 18)

Figure 30 *Knowe Farm, Cumbria, from the SW.* (23.7.84, NMR AP NY 4839/15)

The camp is positioned, at about 125 m above OD, on a gentle SW-facing slope which drops sharply to the River Petteril, providing a natural defence and affording commanding views in most directions, particularly along the valley. The only restriction is to the ENE, where the broad crest of the slope hides a short stretch of the Roman road as it descends into a gully.

The camp, which measures approximately 142 m from NE to SW by 112 m transversely, is not quite rectangular, the NW and SE angles being slightly obtuse while the NE and SW angles are slightly acute. It encloses an area of 1.6 ha (4.0 acres). Each side possessed a gate, more or less centrally placed, protected by a traverse. Just W of the SSE causeway, a slight rise about 36 m long presumably represents the residual rampart. Modern drains cross the site.

NY 43 NE 3   Hesket

Langwathby Moor *Fig 31*

NY 57653342

The incomplete outline of a Roman camp was recorded during aerial reconnaissance in 1992 on Langwathby Moor, just over 100 m E of Langwathby railway station (NMR AP NY 5733/1–6) and 2.5 km NNW of the confluence of the Rivers Eden and Eamont. Situated at about 132 m above OD, it occupies the top of a low NW to SE ridge which separates the Eden valley, some 500 m to the WSW, from the subsidiary valley of the Briggle Beck, just under 1 km to the NE. Its position provides excellent views in all directions. No Roman road network is known in the area, but the Roman fort of Brougham (*Brocavum*), on the main road from York to Carlisle, lies 6 km to the SW.

The cropmarks comprise two complete sides and most of a third. The enclosure, measuring about 98 m from NW to SE, by 86 m transversely, is approximately rectangular. The W angle has a much larger radius than the other corners. A causeway for a gate is visible in each of the NE, SE and SW sides, but no traverses are evident. Both the NE and the SW sides coincide with slight crests, suggesting that the camp may have faced in one or other of these directions.

NY 53 SE 19   Langwathby

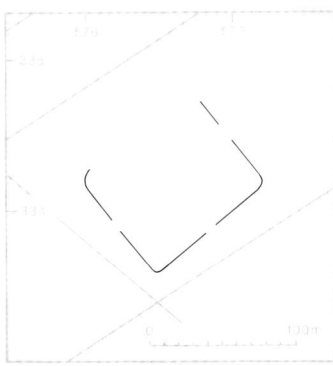

Figure 31 *Langwathby Moor, Cumbria. The field boundary immediately to the SW of the camp has been removed.*

Moss Side 1 and 2 *Fig 32*

1: NY 45626030   2: NY 45696031

A complex of cropmarks at Moss Side, first observed in 1949, consists principally of two superimposed camps (St Joseph 1951, 55; 1965, 78; CUCAP DI 45–8). Of these, the larger, camp 2, possesses what seems best interpreted as an annexe on its N side. The features occupy the almost flat top of a slightly elevated plateau, a little over 30 m above OD, affording uninterrupted views in all directions. The ground falls away gently on the N, S and W sides just beyond the perimeter of the larger camp and its annexe, and there is a peat bog to the NE known as White Moss. The camps lie 1.8 km to the W of Watchclose camp, just over 300 m N of the course of the Stanegate; the Vallum, Hadrian's Wall and Milecastle 61 lie about 400 m to the N.

The smaller camp, 1, is an almost exact parallelogram measuring about 114 m from E to W by 86 m from N to S, and covers an area slightly less than 1.0 ha (2.4 acres). There are centrally placed gates in the shorter E and W sides; that in the former is guarded by a traverse, as may be that in the latter (NMR AP NY 4560/7–8). Though the evidence for the long N and S sides is incomplete, the W part of the S ditch appears unbroken and the W part of the N ditch is virtually so. This suggests that any lateral entrances would probably have lain in the E sector of the enclosure. From this it may be surmised that the camp faced E.

The larger camp, 2, is almost rectangular, measuring 210 m by 187 m, and occupies an area of about 3.9 ha (9.7 acres), excluding its annexe. Opposing gates interrupt the centres of the E and W ditches. No traverse is distinguishable on the E side, but on the W there is a hint that a traverse ditch may coincide with the W ditch of camp 1, as the latter appears to be broader and more substantial at this point (CUCAP AGO 68–9). Opposing lateral gates occupy positions in a 1:2 ratio along the N and S sides; the S gate is guarded by a traverse. Their location may imply that this camp too was E facing.

Immediately N of camp 2 is a slightly trapezoidal enclosure encompassing an area of almost 1.2 ha. The W ditch appears to be a continuation of the W ditch of camp 2. A relatively modern field boundary, now ploughed out but surviving as a cropmark, has obscured the relationship between the E ditch of the annexe and the N side of camp 2. The position of the E side was, however, clearly intended to avoid the N gate of the main camp. There are possible gates in the middle of the E and W sides of the annexe itself. The addition of an annexe to only part of one side of a camp is unusual, but a parallel, possibly of Flavian date, has been recorded at Glenlochar near Castle Douglas, in Stewartry (Frere and St Joseph 1983, 27–9, fig 3).

There is no evidence to clarify the relationship between

Roman Camps in England

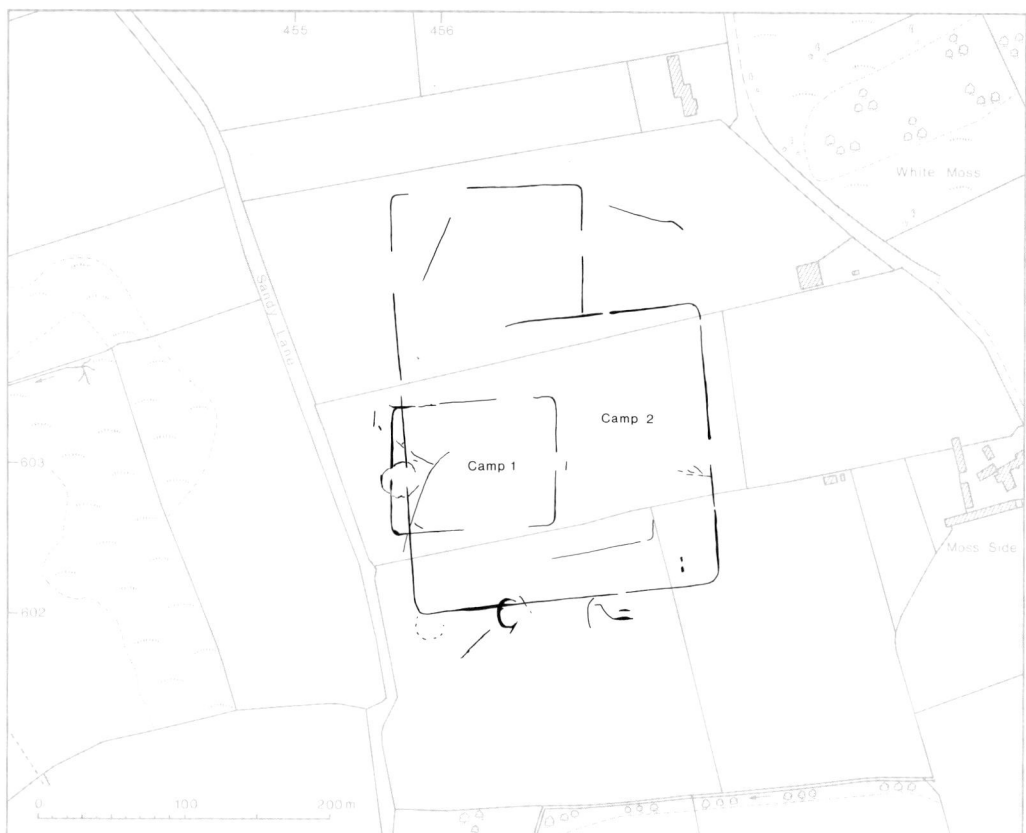

Figure 32 *Moss Side 1 and 2, Cumbria.*

the camps. The clearer definition and more substantial character of the ditches of camp 2 could indicate a later date, the assumption being that a less substantial work is unlikely to have been built across the remains of a stronger and larger one. The argument, however, is not compelling.

NY 46 SE 17   Stanwix

Nowtler Hill 1 and 2 (Grinsdale 1 and 2) *Figs 1 and 33*

1: NY 36275701   2: NY 36005676

The existence of two camps, 300 m apart on Nowtler Hill, a little over 1 km SW of Grinsdale village, has been known for almost two centuries. Plans of them were first made in about 1800 by Daniel Lysons (BL Add Ms 9462, fol 65; Fig 1) and the camps were also noted by John Hodgson (1840, 300). By the early 1850s (MacLauchlan 1857, sheet V; 1858, 79; OS 1st edn 25-inch plan Cumberland XXII.2, 1866) the condition of the surface remains had begun to deteriorate. The camps were subsequently obliterated by ploughing, only to be rediscovered from the air in 1945 and 1949 (St Joseph 1951, 55).

Camp 1 (CUCAP P 59–60), at about 35 m above OD,

Figure 33 *Nowtler Hill 1 and 2, Cumbria.*

occupies the summit of Nowtler Hill, a low rounded rise forming part of a NE-projecting spur overlooking the Eden valley. There are panoramic views in all directions and particularly across the lines of the Vallum and of Hadrian's Wall, respectively some 500 m and 1050 m to the NE.

The defences of this relatively small camp enclose an area of about 0.5 ha (1.2 acres). It is not quite rectangular in shape, the NW and SE sides measuring 78 m and 73 m respectively and the NE and SW sides 64 m. The W and E angles are obtuse, and the N and S angles are slightly acute. There are almost central gaps in the NW, SE and NE sides, the former two being guarded by traverses. Although a traverse in the NE side is no longer visible on aerial photographs, owing to its proximity to the road, its former existence is recorded by both Lysons and MacLauchlan. Lysons' record, however, disagrees with the other older authorities in that it depicts a gate with a traverse on the SW side. In this he may have been in error as the ditch is equally clearly continuous on aerial photographs. It is possible, however, that this apparent continuity is due to the incorporation of the ditches into the more recent drainage system. The camp probably faced NE.

Camp 2 is less than 300 m SW of camp 1. It occupies a very gentle SW-facing slope at a little under 35 m above OD, and immediately SW of Nowtler Hill; a broad low saddle connects it with the site of camp 1. There are extensive views in all directions except to the NE. Here, the rising ground of the hill restricts the view beyond camp 1.

This very small rectangular camp (CUCAP DI 25), aligned ESE to WNW, measures about 57 m by 39 m and covers an area of about 0.2 ha (0.5 acres). According to Lysons, the ditch was interrupted by gates on all four sides, each being guarded by a traverse. For three sides this is confirmed by the evidence of aerial photography, but indications of the traverse on the ESE side have been destroyed by a relatively modern hedge line which cuts through its centre. The position of the opposing gates, in a ratio of approximately 1:2 along the NNE and SSW defences, indicates that the camp faced ESE.

1: NY 35 NE 15   2: NY 35 NE 21   Beaumont

Plumpton Head *Figs 10 and 34*

NY 49903536

The existence of a camp on rolling ground immediately NW of the hamlet of Plumpton Head, has long been known (St Joseph 1951, 54; 1955, 83; CUCAP BRC 6, 7), but it was not until the 1970s that detailed fieldwork by RCHME and repeated aerial reconnaissance was able to establish its full circuit and elucidate its remarkably asymmetrical character (Maxwell and Wilson 1987, 12; CUCAP AZJ 76–8).

The camp lies in the Petteril valley, between about 130 m and 137 m above OD; it is only 60 m W of the main Roman road from York (*Eburacum*) to Carlisle (*Luguvalium*) and just 3.1 km S of the fort at Old Penrith (*Voreda*). Laid out in the form of an irregular polygon, the defences of the camp straddle a broad shallow N to S valley and enclose an area of about 9.5 ha (23.5 acres). Its overall disposition has been chosen with some care and is, in the main, dependent on the line selected for its long W side. This W side, a little over 350 m in length, is sited parallel to and slightly to the W of the summit of a rounded ridge which extends northwestwards from the lip of the flood plain of the River Petteril to a point close to the NW corner of the camp, where it levels out. This ridge provides extensive views in all directions, particularly over the land to the W which is not visible from the adjacent stretch of Roman road. The fact that the camp is not aligned on the Roman road may also indicate that it is earlier than the road, although the topographical factors may have been paramount.

There is evidence for at least two entrances in the W side, each defended by a traverse. The N one, set forward about 22 m, is the more clearly defined; a field boundary has distorted the cropmarks of the second which is set in the centre of the side. Two marks are visible here outside the line of the ditch; of these, the inner one, about 20 m away, may represent the ditch of the traverse. Though the former existence of a third entrance in the S portion of the W side is probable, there is no clear evidence of such at present, despite suggestions to the contrary (Maxwell and Wilson 1987, 12).

The N side of the camp, which, except for its W extremity, lies on mainly flat ground, is the most irregular of all. Its E section is on two separate alignments, and its central part curves uncharacteristically abruptly southwards by about 35 m. These diversions were clearly intended to avoid the boggy ground associated with a nearby gill. This watercourse was still in existence in the mid 19th century (OS 1st edn 6-inch map, Cumberland XLIX, 1867), but has since been ploughed and is distinguishable only as a cropmark. There are no causeways apparent in the N side, but two isolated cropmarks of short ditches may reasonably be interpreted as traverses; one occurs to the W of the curving diversion, about 19 m forward of the ditch. The other lies about 50 m to the E of the E edge of the re-entrant, and about 16 m outside the change in the angle of the circuit, a characteristic position for a gate. It is possible that because of the marshy character of this area there were no corresponding ditch causeways. Alternatively, any former entrance gaps may have been closed in subsequent draining activities.

The well-defined ditch of the E side of the camp, about 170 m in length, is interrupted by three relatively closely spaced, unusually wide gates, each protected by a traverse set roughly 18 m outside the circuit. In 1973 the rampart could just be discerned as a low, spread bank, but ploughing has since completely levelled it. The NE part of this side crosses level ground, but to the SW of the central entrance

Figure 34 *Plumpton Head, Cumbria. The stippled areas represent former portions of the bank which were visible on the ground as soil marks in the mid 1970s.*

it rises to meet a N to S ridge, the N end of which roughly coincides with the SE corner of the camp.

The S side of the camp does not show as a cropmark, but its probable course, approximately 330 m long, including a slight change in alignment about 50 m E of its SW corner, is apparently fossilised in a modern field boundary. From the SE corner of the circuit this crosses a hollow and then rises to join the main ridge at the SW corner of the camp. On the S side of the field boundary, an outward-facing scarp, 0.1 m to 0.7 m high, surmounted by stone from a relatively recent field wall and by rubble collected in field clearance, may represent the remains of the Roman defences.

NY 53 NW 1   Penrith and Hesket

Troutbeck 1, 2 and 3
Figs 35, 36, 37, 38 and 39

1: NY 37932730   2: NY 38902760
3: NY 38392731

A small fort, and three camps that are exceptional in having all their gates defended by *claviculae*, form a group of earthworks that survive to the N and to the NW of the hamlet of Troutbeck, 15 km to the W of the fort at Brougham (*Brocavum*). The position chosen is of strategic importance since it controls one of the principal natural routeways into the uplands of the Lake District from the broad lowlands of the River Eden. A Roman road, leading south-westwards to Troutbeck from the fort at Old Penrith (*Voreda*), probably continued to near Keswick (Bellhouse 1954; Allan and Richardson 1978 and 1980).

The four sites make the most of what level ground there is in this undulating landscape and occupy the gentle S slopes of Lofshaw Hill and its SW spur; these lie between the

Naddles Beck and the Trout Beck, two tributaries of the River Glenderamackin which drains westwards, around the S side of the massif of Blencathra and Skiddaw, to the foot of Derwent Water. The exact date and relative chronology of the four sites is not known, but the similarity of plan of both the fort and camp 2 at Troutbeck with their counterparts at Oakwood, in Ettrick and Lauderdale, which are Flavian in date (Steer and Feachem 1954), may be significant. The numbering of the camps follows that of Lenoir (1977).

Camp 1 (Fig 36), the most westerly of the Roman earthworks, lies at 255 m above OD, about 14 m below the fort and 100 m from its NW corner, on the almost level summit of a spur that extends westwards, parallel with the N bank of the Trout Beck. In contrast to the other three sites, this camp is oriented NW to SE. It is almost rectangular, measuring 205 m from NE to SW by 223 m transversely, and encloses an area of about 4.0 ha (10 acres). The former line of the A66, bypassed in 1974, crosses the S quarter of the site and from it a farm track leads N to Fieldhead. The fence bounding the cutting in which the present A66 runs is immediately outside the S angle of the camp.

For much of its course, the enclosing bank is well preserved, the scarps surviving up to 0.4 m internally and 0.7 m externally, above a ditch 0.2 m deep; the latter is only visible on the surface on the NW and for a short distance on the SW. A discontinuous bank, no more than 0.2 m high, lies approximately parallel to the S half of the SE side. A section cut through the defences in 1955 just to the S of the SE gate, and another cut in 1973 just to the N of the gate, revealed that the ditch was about 1.0 m deep and between 1.4 m and 1.7 m across. A narrow berm, 0.3 m wide, was found in 1955. The bank was found to be 3.0 m and 3.8 m wide in the two sections, and consisted of clay and cobbles upcast from the ditch, retained by inner and outer kerbs of stacked turves (Bellhouse 1956, 32–3; Charlesworth 1974; *Britannia* 5 (1974), 412–13).

The interior is generally level but in the SE it is broken up by shallow, natural watercourses which have scoured away the NE bank to the S of the gate. Each gate was defended by an internal *clavicula*. On the SE, NE and NW, the mounds are 0.5 m, 0.2 m and 0.4 m high respectively; the excavation of the SE gate in 1973 demonstrated that the external ditch closely followed the line of the curving mound (Charlesworth 1974). The position of the NE gate suggests that the camp faced SE. A section cut in 1973 in an attempt to locate an equivalent gate on the SW side rapidly became waterlogged and failed to provide much information. The excavator concluded that the gate lay under the modern road

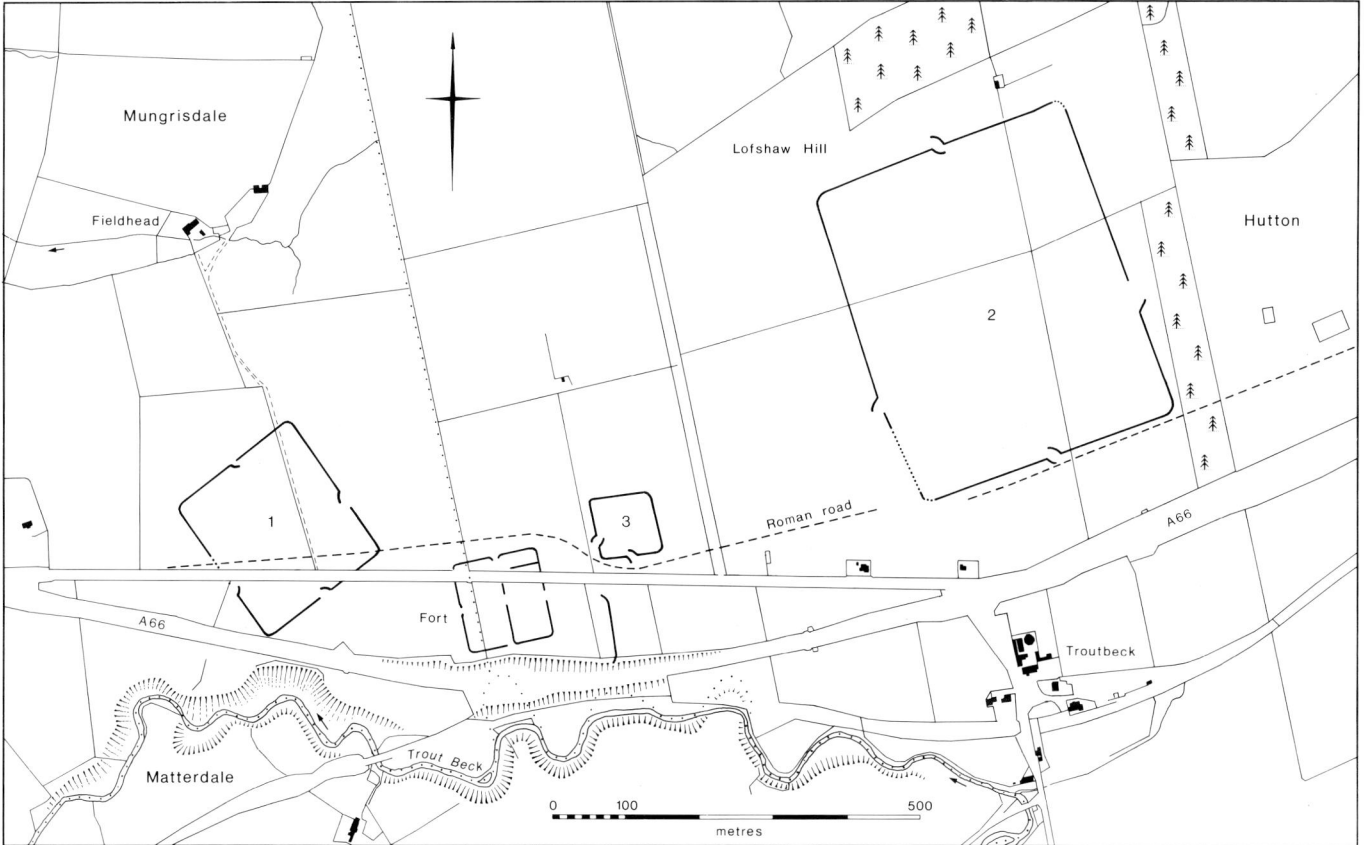

Figure 35 *Troutbeck, Cumbria. Location plan of the fort and camps 1, 2 and 3.*

Roman Camps in England

Figure 36 *Troutbeck 1, Cumbria.*

(Charlesworth 1974). The reason for the NW to SE orientation is unknown; the camp evidently preceded the main Roman road, the course of which cuts across its S half from the E angle (Allan and Richardson 1980). The earthworks of this road are now somewhat confused in this stretch but its general course is clear. Small-scale excavations were apparently undertaken on camp 1 by Manchester University in 1976, and before 1973 by Oundle School and the Brathay Centre. No details have been published.

The easternmost of the camps, 2 (Fig 37), is also the largest, enclosing an area of 9.7 ha (23.9 acres). Its S side is aligned with the contours along the crest of the slope above

Figure 37 *Troutbeck 2, Cumbria.*

Roman Camps in England

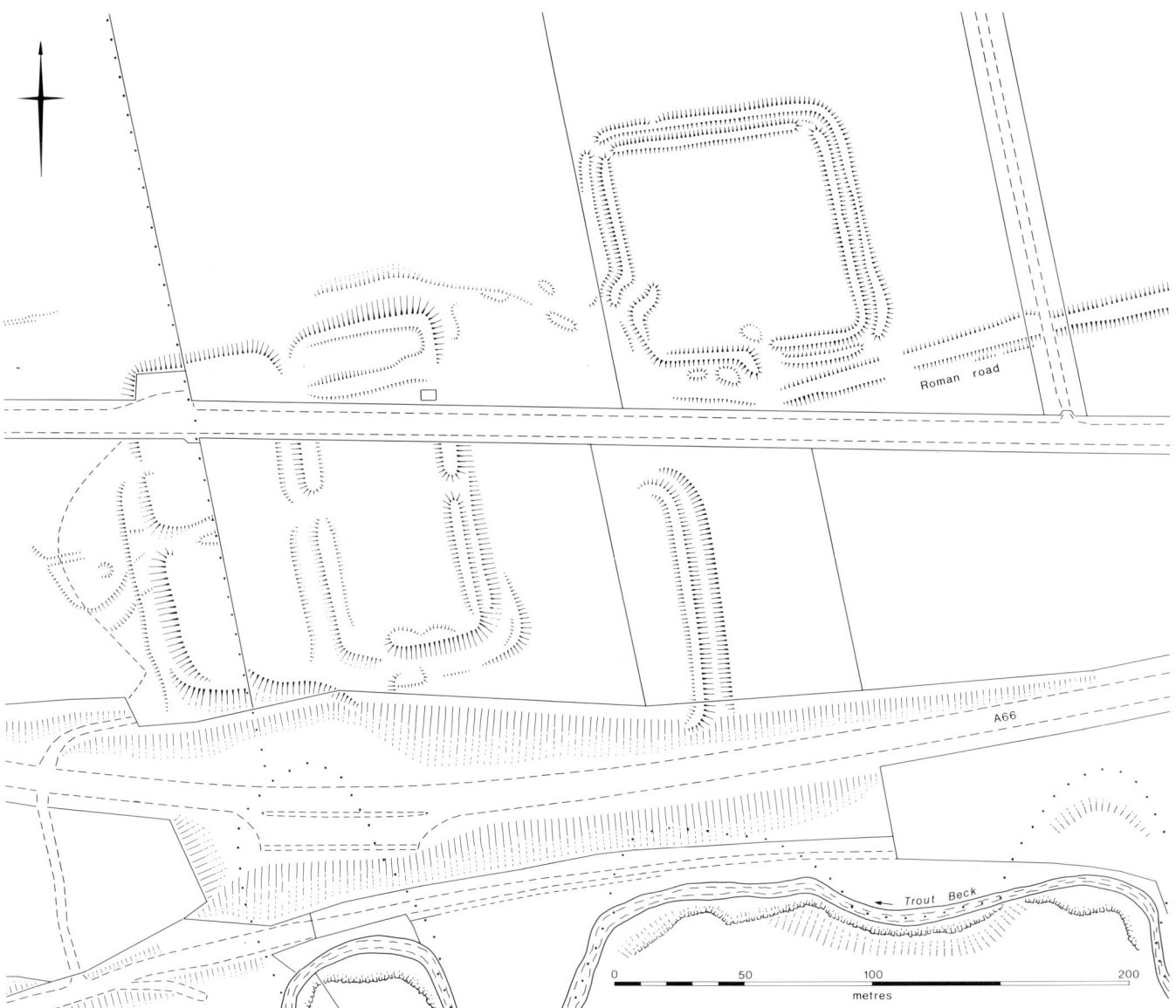

Figure 38 Troutbeck 3, Cumbria, with the fort to the SW.

a shallow valley to the SSE; the course of the Roman road lies immediately outside the camp's defences. The W half of the N side was laid out along the S crest of the almost level summit of Lofshaw Hill itself, at 305 m above OD. The position of the NE angle and the lines of the E and W sides simply served to complete the enclosure to the desired size; the surveyors setting them out were not able to take advantage of any naturally defensible lines. The S rampart, alongside the Roman road, is straight but each of the other three sides is realigned at the gateway. This realignment is most marked on the SSW where, to the S of the gate, the defences turn perceptibly to the E in order that the SW angle should lie on the crest of a hill. None of the angles is a right angle.

Four gates are visible, at least three of them defended by internal and external *claviculae*. The N and S gates are at the central points but the lateral gates are offset, in the ratio 1:2, indicating that the camp faced S. Two-thirds of the W side, to the S of a field boundary that runs from E to W, have been greatly reduced by cultivation, thus, the external *clavicula* of the gate is now barely 0.1 m high; it is most readily identifiable by its vestigial ditch, the line of which has been reused as a shallow drain cutting through poorly developed ridge-and-furrow. Some slight indications of an external bank may have been created by upcast from the comparatively modern drain on the line of the Roman ditch, but since this feature is found elsewhere around the perimeter of the camp it may be an original element in the design. To the N of the field boundary, the ridge-and-furrow (not shown on plan) lies parallel to the defences which, in consequence, are much better preserved. The outer and inner scarps of the bank survive here to heights of 0.7 m and 0.3 m respectively.

Around the NW angle, where the defences climb almost to the crest of the hill, the line of the ditch is visible as a narrow terrace. Some small surface quarries impinge on the Roman earthworks. Where best preserved on this N side, the inner scarp of the rampart is 0.8 m high and the outer scarp of the ditch survives to 0.4 m. The hilltop continues to rise northwards for about 2 m in vertical height, creating a substantial area of dead ground between Lofshaw Hill and Naddles Crag. If the defences had been placed on the N crest of the summit, about 50 m away, this would have been eliminated.

The N gate is in a slight depression; the mounds of its *claviculae* are 0.3 m high but the ditch in each case is almost invisible. A vestigial, unsurveyable, outer mound beside the external *clavicula* may have been reused as a ploughing headland. To the E, the defences descend a gentle slope and are crossed obliquely, and are almost entirely obliterated, by ridge-and-furrow. The ground levels out at a modern field boundary, aligned almost N to S; between this point and the site of the NE angle the land is poorly drained. The arc of

Figure 39 *Troutbeck 1 and 3, Cumbria, from the E. Camp 3 lies in the foreground with the fort, which is cut by a modern road (then the A66), to its SW. Beyond is camp 1, also cut through by the modern road and by the Roman road. Since this photograph was taken the A66 has been realigned to pass immediately to the S of the fort and of camp 1.* (27.11.73, CUCAP BPE 63)

the angle has been eroded away and the defences only reappear on the slightly drier ground to the SE.

The N end of this E side is set on a slight change of slope, from which the land falls gently to the E. The defences are cut by ridge-and-furrow, aligned from E to W; the bank, now 0.1 m high, is spread to a width of 5 m and the ditch is little more than a vegetation mark less than 2 m across. The condition of the earthworks deteriorates further towards the S boundary of this field, set in a gentle dip, and it is difficult to trace any surviving scarps through the rushes in the field beyond. However, the external *clavicula* of the E gate is still relatively well preserved, surviving to a height of 0.4 m.

It is clear that at the SE angle the defences have been much levelled by ploughing; the S rampart, set along a false crest overlooking the valley, is represented by a lynchet up to 0.5 m high which is cut by shallow natural drainage channels. Here the Roman road runs parallel with the side of the camp, its S scarp standing 0.7 m high. The mound of the external *clavicula* of the S gate is visible only as a slight swelling, its tip overlain by the *agger* of a road, apparently later in date, that diverges to pass to the S of a quarry to the W which cuts across the line of the Roman road. The surface features of the last phase of use of the Roman road suggest that, despite the orientation of the camp, the road was constructed later than the defences. This chronological relationship has also been deduced from the course of the road itself (Bellhouse 1956, 35–6). The SW angle of the defences has been ploughed flat, except perhaps for a small elongated mound, 0.2 m high, which may represent the S end of the W side of the camp. To the N of this, the bank has been levelled by cultivation for more than 80 m.

Camp 3 (Fig 38), the smallest of the group, was constructed on the domed summit of the spur at 279 m above OD, immediately to the NE of the fort, which occupies the forward end of the spur above the steeper slopes to the S and W. Before the discovery of the fort (*Britannia* 5 (1974), 413), the camp was variously classified as a fort and a fortlet, probably on the basis that it has an additional outer mound around the defences. Since there is evidence for such a mound at camp 2 there seems no reason to suggest that this much smaller site is not also a camp. Enclosing an area of about 0.6 ha (1.6 acres), it is not quite square but was laid out as a parallelogram, measuring about 105 m across overall.

Where best preserved, the scarps of the inner rampart stand 1.0 m high externally and 0.3 m high internally; the outer mound is up to 0.3 m high. There are two gates on the S and on the W, each defended, as at camp 2, by double *claviculae*. The internal mound on the S has been reduced by ploughing and the external mound on the W is cut by a modern drain. The site is crossed by ridge-and-furrow, aligned from NNE to SSW, but the earthworks remain distinct, except on the W side where the ditch between the ramparts is little more than a vegetation mark. The Roman road from the E, aligned on the E gateway of the fort, passes the S side of the camp, where there is a junction with the Roman road that takes a more awkward route to the N of the fort and then westwards across camp 1. The latter course presumably postdates both the fort and the camp.

1: NY 32 NE 4   Mungrisdale
2: NY 32 NE 3   3: NY 32 NE 2   Hutton

Warcop (Sandford) *Figs 40 and 41*

NY 74081677

The almost complete perimeter of a small camp was recorded from the air in 1949 (St Joseph 1951, 54; CUCAP DO 85–6), less than 1.5 km NW of Warcop. Situated at about

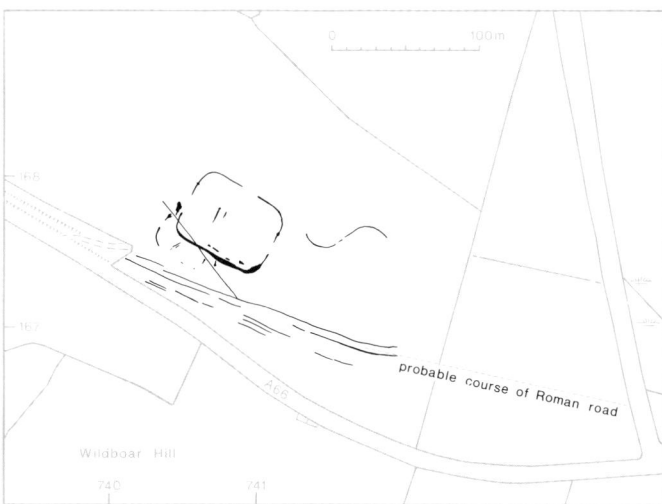

Figure 40 *Warcop, Cumbria.*

Figure 41 *Warcop, Cumbria, from the NW.* (9.7.49, CUCAP DO 86)

155 m above OD, on the main route from York (*Eburacum*) to Carlisle (*Luguvalium*) across the Stainmore Pass, it lies about 5.5 km NW of the fort at Brough (*Verteris*).

The camp was constructed on the gentle SW-facing slope of a spur which descends gradually to the SE; its NE defences follow the fairly broad summit of the ridge. There are good views in most directions, particularly to the W across the Eden valley; to the NW, however, the ridge continues to rise, obscuring this line of sight. The camp, measuring approximately 60 m by 50 m, is more or less rectangular, with each corner rounded in a very broad arc. The unusually large radius of the corners of this camp bears comparison with that of the small camp at Brougham, which is farther to the W along the same road. Enclosing an area of about 0.3 ha, the NE, NW and SE ditches are each interrupted by a relatively wide central gate. No traverses can be distinguished but the ground, which is crossed by field drains, has been under cultivation for a long time, and the cropmarks are not well defined.

The probable course of the Roman road across the Stainmore Pass can be traced as a cropmark less than 20 m S of the camp. To the W it appears as a terrace on the N verge of the modern road, while in the field immediately SE of the camp, a ploughed-down terrace and a hump in the E field boundary apparently mark its position.

NY 71 NW 4   Warcop

Watchclose
(Watchcross or Steadfolds) *Fig 42*

NY 47576019

The existence of a small camp at Watchclose, 1.8 km E of the camps at Moss Side, has long been known. The site, which is now within Carlisle airport, occupies part of an almost level plateau at about 40 m above OD; the ground slopes away gently to the SE and N. The course of the Stanegate, less than 300 m to the N, can be clearly seen, but the line of Hadrian's Wall, almost 1.3 km to the N, is obscured by a low ridge.

When John Horsley visited the site in the early 18th century, the earthworks were described as 'very fair and visible'. By 1783 cultivation had begun to level the remains, a process nearly completed by 1833 (Horsley 1732, 154; Hodgson 1840, 218–19; Richmond and Hodgson 1936).

The NW half of the camp, except for the NW angle of the ditch, is overlain by the SW end of the main runway. The latter is now wider than when the camp was first photographed in 1949 (CUCAP DI 51–2) and accordingly the transcribed cropmarks encroach on the area of the present runway.

The plan determined by excavations in 1935 (Richmond and Hodgson 1936) is confirmed in part by the cropmarks.

Figure 42 *Watchclose, Cumbria.*

Although the rampart had by then entirely gone, the remains of the ditch were found to be 2.4 m wide by 0.9 m deep, enclosing an area of 0.5 ha (1.4 acres). None of the sides appeared exactly parallel, the W one bowing outwards and changing its alignment at the gate. Three gates, one at the centre of each of the W, N and E sides, were all protected by traverses, each of which, according to the excavation plan, lay about 5 m in front of the ditch-terminals. As the S side apparently lacked any gate, the camp presumably faced N. No traces of internal structures were found in the 1935 excavations, but the interior was little sampled.

NY 46 SE 1   Irthington

Willowford *Fig 43*

NY 62546612

This camp lies in pasture at a height of about 155 m above OD on the shoulder of a spur, 350 m S of Turret 48b on Hadrian's Wall. To the N there is an almost precipitous descent to the flood plain of the River Irthing, and to the S to a shallower dry valley. There are extensive views in all directions except to the WSW where the higher ground of the spur restricts visibility.

The camp is an irregular polygon with maximum dimensions of 90 m by 70 m within a shallow ditch up to 0.3 m deep. Erosion has reduced the latter to little more than a narrow terrace in the SW quarter. The only substantial length of rampart to survive is on the NW where it stands 0.3 m high.

The E side of the camp bows outwards, although there is no topographical reason for this; its shallow asymmetrical apex is marked by a gate with a comparatively well-preserved traverse which has a bank 0.1 m high and a ditch

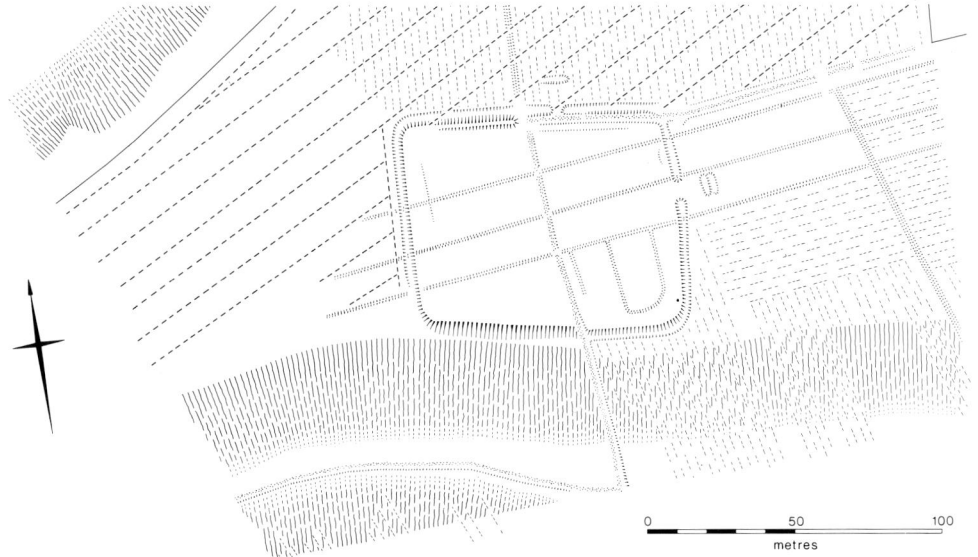

Figure 43 *Willowford, Cumbria.*

0.1 m deep. A second entrance is traceable on the N; this has been mutilated by a later, now ruinous, wall of stone and turf which extends along part of the line of the rampart, and by a buried drain which cuts across the causeway. The traverse is reduced to a barely discernible ditch; this is overlain by narrow ridge-and-furrow and has been disturbed at its W end by another buried drain. On the S, where the rampart lies along the crest, the ground falls away so steeply as to make the provision of an entrance there impractical.

Later agricultural activity can be seen in and around the camp. The ruinous wall turns to bisect the interior from N to S and three parallel earthen banks, 0.1 m high, cross the camp from E to W, overlying the Roman defences. In the SE quarter there are two similar banks, one of which forms a small enclosure. Narrow ridge-and-furrow extends to the outer edge of the ditch on the N and SE and appears to be contemporary with or later than the parallel banks. On the N and W a modern system of buried drains, designed to avoid the camp, has impinged on the defences in places. A glacial erratic boulder, known as the Greystone, lies within the SE angle of the camp.

NY 66 NW 7   Upper Denton

Devon

Higher Kingdon (Alverdiscott)
Figs 44 and 45

SS 49262548

The greater part of the perimeter of a camp has been recorded as cropmarks to the N of Gammaton Moor, at the N end of a ridge which forms some of the highest ground on the E edge of the Torridge valley (St Joseph 1977, 126, fig 1; CUCAP BUN 48). The S half of the camp occupies the gentle E knoll of a local summit, at about 150 m above OD. The knoll is aligned from E to W and gives extensive views in all directions. The SW slope of the lower W knoll has been cut into by the triple ditches of an enclosure. These earthworks, now levelled, have consistently produced much more pronounced cropmarks than that of the camp (Silvester 1978, 252–3). The relationship between the two sites is not clear.

Figure 44 *Higher Kingdon, Devon, from the NE. The ditch of the camp, here seen as a 'reverse' cropmark, is obscured in places by former field boundaries and other features of geological origin. The ditches of the prehistoric enclosure to the SW are clearly visible.* (18.7.75, CUCAP BUN 48)

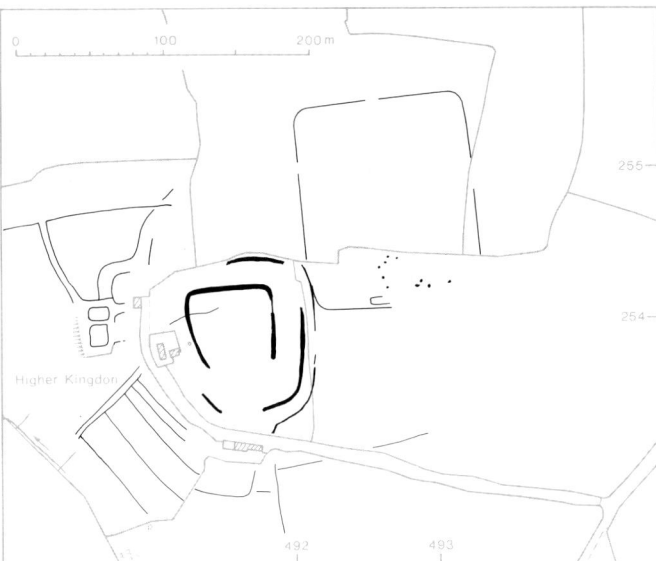

Figure 45 *Higher Kingdon, Devon. The well-marked triple ditches to the E of Higher Kingdon Farm are probably of prehistoric date. The cropmarks to the W and SW of the farm relate to the medieval hamlet of Higher Kingdon; other cropmarks in the vicinity of the camp are geological in origin.*

The topography and the wholesale removal of former field boundaries have made the transcription of the cropmarks particularly difficult. Nevertheless, it seems that the camp enclosed an area of about 1.6 ha within its ditch. The excavation of a drainage trench in 1978 across the S and W sides suggested that the ditch was about 1.3 m wide; however, the upcast material had been completely levelled and below the plough-soil the ditch only survived to a depth of 0.5 m (Silvester 1978, 251–2).

The layout of the camp is rather unusual in relation to the topography. The W side was set out so as to cut across the slight saddle between the knolls, immediately outside the triple-ditched enclosure. The S defences, positioned down the hillside, would not have been intervisible with the rest of the perimeter or with most of the interior. These cropmarks are very faint and thus no SE corner has been transcribed.

A simple gate is visible close to the centre of the N side, which itself seems to have been realigned slightly at this point; the recorded line of the S ditch may suggest a similar arrangement there. An apparent gap in the cropmark of the W ditch may perhaps also indicate the presence of a gate; on the E side, however, a former field boundary crossed the defences, obscuring the cropmarks.

SS 42 NE 24   Alverdiscott

North Tawton *Fig 46*

SS 66350060

Fragments of at least one camp have been identified in the vicinity of The Barton, within a large multi-period complex of cropmarks on the E bank of the River Taw (Griffith 1984, 20–5). The site lies in gently rolling countryside, immediately adjacent to the river-crossing of the Roman road leading westward from Exeter.

The largest and most coherent feature, camp 1, is situated near the top of a slight rise at about 140 m above OD, and about 500 m to the N of the Roman fort and its annexe which survive as rather eroded earthworks. From camp 1 visibility is unrestricted except to the E, where the ground continues to rise gently for another 500 m. To the N of the road (A3072) between The Barton and de Bathe Cross, the N ditch of camp 1, and part of the E one, can be traced on aerial photographs (CUCAP BTR 18–21). The N side, which occupies a shallow dip, may have been aligned to meet at a tangent the earthwork of what is now only a double ring-ditch, although the nature and date of this cropmark are not known for certain. A possible NW angle can be traced on photographs immediately E of the field boundary to the N of The Barton. If this is accepted, it would give the N side a total length of just over 420 m; the W defensive ditch would thus have lain as much as 60 m to the E of a W-facing scarp which descends gently to the flood plain of the River Taw.

Only approximately 200 m of the E ditch of the camp can be determined, but it occupies the highest part of the site, and the whole of the probable defensive circuit would have been visible from a point roughly midway along it. None of the breaks in the ditches can be identified as a gate. A possible position for the S ditch would have been between 20 m and 30 m to the S of the A3072, just to the N of the crest of a gentle S-facing slope roughly parallel with the N side; the SW corner of the camp would thus have been immediately S of The Barton (SS 66270056) where the ground begins to drop away more steeply to the W. Within these hypothetical limits, the camp would have covered about 10 ha (25 acres).

Just over 20 m N of the N side of camp 1, an interrupted ditch running from E to W has been claimed as the N side of another camp which, from its position, would have overlapped camp 1. However its putative NW angle, at SS 65910073, and W side, as published by Griffith (1984,

Figure 46 *North Tawton, Devon, with the fort to the S. The Roman road to the N of the fort is visible as a parch mark.*

21), could not be verified from the aerial photographic evidence. The topography is quite unsuitable for a camp, since the proposed line of the W side lies on the actual flood plain of the River Taw while the N ditch descends the river scarp to meet it.

An acute rounded angle can be seen among cropmarks about 120 m N of camp 1, but there is insufficient evidence to support its identification as part of a camp. It lies on level ground about 60 m E of the river scarp, and if Roman and military in origin, it would almost certainly have stopped short of it.

Between The Barton and the fort is another multi-period complex of cropmarks. No additional camps are apparent, but there is evidence of the NW corner of a substantial double-ditched compound of Roman military character, within which a smaller two-period enclosure of fortlet size has been laid out (Griffith 1984, 20–4; Maxwell and Wilson 1987, 3–4; NAR SS 60 SE 23). Clearly the river-crossing at North Tawton constituted a position of great strategic significance and its installations reflect a sequence of changes which probably extended over a considerable period.

SS 60 SE 18   North Tawton

County Durham

Bowes Moor *Fig 47*

NY 92971251

Immediately to the N of the signal station or watch-post on Bowes Moor which was occupied in the late 3rd or early 4th century (Annis forthcoming) are the very slight remains of a small square camp, first identified from the air in 1979 (CUCAP CKQ 4–8). Measuring only 56 m across inside the ditch, the camp lies at 400 m above OD, on almost level ground which slopes very gently to the SE. Its S side is about 60 m from the line of the Roman road from York (*Eburacum*) to Carlisle (*Luguvalium*), now the A66, and it is separated from this main route over the Stainmore Pass by the earthworks of the signal station, as little as 8 m away. The two enclosures are axially offset from one another. Although there are good views from the site along the road, to Rey Cross in the W and to Vale House in the E, the valley of the River Greta lies in dead ground to the S.

On the surface, much of the perimeter is reduced by a thin layer of overlying peat to a single scarp of minimal height. The line of the ditch is just traceable as a faint depression no more than 0.2 m deep; a short length of the inner scarp of the internal bank survives as a slight earthwork along the S side. The E perimeter was sectioned, close to the SE corner, in 1990 (Annis forthcoming). This revealed that the ditch here was 0.9 m wide and 0.2 m deep; the bank was found to be 1.9 m wide and 0.3 m high, the upcast material being held in place by a turf revetment. There are now no signs on the surface of any gates. A short length of ditch, which may be a later drain, extends southwards for a few metres from the SW corner.

The rounded corners of the earthwork, its layout parallel to the Roman road and its proximity to the signal station are not in themselves sufficiently strong criteria with which to argue for a Roman date. Association with the signal station is, however, suggested by the position of the larger enclosure; unless it is also Roman in date there would seem to be no need not to set it in a more convenient position beside the road. Camp and signal station may, therefore, have been in contemporary use.

NY 91 SW 9   Bowes

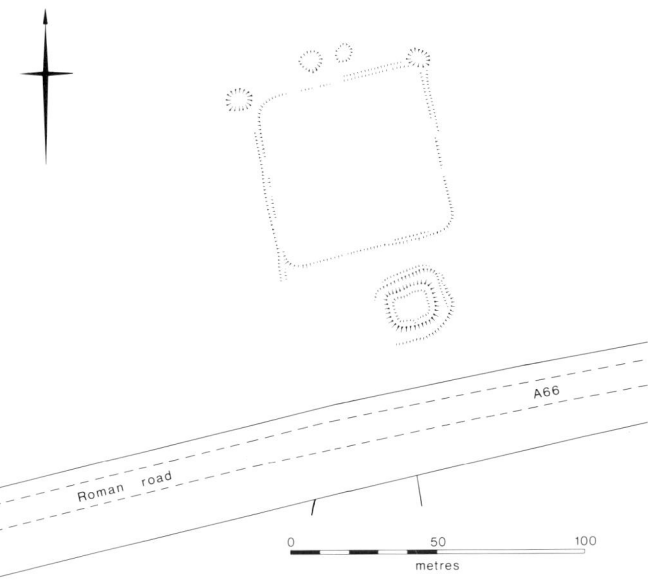

Figure 47 *Bowes Moor, County Durham, with the watch-post or signal station to the S, as surveyed in 1990 before the A66 became a dual carriageway.*

Rey Cross *Figs 5 and 48*

NY 90021240

One of the most impressively defended camps in Britain was constructed at 447 m above OD on the summit of the road over the Stainmore Pass, the route across the Pennines, now the A66, that links Teesdale with the Eden valley. The main Roman road from York (*Eburacum*) to Carlisle (*Luguvalium*) and into western Scotland used this pass, linking the local forts at Bowes (*Lavatris*) and at Brough under Stainmore (*Verteris*). The defences were thrown up on the shoulder of Buzzard Hill which extends southwards, creating at this point a steep slope down to the N bank of the River Greta. The W defences of the camp were laid out along the crest of this shoulder so as to take full advantage of the unrestricted view over the watershed, 2 km to the W. Similarly, the S defences occupy the crest of the rocky hillside above the river, eliminating any dead ground on this side. The positions of these two sides and the length of the S one were dictated by the topography (*contra* Richmond and McIntyre 1934, 51) but there were no such strong factors determining the alignment of the N and E portions of the perimeter. As a result, none of the corners of the camp is a right angle; the N side was perhaps intended to be parallel to that on the S, but on the E this was not even attempted. The E side was probably only prevented from being at right angles to the other two by the need to avoid some marshy ground; there was no disadvantage in this, however, and the position gives extensive views to Bowes and beyond. To the NE and N the ground is relatively level, descending only gradually into the head of Deep Dale and, farther away, into Baldersdale.

The camp encloses a comparatively level area of 8.1 ha (20 acres), which slopes only very gently from the NW quarter towards the S and E. To the S of the modern road the ground is more broken and there are gullies and ribs of rock within the interior. The rampart forming the perimeter is unusually massive, still standing up to 1.8 m high in the centre of the S side and measuring as much as 11 m wide across its base. It is evident that a substantial quantity of stone was used in its construction; surface indications suggest that the material was not, in the main, derived from a conventional outer ditch but may have been gathered or scraped up from either side. However, the excavation in 1990 of the short length of rampart that was due to be destroyed in the construction of the S carriageway of the modern road revealed the presence of a berm about 1 m wide and a substantial but very irregular ditch, up to 2 m wide and 0.8 m deep, of which there was no trace on the surface. MacLauchlan (1849, 351), writing of the contemporary quarrying, said that a ditch had not been identified, but this view may have been based on surface observations alone. Only along part of the N side and next to the most northerly of the E gates are there any surface signs of an external ditch, here no more than 0.4 m deep. In 1989, probing through the peat at the NW angle by RCHME suggested that there might have been a short length of external ditch there, perhaps as much as 0.8 m deep, its centre being about 4.7 m from that of the rampart.

Each of the nine gates that can still be identified was defended by a traverse, the mounds of which are oval rather than bar-shaped. These now vary in height: those on the S are 1.4 m high, and the northernmost example on the W side survives to a height of 1.6 m; outside the E and W central gates they are 1.2 m and 1.0 m high respectively, but at the N gate on the E and along the N side the traverses are only between 0.4 m and 0.6 m high. These latter measurements may well be affected by the presence of the raised peat bog which is here at least 0.4 m thick. None of the traverses now exhibits any sign of an attendant outer ditch. It is likely that the N carriageway of the modern A66, shown on the plan before the construction of the S carriageway began in 1991, and which follows the line of its Roman predecessor, entered and left the camp through two further gates. Excavation, however, has suggested that the easterly of these gates may have been slightly farther to the S or may have been widened subsequently. Some cobbling, perhaps that of a road, and some small post-holes seem to have been stratigraphically later than the rampart (Robinson forthcoming). Apart from the poorly preserved W example along the N side, each gate is flanked by inturned rampart-terminals, unusual features which seem to belong exclusively to forts and camps constructed in the 1st century AD (Jones 1975, 118).

The rampart shows little variation in form, although it is noticeably broader at the NW and SE angles; in the centre of the S side and close to the central gate on the W it also has a markedly flat top, 2.0 m across. In the W third of the N side the rampart is only visible intermittently through the peat bog. Although this ground in itself may have provided some natural defence, especially in wet weather, it is nevertheless surprising that probing does not suggest the survival here of any substantial features below the surface. This is particularly unexpected when contrasted with the proportions of the rampart elsewhere.

Along the W portion of the S side the rampart is impressive, standing 1.5 m high internally and forming a false crest above the Greta valley. Despite the evidence for a ditch elsewhere, the material here seems to have been scraped up from the interior, an impression accentuated by the presence of a sinuous, natural scarp immediately to the N. However, some of this rampart may not be artificial: it seems that the constructors may have chosen to cut back the N side of another natural rock spine to form the rearward scarp. This may also be the most likely explanation of what appears, at first glance, to be a single course of outer facing-stones, 4.0 m long, which again is probably a natural rock outcrop. The traverse mound of the W gate here seems to have been carved out of another such spine of rock.

Knowledge of the interior of the camp is limited. Blanket bog has invaded much of the NW and as much as a quarter of the interior has been removed by surface quarrying for limestone, apparently in the early 19th century between the visits made by Roy (1793, 73–4, pl XVII) and MacLauchlan (1849, 350–1). However, when small portions of the area to the S of the modern road were excavated in 1990 some randomly distributed stake-holes were identified, associated with 4th-century pottery (Robinson forthcoming). In the 19th century some pottery was found by the quarrymen in the vicinity of the mound on the summit, to the N of the Rey Cross itself, but the character of the sherds was not recorded (MacLauchlan 1849, 351). The irregular shape of the camp and the provision of only two gates on the topographically restricted S side must have made the internal planning awkward. Richmond and McIntyre (1934, 54–6) attempted to resolve this presumed problem, but their suggestions are not readily verifiable and the calculations do not seem to take account of the broken ground along the S side. It is unlikely that this area was ever intended to be occupied,

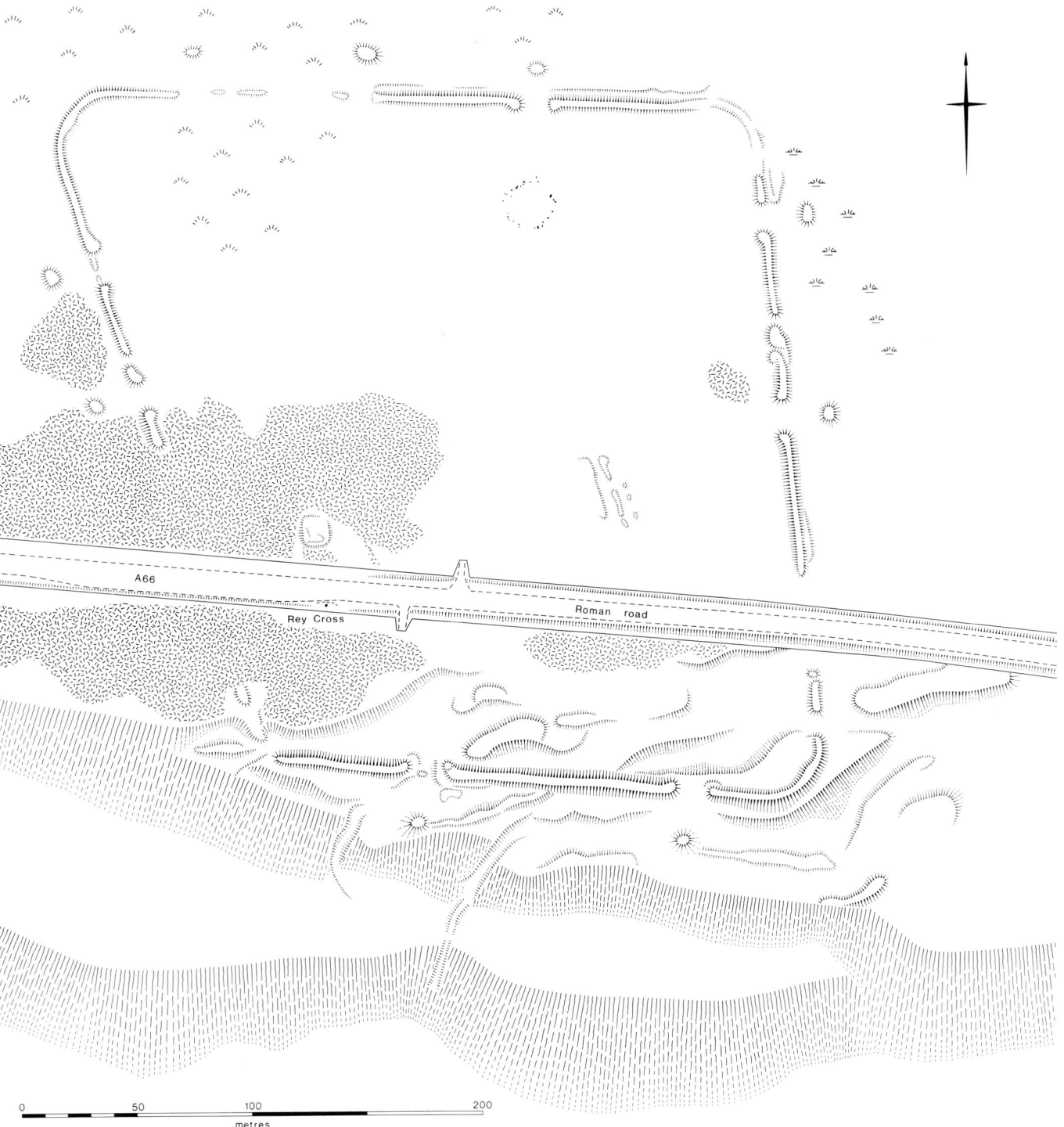

Figure 48 *Rey Cross, County Durham, as surveyed in 1990 before the A66 became a dual carriageway and before the Rey Cross was moved. The stipple indicates areas of quarrying. A circle of stones, possibly prehistoric in date, lies in the NE quadrant.*

although it was necessary to include it within the defences in order to place the perimeter on the most advantageous topographical line.

Despite the massive size of the defences, the camp does seem originally to have been for temporary occupation only. This is suggested by its carefully chosen, albeit awkward, defensive position and the fact that it lies halfway between the forts at Bowes and Brough, each less than 12 km away. In Richmond's phrase, this was 'a superb example of *castra aestivalia*, placed at the gate of Cumbria by an army intending to march deep into that territory the next day'

(Richmond and McIntyre 1934, 52). It would appear that this initial occupation took place early in the Roman conquest of the North, probably in the Flavian period. This is suggested by the inturned terminals of the rampart at the gates, which seem to be a Flavian characteristic (Jones 1975, 118), and by the realignment of the Roman road (noted by Richmond and McIntyre 1934, 57) at the point where it crossed the E rampart. This realignment indicates that the camp already existed when the road, conventionally thought to be late 1st-century in date, was surveyed and constructed. In addition, because sufficient land exists close to the forts at Bowes and Brough for a camp of this size, it would seem that this position, high on the pass, would only be preferable in the period before either of those forts was established, sometime in the 70s or 80s.

Whatever the initial date of the camp, there is little doubt that the defences, astride this important Roman road, were reused. Late 3rd or 4th-century pottery was found in the upper fill of the ditch and within the interior in 1990 (Robinson forthcoming), and some of the gates — those on the S, and the N ones on the E and W sides — show signs of having been blocked. This is most obvious on the W, where the N gate has been closed by a low bank standing 0.5 m high and consisting mainly of stone. At the other gates that seem to have been blocked, only a small number of boulders survive in position, continuing the line of the rampart across each gap. The date of this work is unknown.

Three features within the interior should be mentioned briefly. The first is Rey Cross itself (NY 81 SE 4) a simple shaft reduced to a stump. Its history as a boundary stone, from at least as early as the late 13th century, has been set out by Collingwood (1927; Robinson forthcoming) but the name itself is Scandinavian, and therefore the Cross is presumably much older (Smith 1928, xlvi). (With the building of the dual carriageway, the Cross was moved some distance to the E, outside the area of the Roman camp.) A few metres to the N, on the opposite side of the line of the Roman road and on the summit, is what appears to be a square mound, 0.8 m high and about 15 m across. It is surrounded by quarrying on all sides except the SE. Recorded by Hutchinson (1776, 15) and by Roy (1793, 74), it seems to have been respected by the quarrymen. Its origin is uncertain. It could have been sepulchral but the most closely comparable earthwork in the vicinity is the signal station adjacent to the camp on Bowes Moor, 3 km to the E (Annis forthcoming). If there was a chain of signal stations over the pass (Farrar 1980) perhaps this mound, which when seen from Bowes Moor is on the skyline, was a part of that system.

In the NE quarter of the camp is an irregular group of recumbent stones which, it has been suggested (Vyner pers comm), may have been a stone circle. It is possible that this is what MacLauchlan (1849, 350) thought was a 'tumulus';

he gave no description of it but if the identification was correct then the material within the kerb has been robbed. Its significance here is that any comparatively early structure in this position could have interrupted the line of the internal road, running from gate to gate, in between the tents of the Roman camp.

NY 91 SW 2   Bowes

Sandforth Moor *Fig 49*

NZ 20562104

Parch marks of what may have been a small camp were recorded in 1978 (Selkirk 1980, 16; NMR AP NZ 2021/1). The site is on a gentle S-facing slope just below the top of a low E to W ridge. From the crest line there is good visibility in all directions and, in particular, over a considerable length of Dere Street, now the B6275, towards the fort at Piercebridge only 5.5 km to the S.

The S ditch, about 84 m long, and parts of the E and W sides are known, but the field is traversed by well-developed narrow ridge-and-furrow; this is likely to have bitten more deeply into the higher part of the slope, destroying any evidence of the N side. No entrance gaps can be identified. The apparent gap at the W end of the S side is probably the result of ploughing. By analogy, the most likely line for the N defensive ditch would be along the narrow crest of the ridge itself, which runs parallel to the S side of the enclosure and within 10 m N of the point where evidence for the W ditch fades out. If so, the camp would have measured between 90 m and 110 m from N to S, probably enclosing within the ditch an area of between 0.8 ha and 0.9 ha (1.9 acres and 2.4 acres).

NZ 22 SW 35   Summerhouse

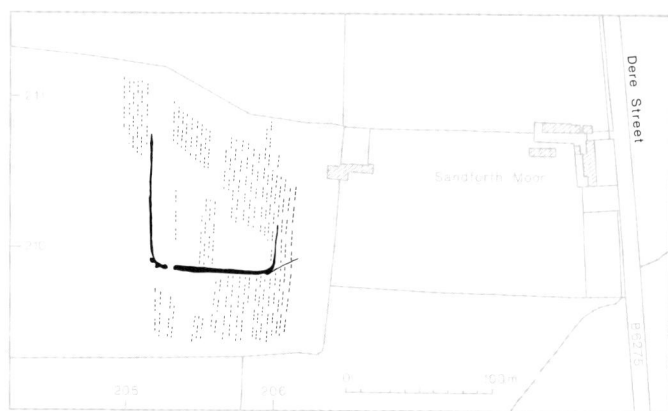

Figure 49 *Sandforth Moor, County Durham.*

Hereford and Worcester

Brampton Bryan *Figs 50 and 51*

SO 37957240

The camp at Brampton Bryan is the largest and westernmost of the group around Leintwardine (*Bravonium*) (St Joseph 1965, 85; 1969, 120, fig 6; 1973, 235; CUCAP AST 29–30). It is situated 500 m to the E of Brampton Bryan, and occupies a prominent position on a slight W to E ridge, at a little over 130 m above OD, and immediately above the broad flood plain of the River Teme to the N. From the site of the camp there are good views in all directions, especially to the W up the River Teme and to the N up the River Clun.

The cropmarks are generally rather indistinct, but the NE angle, most of the S, E and W sides, and a fragment of the N side at the NE corner are known, enclosing an irregular quadrilateral area of about 23 ha (57 acres). On the S side the causeway of the gate seems reasonably clear (CUCAP AYA 6). It lies about 230 m from the SE angle and roughly 335 m from the SW angle, and is thus positioned in a 2:3

Figure 50 *Brampton Bryan, Hereford and Worcester.*

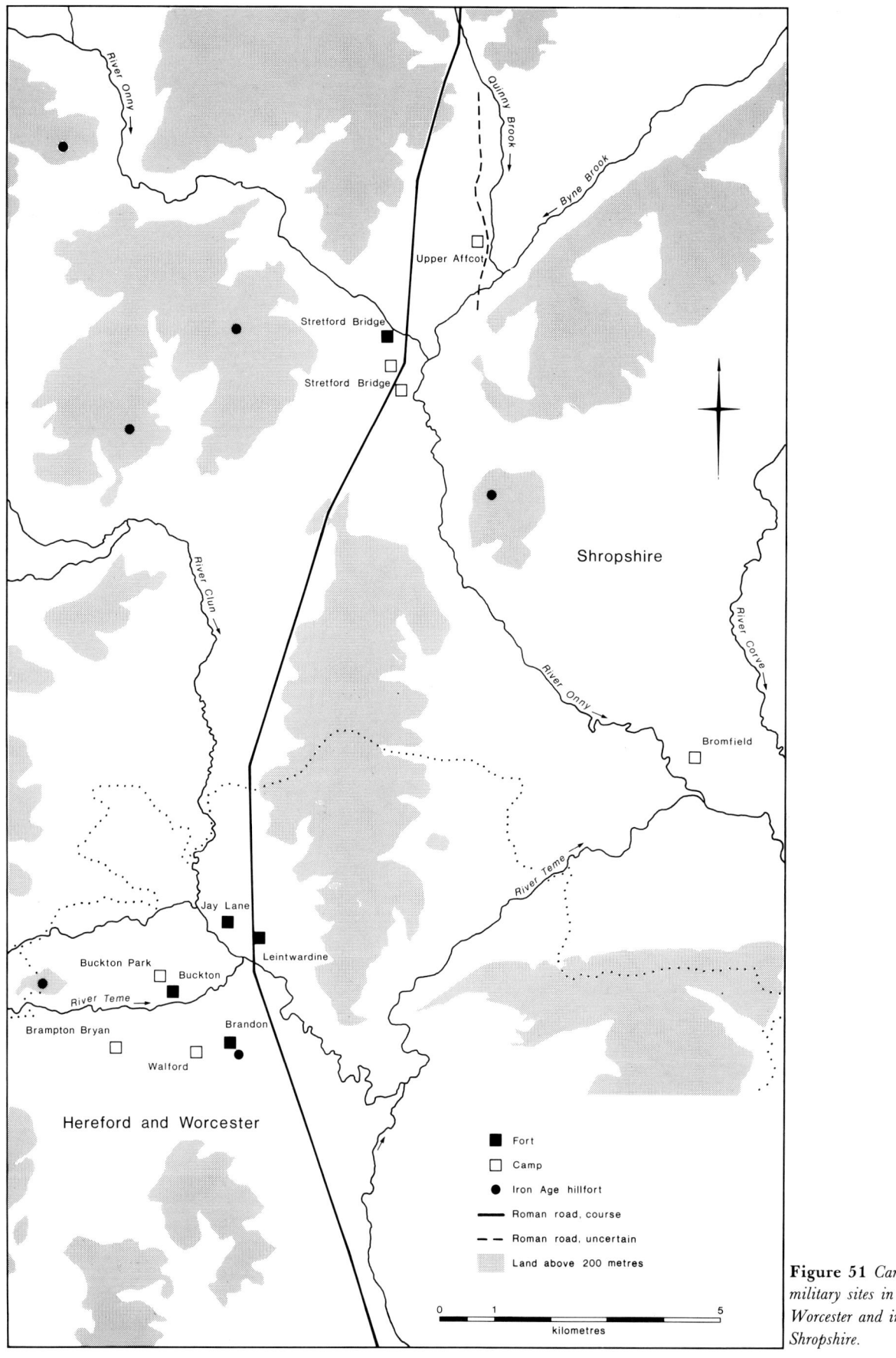

Figure 51 *Camps and other military sites in Hereford and Worcester and in southern Shropshire.*

ratio along this side, perhaps suggesting that the camp faced ESE. The cropmark of the traverse apparent here is only about 7 m out from the perimeter and thus access to the camp interior would have been very restricted. The position of the NW angle is not known for certain, but a break in the ditch on the W side may mark a gate lying close to the centre of the defences there. On the E, the modern road seems to have utilised a central break on that side.

The overall shape of the camp is partly determined by the topography. The S side occupies a break in slope just below the crest of a natural S-facing scarp which drops gently to an unnamed tributary of the River Clun. This scarp turns sharply N at the presumed position of the SE corner of the camp and continues along the E side as far as the modern road; its presence may explain the slightly acute SE angle. To the N of the road, the perimeter ditch lies back from the scarp. The W defences also coincide with a change in slope as the ground which rises westwards within the interior levels off towards Brampton Bryan. The line of the N side is unclear. Cropmarks to the N of the steep scarp here do not conform to the expected position or layout of a NW angle. It seems likely that the camp was restricted to the land to the S of the scarp; the N defences may be partly masked by modern field boundaries, some of the more easterly of which may preserve their line.

SO 37 SE 19   Brampton Bryan

Buckton Park *Figs 51 and 52*

SO 38897356

Evidence of a possible camp has been recorded from the air, some 370 m W of Buckton Park in the valley of the River Teme (St Joseph 1961, 124; CUCAP ZV 56). With Buckton fort, 150 m to the SSE, it occupies a low but pronounced eastward spur at just under 130 m above OD, about 1.5 km

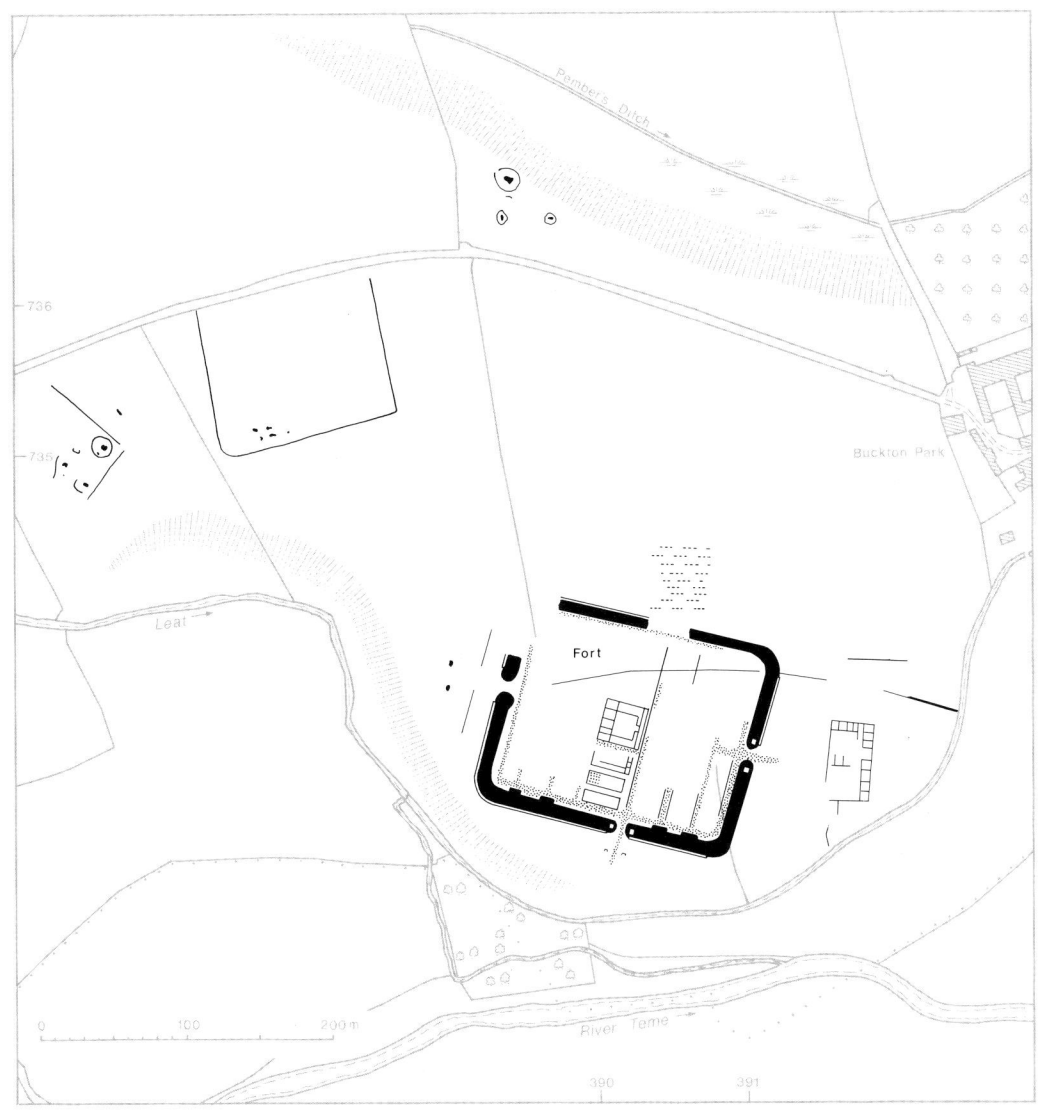

Figure 52 *Buckton Park, Hereford and Worcester, with the fort to the SE. The areas of stipple within the fort show the parch marks of roads.*

W of the confluence of the Teme and the Clun. This spur is defined on the N by a scarp of some 4 m, between Pember's Ditch and the track leading WNW from Buckton Park, and on the S by a scarp 3 m to 7 m high, above a former mill leat and the former course of the River Teme.

The cropmark evidence for the possible camp is equivocal. It comprises the ditch of a complete S side, approximately 122 m long, and about 100 m each of the E and W sides. The SE corner is unusually rectangular for a camp, and the SW is rather poorly defined on the aerial photographs, largely because of its proximity to a field boundary. In the middle of the S side there is a faint hint of a break that might be a gate but this is too poorly defined to be plotted and could be the result of geological factors.

The identification of the cropmarks as those of a possible camp would be in considerable doubt were it not for their characteristic and convincing topographical position. They occupy a gentle N-facing slope at the neck of the spur, which steepens near the SW corner. There is no certain indication of how much farther to the N the putative camp may have extended; however, between 50 m and 70 m to the N of the drive to Buckton Park, the slope increases a little, suggesting that the N side may have lain to the S of this point. A very rough estimate might indicate a N to S dimension of less than 160 m and a defended area of about 1.9 ha (4.7 acres). The camp appears to have faced N. Although it commanded extensive views in all directions, especially to the W, along the Teme valley, effectively the camp would have been concealed from the S.

Frere (1987, 50; Frere and St Joseph 1983, 98) has suggested that it might have served as a labour camp for the fort, but this association is unproven. Limited excavation of the fort revealed two periods of occupation: in the first phase, in the late 1st century, the fort was of timber construction but it was subsequently rebuilt on a different axis and with stone defences (Stanford 1970b, 238–58).

SO 37 SE 21   Buckton and Coxall

Shurnock (Inkberrow) Figs 53 and 54

SP 02826023

The site of a probable camp was recorded in 1975, approximately 650 m SSE of the hamlet of Shurnock (CUCAP BUI 25–8). It occupies the tip of a NE-facing spur, at about 85 m above OD, on the lip of a steep valley some 10 m to 15 m deep. Though overlooked from the N and SW, the site provides uninterrupted views down the valley of the Brandon Brook to the W. To the NE and NW can be seen the line of the Salt Way from Droitwich, which passes within 330 m to the NE of the camp. Important in the medieval period, this route appears to have followed approximately the line of the Roman road to Alcester, which is less than 7 km to the SE and which appears to have been preceded by a fort or other early military establishment.

The area enclosed within the camp ditch measures about 72 m from WNW to ESE by at least 52 m transversely; roughly at the centre of the bowed E side there is a gap approximately 8 m wide. It is uncertain how much of the steep scarp immediately N of the camp has been eroded since the Roman period, but the N ditch must have lain quite near its edge, very close to the natural crest. There is a very faint hint on the aerial photographs, too tenuous to plot, of part of the arc of the NE angle. It is possible that the enclosure might have been trapezoidal in shape for no

Figure 53 *Shurnock, Hereford and Worcester.*

Figure 54 *Shurnock, Hereford and Worcester, from the N. (12.7.75, CUCAP BUI 25)*

evidence of the NE or the NW angles or of the WNW side is visible in the scarp. The interior is relatively level, although a natural hollow runs from N to S roughly through the middle. A series of parallel field drains cuts across most of the interior and extends to the S. The E side of the camp makes use of the natural slope, here rather less steep, but the ground is level outside the S ditch and there is a very slight rise beyond the W side.

SP 06 SW 26   Inkberrow

Walford Figs 51 and 55

SO 39417223

About 350 m SE of Walford the almost complete outline of a large camp is known from cropmarks (St Joseph 1961, 124; 1965, 85; CUCAP BGD 94). It occupies a slight but pronounced spur on the S side of the Teme valley at approximately 130 m above OD. The position commands excellent open views to the N, NW and W. The Roman military establishments at Leintwardine (*Bravonium*), Buckton and Brampton Bryan are all clearly visible; only 400 m to the E, within the Iron Age hillfort known as Brandon Camp, excavation has revealed part of a campaign supply base (Frere 1987). The position of the defensive circuit appears to have been carefully selected so that its NW and SW ditches lay close to pronounced natural scarps. Both the NW and the SE sides coincide with local high points, but outside the latter the terrain falls away more gently into a slight hollow before rising again towards higher ground. A similar slight valley separates the NE defence from the hill occupied by Brandon Camp.

The Roman camp is almost a parallelogram, measuring approximately 390 m from NW to SE by 250 m transversely, and encloses about 9.7 ha (24 acres). Its W corner, the only part of the circuit not attested by cropmarks, appears to have been removed by quarrying, but no trace is discernible in the quarry face. The NE and SW ditches are slightly bowed, the alignment of the former, and most likely the latter, apparently pivoting slightly on the gates. There seem to have been four entrances. A gate in the centre of the SE side is partly overlain by the modern B4530 road. On the NW

Figure 55 *Walford, Hereford and Worcester.*

side, the gate may have been just to the W of this road. However, an interruption in the cropmark of the NW ditch about 30 m SW of the road could be attributed at least partly to local variations in geology or to natural drainage features which are apparent on the aerial photographs. The NE and SW entrances are almost, but not exactly, opposite one another, the former located in a ratio of 1:2 along the NE side, while the siting of the latter only approximates to this formula. The camp, therefore, presumably faced NW. There is a pronounced kink in the modern hedge line beside the S corner of the camp, suggesting that its ditch may still have been visible as an earthwork when the field boundary was laid out.

Within the camp, the fragmentary cropmark of an enclosure with rounded angles has been recorded centred at SO 39367232. This is unlikely to be another camp. Just inside the NW ditch of the camp, broad alternating dark and light bands, visible as cropmarks but not illustrated, are probably of geological origin. An irregular linear feature outside the E corner of the camp is a pit alignment, perhaps aligned on what seems to have been a round barrow.

SO 37 SE 18   Adforton

Lincolnshire

Ancaster *Fig 56*

SK 97954446

The cropmarks of a camp on the W crest of a gentle spur that forms the N side of the Ancaster Gap, at about 60 m above OD, were recognised in the drought of 1976 (CUCAP BQQ 39–43). The camp lies near the junction of two natural routes, one linking the basin of the River Trent with the regions about The Wash, and the other, followed by Ermine Street which passed less than 550 m to the E, running from N to S along the limestone ridge. The pre-Flavian Roman fort and later town of Ancaster lay about 600 m to the SSE on the valley floor (Todd 1981).

The site clearly took advantage of the panoramic views to the W, SW and to the immediate S; to the N, however, the ground continues to rise to about 80 m above OD. The spur itself creates dead ground immediately to the SE.

The camp, which measures just over 400 m from N to S by 282 m transversely, encloses an area of a little under 11.3 ha (28 acres). Its S half has been damaged by the railway cutting and a former quarry, now a rifle range. The position of the SW angle and a hint of a turn in the W end of the N ditch, suggest that the recognition of the W side from the air has been prevented by the almost coincident modern field wall. The probable position of this W ditch occupies the crest of the W side of the spur, and this topography may have dictated the alignment of the whole camp. An interruption in the line of the N side may be a gate, since it occupies a central position. Unfortunately the equivalent point on the S is masked by one of two small quarries now evident only as cropmarks. One of a series of former field boundaries, running N to S and aligned on those surviving N of the railway, meets the ditch of the camp at this point. Other fainter marks may be relatively recent in origin.

SK 94 SE 31 Ancaster

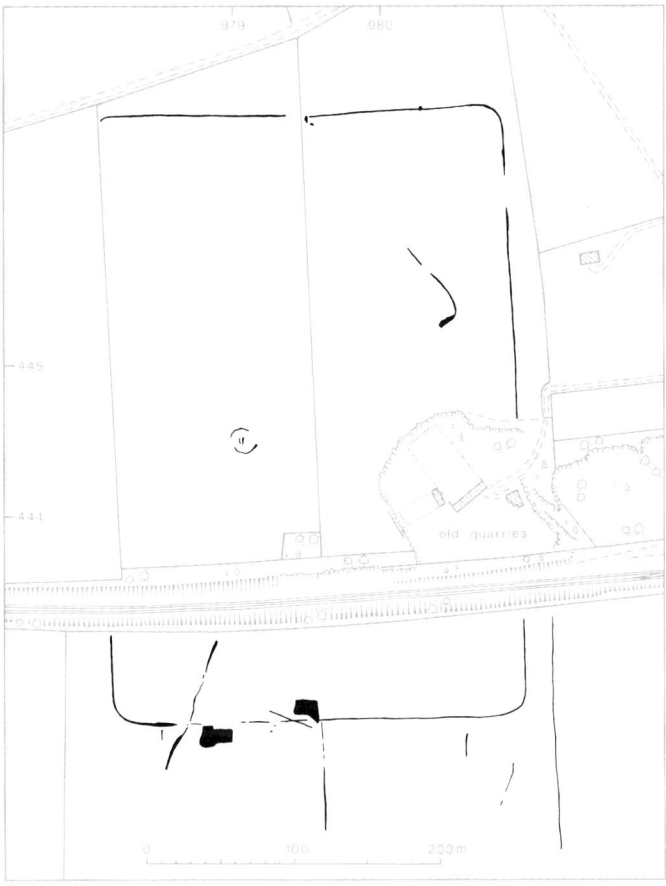

Figure 56 *Ancaster, Lincolnshire.*

Newton on Trent 1 and 2 *Fig 57*

1: SK 82517336   2: SK 82527332

Aerial reconnaissance has located fragments of two possible camps (St Joseph 1969, 104; 1977, 128; CUCAP BUQ 15–17) and a vexillation fortress with outworks (St Joseph 1965, 74–5; 1973, 214; Bishop and Freeman 1993, 187–9) on Newton Cliff, on the E bank of the River Trent. The fortress occupies an elevated position at the W end of a ridge, at 24 m above OD. The whole complex is sited on the highest ground close to the river in this region; it commands the present river-crossing at Dunham on Trent, and provides views southwards along the Trent valley.

Three sides of the double-ditched vexillation fortress (SK 82367372) are known; the fourth, W, side, if such existed, has been lost to river erosion. The area enclosed is likely to

Roman Camps in England

Figure 57 *Newton on Trent 1 and 2, Lincolnshire, with the vexillation fortress and its defensive outworks to the N.*

have been at least 12 ha (30 acres). There was a defensive outwork comprising a polygonal envelope of ditches on the three sides, with perhaps a simple gate on the N and S sides; on the E a more complex system, with staggered entrances, is discernible. Nothing remains on the ground, except for a very slight rise on the line of the NW part of the inner defence close to a Second World War observation post. It has been suggested (D Wilson 1984a, 58, 60, group 3) that outworks of the kind seen around this fortress may be interpreted as a temporary defence for the construction party.

To the S of the fortress, two linear cropmarks seem to represent portions of the perimeters of two camps. They lie at 25 m above OD, on the S side of the slight hollow surrounding the high ground occupied by the fortress. Their position commands good views to the N, and particularly to the E, but to the S the line of sight is obscured by a rise.

The broader, more northerly, ditch of camp 1 is about 280 m long and has a *clavicula* close to its W end (CUCAP BUQ 15, 17; BVB 2–9). The same aerial photographs show a second, narrower ditch belonging to camp 2, between 40 m and 50 m to the S of the first, and not quite parallel with it. It is at least 150 m long and has a rounded angle which turns southwards at its E end. Less than 280 m to the S of this line the cropmark of another ditch has been recorded. Its breadth is approximately the same as that of camp 1, about 335 m to the N, to which it appears to be parallel; it could, therefore, have formed part of the S side of this camp.

The detailed topography here is not sufficiently striking to provide clues as to the approximate area enclosed by either camp. The overall position of the camps is markedly inferior to that of the fortress, suggesting that the construction of the fortress had had priority.

SK 87 SW 27   Newton on Trent

Norfolk

Horstead *Fig 58*

TG 25851931

Aerial reconnaissance has recorded the almost complete outline of a camp immediately W of Horstead, on a gravel terrace on the S edge of the Bure valley (Edwards 1976, 261–2, pl XXVIII; 1978, 100; NMR AP TG 2519/3–03). The site occupies the level top of a slight spur at about 10 m above OD. From this point there are open views in most directions, although to the N the river is obscured by another slight crest, now occupied by the B1354 Horstead to Aylsham road.

Within its ditches, the camp measures approximately 365 m from NE to SW by 255 m transversely, a total area of about 9.5 ha (23.5 acres). The E angle appears to be rather smaller in radius than the N and W corners. Most of the perimeter can be plotted, except for the S part of the SE side where a damp hollow has so far failed to produce cropmarks even in periods of drought. The NE, NW, and SW sides are roughly at right angles to one another, but the position of the S angle suggests that the missing S part of the SE defensive line must veer slightly to the SW. This apparent misalignment, presumably skirting the hollow, was probably deliberate.

The camp apparently faced NE, but only one gate is clearly visible, just to the S of a hedge line on the NW side; it occupies a characteristic position, dividing the interior of

Figure 58 *Horstead, Norfolk.*

the camp across its axis in the ratio of 1:2. On the SW, Frettenham Road probably crosses the defensive circuit at, or close to, an entrance. The cropmarks of the NE and SE sides are insufficiently clear for entrances to be distinguished with any certainty.

The NE side and the E corner of the camp are almost on the 10 m contour and it is this crest which seems to have dictated the orientation of the defensive circuit. The W boundary of the relatively modern wood makes a marked kink at a point exactly coincident with the NE ditch of the camp, suggesting that its defences may have been visible when this field boundary was laid out. There is, however, now no trace of any earthworks in the very disturbed ground within the wood, or indeed elsewhere.

Within the NW third of the interior of the camp, and to its S, an extensive spread of pits has produced strong cropmarks. A D-shaped enclosure, measuring 40 m across and with an entrance on the NW, may represent a native settlement of Iron Age or Romano-British date. It appears to be associated with several ditched trackways and boundaries, but has no direct relationship to the camp.

TG 21 NE 9   Horstead with Stanninghall

Northumberland

Bagraw *Fig 59*

NY 84999650

The camp at Bagraw in Redesdale, approximately equidistant from the forts at Blakehope and High Rochester (*Bremenium*), is situated at 200 m above OD, along a relatively flat-topped but locally prominent ridge, aligned NW to SE. The camp overlooks the valley of the Rede immediately to the W, and is protected by the steep-sided ravine of the Bagraw Burn on its SE flank. The modern A696 road cuts obliquely across the SW quarter; its Roman predecessor, Dere Street, runs parallel with the SW rampart of the camp and only 5 m outside it, following the line of the ridge. To the S of the modern road, the line of Dere Street survives as a terrace in the hillside, with a single scarp 0.5 m high; to the N it is a cambered linear mound up to 11 m wide and 0.4 m high. The relative chronology of the camp and the Roman road cannot be demonstrated from fieldwork alone, since the alignments of both are determined by the topography. The likelihood is that the road preceded the camp although the absence or poor survival of entrances also makes this difficult to prove.

The earthworks are extremely unusual, consisting of two elements, set end to end. The layout of these two parts, although superficially rectangular, is most irregular. The E and W sides of each part lie parallel to one another but are realigned by about three degrees close to their midpoint. Of the three short sides, aligned approximately NE to SW, the S and central ones are approximately parallel but the N side is markedly askew. Thus the N element of the earthworks is a trapezium, whereas the S one is a parallelogram. This difference in layout may be significant in the determination of function and relative chronologies.

The N part occupies an area of 3.6 ha (8.9 acres). Its N side has an abraded outer ditch 0.3 m deep; the rampart here is up to 0.4 m high but towards its W end it is reduced to a single scarp. The N part of the E side is better preserved within a plantation, the rampart standing 1.1 m above the bottom of the ditch which is as much as 0.7 m in depth. The S side, the medial feature of the earthworks as a whole, has been disturbed by tracks but the rampart survives to a maximum height of 0.8 m high and the ditch is 0.3 m deep.

On the W, however, no ditch survives alongside Dere Street, but the rampart stands up to 1.1 m high externally and 0.5 m internally. A later bank and ditch cut across the defences and the line of the road; their function is unclear.

Two gates are clearly visible: on the E, to the N of the central point of this side, there is a narrow gap, now only 3 m wide, guarded by a traverse mound 0.4 m high; on the S, a traverse mound of similar height, with a fragment of an outer ditch, 0.4 m deep, protects a gate 6.5 m wide. This gate is about 5 m off-centre and from it the low *agger* of a road, no more than 9 m wide and 0.3 m high, runs northwards at a slight angle to the axis of the camp. The point on the N side towards which this road is heading has been severely scoured and abraded and no gate can now be identified on the surface. The line of the W rampart is broken approximately opposite to the gate on the E side but no unequivocal Roman features survive here.

The S part of the earthworks, enclosing 3.5 ha (8.6 acres), is more difficult to interpret. The E side has been eroded by the steep slopes above the burn but where it survives at all the ditch is as much as 0.4 m deep; the rampart stands 1.4 m high externally and 0.4 m high internally. The fragment surviving at what appears to be the SE angle is not on the same alignment as the larger portion to the N, perhaps suggesting that an adjustment had to be made to position the earthworks on the crest of the natural slopes. The W side of the enclosure, a bank 1.0 m high, is featureless. As in the N part, no W entrance is visible, but it is conceivable that the whole of this side may have been reused as a later boundary bank, thus blocking any possible Roman gates. The passage of the modern road through the short S side, slightly to the E of its midpoint, may suggest the former presence of a break in the earthworks here. Otherwise, however, this portion of the perimeter is somewhat confusing. It seems that a drain has been cut inside what appear to be Roman defences and the upcast deposited on its S side. To the S stand the broken remains of what seems to be the Roman rampart, still up to 1.0 m in height.

The junctions between the two parts of the earthworks have been much disturbed and thus their relative chronology is in doubt. MacLauchian's proposal (1852a, 32) that the camp was doubled in size is not entirely satisfactory, for the traverse outside the 'medial' defences is unlikely to have survived if the S half was subsequently occupied. It is possible,

Figure 59 *Bagraw, Northumberland.*

Roman Camps in England

however, that the S part of the earthworks played a subsidiary role, forming an annexe to a contemporary or slightly earlier camp to the N, the semi-permanent status of which may be indicated by its well-developed quasi-axial roadway. The irregularities of layout, especially the difference in alignment between the E and W sides, rule out the suggestion (Richmond 1940, 120) that this was one elongated camp which was subsequently divided into two.

NY 89 NW 20   Rochester

Bean Burn 1 *Fig 60*

NY 75696602

Less than 450 m to the ESE of the large camp around the farm at Seatsides are two much smaller ones, 120 m apart. The remains of the more easterly of the two camps are situated at 213 m above OD in flat pasture at the bottom of a gentle S-facing hill slope in the valley of the Bean Burn. The area has been extensively ploughed, as evidenced by ridge-and-furrow, and more recently, with the result that the earthworks have been reduced and spread.

The camp was symmetrically planned and encloses an area of about 0.3 ha (0.7 acres). The earthen rampart is best preserved on the NW where it survives to a maximum height of about 0.4 m. There are four gates, visible as slight depressions in the rampart at the centre of each side. A traverse is still discernible outside both the N and the S gates. Each of these traverses consists of a low bank about 0.2 m high and 7 m long, but their ditches, like the ditch around the camp itself, have been levelled by cultivation. Apart from the overlying ridge-and-furrow and a shallow watercourse which cuts through the E gate, there are no internal features.

NY 76 NE 20   Henshaw

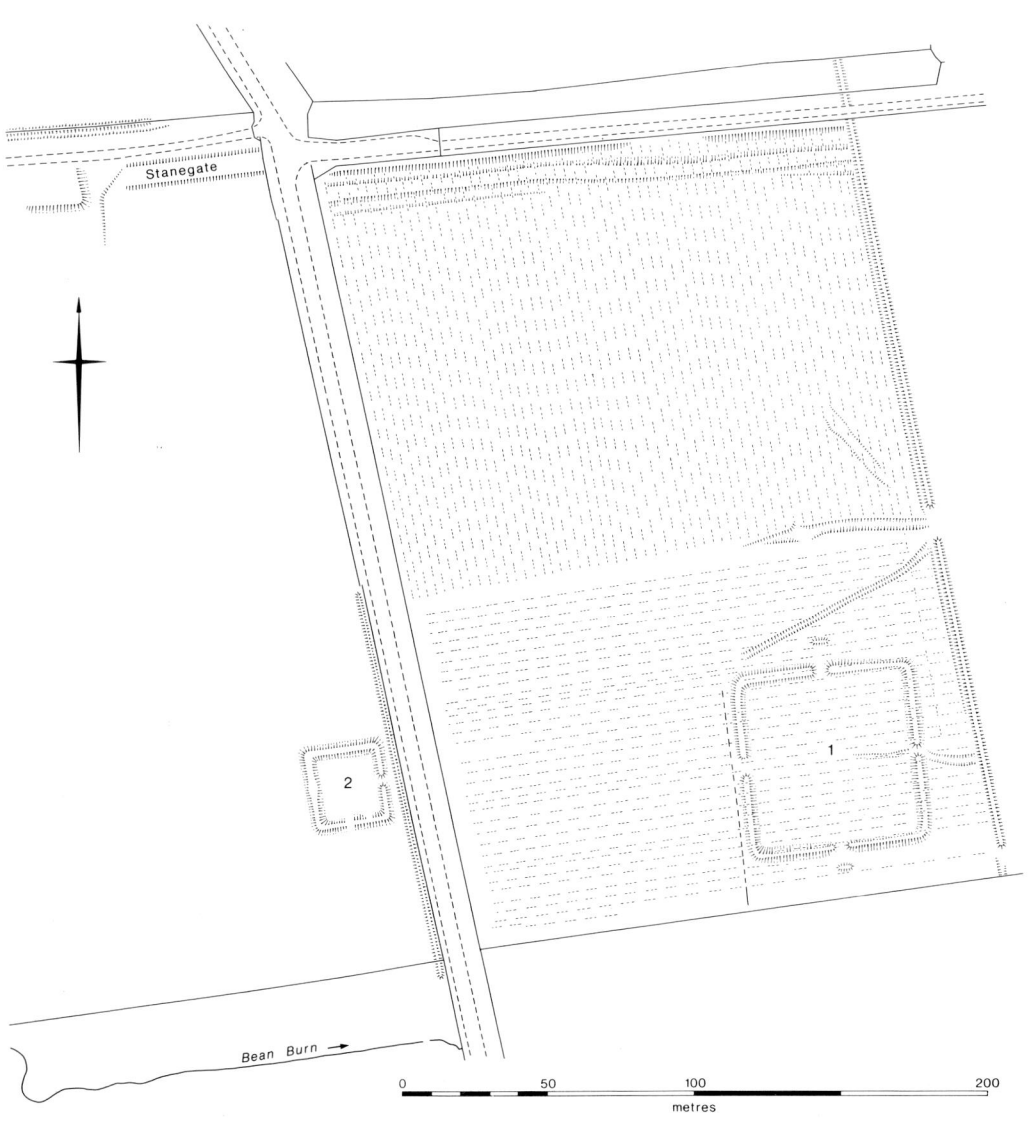

Figure 60 *Bean Burn 1 and 2, Northumberland.*

Bean Burn 2 *Fig 60*

NY 75526600

This very small camp is situated on level ground at 221 m above OD, near the bottom of a gentle S-facing hill slope, 120 m W of Bean Burn 1. Though at present under pasture the field has recently been ploughed and traces of ridge-and-furrow are still just discernible, oriented approximately N to S.

The camp survives as a square, low, earthen-banked enclosure, measuring only 19 m across internally and covering an area of less than 0.04 ha (0.09 acres). The remains of the rampart are only about 0.2 m high on average and have been spread to a width of about 6 m all round. It is best preserved at the N end of the E side where it stands 0.5 m in height.

No characteristic Roman features are now visible but in 1966 the Ordnance Survey recorded the presence of 'four opposing gates and traces of *claviculae* on the south and east sides'. Only two entrances can now be identified with any certainty. The best preserved is in the E where there is a roughly central gap, about 4 m wide, the N side of which has a slightly wider swelling on its inner edge. In the centre of the S side of the camp a less well-defined gap also has, on its E side, a suggestion of an internal swelling to the rampart. These may be the remains of *claviculae* but they are now too indefinite for classification as such. There are very slight depressions in the rampart roughly central to the other two sides which could mark the positions of gates. A later field bank runs beside the E rampart, parallel with the modern road.

NY 76 NE 17   Henshaw

Bellshiel *Fig 61*

NY 81859985

A camp, which encloses an area of 15.9 ha (39.4 acres), occupies a broad domed summit to the W of Dere Street, above the steep slopes on the E bank of the Bellshiel Burn, close to its confluence with the River Rede. Within the interior the ground slopes gently to the E towards Dere Street and the Sills Burn; the view takes in both the Rede and the Bellshiel Burn valleys and the fort at High Rochester (*Bremenium*), 1.5 km to the SE. To the N, the horizon is formed by Bellshiel Law, just over 1 km away.

The hilltop, which is up to 252 m above OD, has been cultivated for a limited period in the past, the greater part of the interior of the camp being covered with ridge-and-furrow. A number of boundary banks, some probably contemporary with this ploughing and others apparently later in date, make the initial identification of the surviving Roman earthworks difficult in some sections. The prominent mounds of upcast, piled around bell-pits (p on Fig 61) sunk for the extraction of coal, evidently postdate the cultivation. The summit of the hill is approximately marked by a prehistoric cairn (c), 8 m in diameter and 0.8 m in height, which has a modern military trench cut around its N arc. From this point the ground falls gently away down slightly convex slopes. Intervisibility is, therefore, restricted within the camp and this may have made the setting out of the defences somewhat difficult.

The E and W sides are parallel but those on the N and S are realigned at gateways. Only the NW angle is not a right angle. The E side is approximately 15 m longer than the W one. The latter runs along the crest of the hill above the Bellshiel Burn; it is overlain along its S half by the remains of a boundary bank 1.5 m high that contains large quantities of stone. To the N, this later line diverges, leaving the ragged discontinuous remains of the Roman defences exposed around the NW angle. The ploughing of the interior of the camp has reduced the rampart here to a series of mounds which stand 1.3 m high externally and no more than 0.4 m in height internally. The W end of the N side is even less well preserved, the fragmentary rampart being no more than 0.7 m high externally and 0.2 m high internally. Nowhere in this NW quarter is the ditch any more than 0.3 m deep. Immediately to the E, two relatively recent quadrangular enclosures, bounded by banks of earth and stone, overlie or utilise the Roman defences and are associated with the gently curving bank and ditch that crosses the camp from N to S. In the westerly of these two enclosures the preservation of the ramparts progressively declines, due to the ridge-and-furrow which itself seems to predate the enclosure. There is a slight inturn of the scarp of the rampart here but there is no firm indication that this is a remnant of a Roman gate. Farther E, the defences are overlain by a boundary bank which is 1.2 m high on its N side, up to 0.5 m high to the S and 2.5 m broad. The NE angle of the camp lies in poorly drained ground outside the later field system. Here the Roman rampart is spread to a width of 4 m; its external scarp survives to a maximum height of 1.2 m and on its inner side the rampart is up to 0.4 m high. The ditch, which is 0.7 m deep, has been further deepened for a modern drain. Much of the E side is again overlain by the continuation of the boundary bank which, for some of its course, is flanked by drains; from the SE angle the bank continues southwards beyond the camp.

The W quarter of the S defences is overlain by a boundary bank and by later industrial activity. Elsewhere, most of this side has been severely reduced by ridge-and-furrow. However, some fragments of the rampart have survived virtually intact and still stand up to 1.3 m high externally and 0.6 m internally. No ditch is visible on this side, perhaps because the rock is too close to the surface. This is certainly

true towards the W end, as can be seen in the rock-cut coal-shafts (p on Fig 61), but elsewhere modern soldiers have managed to cut two shallow trenches (t). Nevertheless, any Roman ditch which had been dug here would have been filled by the ridge-and-furrow ploughing.

Only two gates through the defences are readily recognisable. At the central point of the E side the comparatively well-preserved ditch of a traverse survives outside the line of the rampart. The ditch is only 0.4 m deep but, partly because it is set on a slight eastward slope, the outer scarp of the mound is still 1.0 m high; the inner scarp now measures only 0.2 m in height. The position of the gate itself is obscured by the later boundary bank. The only identifiable S gate was defended by an internal *clavicula*. Apart from the loss of its tip, trimmed away by ploughing, this *clavicula* is strikingly well preserved, standing up to 1.0 m high and revealing that its bank contains large amounts of stone. The other gates are now more difficult to identify. At the central point of the W side the later boundary bank abruptly leaves the Roman line, suggesting that the defences were interrupted here in some way, perhaps for a gate. A slight scarp, barely 0.2 m high and not surveyable, could conceivably represent the last vestige of a traverse, although this is markedly closer to the rampart than the better preserved example at the equivalent point on the E. At the central point of the N side the defences change alignment slightly. This commonly happens at a gate but at Bellshiel this position coincides with a slight crest which forms the skyline when seen from the NE angle. It is thus likely that this was simply a surveying point at which a slight error was made in the laying out of the camp. A similar realignment seems to occur at the centre of the S side although here there is no topographical feature that might have influenced the design. A gate might be expected through the N rampart opposite the S *clavicula* but here again there are no clear indications. In the W half of the S side, there is a mound lying at an angle to the line of the defences; on plan, this may appear to be superficially similar to an external *clavicula*, but it is a tip, 2 m high, thrown up from the adjacent coal-shaft (p) immediately to the W.

NY 89 NW 3   Rochester

Figure 61 *Bellshiel, Northumberland, overlain by ridge-and-furrow and by later field boundaries. The dashed line crossing the E edge of the camp marks the line of a modern pipe-trench. A cairn (c), coal-pits (p) and modern military trenches (t) are also shown.*

Birdhope 1, 2 and 3 *Figs 12 and 62*

NY 82679883

Three superimposed camps lie on one of the largest areas of relatively level ground adjacent to Dere Street between North Tynedale and the Border. The site is immediately to the W of the deeply cut valley of the Sills Burn, 350 m to the WNW of the fort at High Rochester (*Bremenium*). Two-thirds of the site slopes gently to the N; in the S portion, however, between the well-preserved earthworks of camp 2 and the modern military buildings of Redesdale Camp, there is a slight but rather poorly drained fold in the ground. Farther S again, beyond the modern camp, the land falls steeply to the haughlands of the River Rede. The outlook from the Roman camps extends northwards along Dere Street to Thirlmoor and southwards across Redesdale, but to the E higher ground around High Rochester cuts the line of sight.

Camp 1, the largest of the three, seems to have been set out as a parallelogram enclosing an area of 12.3 ha (30.4 acres). The line of the E side lies very close to the rapidly eroding slopes, 20 m high, above the Sills Burn; the Roman defences here are overlain by a later boundary bank up to 0.7 m high. A gap in this bank, nearly 40 m to the N of the point where the eroding river-scarp comes closest to the defences, may mark a gate although this cannot now be proven from fieldwork alone; at the equivalent position on the W there is a gate defended by a *clavicula*. The N side of the camp is barely traceable, having been almost levelled by cultivation or concealed by the growth of peat. The rampart only survives as a slight rise about 2 m wide, its better preserved external scarp being nowhere more than 0.2 m high. The line of the ditch can be traced intermittently as a vegetation mark. The area of the NW angle lies in very poorly drained ground and the earthworks here are probably covered by peat. Much of the W side is marginally better preserved; the defences there are 5.5 m across overall, and consist of a bank and ditch measuring 0.3 m in height and depth respectively. As so often elsewhere, the defences are slightly realigned at the single relatively well-preserved gate, to the S of which the ditch has been partly recut as a modern drain. Beyond the slight natural fold in the SW quarter of the camp, the SW angle of the defences would have been on slightly higher ground with a restricted view of the land beside the River Rede.

The modern camp has destroyed all trace of the SW angle of its predecessor, the earthworks of which reappear to the E, immediately before what may have been a gate, set at the central point on this S side. The bank here stands to a height of 0.2 m at best and the ditch, 0.1 m deep, is little more than a vegetation mark. It has been suggested that the slight mound, 0.1 m high, just inside the line of the bank at the postulated gate, is the last remnant of a *clavicula* (Richmond

1940, 122, fig 33). The only relatively well-preserved gate is that on the W where the mound of an internal *clavicula* survives to a height of 0.4 m. The point at which it sprang from the perimeter has been destroyed by a modern military installation. There is no sign of the external traverse shown here by MacLauchlan (1864, 64, sheet V). This gate lies just over 30 m to the N of the central point of the W side, suggesting that the camp faced N towards Dere Street about 80 m away. The slight inturn of the scarp marking the defences on that side could be the last remnant of a *clavicula* if three equally spaced gates were originally provided facing the road.

Inside the camp and outside its SE angle there is a small cluster of bell-pits (p on Fig 62) dug for coal. Amongst these are the faint earthworks (b) of several small, rectangular, earthen, Roman mausolea and some simple, circular barrows which are probably contemporary. Richmond (1940, 122) was less accurate than MacLauchlan (1852a, 35) as to their origin for he considered that these were 'rectangular pits for shelter or storage, sometimes associated with mounds to shield them and the tents from wind and rain'. From this he deduced that camp 1 was semi-permanent. However, from their positions, these burial mounds evidently postdate the construction and use of camps 1 and 2; it is clear that this area, overlooked by the fort at High Rochester, was used as an extension to the partly excavated Petty Knowes cemetery, to the E of the fort, which seems to have been receiving burials from the early 2nd century to the early 4th century (Charlton and Mitcheson 1984).

Camp 2 is extremely well preserved. Almost exactly rectangular, it encloses an area of 3.1 ha (7.7 acres); its S side is set along the gentle forward crest that overlooks the hollow to the SW and which probably determined the orientation of the camp. The outer scarp of the rampart on the S side stands 1.3 m high, above a ditch 0.5 m deep which has been incorporated into the modern system of field drains. The inner scarp of the rampart is 0.5 m in height. In their S half the E defences are almost equally well preserved, although the ditch has been further disturbed and deepened by modern drains. To the N of the gate on this side, however, the state of survival rapidly declines, perhaps due to the growth of peat, and the bank is no more than 0.4 m high. A section cut through this bank in the 1930s revealed that it was built of turf (St Joseph 1935, 240). On the N side the bank stands 0.8 m high and the ditch is 0.3 m deep, but on the W the measurements are 1.1 m and 0.6 m respectively, with the inner scarp of the bank being 0.7 m high.

There are four gates, each defended by a traverse. The N one is reduced to a single scarp 0.1 m high, but at each of the other gates both the mound and the ditch survive; the forward scarps of the E, W and S mounds are 0.5 m, 0.6 m and 1.0 m high respectively, and their rear scarps 0.3 m, 0.4 m and 0.1 m in height. The ditch of the E example, which is immediately adjacent to a later barrow, is now visible as little more than a change in the vegetation, although the other two survive to a maximum depth of 0.4 m. Once again, the positions of the W and E gates suggest that the camp faced N, towards Dere Street. The W gate is offset a few metres to the E of centre, although the reason for this is unclear.

The SW angle of a third camp, 3, apparently enclosed by camp 2, can be traced, with some difficulty, on the ground. Its perimeter bank is nowhere more than 0.3 m high externally. The ditch, which is visible on the W, is no more than 0.1 m deep. The two surviving sides of this low earthwork lie almost parallel to those of camp 2; therefore the S side could have exploited to some extent the same slight topographical advantage provided by the gentle crest on which it was constructed, although neither camp had the extra outlook into the valley bottom of the Rede that would have been possible from the postulated position of the W angle of camp 1. An aerial photograph, taken in 1937 (NMR AP NY 8298/1; Fig 12), shows that the NW side of camp 3 extended for a total length of 150 m to a NW angle. This is not verifiable on the ground but the evidence suggests that the camp would thus have enclosed an area of at least 2.1 ha (5.2 acres).

It is clear from the good preservation of camp 2 that it must have been later in date than camp 1. By the same token, it seems likely that camp 3 is earlier than camp 2. The junctions between these last two have not survived on the surface but the line chosen for the SW perimeter of camp 2 is a slight improvement, topographically, when compared to that of camp 3 almost immediately to its rear. Nothing can be said of the gates of camp 3 nor of its relationship to camp 1.

NY 89 NW 10   Rochester

Brown Dikes *Fig 63*

NY 83987029

This camp is situated in a dominant position at the SE end of a ridge known as Brown Moor, at a height of 245 m above OD and 500 m to the S of Hadrian's Wall. The ground, which is in permanent rough pasture, slopes gently away in all directions except the NW; here there is a slight rise to the summit of the ridge but this is not sufficient to block the panoramic view.

The camp is almost perfectly square with sharply rounded corners. It measures 67 m across the interior, giving an area of 0.4 ha (1.1 acres). The generally well-preserved earthen ramparts are about 5 m wide and 0.2 m high above the

Figure 62 *Birdhope 1, 2 and 3, Northumberland. Roman barrows (b) and comparatively recent coal-pits (p) are shown.*

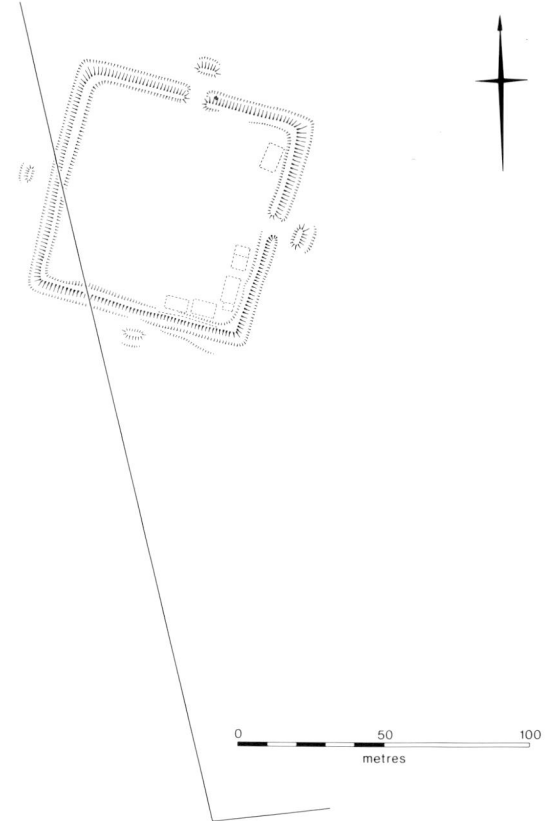

Figure 63 *Brown Dikes, Northumberland. The footings of later rectangular buildings lie along the E and S sides.*

interior. The ditch is 3 m wide and its inner scarp is up to 1 m deep along the N side where it is best preserved.

Gates in the centres of the N and E sides are defined by breaks about 5 m wide. Each is defended by a well-defined traverse, 0.4 m high, with a shallow outer ditch 2 m wide and 0.3 m deep. There is a similar traverse in the centre of the S side and another just S of the centre of the W side; neither is as well defined as those on the N and E, but both are obvious. There is no corresponding break in the rampart on either the S or W sides. The point in the W side where the gate should have been is overlain by a modern drystone wall but there is no clear sign, in the later phases of activity on the site, that either the rampart or the ditch were interrupted. There is a slight but ill-defined break in the outer scarp of the ditch behind the traverse on the S side.

The interior of the camp, which is slightly domed, is covered by clumps of thicker tussock grass. No demonstrably Roman internal features are visible. Set inside the S corner are the remains of four rectangular structures, probably shielings, with another inside the E corner. The footings of these structures are very slight, consisting of low turf banks measuring 1.4 m wide but no more than 0.3 m high and averaging 8.4 m by 5.7 m externally overall.

Immediately to the S of the two structures against the S side, along the top of the rampart, is a very slight raised line of tussock grass, no more than 0.1 m high and 0.2 m wide and shown as a dashed line on the plan. This may possibly be the remains of some fence or wind-break associated with the shielings.

The camp was one of only two noted by Horsley (1732, 146, map 6), the other being Watchclose, Cumbria; he made no mention of the shielings which were probably already hard to trace.

NY 87 SW 13   Newbrough

Burnhead *Fig 64*

NY 70986696

This camp lies at a height of about 190 m above OD on a N-facing slope in rough pasture, some 60 m NE of Hadrian's Wall and 850 m NNW of Burnhead. It encloses an area of 3.5 ha (8.6 acres), and is only approximately rectangular. The E and W sides are parallel and the N side is at right angles to them. The E defences are 8 m longer than the W, and those on the S bow outwards slightly towards the entrance. Later field banks of earth and stone, themselves denuded and spread, occupy the summit of the rampart on the E and W, and accentuate its height to as much as 0.9 m. The Roman ditch, now up to 0.7 m deep, has been recut to form part of the drainage system on the hillside, and the E side is further obscured by a ditch and upcast bank associated with the public road alongside the camp. The best-preserved stretch of the defences, apparently unaffected by later works, is on the N, on the lip of a shallow valley, where the rampart is 0.2 m high internally and up to 1.4 m high externally; the ditch, partly recut, has an external scarp 0.3 m deep. The metalled farm road to Great Chesters crosses the camp, cutting through the E and W ramparts, and there are further minor mutilations to the defences that have been caused by cattle, drainage ditches and other modern agricultural activities.

The camp faces N, and the S defences occupy the crest of the natural slope. There is a gate in each of the four sides. A drainage ditch now passes through the N entrance, truncating the W side of the traverse, which survives as a bank 0.1 m high with slight traces of an outer ditch 0.1 m deep. A slight bulge on the inner face of the rampart may indicate the former presence of a recessed gate, or may be the remnants of an *ascensus*; the interpretation is made more difficult by the spoil upcast from the two modern ditches that join at this point. At the S entrance the original ditch has been recut and extended across the causeway, and the break in the rampart seems to have been partly filled with this later upcast. The traverse is well preserved: its bank stands 0.4 m high, 0.8 m above the base of its outer ditch, which is 0.4 m deep; some stone debris has been piled on the summit of the bank. The public road has presumably destroyed the

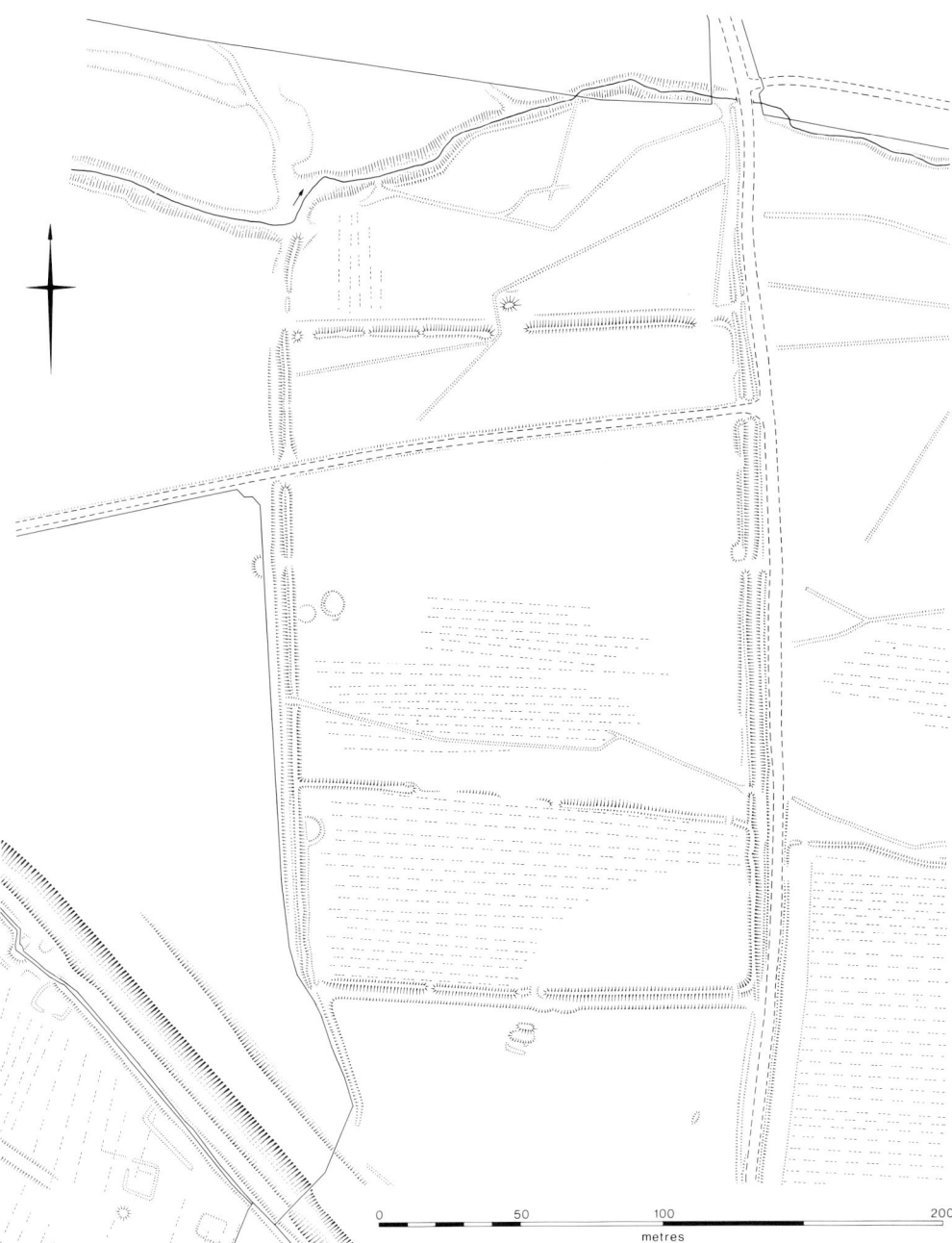

Figure 64 *Burnhead, Northumberland. Hadrian's Wall lies under the field boundary that runs obliquely across the SW corner of the plan. The ditch of the Wall, and the glacis mound to the N, are clearly visible.*

traverse at the E entrance; an inward swelling on the N side of the gap through the rampart could be a vestige of a recessed gate or of an *ascensus*, but the area is disturbed and the feature may be simply the result of the displacement of rampart material. A later field bank partly blocks the W entrance gap, and the modern drainage ditch has cut through the causeway. The traverse here survives only as a spread mound, 0.3 m high, against the wall in the adjacent field; its ditch has been levelled but is marked by a change in the vegetation.

Evidence of ridge-and-furrow cultivation occupies two-thirds of the interior of the camp. This ridge-and-furrow is probably contemporary with the bank that lies parallel to it and that forms the N side of a small field in the S third of the interior. Three small, curvilinear earthworks, each defined by banks, lie close to the W rampart. The relationship of these earthworks to the ridge-and-furrow to the E and to the Roman defences cannot be demonstrated from ground inspection alone, but they resemble the post-medieval limekilns in the area (*see* Milestone House camp). There are, however, no obvious remains of any associated quarrying in the vicinity, although a seam of limestone does cross the camp from E to W.

NY 76 NW 19   Greenhead

Carham Fig 65

NT 79853770

Cropmarks noted in 1961 less than 600 m to the S of Carham appear to show portions of two possible sides of a camp with an entrance gap and external traverse (CUCAP ADZ 41–4). They lie between about 60 m and 70 m above OD at the W end of a ridge which provides extensive views over Tweeddale.

The cropmarks of the SW ditch of this possible camp are approximately 220 m long but are broken for about 24 m by a causeway for a gate; a possible traverse, roughly 20 m in length, is set about 18 m to the SW of it. The cropmarks are not of good quality, and there is a mark similar to the suggested traverse only 15 m to the SE. A cropmark extending from the presumed traverse north-eastwards probably represents a modern drain. The cropmark of another straight ditch line, approximately 100 m long, has been recorded close to the SE side of Dunstan Plantation (CUCAP ADZ 43). Lying at right angles to the ditch described, this could be a fragment of the NW side of a camp; this receives some support from the topography, for the slope of the ground is more pronounced immediately to its N. Elsewhere the terrain falls away quite gently in all directions except the E, where it rises slightly towards the summit of the ridge, some 400 m E of the probable SW ditch.

The strategic location and the local topography of the cropmarks tend to favour their classification as a camp. However, particular caution is necessary in the interpretation of the evidence in this case, as the Scottish army is said to have camped hereabouts in 1296; it might have dug similar ditches, or may have deliberately reused earlier defences.

NT 83 NW 10   Carham

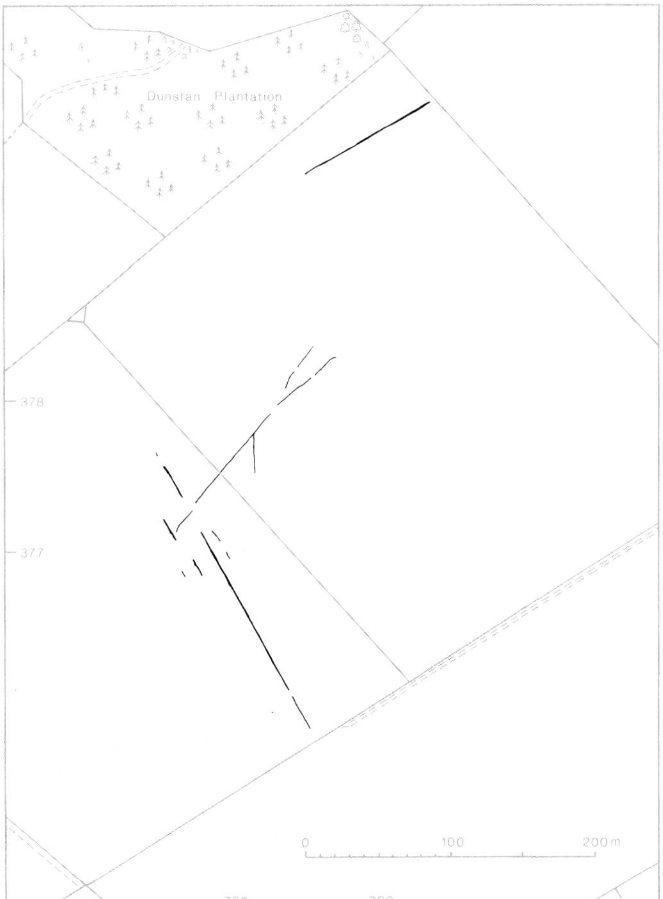

Cawfields Figs 66 and 67

NY 71386693

Occupying the summit and the gentle N-facing slope of a broad ridge above the E bank of the Caw Burn at about 190 m above OD, this camp encloses an area of 0.6 ha (1.5 acres). Now under permanent pasture, it has been severely reduced by ridge-and-furrow which crosses the camp from N to S. The rampart is best preserved along the N side where it survives to a maximum height of 0.6 m internally and 1.3 m externally; part of the S side, which was laid out along the crest of the ridge, has been reduced to an

Figure 65 *Carham, Northumberland.*

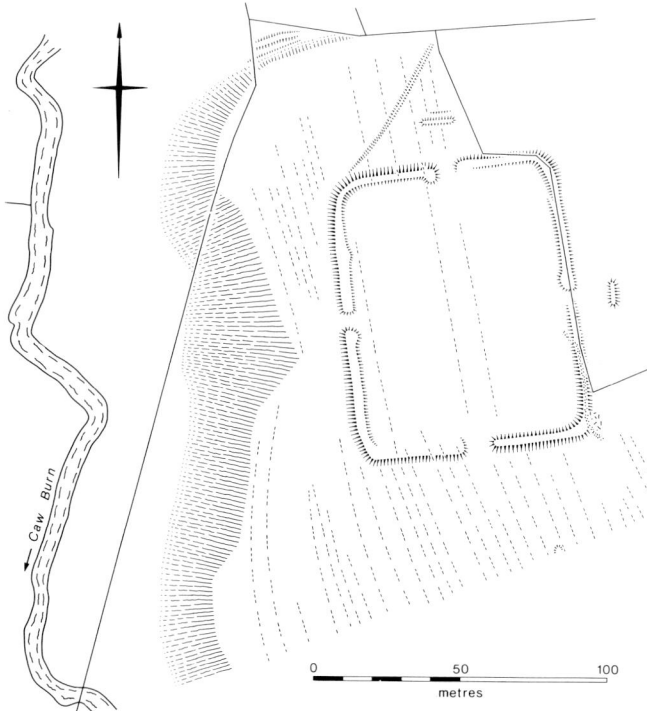

Figure 66 *Cawfields, Northumberland.*

Figure 67 *Cawfields, Northumberland, from the N. The traverses on the N and E are visible as is the mutilation of the S side by later ridge-and-furrow cultivation. Hadrian's Wall and Milecastle 42 lie in the middle distance although the W continuation of the Wall has been destroyed by Cawfields Quarry. Beyond, in the background, is the Vallum.* (16.1.73, CUCAP BLL 29)

outward-facing scarp only 0.4 m high. Nowhere is there any trace of an external ditch. There is an entrance at the midpoint of each side. No traverse survives outside either the S or the W gates; the traverse on the E has suffered from cultivation and its ditch is visible only as a vegetation mark. The N traverse, however, is in good condition, despite the ridge-and-furrow: its bank still stands to a height of 0.6 m above the bottom of the ditch, which is 0.2 m deep. On the right-hand side of the N, E and W entrances the rampart broadens towards the interior. This may indicate that the camp was provided with readily defensible inturned gates; alternatively, but rather less likely, a rectangular *ascensus* may have been built to allow access to the top of the bank. The N example is the best preserved. Modern field boundaries follow the line of the rampart along stretches of the E and N sides; the land to the E has been ploughed regularly and the outer edge of the rampart has thus been truncated. At the SE corner the rampart is overlain by the footings of a wall, 1.3 m wide, and by a dump of building debris. The interior of the camp is featureless except for traces of ridge-and-furrow; the slight unevenness of the ground may indicate that it was formerly overgrown with woodland or scrub.

NY 76 NW 20   Haltwhistle

Chapel Rigg *Figs 11 and 68*

NY 64596542

A well-preserved camp, with unusual gates and an outwork, occupies the summit of an E to W ridge at 190 m above OD. To the W and SW of the camp this ridge is cut by a steep-sided gully drained by an unnamed tributary of the Tipalt Burn. Except to the E, where the gently ascending ridge curtails visibility some 200 m from the camp, there are extensive views all round, notably to the N and NE towards Hadrian's Wall and the Stanegate.

Roman Camps in England

Figure 68 *Chapel Rigg, Northumberland with its sinuous outwork to the SW.*

The camp is rectangular, measuring 87 m from E to W by 69 m transversely within a rampart and ditch enclosing an area of 0.6 ha (1.5 acres). The S defences are aligned along the S false crest of the ridge, the N crest line of which is approximately on the long axis of the camp; to the N of this the interior slopes gently to the N. There are no signs of modern drainage or of any cultivation, with the result that the surface of the site is largely obscured by a very heavy growth of rushes.

Around the whole perimeter the ditch is silted up and in many places it is waterlogged; nowhere is its counterscarp more than 0.3 m high. On the N and E sides, hillwash has masked the earthworks, so much so that the principal surviving feature is an outward-facing scarp no more than 0.6 m high; on the N the ditch is barely distinguishable. The S and W defences, by contrast, are in unusually good condition. They survive as a bank and ditch, the former being 0.5 m high internally and standing to a maximum height of 1.4 m above the bottom of the ditch. Here the defences measure 9.0 m across overall. Around the SW angle, between the entrances, the line of the rampart is emphasised by an abrupt change in vegetation: the surviving bank is covered with grass, whereas rushes predominate over the remainder of the site.

Centrally placed in each of the four sides of the camp is a gateway protected by the unusual combination of a traverse and an internal *clavicula*. The W *clavicula*, although obscured by rushes, is in particularly good condition, its bank standing up to 0.8 m high; the E example, however, is so reduced as to be unsurveyable. Each traverse is 12.0 m long; those on the N and W have a bank and ditch surviving to a height of 0.1 m and a depth of 0.3 m respectively, but little more than the ditch, up to 0.2 m deep, is traceable in the S and E examples.

From a point 19 m W of the W traverse, a well-defined scarp extends along the lip of the gully, merging occasionally with the natural slopes and fading out 22 m SW of the traverse of the S gate. Standing to a maximum height of about 0.6 m, it is marked by the same vegetation change as the rampart of the camp itself. This suggests that the scarp is the remnant of an artificial bank, which seems to have been provided only along that portion of the crest beyond which the floor of the gully forms dead ground when seen from the rampart of the camp. From this scarp, however, there is an unrestricted view down to the burn and it seems most likely that the bank was an outwork contemporary with the camp. Both the arrangement of the gates and the provision of an outwork is extremely unusual and may be indicative of the circumstances in which the camp was constructed. There is nothing to support the suggestion that this was a practice camp (Bennett 1980, 154).

NY 66 NW 32   Thirlwall

Chesters Pike *Fig 69*

NY 70696717

In gently sloping ground at the foot of the SE flank of Chesters Pike, at about 198 m above OD, there are the abraded remains of a camp. It lies in permanent pasture, immediately to the N of an unnamed tributary of the Caw Burn, 350 m N of the fort at Great Chesters (*Aesica*). The camp encloses an area of approximately 0.5 ha (1.3 acres). The S and E ramparts are reduced to low mounds and are barely perceptible, having been mutilated and obscured by modern fences and banks, by buried land drains and by cultivation. On the N and W sides the rampart has also been spread by ploughing, to a general width of about 8 m, but it still survives to a maximum height of 0.6 m. No ditch is now discernible, although at the S end of the W side an old watercourse or drainage channel lying parallel to the rampart must occupy the line of the original Roman ditch. No entrance can be seen in the S side where the remains are particularly indistinct; access here is restricted by the close proximity of the steep bank of the stream.

There seems to have been an entrance approximately in the centre of each of the other three sides. The E example is visible as little more than a lowering in the fence line; the absence of a traverse may be explained by the existence of ridge-and-furrow in the adjoining field to the E of the camp. Though much abraded, traverses are clearly visible on the N and W; the ditch of the latter traverse is emphasised by the presence of the later watercourse. On the E side of the N entrance the rampart bulges outwards, or appears to have turned through a right angle, for a distance of 2.5 m (cf Jones 1976, 23); however, here it survives only to a height of 0.2 m.

The projected line of the aqueduct to Great Chesters fort crosses the field about 40 m to the N of the camp but no trace is visible on the surface.

NY 76 NW 46   Greenhead

Chew Green I and III
Frontispiece, Figs 70 and 71

I: NT 78800843   III: NT 78690866

The two camps at Chew Green lie on the bank of the River Coquet between two of its tributaries: the Chew Sike on the E, flanked by steep slopes, and the gentler descent to the March Sike on the W. Around a low knoll, at 442 m above OD, there is a habitable area of at least 15 ha (37 acres), the largest stretch of comparatively level ground beside Dere Street before it climbs to the ridge which marks the border with Scotland, at Brownhart Law. In addition to the two camps (I and III), the earthworks include those of a semi-permanent fort (IV), a fortlet (V), and the *agger* of the Roman road, as well as later remains. The Roman earthworks are as complex as they are remarkable and the sequence is not wholly clear, despite the excavations of 1936 (Richmond and Keeney 1937). Here, only the two camps are described in detail; for clarity, the numbering system used by Richmond and Keeney has been retained.

Camp I, the largest element on the site, is almost square and enclosed an area of about 7.7 ha (19 acres). The NE and SW sides are parallel and the W and the N angles are right angles. The camp faced NE towards Dere Street but its size, and the dimensions chosen, determined that the rear rampart had to take in lower ground, especially at the S angle, which is 10 m below the S corner of the later fort (IV). A camp of more elongated plan would have made better use of the level land available to the NW.

The earthworks are most impressive on the SE side where the outer scarp of the rampart stands 2.0 m high above the bottom of the ditch which is 0.4 m deep. The outer scarp of the rampart is accentuated here by the slope of the hill, but nowhere does the inner scarp survive to more than 0.5 m in

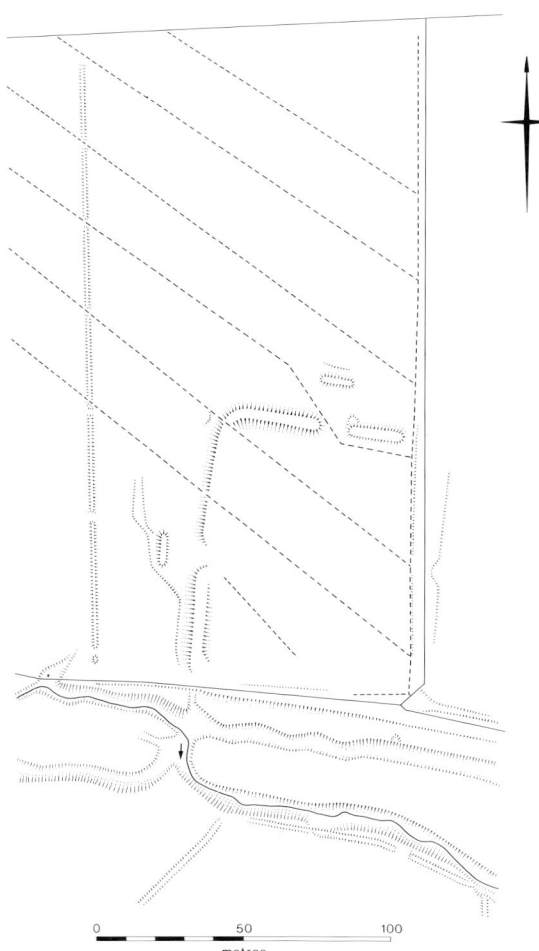

Figure 69 *Chesters Pike, Northumberland.*

height. For a short distance on the SW the defences are covered by the counterscarp bank of the later fort. Farther NW, immediately to the SE of the SW gate, a small counterscarp bank would normally be interpreted as a part of the natural hillside, an effect of the ditch being cut into the slope. However, Richmond's section through the defences at this point revealed what the excavators interpreted as a low glacis mound of upcast. The ditch here was said to be 8 ft 3 ins (2.5 m) wide and 3 ft 9 ins (1.1 m) deep, including a basal channel. The main rampart, 10 ft (3.0 m) wide, was laid on a foundation of turf and had a low forward kerb and a rear capping, each also of turf, which retained a core of rock brash (Richmond and Keeney 1937, 133–5; the measurements given in the text do not agree with the published section). Towards the W angle, where the ground is crossed by a series of drains, the preservation of the defences of camp I becomes markedly poorer as the ground levels out. Here the defences survive only as a broad bank spread to a width of about 3 m, its smooth outer scarp nowhere more than 0.5 m high; the line of the ditch is marked by a change in the vegetation.

On the NW side, the earthworks appear to be out of alignment around the junction with the SW side of camp III; this may be an illusion caused by the drains that cross the defences here at a very oblique angle, but the distortion is shown on Robert Tate's plan of 1810 (Alnwick Castle Archives: Sir David Smith's Collection, Northumberland Atlas 2:–187a/2). Nevertheless, the cutting of the drains makes it impossible to determine, from the surface remains alone, the sequence of construction of camps I and III, the perimeters of which intersect at this point; natural scouring down the hillside has largely contributed to the impression, apparently erroneous, that the ditch of camp I cuts through the bank of camp III. To the NE, a section of the rampart of camp I has been almost levelled (*pace* Richmond and Keeney 1937, 136) to the W of the gate on this side. The slighted rampart is only 0.1 m high; the remainder of the material was probably pushed into the ditch. The latter is only 0.2 m deep and seems to have been recut as a modern drain; upcast material has been spread outside the ditch for a distance of 3 m.

The single gate on this NW side is on the SW edge of the broad summit between the two burns; to the NE, the preservation of the defences is much better, and here the outer scarp of the rampart stands 0.9 m above the bottom of the ditch, which is 0.4 m deep. The inner scarp of the rampart is 0.5 m high. Richmond and Keeney (1937, 136) stated that their trenches at the NE junction with camp III showed that the rampart of camp I had been cut through by the ditch of camp III, which was therefore later in date. Immediately adjacent to this intersection, the NW half of the NE side of camp I is crossed and overlain by the low earthworks of medieval enclosures. The ditch of the camp seems to have been recut in places as a drain and the rampart was probably reused as part of the later enclosures; despite this, the outer scarp of the rampart survives to a height of 0.7 m although its inner scarp and the ditch are each only 0.2 m in height and depth respectively. The SE half of this NE side of camp I evidently determined the position and alignment of the NE side of the later fortlet (V), and of the two 'annexes' which overlie the E angle.

The NE gate of camp I probably lay at the crest adjacent to Dere Street and should be overlain by the N angle of the fortlet (V). The other three gates are, however, visible. The SW gate, set almost exactly at the centre of that side, is on the crest of the ridge; no external traverse can be seen and thus the inner side of the gate was chosen for investigation in 1936, when the springing of a *clavicula* was apparently identified 'in the requisite position, bedded upon an extra thickness of turf, as in the main rampart' (Richmond and Keeney 1937, 134). The NW gate is now little more than an interruption in the line of the ditch, with the slight stub of an internal *clavicula*, up to 0.2 m high, still apparent. A trial trench across the expected position of this *clavicula* in 1936 again revealed laid turf (Richmond and Keeney 1937, 134). In the comparable position on the SE side, a broad gap immediately to the NW of the SW defences of the more southerly 'annexe', to the S of the fortlet, was probably an original gate into camp I, and may have remained in use throughout the active life of the site.

Camp III is a parallelogram of much more elongated form than camp I, enclosing an area of 5.5 ha (13.7 acres). The shape chosen makes better use of the ground available and the camp occupies the whole of the broad crest of this gentle ridge between the March Sike and the Chew Sike. It was necessary, however, to overlap into camp I and, in doing so, the NW defences of camp I were partly levelled for a short distance where these crossed the central axis of camp III. The ground within the SE half of camp III is almost flat but in the NW the land rises to approximately 460 m above OD, only about 20 m below the height of the watershed.

Although the outline of the camp is clear, the earthworks are not particularly well preserved on the surface; they survive best on the SW side close to the W angle, where the rampart stands 0.5 m internally and 1.4 m above the bottom of the ditch, which is 0.7 m deep. For most of this SW side the defences are almost overwhelmed by the growth of peat, leaving only the slight outer scarp of the rampart frequently no more than 0.1 m high. Elsewhere on the perimeter, the rampart averages 0.7 m in height externally and 0.4 m internally; the ditch is usually about 0.4 m deep. Round the E angle, the scene of much post-Roman activity, the earthworks are reduced to a bank 0.4 m high and the ditch is barely discernible. When sectioned in 1936, just to the SE of the NE junction with camp I, the ditch was found to be 'V-shaped, 7 ft 6 ins (2.3 m) wide from lip to lip and 3 ft

Figure 70 *Chew Green I and III, Northumberland, with fort IV and fortlet V.*

(0.9 m) deep'. The rock brash that made up the rampart, 2 ft (0.6 m) high, was held in place by turf kerbs, the larger forward one enabling a steeper face to be built on this side. Again, these measurements do not agree with the published section (Richmond and Keeney 1937, 135–7). At the N angle good use is made of the natural defences provided by a small gully that drains into the Chew Sike.

At least three gates are visible, the best preserved, despite disturbance by modern drains, being that on the NW. Here the ground rises steadily to the skyline, only about 150 m away; the gate is protected by a traverse, the mound of which is 0.3 m high. The ditch of this traverse is marked only by a change in the vegetation, about 1.5 m wide. At the gate at the SE end of the SW side, in an area almost submerged in peat, the traverse mound is 0.6 m high externally and 0.2 m high internally with, once again, an external ditch about 2 m wide marked by a change in the vegetation. In the centre of the SE side there is a gap for a gate through the bank and a causeway across the ditch; excavation by Richmond and Keeney (1937, 137) found no sign of any traverse but the counterscarp bank of the fort (IV) lies only 8 m away, making any such provision unnecessary. Certainly, there seems to have been a gate about 75 m NW of the E angle, where the ditch seems to stop at a point opposite to the gate in the SW side. This area, however, is very disturbed; a possible fragment of a traverse mound, 0.6 m high on its SE side, survives about 9 m outside the defences. Given the proximity of Dere Street, it is surprising that this seems to be the only gate opening on to the road. There is no evidence for the gates postulated on the inaccurate plan published by Richmond and Keeney (1937, pl xx). The camp, therefore, seems to have faced SE, its main gate opening almost directly on to the defences of the fort (IV). The relationship between camp III and the fort seems to have been close; both are evidently later than camp I. The excavators suggested that the small mound, 5.2 m long, 1.7 m wide, and 0.3 m high, on the SE lip of the ditch of camp III, was a traverse mound of the NW gate of the fort (Richmond and Keeney 1937, 138). In Richmond's excavation notebook (No. 19), now in the Ashmolean Museum, Oxford, there is an unpublished section which shows a turf base to this mound. Its position and orientation are only comprehensible if the initial construction of the fort preceded that of camp III.

The description and interpretation of the two camps cannot be separated from that of the other elements of this complex landscape, of which one of the most intractable puzzles is the relative chronology of its components. It is immediately evident that the earthworks are of more than one period, but little dating evidence was recovered by excavation. Samian and coarse wares spanning much of the 2nd century were present, and there was one piece of cooking-pot, said to be of Flavian type. None of the sherds was stratified except those of a Dragendorff 33 and the unpublished rim of a mortarium (Richmond and Keeney 1937, 142; Richmond Notebook 19, Ashmolean Museum); both of these were in a layer associated with burnt timber and apparently sealed by wattle and daub within the interior of the fortlet (V). Given the medieval occupation of the site, which was not commented upon by the excavators, even these sherds may have been *ex situ*.

The form of the earthworks provides few clues. The relatively square plan of camp I seems to be an early characteristic and here this is demonstrated stratigraphically. The similarity of the first phase of the fort (IV) to site A at Cawthorn, North Yorkshire, suggests that it was built no later than the early second century. At the other end of the likely sequence, the closest parallel to the triple ditches of the fortlet (V) is probably the final period at Cappuck in Roxburgh, built sometime after about AD 160 and perhaps as late as the 3rd century (Richmond 1951; RCAHMS 1956, 381–3 no. 803; Hartley 1972, 40; Daniels 1978, 306); Cappuck is the next post to the N along Dere Street, and was the link between Chew Green and Newstead in Tweeddale.

The remaining earthworks are described briefly to set the camps in context.

'Fortlet' II. The ditch of this postulated fortlet is known only from Richmond's trenching which traced it, apparently, on the SW, NW and SE within the later fortlet (V). It was said to enclose an area of 52 m by 40 m within its ditch, which seems to have been slighter than the excavators' published description suggested; no trace of an attendant rampart was identified (Richmond and Keeney 1937, pl XXI, 145–6, 148–9; Richmond Notebook 19, Ashmolean Museum).

Fort IV. The form of the earthworks, consisting of a relatively weak rampart and a broad counterscarp bank, the internal roads (NMR AP NT 7808/18/85; CUCAP BD 9–10; Richmond and Keeney 1937, 139), and the massiveness of its defences, which on the SE side still present a scarp 3.0 m high, set this site apart from Roman camps. It most closely resembles site A at Cawthorn, which is of almost exactly the same dimensions. Each seems to have been semi-permanent in character and they are better classified as forts than as camps.

The excavations revealed that although the SW and NW gates had originally been defended by internal *claviculae*, these were evidently replaced by external traverses (Richmond Notebook 19, Ashmolean Museum). This suggests that the fort was reoccupied, perhaps more than once and probably on a temporary basis, at some time during the Roman period. In this geographical position this should not be unexpected. The fort evidently postdates camp I and, judging by the awkward arrangement of its principal gate, on the NE, it seems also to be earlier than the fortlet (V). The '*ballistaria*' identified by Richmond are unimpressive as earthworks and their position is militarily nonsensical; the identification must be treated as doubtful (cf Campbell 1984, 82).

The fortlet (V) was square on plan and was defended by

Figure 71 *Chew Green, Northumberland from the SE. The deep defences of the fortlet, V, and the two earlier 'annexes' stand in the centre of this view. To the W are the well-marked defences of the fort, IV, lying within the perimeter of the larger camp I. To the NW of the fort, and overlapping camp I, are the defences of the smaller camp III. The line of Dere Street leads away from the camera and crosses the Chew Sike at upper right. (27.7.67, CUCAP ATH 20)*

a principal rampart, outside which lay a broad berm. Two less prominent banks divide the three ditches, providing considerable defence in depth. There was a single gate on the NE. The fortlet is overlain by later enclosures, especially on the SE.

The chronological relationships between the fortlet (V) and the other landscape components cannot be resolved without further excavation. Topographically, however, the putative earlier fortlet (II), which may or may not be later than camp I, is likely to be earlier than the fort (IV). Between the fort and camp III the timescale must have been sufficient to allow for the initial occupation of IV, when it was defended by *claviculae*, and then its disuse. The orientation of the NW traverse mound of the fort suggests that camp III was constructed next in the sequence and was followed by the reoccupation of IV, its gates modified by the removal of the *claviculae* which were replaced by traverses. This overturns the sequence proposed after the excavations in 1936 (Richmond and Keeney 1937). However, none of this is dated, and the suggestion that the fort (IV) may have had a role during the construction of Dere Street must remain a possibility; the stimulus for the reuse of the site, which may well have happened more than once on so important a road, is unknown. Fortlet V may have been constructed before or after this apparent reuse of the fort.

The relationship of the fortlet (V) to the two 'annexes' on the SE is also quite unclear. However, these share a common alignment of their NE sides and it seems probable that they preceded the fortlet, especially since the interior of the NW 'annexe' is disproportionally small in relation to its defences and appears to have been overlain by the fortlet. It seems unlikely that there could have been an entrance into this more northerly 'annexe', close to its N angle, as Richmond claimed, but the whole area is now so obscured by later activity that certainty is impossible. The sequence of construction is not clarified by the earthworks which, at the junctions between the two 'annexes', seem to offer conflicting information. The very steep slopes within the interior of the more southerly 'annexe' makes its use as a 'waggon-park' (Richmond and Keeney 1937, 144) most implausible. For any such function the use of the level ground immediately to the NW would have been vastly preferable.

Uncertainty also surrounds the relationship between the Chew Green site and the undated small fortlet, apparently a watch-post or signal station, on the E shoulder of Brownhart Law (RCAHMS 1956, 378–9, no. 798). Visibility between the two sites is blocked by a ridge about 130 m to the S of this fortlet on the watershed, but a tower only 12 m high, or two of 6 m, would have made them intervisible.

As a convenient halt on the route over the hills, Chew Green had a long history of later use. As early as 1249 it was formally established as a trysting-place for the settlement of cross-Border criminal cases (Ridpath 1810, 138). This activity probably centred on the small building, apparently a Norman chapel, the site of which is marked by confused, roughly rectangular earthworks in the centre of the fortlet (V). The chapel was excavated in 1883 (*Proc Soc Antiq Newc* 3 ser **4** (1909–10), 162; Bosanquet 1925, 68). Small enclosures, probably for stock, bounded by banks up to 0.5 m in height, were built beside Dere Street. In places they overlie the Roman earthworks but are otherwise undated. They are concentrated to the NW of the fortlet (V) but there are others in the N quarter of the fort (IV) and also to the SE of the fortlet. One bank follows the SE counterscarp of the fort and forms part of an enclosure beside the river. There are traces of platforms, which might have been occupied by timber buildings, immediately inside and outside the S angle of the fortlet (V). The footings of two small structures, apparently a building and a small pen, survive on top of the *agger* of Dere Street, just to the S of the point where the road crossed the Chew Sike and immediately NE of the NW part of camp III. Later road-users had to cross the burn about 30 m downstream. On the NE bank, immediately opposite, are the earthworks of the Chew Green inn, which stood among the braided hollow-ways of Dere Street and its successors. It may have remained open as late as the 1770s when the earthworks were planned by Roy (Frontispiece; Macdonald 1917, 202, 215–16, pl XXX).

NT 70 NE 3   Alwinton

Coesike West 1 and 2 and Coesike East *Figs 72 and 73*

West 1 and 2: NY 81797011
East: NY 81897023

Three camps survive in permanent pasture close to the modern B6318 road and to the S of the Coesike Burn. The largest, Coesike West 1, contains the vestigial remains of a smaller camp, Coesike West 2; Coesike East lies some 85 m to the NE.

Coesike West 1 is situated towards the E end of a low spur, at about 240 m above OD, some 215 m S of the Vallum; it has commanding views to the E and W along the line of Hadrian's Wall, SE into Tynedale and to the N. It measures 55 m across and encloses a rhomboidal area of 0.2 ha (0.6 acres). The defences are in a good state of preservation. The maximum internal height of the rampart and the external scarp of the ditch are both 0.3 m. Where

Figure 72 *Coesike West 1 and 2 and Coesike East, Northumberland.*

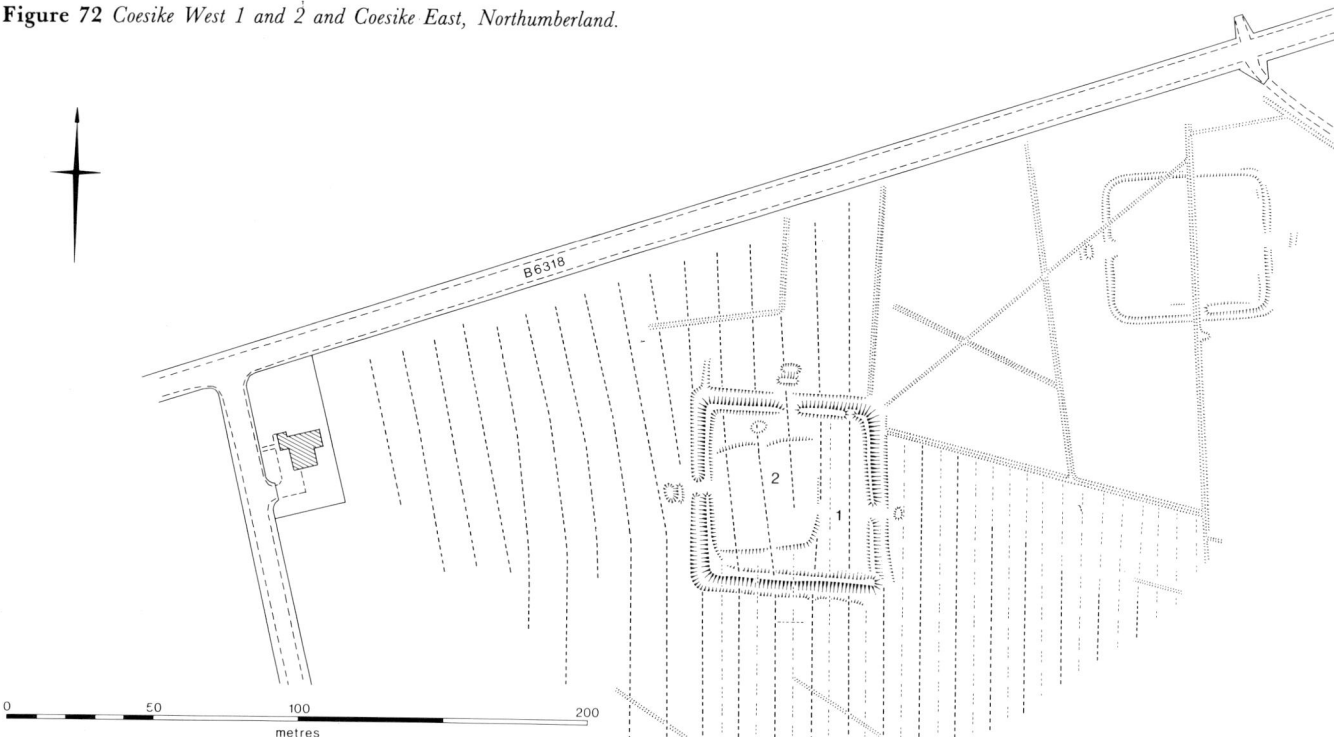

Figure 73 *Coesike West 1 and 2 and Coesike East, Northumberland, from the S. Traces of camp 2 are just visible within camp 1.* (4.2.71, CUCAP BEW 79)

best preserved, along the S side, the rampart is 1.0 m high above the base of the ditch. There are three entrances, each defended by a traverse, in the N, E and W sides. The N and W examples occur at medial points along the ramparts, whereas the E entrance is displaced slightly to the S. The N and W traverses each consist of a bank, up to 0.3 m high, and an external ditch 0.1 m in maximum depth; the E traverse is reduced to a low amorphous bank. Narrow ridge-and-furrow cultivation encroaches on the outer edge of the ditch on the S side and can be seen on aerial photographs to have extended over the ramparts and into the interior (CUCAP BAX 88; BEW 79; Fig 73). Later drainage channels, utilising some of the furrows of this cultivation, cross the camp from N to S, and have caused some disturbance to the defences.

Within the interior of this camp there are the remains of a smaller camp, Coesike West 2, which is in an extremely poor state of preservation. This smaller camp seems to be the earlier of the two as its W defences appear to be overlain by those of the larger one. Elsewhere its rampart is reduced to a discontinuous outward-facing scarp, measuring 0.3 m in maximum height on the S side; it is barely traceable on the N and has been almost totally destroyed on the E, where it has been mutilated by the later drainage system. No ditch is visible. There are a number of breaks in the rampart, the interpretation of which is confused by the later drains. Only one entrance can be tentatively identified: it is marked by an amorphous mound, less than 0.1 m high, which is almost certainly the remains of a traverse, about 3.0 m outside a gap in the N rampart. The camp may have been approximately square, measuring about 34 m from crest to crest, and enclosing an area of about 0.1 ha (0.2 acres).

Coesike East camp is on level ground some 6 m below the spur occupied by Coesike West 1 and 2, and in the same large pasture field. Though visibility is more limited than from its neighbours, there are open aspects along the line of the Wall to the W and E and restricted views to the N. It measured 50 m from W to E by 45 m transversely and its more regular layout must have enclosed an area of approximately 0.2 ha (0.4 acres). The rampart, now surviving to a maximum height of 0.1 m, has been almost entirely destroyed but a slight ditch, 0.1 m deep, is traceable for most of its course. There is some stone in the make-up of the rampart, presumably upcast from the ditch, and there are a number of boulders in the camp interior. The three entrances, each with traces of a traverse, lie at the midpoint of the E, W and S sides. The best example is on the W where the causeway is 4.0 m wide, and the traverse comprises a bank 0.1 m high with an external ditch 0.1 m deep; both are truncated at the N end by a modern drainage ditch. All that remains of the E traverse is the ditch, 6.0 m long and 0.1 m deep; the bank outside this ditch appears to be natural, and is probably a turf-covered outcrop. A second modern drainage ditch with its bank of spoil, which bisects the camp from N to S, has cut through the S entrance partly obscuring it, and has obliterated the W half of the traverse there. The same drain crosses the medial point in the N side and may have destroyed all traces of an entrance here, though there is no evidence of a causeway or of a traverse at this point.

NY 87 SW 14   Haydon

Roman Camps in England

Crooks *Figs 74 and 75*

NY 63616561

On the N edge of Thirlwall Common, at 190 m above OD and 450 m S of Crooks, are the somewhat reduced earthworks of a camp. The axis of the camp lies along a low ridge that extends NNE from Wardoughan. The position is unusual for although there is an open outlook to the S and E, visibility from the site is severely restricted elsewhere. On the N, the ground falls into a shallow depression but then rises to another low crest only 60 m away. The W side of the camp is on the E edge of the broad crest of the hill but the slopes to the Poltross Burn produce dead ground within a distance of about 90 m. Thus, despite their proximity, the fortlet at Throp and the closest sections of the Stanegate and of Hadrian's Wall are all invisible from the camp. Bearing in mind the position of the W defences, the camp may have faced E although this cannot be proven from fieldwork. Certainly the tactical considerations that have been implied elsewhere are an illusion (Bennett 1980, 160).

The principal surviving earthwork is the ditch of the camp. This is up to 0.7 m deep and is narrow and sharply defined; this must be due, in part, to its incorporation into the system of mole-drains which form a herring-bone pattern across the site. The internal rampart, on the other hand, has been almost entirely levelled, its material spread for up to 6 m into the interior; the remnants, which probably include silt from a relatively modern clearing of the ditch, stand no more than 0.2 m high and are best preserved close to the

Figure 75 *Crooks, Northumberland, from the SW. The traverse to the S is still well marked, as is the system of modern mole-drains. The photograph shows the site before much of the rampart was levelled.* (4.2.71, CUCAP BEW 25)

NW angle. The reason for this levelling is unclear since neither the interior of the camp nor the surrounding ground show any other sign of former cultivation.

The area enclosed by the ditch amounts to 0.9 ha (2.2 acres). There are four gates, one in the centre of each side, and each defended by a traverse. Apart from the N one, which is badly disturbed by a drain, the upcast mound of each traverse stands 1.6 m high; their ditches are now nowhere more than 0.4 m deep. The mound of the W traverse has been dug into, as has the levelled rampart just to the S of the E gate.

NY 66 NW 33   Thirlwall

Dargues *Figs 76 and 77*

NY 86009376

This camp lies between 158 m and approximately 175 m above OD on the gently sloping NE-facing side of the Rede valley. It has extensive views down the valley to the SE but the slight rise at Blakehope, 600 m to the N, partly blocks lines of sight in that direction. Almost immediately to the S of the camp the steep-sided valley of the Dargues Burn affords excellent protection. On the SW side there is good visibility to the W and up the Dargues Burn. Across the latter and 500 m to the SE is the native settlement at Garret

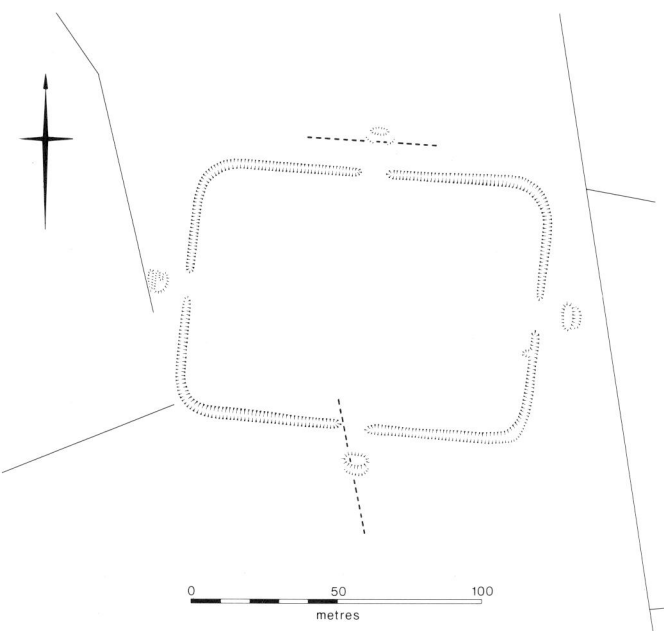

Figure 74 *Crooks, Northumberland. Most modern mole-drains have been omitted from the drawing.*

Figure 76 *Dargues, Northumberland.*

Shiels (NAR NY 89 SE 3), beyond which visibility is obscured by rising ground.

The camp, which faces NE, is an almost regular playing-card shape and its NE rampart is approximately aligned on Dere Street, 40 m to the E, on the far side of the modern A68 road. It encloses an area of about 5.9 ha (14.5 acres). The NE and SE sides were probably slightly shorter than those on the SW and NW, but they cannot be measured precisely due to the destruction of the E corner of the camp by the farm buildings at Dargues. There are four opposing entrances,

Roman Camps in England

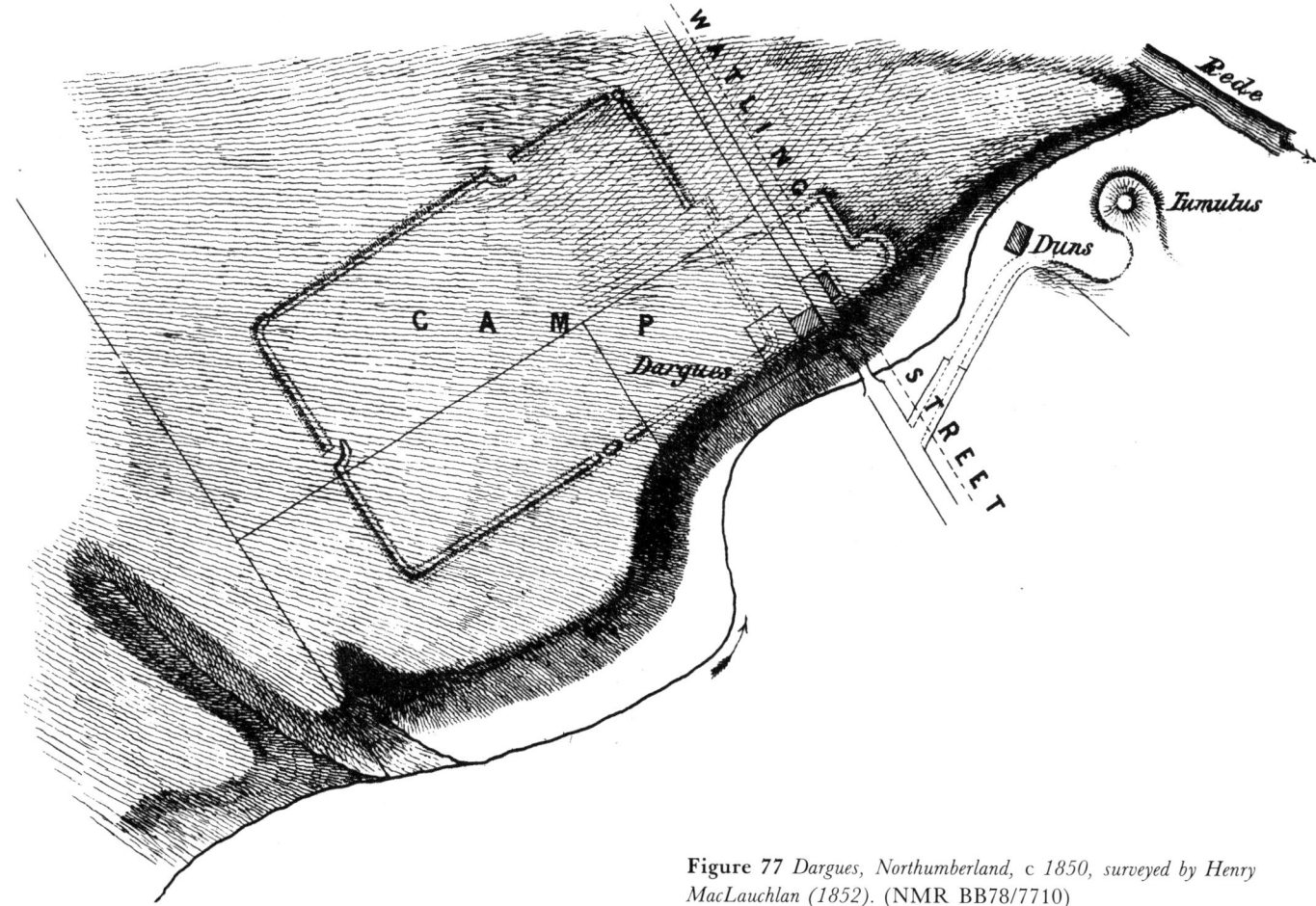

Figure 77 Dargues, Northumberland, c *1850, surveyed by Henry MacLauchlan (1852).* (NMR BB78/7710)

each protected by an internal *clavicula*. These entrances are centrally placed on the shorter NE and SW sides but are offset approximately 53 m to the NE on the long axis. No structures are visible in the interior which is cut by numerous drainage ditches of varying age, some partly obliterated by the growth of peat.

The SW rampart is now flat-topped but is fairly well preserved, averaging 0.2 m in height with a ditch 0.3 m deep, and is carefully sited on the crest of the hillside. Farther to the SW, the ground levels out and then begins to drop slightly to the W. In the S corner the ditch is silted and distorted at the junction with a modern drainage ditch but the spread rampart is still 0.4 m high. The bank of the SW *clavicula* stands up to 0.5 m high, but its ditch is now defined by little more than a change in the vegetation. Despite the damage caused at one point by the cutting of a drain, the rampart at the W angle survives to a height of 0.7 m above the bottom of the ditch; the latter is almost obliterated.

On the NW the ditch partly follows the line of a slight natural dip; it has been widened by water-scouring and substantially infilled by rotavation and drain-laying. This has also badly mutilated the front of the rampart which here averages 0.3 m in height. The bank of the *clavicula* stands

0.4 m high and is the best preserved although its tip has been truncated by a drain.

The N stretch of the NE rampart is as much as 0.6 m high and the ditch here is up to 0.4 m deep, but the flat-topped rampart has frequent breaks caused by natural and modern drainage. These agencies have also largely destroyed the *clavicula*, but its springing-point from the rampart is clear and two slight swellings beyond may also have formed part of it. Immediately S of the *clavicula*, farming activities have mutilated the rampart, pulling it forward into the ditch. In the field to the N of Dargues farmhouse, the rampart has been spread and distorted by ridge-and-furrow and it is totally obliterated immediately adjacent to the farmhouse by disturbance resulting from the construction of a large barn. No Roman structures were identified at the time of this development in the 1980s (inf P Austen, English Heritage).

In the field immediately W of the farmhouse, the SE rampart is very eroded and is now only about 0.1 m high; the general line of the ditch is clear but it is in poor condition, having been distorted and eroded by water. The bank of the *clavicula* is 0.2 m high, but its ditch has been somewhat deepened by water-scouring. In the next field to the SW, the rampart is 0.4 m high and the ditch is up to 1.0 m deep;

however, both have been accentuated by the recutting and maintenance of the ditch as a drain: spoil has been deposited externally, to form a small but sharp bank, and internally as an addition to the top of the rampart.

East of the A68, the line of Dere Street is indicated by an *agger* up to 0.1 m high, with scatters of cobbles and stones where the ground is eroded. Beyond and roughly parallel to the *agger* is a much reduced headland. East of the cottage on the E of the A68 is a disturbed area of rock and stone but no obvious pattern of structural remains can be discerned. The feature depicted here by MacLauchlan (1852a, 29–30, map 5; Fig 77) seems best interpreted as being partly of natural origin and partly a continuation of the ploughing headland to the NW.

NY 89 SE 10   Rochester

East Learmouth *Fig 78*

NT 87053698

Aerial reconnaissance has recorded the almost complete outline of a large camp some 600 m ESE of East Learmouth (St Joseph 1961, 120; 1973, 215; CUCAP AAC 2–7). It lies in undulating ground, on the top and the NW side of a spur, between about 52 m and 73 m above OD. From the highest point there is good visibility to the E, N and W, especially towards the River Tweed to the NW.

The camp is not quite rectangular, measuring between 300 m and 318 m from N to S by about 445 m transversely; it encloses an area of about 13.6 ha (33.6 acres). Only the W side is approximately straight, for the others all pivot slightly at the gates, a feature observed on a number of other camps. Three entrances can be distinguished, each with a traverse set about 10 m to 12 m outside the ditch. The approximate position of the missing S entrance can be surmised opposite the N gate and just W of the road, in the area suggested by the change in the alignment of the S ditch. The E and W gates are centrally placed. The N and S entrances, however, are not precisely positioned in the characteristic 1:2 ratio along the E to W axis, so that the camp, which faced W, would have had a proportionately small *praetentura*.

The lack of symmetry in the layout of the camp is largely a reflection of the local topography. The N and S defences occupy broad E to W ridges. The highest point occurs midway along the S side. The N defensive line lies below the summit of the ridge and has a gradual fall from E to W. Two slight hollows impinge on the E and W defences, the lowest point of the camp being just N of the gate in the W ditch. Because of this uneven ground, only the NW and SW corners of the camp are intervisible, hence, perhaps, the straightness of the W side. The location of the camp, which is less than ideal, may have been dictated by the need to select the driest ground in an area where there are a number of peat bogs.

In the NW quadrant of the camp, three sides of an

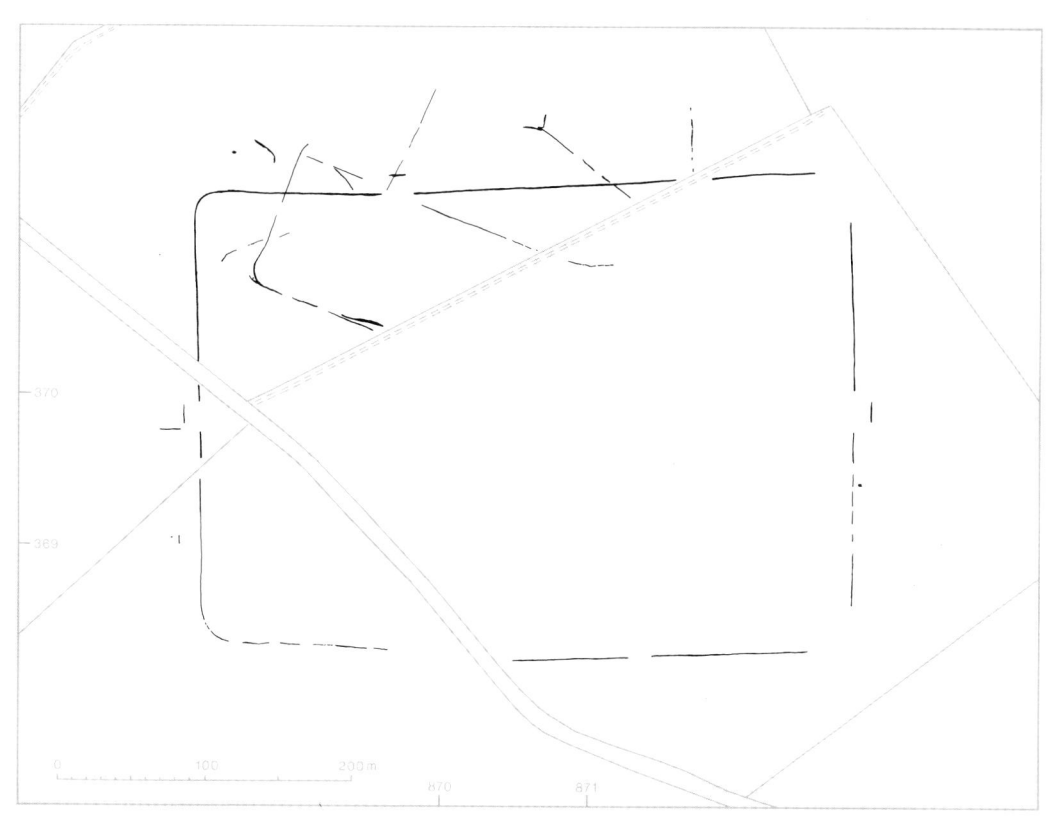

Figure 78 *East Learmouth, Northumberland.*

enclosure are visible as cropmarks. The rather sharp corners and slight irregularities in the layout of this enclosure argue against its acceptance as another small camp. Some of the adjacent fine cropmarks could represent drains.

NT 83 NE 14   Carham

Farnley 1, 2 and 3 *Fig 79*

1: NY 99476314   2: NY 99586312
3: NY 99806310

Three camps, of differing size and orientation, have been recorded lying close together on an undulating terrace at about 67 m above OD (CUCAP ATH 5; St Joseph 1951, 53). To the N is the steep scarp down to the haughlands and the S bank of the River Tyne; to the S, beyond the line of Dere Street, 250 m away, the ground rises steeply to Prospect Hill. There are extensive views upstream and downstream, from the sites of the camps, including the Flavian supply base at Red House and the fort at Corbridge (*Coria*), respectively about 3 km and 2 km NW up the valley.

Camp 1, the most westerly and apparently the smallest, measures only about 75 m across; its S side is masked by the modern A695 road and by the gardens of Farnley Grange. Parching, presumably marking the line of the camp's internal bank, was still visible in 1949 (CUCAP DS 11), but subsequent photographs show only the ditch. No gate can be discerned in either the E or the W sides; on the N the cropmarks are too faint to be certain whether or not an entrance existed.

The central camp, 2, is larger, about 100 m across; its S side is also overlain by the road and gardens. A gap, rather wide and off-centre but perhaps a gate, can be distinguished in its N side. No traverse is evident.

The outline of camp 3, the most easterly, is almost completely known except for its SE corner. Measuring about 160 m from WSW to ENE by 102 m transversely, it covered over 1.6 ha (4.0 acres). A gate is visible in both the W and the N sides, the latter at the position appropriate to a 2:1 ratio, but the probable sites of opposing E and S entrances are cut and obscured by a field boundary and drain. There are no indications of any traverses. The arrangement of its entrances appears to imply that the camp faced ENE away from Dere Street. It may, therefore, have predated the establishment of this road.

The detailed positioning of camp 3, and perhaps of the other two camps, seems to have subtly exploited minor topographical features. Part of the terrace on which the camps are sited rises gently to the N. The S side of camp 3 lies close to the crest of this slope and appears to be aligned along it. Although the line of this crest can no longer be traced as a distinct feature to the S of the modern road, general differences in ground level suggest that the S sides of camps 1 and 2 may perhaps have utilised this natural rise in a similar way, and that this may also have determined their overall alignments.

NY 96 SE 22   Corbridge

Figure 79 *Farnley 1, 2 and 3, Northumberland.*

Featherwood East *Fig 80*

NT 82020563

This fairly well preserved camp lies on the E side of Dere Street, and faces the road. It is situated on a gently sloping E-facing spur between the headwaters of the Ridlees and Southhope Burns, 7 km N of the fort at High Rochester (*Bremenium*). The highest point of the camp, at about 430 m above OD, is at the NW corner, and the ground falls away to about 380 m at the SE corner. The NE, SE and SW angles lie on opposite sides of the spur and the convex slopes mean that there is no point from which the whole of the interior is visible. The result is that the camp occupies a much less advantageous topographical position than its neighbour, Featherwood West, 250 m to the W.

The area enclosed, 15.9 ha (39.4 acres), is almost precisely the same as that at Featherwood West. This, together with the markedly inferior position occupied by the E camp, may suggest that the two were contemporary; it is even possible that each may have held half of a single force. The views to the NE and SE over the Ridlees valley are unobstructed; Kyloe Knowe and Ridlees Cairn, over 1 km away, block the view to the S, but the only serious restriction is immediately to the W, where the S spur of Foulplay Head, carrying Dere Street, forms the horizon. So long as the W camp was also occupied, this flank would have been covered.

Only the two S angles of the camp are intervisible. The N and S sides, however, are both straight and almost exactly parallel. The W and E sides, which cross the axis of the spur, are realigned once and twice respectively. On the W the realignment occurs at the gate which is about 50 m S of a local crest. On the E the line was changed on either side of the gate, at the two local horizons visible from the gate itself.

On the W the rampart is now rather ragged but still stands 0.7 m high externally and 0.5 m high internally. A modern drain occupies the approximate line of the Roman ditch and cuts through the causeway of the central gate. On the other three sides, modern drains also occupy the line of the ditch for much of its course and cut through the defences at frequent intervals. Tank-tracks and the road to Ridleeshope have levelled the earthworks which have also been damaged by shell-bursts. Nevertheless, between the E entrance and the modern road, where the ditch is 0.2 m deep, the internal and external scarps of the rampart still stand to a maximum height of 0.3 m and 1.5 m respectively; the earthworks on the N and S sides also survive to similar dimensions, where best preserved.

Three of the traverses guarding the gates are also well preserved, their mounds surviving up to 0.5 m high internally and 0.9 m externally; the ditch of the W one is still 0.5 m deep. The E traverse has been mutilated by the passage of tanks, and the ditch is only visible as a vegetation mark. The adjacent gate has also been eroded and distorted by the run-off of surface water.

The interior of the camp has suffered from modern drainage, from military activity and from the presence of a large quarry in the NE quarter, just above the crest of the steeper slopes. Immediately to the E of the quarry, a vestigial bank, about 2 m wide and no more than 0.2 m high, runs N, well beyond the Roman defences (RAF 106G/UK 628 4060–1). The point of junction is disturbed and the function of the bank and its chronological relationship to the camp is uncertain.

NT 80 NW 4   Alwinton

Featherwood West *Fig 81*

NT 81350577

The remains of a large camp enclosing an area of 15.6 ha (38.5 acres) lie on the exposed summit of Foulplay Head at 460 m above OD, 7 km N of the fort at High Rochester (*Bremenium*). This site offers the best position for a camp of any size along the line of Dere Street between the camps at Silloans and at Chew Green. It is markedly superior to the site of its neighbour, Featherwood East, with which it may be contemporary. There are excellent views north-eastwards to the modern Border, southwards into Redesdale and eastwards into Coquetdale; only to the SW is the line of sight limited, by the saddle close to the W corner of the camp, from which the land rises again to Loan Edge, 750 m away. Despite the advantage of this site, the topography has still put constraints on the layout of the camp. The NE rampart is aligned approximately parallel to Dere Street towards which the camp seems to face, despite there being an extra gateway on the NW side. The NW defences of the camp are positioned on a forward slope so as to command the valley of the Cottonshope Burn without leaving dead ground close at hand. The angle between these two sides, only about sixty-three degrees, dictated a trapezoidal plan. The N angle of the defences is at the highest point and from the almost level N quarter of the camp the land gradually falls away to the S angle some 50 m below. Evidently some difficulty was experienced in laying out the camp for the SW side alone is straight and only the SW parts of the NW and SE sides are parallel. Minor realignments occur at the NE entrance and at the more northerly of the two gates on the NW. On the SE, adjustments to the line were made at about 180 m from the E angle, at the postulated position of the single gate here, and also at a point 125 m from the S angle. It is significant that both of the NW gates and the SE gate are positioned at local crests.

Along the NE side the rampart has been damaged by a hollow-way that runs behind and partly on top of it, breaching the N angle. Towards the E angle, the bank measures only

Roman Camps in England

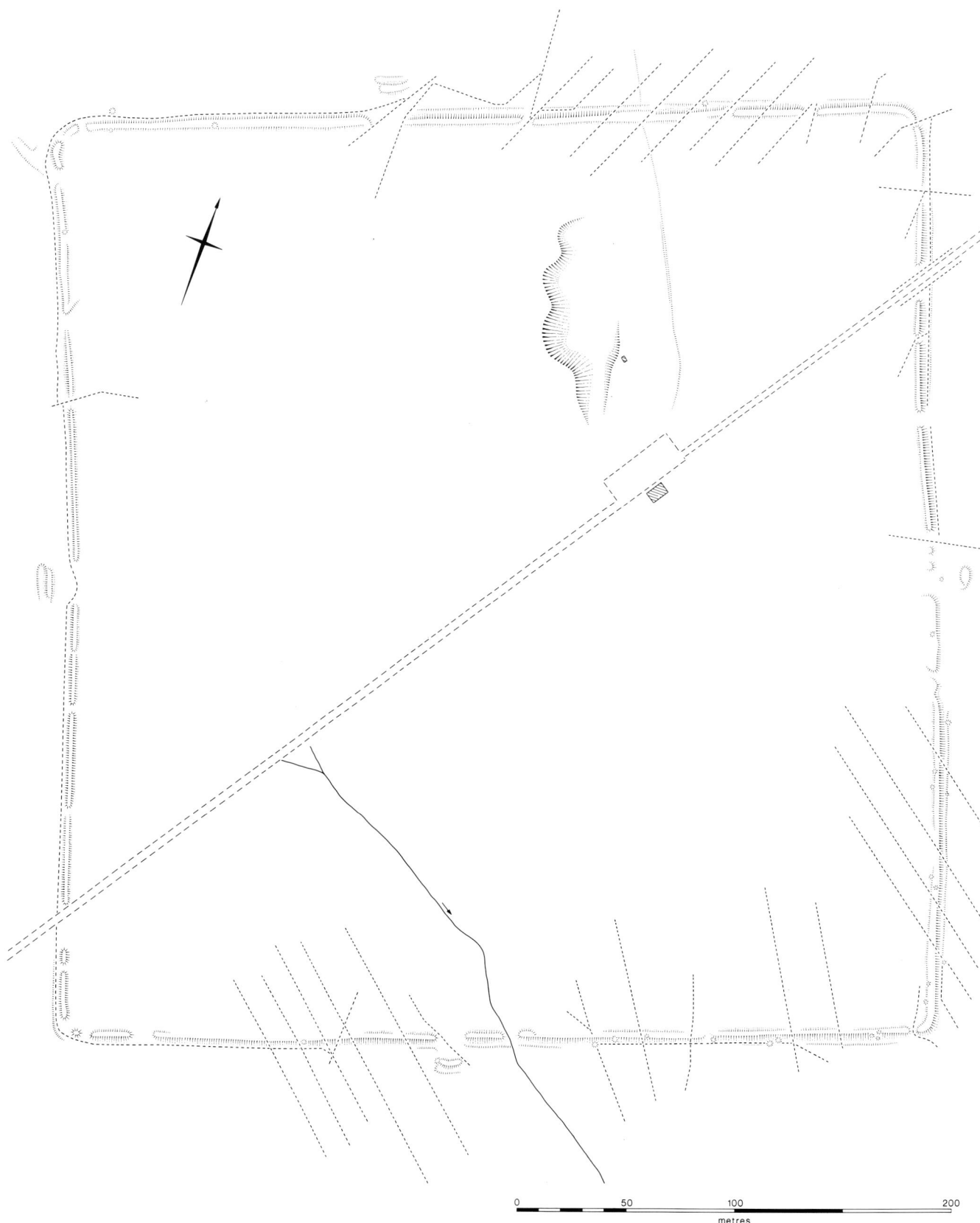

Figure 80 *Featherwood East, Northumberland. Modern drains are shown only where they intersect with the perimeter of the camp.*

Figure 81 *Featherwood West, Northumberland. Modern drains are shown only where they intersect with the perimeter of the camp.*

Northumberland

0.3 m in height but to the NW of the gate it stands 0.5 m high internally and 0.9 m above the bottom of the ditch. On this side the latter is up to 0.6 m deep. For much of the long NW front, however, the ditch is now represented by little more than a minimal outer scarp; only to the S of the more southerly of the two gates does it attain a depth of as much as 0.4 m. In contrast, the outer scarp of the rampart here, set on a forward slope, is impressive, surviving to a maximum height of 1.7 m; the inner scarp is poorly preserved and nowhere exceeds 0.3 m. On the SW, the defences are fragmentary and are cut and utilised by modern drains. Where best preserved, to the NW of the single gate on this flank, the inner scarp of the rampart is only 0.1 m high, although externally it stands up to 1.4 m. The ditch here is no more than 0.4 m deep. Much of the SE side is also in poor condition, cut by drains and natural gullies. The sections surviving best are on either side of the presumed position of the gate; the rampart still rises up to 1.1 m above the bottom of the ditch here although the inner scarp of the bank and the outer scarp of the ditch are no more than 0.4 m in height and depth respectively.

Each of the five gates seems to have been protected by a traverse. MacLauchlan (1852a 39; 1852b, pl VI) suggested the additional presence of an internal *clavicula* on the NE. However, although there is a slight scarp in the position that he indicated, such a provision would have been an aberrant arrangement: any internal *clavicula* should have been on the other side of the gate. The best-preserved traverses are the two on the NW, the mound of the N one standing to a height of 1.2 m and that of the S one to a height of 1.0 m. Their ditches are now largely silted up, and the mound guarding the more northerly of the two gates is mutilated at its N end. The traverse on the SW side is only just perceptible on the ground (NMR AP NT 8105/1–2) and that on the NE side has been severely mutilated, apparently by a modern military trench. MacLauchlan (1852a 39; 1852b, pl VI) thought he could discern a traverse on the SE and marks it on his survey at the point where a gully cuts through the defences. Slight swellings in the expected position are so gentle as to be unsurveyable. Without excavation, certainty is impossible but a gate here would probably correspond to the more northerly gate on the NW side. Apart from the poor drainage, there is no other topographical reason for the omission of a second gate on the SE flank.

The interior of the camp is featureless except for some modern drains and scattered shell-holes predating 1945 (RAF 106G/UK 628 3060–1). The overall plan of the camp and the provision of the extra gate in the W half of the NW side must have made a standard arrangement of the interior almost impossible.

Outside the NE flank of the camp the course of Dere Street is not now readily apparent; later hollow-ways near the N corner of the camp seem to have departed slightly from the expected line.

NT 80 NW 7   Rochester

Fell End *Figs 13 and 82*

NY 68546549

A large camp, at present in unimproved pasture, straddles one of a series of E to W ridges 1.7 km E of the fort at Carvoran (*Magnis*). It measures 360 m from E to W by 240 m transversely, and encloses an area of about 8.7 ha (21.5 acres). The highest point of the ridge is close to the W side of the camp at 250 m above OD, but the lowest points on the N and S ramparts are respectively 17 m and 21 m lower. The Stanegate follows the crest of the ridge and bisects the camp from E to W.

The defences are generally well preserved although there are sections, notably at the medial points on the E and W sides, which have been destroyed by extensive surface quarrying, by the Stanegate and by adjacent later hollow-ways. The S, E, and W defences have fairly consistent dimensions: the rampart is 0.1 m to 0.3 m high internally and stands 0.7 m above the base of the ditch; the latter has a counterscarp of between 0.1 m and 0.2 m. There are faint and intermittent traces of what conceivably may be an upcast outer bank (cf Oakwood, Ettrick and Lauderdale; RCAHMS 1957, 99–102). The N defences lack this consistency. The part to the E of the entrance, which lies at the top of a steep natural escarpment, is affected by soil slumping and peat growth; of this stretch of rampart only a discontinuous outer scarp, up to 0.7 m high, or at best, a low tussocky bank, survives. To the W of the entrance the defences utilise the crest of a steep escarpment with good visibility N to Hadrian's Wall. Here the rampart is 0.2 m high internally and up to 1.3 m above the ditch; the latter is marked by a terrace with a slight counterscarp bank measuring 0.1 m in maximum height at the top of the natural slope. It is possible that this stretch of the defences may have been refurbished at a later date. The evidence for this is the unusual height of the rampart, notwithstanding its enhancement by the ground configuration, the sharpness of the outward-facing scarp, and the existence of a series of scoops cut into the line of the ditch, some of which impinge upon the rampart. Whether this represents a strengthening of the defences during the Roman occupation or much later reuse is unclear.

Only two entrances can now be identified and these are approximately central to the N and S sides. The former is visible as a gap, 9 m wide, partly obscured by peat growth. A bulbous end to the rampart on the W side might possibly be the remains of an *ascensus*, but the area is too disturbed for certainty. There is a traverse some 2.5 m outside the outer edge of the ditch; its bank survives as a N-facing scarp, 1.1 m high, and its ditch as an external terrace in the steep natural escarpment. The modern drainage ditch that utilises the gap provided by the gate has eroded the scarp of the traverse and material from it has washed on to the terrace. This N entrance, opening directly on to the steep escarpment, would have had limited practical use. The S entrance is about 11 m wide and is guarded by a traverse lying 7.5 m outside the line of the perimeter ditch. The bank of this traverse is only 0.1 m high internally but stands 0.7 m above the bottom of its external ditch, which is barely discernible. Both entrance and traverse are mutilated by the ridge-and-furrow cultivation that extends from the bank and ditch of an old field boundary within the camp across the S defences, fading out close to the modern road.

The central portions of the E and of the W rampart, where an entrance might have been expected, have each been disturbed or destroyed by the Stanegate, and by later quarrying and hollow-ways. Indeed, the course of the Roman road itself is difficult to establish with certainty. Its general course, along the crest of the ridge, is clear, however; the turn to a more northerly line beyond the W end of the camp is made necessary by the topography in the descent to the fort at Carvoran.

The breaks in the rampart caused by this zone of destruction are 31 m wide on the E and 36 m wide on the W. The relationship between the camp and the Roman road cannot, therefore, be demonstrated on the ground. Nevertheless, the passage of a road through the centre of a camp, utilising a large proportion of the restricted amount of level ground available, would have disrupted the internal layout. It is therefore likely that the coincidence of axis between the camp and the road is a product of the topography, and that the camp had gone out of use before the Stanegate was constructed. The shallow quarries running approximately parallel to the general line of the road on either side are not

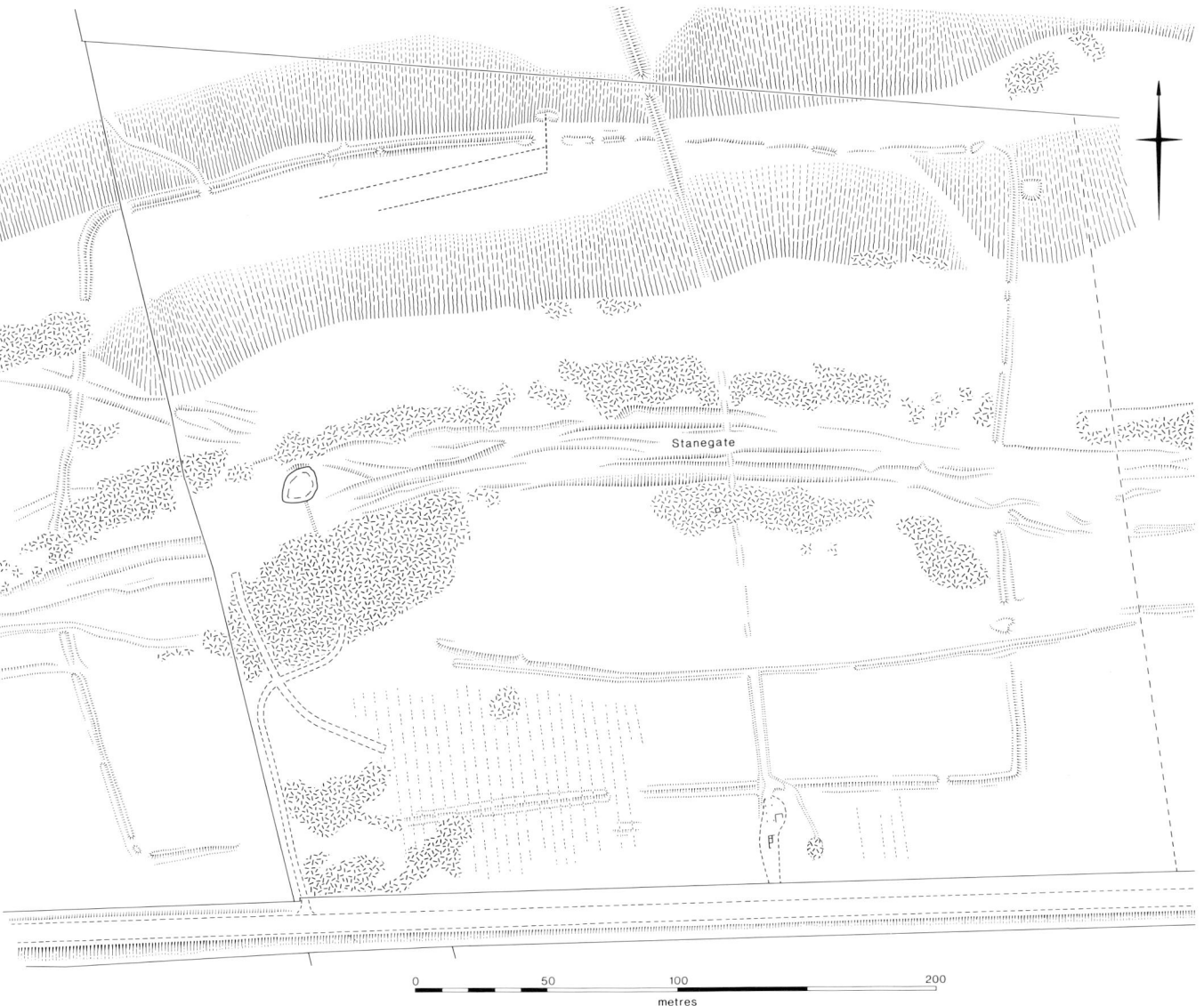

Figure 82 *Fell End, Northumberland. The stipple indicates areas of quarrying; a colliery tramway crosses the camp from N to S.*

Roman Camps in England

Figure 83 *Glenwhelt Leazes, Northumberland.*

directly associated with it. Although some of the hollow-ways may be the result of quarry traffic, the quarries themselves are comparatively recent and follow outcrops of sandstone which on this site consist of a ganister, known as the Firestone Sill; these outcrops extend to the WSW and diverge from the line of the road to the W of the camp (inf British Geological Survey; CUCAP AKI 72–3). Of all the trackways, one just to the N of the centre of the W side of the camp appears to be cut by the Roman defences and thus to predate them. It survives, within an area of quarrying, for a distance of about 30 m; it is 4 m wide and 0.2 m deep.

The greater part of the interior of the camp occupies the sloping ground to the N and S of the ridge. On the N the hillside is in places so steep, with a 25 per cent gradient, that the usable space within the rampart would have been restricted to a maximum area of only 7.5 ha (18.5 acres).

The irregular plan of the camp is unusual and the internal angles of the rampart lack uniformity, that on the SE being especially sharp. Like the example at Milestone House, 4 km to the E, the layout seems to have been partly dictated by the topography. Thus in its W half the N rampart was constructed along the crest of the steep natural scarp, economically utilising its defensive potential. Nevertheless there is a regularity in the plan, for each of the four major sides is composed of two portions which articulate about each entrance.

The bed of a tramway extends from the site of a disused colliery behind Peatsteel Crags, 120 m to the N; it crosses the camp from N to S, to reach a loading bay beside the modern road. The bay itself is reduced to some concrete foundation posts and the remains of a platform amidst coal refuse. Alongside the tramway, in an old quarry within the camp, is a roofless brick-built structure which may have been an engine house. Neither colliery nor tramway appears on large-scale maps until 1956 (OS 6-inch).

NY 66 NE 14   Haltwhistle

Glenwhelt Leazes *Figs 83 and 84*

NY 65606560

This camp is prominently situated at about 165 m above OD on the E end of a spur overlooking the gap in the Whin Sill escarpment cut by the Tipalt Burn, and has excellent views all around. It lies 850 m W of Carvoran (*Magnis*), 175 m S of the Vallum and only 40 m S of the Stanegate and is easily approached from all sides except the E, where the ground falls away steeply to the modern road. Formerly covered by rough grassland and improved pasture, the area is now occupied by Haltwhistle Golf Course and most of it has been extensively drained and re-seeded. Several old field boundaries have been partly uprooted and levelled, but elements of a former agricultural landscape can still be traced. As a result of all these activities the camp is now in poor condition although, remarkably, most of the principal features survive in varying states of preservation: a rampart and outer ditch, and four gates, each of which has the unusual combination of an internal *clavicula* and an external traverse.

The camp is an almost perfect rectangle, the interior of which measures some 150 m from N to S by about 80 m transversely, an area of 1.2 ha (3 acres). The defences are best preserved to the E of the N gate; here the rampart is about 4 m wide and 0.7 m high above the interior, and the outer ditch is 3.0 m wide and 0.5 m deep. The NE corner has been cut through for a path. The N end of the E rampart has been encroached upon and greatly reduced by ridge-and-furrow; a headland running parallel to the rampart overlies its E edge. To the S of the E gate the defences are crossed by a later boundary bank; farther S again the rampart has been spread to a height of only 0.2 m and the ditch has been levelled for a distance of about 50 m. The ditch is visible once more around the SE corner and here the rampart is better preserved, its outer scarp surviving to a height of 0.7 m; it is crossed by another hedge bank just to the E of the S gate. From this gate, along the remainder of the S side and up to the W gate, the rampart has been much

Figure 84 *Glenwhelt Leazes, Northumberland, from the E. The photograph shows the camp and its landscape before it was further encroached upon by Haltwhistle Golf Course. As a result, elements of the post-Roman landscape since destroyed are still visible. The curving line of the Stanegate lies between the camp and the Vallum (upper right). (4.2.71, CUCAP BEW 38)*

reduced, surviving only to a maximum height of 0.2 m, although its general line is quite clear; the ditch has been mainly infilled. To the N of the W gate the rampart is better preserved and is about 0.3 m high; in this stretch the ditch has been recut as a modern drain which slices through the NW corner of the camp, mutilating the defences.

The four gates, the positions of which are clearly marked, are of exceptional interest in that each has a traverse and also an internal *clavicula*. The *claviculae* are all much reduced in height; the N example is the least damaged, being a maximum of 0.5 m high. In contrast, the W one is visible only as a slight scarp some 0.2 m high. The four traverses are in a broadly similar state. The N one is again relatively undamaged, its rampart standing about 0.7 m above the bottom of the outer ditch, whereas the bank of the E traverse, only 0.3 m high, is overlain and mutilated by ridge-and-furrow; no trace of its ditch survives on the surface.

The interior, generally level, has been ploughed and drained in recent times and may once have been covered by ridge-and-furrow. Part of what appears to be a hollow-way, apparently earlier than the camp, cuts across the S half of the interior from the NW to the SE corner (CUCAP BEW 38; Fig 84).

The construction of the golf course has levelled a stretch of the Stanegate for a distance of about 30 m some 250 m to the NW of the camp. Elsewhere the road is generally well preserved. To the N of the camp it curves north-eastwards, and is overlain by ridge-and-furrow, but it can be seen to turn abruptly SE on the crest of the steeper slope (CUCAP BEW 38). These changes of direction conform to the general line of the Stanegate to the W of Carvoran and are necessary in order to negotiate the crossing of the Tipalt. Whatever the exact chronological relationship between the road and the camp, it is most unlikely that the Stanegate was constructed on this more northerly line simply to avoid an occupied camp (cf Bennett 1980, 157, 160).

NY 66 NE 13   Greenhead

Greenlee Lough *Figs 7 and 85*

NY 77466955

About 1.5 km NW of the fort at Housesteads (*Vercovicium*) a Roman camp was constructed over the remains of a field system apparently associated with a late prehistoric enclosed settlement. Situated at approximately 240 m above OD, the camp lies on the smooth S-facing dip slope of the rocky escarpment that plunges into Greenlee Lough to the N. The position is strengthened by the short gorge, 120 m W of the camp, through which the Jenkins Burn flows out of its shallow valley and into the Lough. Over the area of the camp the ground falls gently to the S for a vertical distance of 6.5 m from NW to SE. One third of the camp, to the N of a slight gully, is on sandstone and is covered by a thin layer of peat which reduces the definition of the earthworks there; the remainder overlies limestone.

The camp, which measures approximately 142 m from NW to SE and 118 m from SW to NE and which encloses an area of 1.4 ha (3.6 acres), is not an exact rectangle. Although the S corner is a right angle, the SW side is about 4 m shorter than the NE rampart which appears to bow slightly outwards close to its midpoint. On the surface the rampart measures up to 0.6 m high and the external ditch is 0.4 m in depth. When excavated in 1984 the ditch was found to have been V-shaped, measuring 1.9 m in width and 0.8 m in depth. The clay rampart was 2.2 m thick and 0.4 m high with a kerb, built of turf, 0.8 m wide; it was separated from the ditch by a narrow berm (*Britannia* **14** (1984) 279–80; Welfare 1986).

The remains of two gates can be identified, set approximately at the midpoints of the NW and SE sides. Each was defended by an internal *clavicula*. At the NW gate the causeway has been cut through by a comparatively recent drain. An inturned scarp to the S of the modern track on the NE side might be the last trace of another *clavicula*, but there is nothing distinctive to be seen in the equivalent position on the SW, the area around which has been disturbed by the track, the building of a field wall and by ploughing.

The interior of the camp is occupied by remains that are not of Roman date. To the N of the modern track are the footings of a rectangular building, now only 0.2 m high, and, farther N, the remains of a rectilinear sheepfold made of turf; between them is a shallow gully containing solution hollows which seems to mark the division between the underlying sandstone and limestone. Another building stood S of the track, over and across the low narrow ridges and shallow furrows of the prehistoric cord-rig cultivation that covers much of the hillside. The excavations confirmed that this cultivation was earlier in date than the construction of the camp. Field banks are aligned with the cord rig, approximately from N to S, within and to the E of the camp. It may be that these fields were associated with the circular stone-built settlement 70 m to the SW of the camp. From this settlement the banks and scarp defining a trackway, just visible through the ill-developed post-medieval narrow ridge-and-furrow, extend eastwards across the S third of the interior of the camp. The numerous small, shallow depressions in this area seem to be solution hollows that have formed over the limestone. A small hillfort lies 500 m to the NE, on the crest of the steep scarp down to the Lough. It is overlain by the footings of several shielings (RCHME 1970, 23–4, 33–4, pl 8).

NY 76 NE 24   Bardon Mill

Figure 85 *Greenlee Lough, Northumberland. The camp was constructed across a field system apparently associated with the settlement to the W; to the NE a hillfort is overlain by medieval shielings.*

Grindon Hill Fig 86

NY 82426788

This small camp, situated 40 m S of the course of the Stanegate, 5.5 km E of Vindolanda, lies at the E end of a narrow flat-topped ridge at a height of about 230 m above OD. The views are extensive in all directions except due N; there the ground falls gently away into a shallow hollow between the camp and the Stanegate, before rising to the summit of a small hill only 400 m away.

The N and S sides of the camp coincide with the crests of the natural ridge; the defences measure approximately 40 m from N to S and from W to E and have been laid out as a parallelogram enclosing an area of 0.1 ha (0.3 acres). Now in permanent pasture, the site has been severely reduced by narrow ridge-and-furrow cultivation. On the N and S the underlying earthworks of the rampart can be distinguished only with difficulty for the ploughing has cut across them at right angles. On the E and W the rampart is traceable as low swellings, no more than 0.2 m high, in the plough ridges, which share the same alignment. Slight changes in vegetation mark the line of the external ditch where this coincides with a furrow; this is best seen in the S half of the W side.

The exiguous remains of the rampart fade out altogether at the central point of each side, although the effects of the later ploughing have somewhat masked this on the E. Barely perceptible rises in the plough ridges, no more than about 0.1 m high, almost certainly mark the position of traverses on E and W.

NY 86 NW 3   Haydon

Grindon School Fig 87

NY 81386978

The ploughed-down remains of this small camp lie in an unusual position towards the bottom of the shallow valley of the Settlingstones Burn, 400 m S of the Vallum and at about 235 m above OD. The situation lacks any natural defences. Although the views are open to the E, the camp is dominated by a false crest, 100 m to the N and 13 m higher, which seriously restricts visibility. So, to a lesser extent, does rising ground to the S and W. The camp is approximately square and measures only 32 m across internally. Despite being under close-cropped pasture at the time of survey, details of the camp are barely discernible, due to the ridge-and-furrow that extends across the site from N to S; modern farming activities have also contributed to the erosion of the site although it was already seriously abraded by 1930 (NMR AP NY 8069/1/1 – 2). The E rampart is damaged by furrows and the S one is reduced to a spread mound 0.1 m high; even the better preserved sections of rampart in the N and W are denuded and do not exceed 0.3 m in height. At the NE and

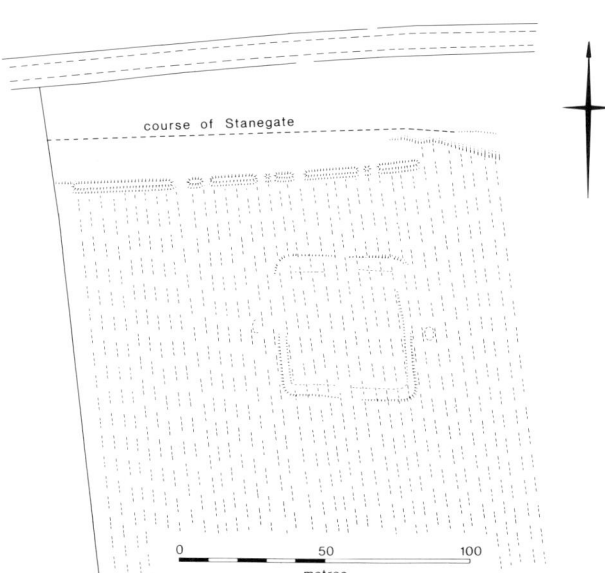

Figure 86 *Grindon Hill, Northumberland.*

Figure 87 *Grindon School, Northumberland.*

NW corners there are traces of an outer ditch which now measures only 0.1 m in maximum depth. Despite the small size of the camp, there is an entrance in the centre of each side. The amorphous remains of ploughed-down traverses survive outside the N, E and W gates as low swellings no more than 0.1 m high; none can be seen on the S. A modern ditch cuts diagonally across the N rampart.

NY 86 NW 1   Haydon

Haltwhistle Burn 1, 2, 3 and 4
Figs 88 and 89

1: NY 71456629   2 and 3: NY 71606635
4: NY 71396645

The Stanegate, the Roman road from Corbridge (*Coria*) to Carlisle (*Luguvalium*), had to negotiate the steep and narrow valley of the Haltwhistle Burn just to the S of Cawfields; from about AD 105 this crossing-point was guarded by a fortlet (Gibson and Simpson 1909; Breeze and Dobson 1985, 8). Some of the internal features, excavated in 1908, including a barrack block and officers' quarters, are still visible as earthworks. Externally, the defences were strengthened by the provision of an outwork (cf D Wilson 1984a). The Roman road almost clips the SE corner of this outwork and turns W at each of the crests above the burn, which was crossed at a slight angle.

To the N lay Burnhead Crag, along the crest of which Hadrian's Wall was built; the Crag was removed by quarrying in the 20th century. The Vallum here lay close to the Wall, at the foot of the dip slope on the S side of the Crag. Between the Vallum and the fortlet three camps were constructed, one of which was later halved in size. The chronological relationship of the camps to the other features of Roman date in the immediate vicinity is unknown. The area around the fortlet has been disturbed by watercourses and by the tracks and tramways associated with the 19th-century ironstone mines 400 m to the E. The scarps on the E bank of the burn have also been extensively quarried away.

Camp 1 lies about 40 m to the N of the outwork around the fortlet and occupies the summit and N-facing slopes of a low ridge which extends W towards the Haltwhistle Burn. This siting, at about 190 m above OD and slightly above the level of the fortlet, ensures good all-round visibility and probably dictated the general form and orientation of the camp. The highest point of the interior is in the SE, some 6 m above the NW corner.

The camp faced E and is rectangular in plan, measuring 147 m from E to W and 84 m from N to S. It enclosed an area of 1.0 ha (2.5 acres). Where best preserved, in the SE, the rampart is 0.1 m high internally and has an outer scarp rising 0.7 m above the base of the ditch. The latter, which averages 0.2 m in depth, has been partly destroyed by a hollow-way at the SW angle, and scouring from a seasonal watercourse has removed a section of the N side close to the NW angle. Silting has levelled the ditch in the NE, on either side of the public road to Burnhead and Cawfields. Excavations across the SE angle in 1907–8 (Gibson and Simpson 1909, 259–60, pls I and IV) revealed that the ditch was 4 ft (1.2 m) wide and 2 ft (0.6 m) deep, and that its centre-line was 8 ft (2.4 m) outside that of the rampart. The two elements may have been separated by a narrow berm. Turf had been used for the foundation of the rampart and for a forward revetment — more turf, the excavators estimated, than would have been provided by stripping the area of the ditch alone. The body of the rampart, which stood 2 ft 2 in (0.66 m) above the old ground surface, was composed of material upcast from the ditch.

Two entrances are readily traceable. That on the W is mutilated by surface quarrying and trackways; the traverse has survived to a height of 0.2 m, although the N half of its ditch has been levelled. The S gate is better preserved: the bank of the traverse is 0.4 m high externally but the ditch has been eroded by a former watercourse. A trench, the line of which is still discernible, was cut through this entrance and revealed that the bank of the traverse was constructed in the same way as the rampart (Gibson and Simpson 1909, 260). The public road to Burnhead and Cawfields crosses the N and E defences at the points precisely opposite the S and W entrances of the camp. Although there is now nothing to be seen it is likely that, in its original form, the road utilised the former Roman entrances.

A short stretch of bank and ditch close to the SE angle is not on the recorded alignment of the excavation trench there but may be relatively recent in date. Apart from slight traces of modern drainage channels extending down the slope, the interior of the camp is now featureless. The areas of possible cord rig visible on aerial photographs (CUCAP K 17 AB 269–70; T 80–1) inside and immediately to the E of the SE quarter could not be confirmed on the ground surface. Nevertheless it may be that the groove revealed by excavation in the old ground surface 5 ft 6 in (1.68 m) inside the centre-line of the rampart (Gibson and Simpson 1909, 260, pl IV) was a furrow forming part of that earlier arable landscape.

Camps 2 and 3 lie on an almost level shelf 30 m to the ENE of camp 1 and 3.5 m below its highest point in the SE. Camp 2 is square on plan, measuring 94 m across and enclosing an area of 0.7 ha (1.7 acres). At a later date it was divided into two by a rampart and ditch that extends E to W across the axis. The secondary camp thus formed, camp 3, occupies the N half of its predecessor and takes in an area of only 0.3 ha (0.8 acres). The rampart of each camp stands to a maximum height of 0.3 m internally and the external ditch is now no more than 0.3 m deep.

There are three entrances to camp 2 visible at medial points in the N, S and E sides respectively; each has the remains of a traverse comprising a bank up to 0.3 m high and a ditch up to 0.1 m deep. The N and S entrances have

Roman Camps in England

Figure 88 *Haltwhistle Burn 1, 2, 3 and 4, Northumberland, with the fortlet, within its outwork, to the S. A section of Hadrian's Wall was destroyed by Cawfields Quarry, on the N edge of the plan. The stipple indicates other areas of quarrying. Some prehistoric cord-rig cultivation is shown to the S of camp 2.*

Figure 89 *Haltwhistle Burn 1, 2, 3 and 4 and Markham Cottage 1 and 2, Northumberland. Vertical photograph, with N to the top, taken 16.1.73. On the right, Hadrian's Wall and Milecastle 42 are visible. To the NW of Cawfields Quarry the ditch of the Wall is still well preserved. To the S of Hadrian's Wall is the Vallum. The* agger *of the Stanegate is also visible, just above the modern road. To the NE of the point where the Stanegate crosses the Haltwhistle Burn is a fortlet set within its outwork. Immediately N of this is Haltwhistle Burn camp 1, with camp 2 (which was later modified to form camp 3) farther to the NE. The very small camp 4 lies between the Vallum and camp 1. To the W of the Haltwhistle Burn, Markham Cottage 2 is clearly visible, set inside the faint remains of Markham Cottage camp 1. The latter has been extensively overploughed with ridge-and-furrow.* (CUCAP K 17 AB 270)

been widened by the incursion of seasonal watercourses; in the N the watercourse has destroyed the ditch of the traverse. The E entrance to camp 2 is effectively blocked by the SE corner of camp 3 but excavations in 1907–8 confirmed the existence of the causeway at this point (Gibson and Simpson 1909, 261). Old trackways have denuded and truncated the bank of the E traverse and the end of the ditch on the S side of the centrally placed entrance to camp 2. There is no sign of the W entrance because the appropriate stretch of the W rampart has been eroded by a broad seasonal watercourse; the putative position for a traverse is occupied by the track that skirts this side of the camp. An unusual feature of camp 2 is the closeness of the traverses to the line of the defences, the distance between the inner edge of the traverse bank and the outer edge of the ditch being only about 1.5 m.

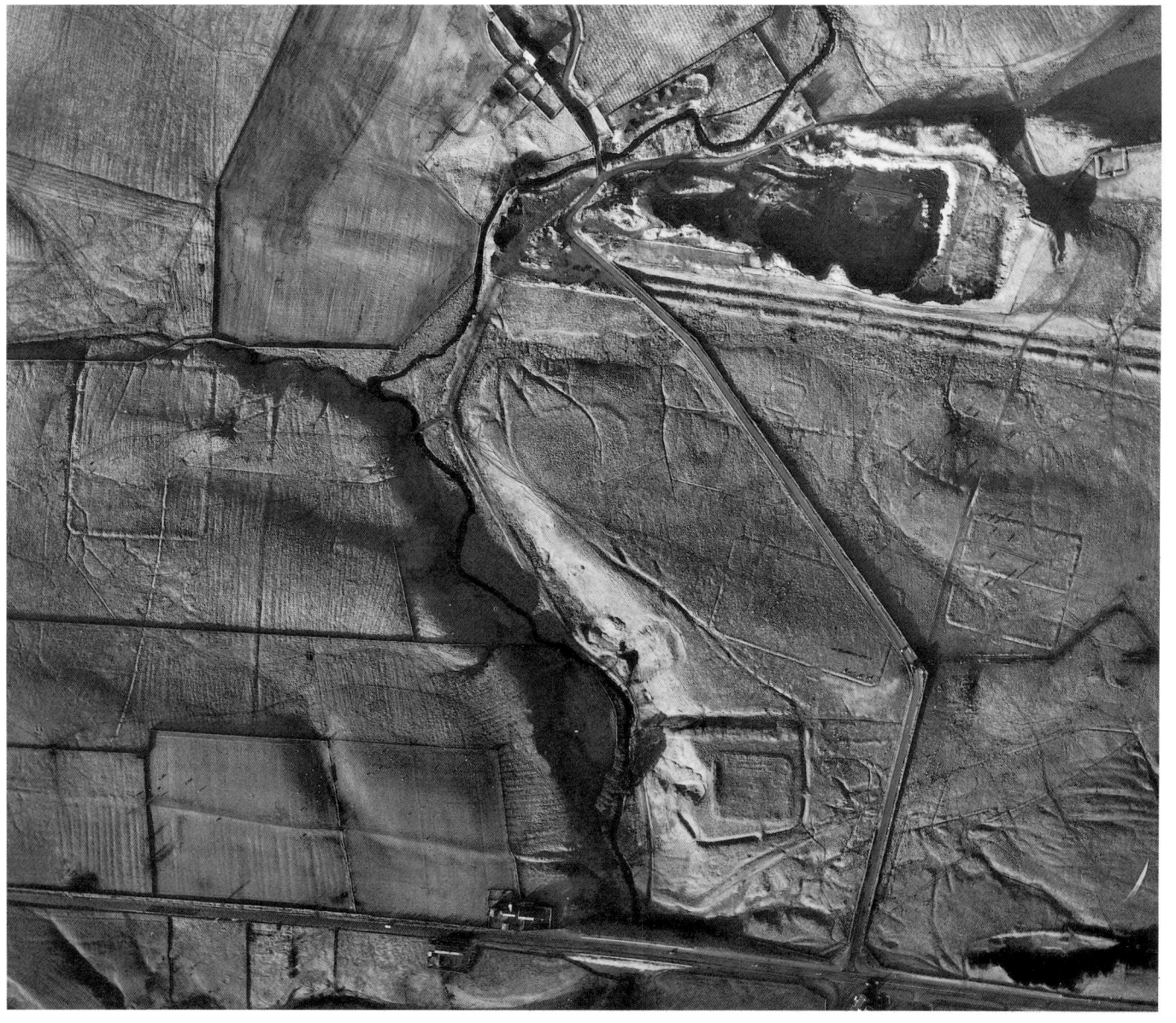

Roman Camps in England

The E rampart and ditch of camp 3 may have been reconstructed for they appear to be offset by about 1 m from those of the earlier earthwork (Gibson and Simpson 1909, 261). The camps share a common N entrance but the new S rampart was provided with a gate at the midpoint. The well-preserved traverse lies about 3.5 m beyond the outer lip of the ditch of the camp. The defences are somewhat mutilated by natural drainage and a grass track bisecting the camp has cut the E and W ramparts. There is, however, no evidence of entrances on either of these sides. Within the camp are the turf-covered remains of two structures of unknown purpose each 0.1 m high. One is approximately square and is bounded by a bank with two stones exposed in the NE corner; the other is U-shaped with a depression in the centre. An area of cord-rig cultivation, presumably prehistoric in date, survives to the SE of camp 2.

Camp 4 is exceptionally small and is situated 45 m S of the Vallum, at a height of about 180 m above OD, close to the bottom of a shallow valley. It occupies the lowest lying and most poorly drained site of any of the camps in the Haltwhistle Burn group. Although it enjoys comparatively wide views to the E and W, the camp would have been immediately overlooked from the N by the former Burnhead Crag along which Hadrian's Wall was constructed.

Only slight traces of the rampart are discernible, for it is no more than 0.1 m in height and is spread to a width of about 3 m; it encloses a tiny area measuring approximately 19 m from E to W by 16 m transversely. The depth of the silted external ditch ranges from 0.1 m to 0.2 m. There are two opposed entrances, on the E and on the W, each approximately 3.5 m wide; no evidence of traverses or *claviculae* has been noted. Because of its weak defensive position the camp is unlikely to predate Hadrian's Wall.

1: NY 76 NW 13   2 and 3: NY 76 NW 12
4: NY 76 NW 44   Haltwhistle

Lees Hall *Fig 90*

NY 70466567

The siting of this camp, and the provision of an outwork, are most unusual. The defences enclose the upper reaches of a small stream, now piped underground for much of its course, which runs from W to E almost along the axis of the

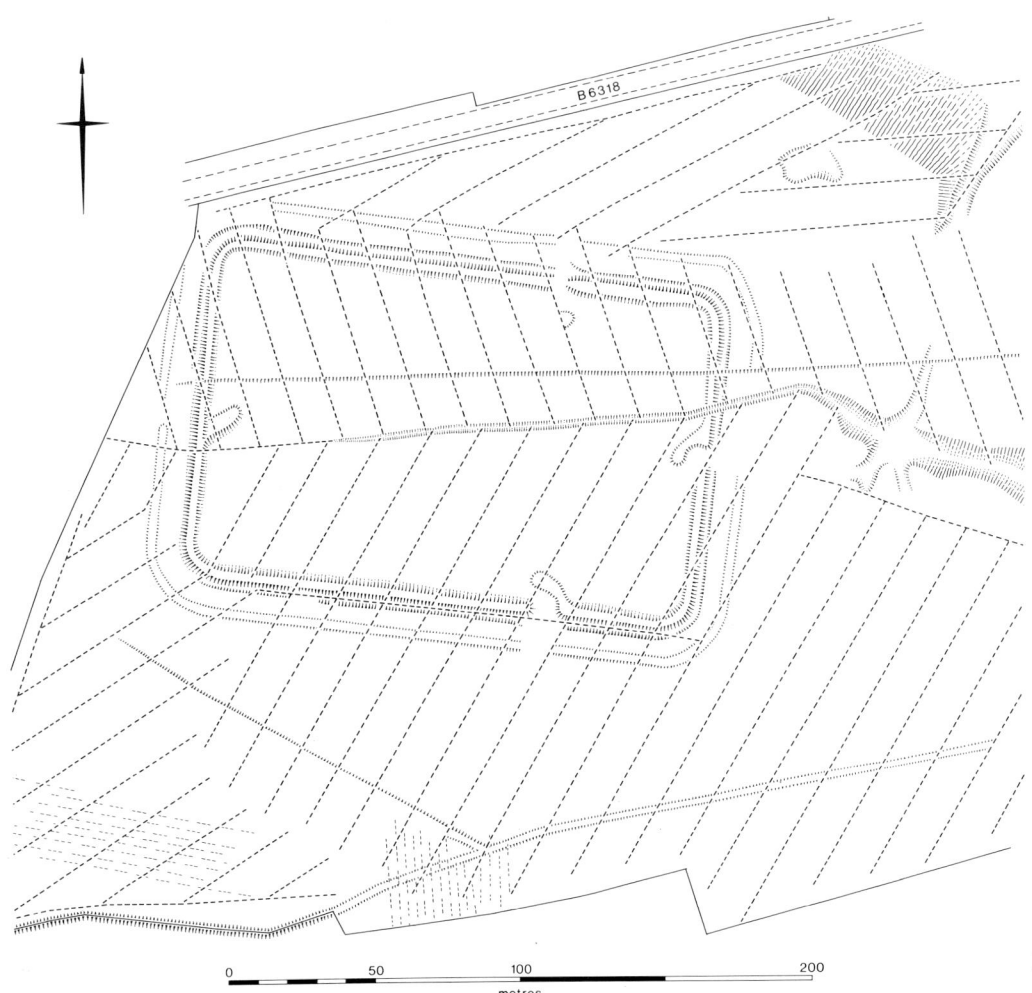

Figure 90 *Lees Hall, Northumberland.*

camp, dividing the broad SE flank of Haltwhistle Common into two spurs. To the W of the camp, which lies at about 200 m above OD, the ground continues to rise very gently; the position of the W rampart above a slight change of slope does, however, allow a restricted outlook in this direction. The views from the interior, except towards the E, are not extensive. From the position normally occupied by the headquarters — here partly occupied by the bed of the stream — the ground rises for about 2 m to both the N and the S ramparts. The N rampart has the most commanding views; it lies, in part, on the crest of the N spur overlooking the line of the Stanegate, only 120 m away, and beyond to the crags occupied by Hadrian's Wall between Walltown and Winshields. In contrast, the S rampart is only about 80 m from the crest of the higher ground forming the S spur of the hill; all views in this direction, across the valley of the South Tyne, are therefore blocked.

Despite its proximity to the Stanegate, the camp faces almost due E. It measures 175 m from W to E and 110 m from N to S and encloses an area of 1.7 ha (4.2 acres) within an earthen rampart which averages about 0.3 m in height and is nowhere more than 0.5 m above the interior; it is spread to a width of about 6 m. The external ditch, about 0.4 m deep and some 3 m wide, survives throughout its length except around the SW angle. As a whole the defences and the interior of the camp have been badly damaged, especially by a system of drains cut in 1976 (Austen 1977).

There were four gates, each one slightly offset from that on the opposite side and each defended by an internal *clavicula*. The N *clavicula*, the presence of which was noted in Ordnance Survey records (NAR NY 76 NW 18) has been almost entirely destroyed by a drain; the other three survive to a height of about 0.3 m. The line of the ditch is broken for a causeway opposite each of the N, E and S gates although on the S it has been cut through by a modern drain (Austen 1977). On the W, where the ditch is no longer evident, there is now no trace of a break in the rampart; this entrance seems to have been blocked at a secondary stage.

The outwork consists only of a bank with no attendant ditch. Apart from a slight irregularity in its alignment around the NE angle, it lies parallel to the rampart of the camp and about 13 m outside it. The bank is in poor condition and in some places is barely discernible, but on the S side it is clearly visible on vertical aerial photographs taken in 1946 (RAF 106G/UK 1392, 4186–7). The NW corner has been completely destroyed but elsewhere it averages about 0.2 m in height and is spread to a width of about 3.2 m. On the N, W and S there is a break in the bank opposite each entrance; another gap probably existed outside the E gate although it is now impossible to confirm this without excavation. Outworks are known to have been provided around Roman forts in Britain (Wilson 1984a) but for a camp the provision of such an encircling outwork seems to be unique. The existence of an outwork here must throw some doubt on the classification of the site, although it is unknown whether the inner and outer defences are strictly contemporary. Its position, which has no natural strength on the S, may have prompted the provision of this extra line of defence. Either way, it is not likely to have been a temporary encampment or fortification and occupation may have been for a season or more. If the blocking of the W entrance took place in Roman times this would suggest more than one period of use.

A relatively early date for the initial construction may be indicated by the presence of *claviculae*. Proof is lacking, but since the fortlet beside the Haltwhistle Burn, 1 km to the ENE, was not occupied before *c* AD 105 (Breeze and Dobson 1985, 8), it is conceivable that the earthworks at Lees Hall are those of a predecessor. If so, they might be early Flavian, or even Agricolan, in date.

A lynchet, 0.5 m high, crosses the N half of the camp and overlies the E and W ramparts. This is probably the remnant of an old field boundary, similar to and contemporary with others to the S of the camp. There are faint traces of ridge-and-furrow to the SW, and 65 m to the E of the camp a hollow-way cuts across the natural gully.

NY 76 NW 18   Haltwhistle

Limestone Corner *Figs 91 and 92*

NY 87677136

A small camp, partly excavated in 1912 (Newbold 1913, 71–4), occupies a gentle S-facing slope under permanent pasture at the S edge of the summit at Limestone Corner, some 200 m S of Hadrian's Wall and 105 m S of the Vallum. There are commanding views along the Wall to the W as far as Steel Rigg, to the E into North Tynedale, and S to the valley of the South Tyne; visibility to the N is restricted by the hill summit.

The camp is not quite square; the N side measures 48 m, the S 50 m, the W side 49 m and the E side 44 m. It encloses an area of about 0.2 ha (0.6 acres) within a low rampart which survives mainly as an outward-facing scarp; the latter is up to 0.6 m high, above the bottom of a shallow ditch, at best 0.1 m deep. The ditch is traceable around most of the perimeter, but it may not have been continuous; certainly its course is interrupted at the NW corner by an outcrop of dolerite. As a result of later occupation of the interior of the camp, the inner scarp of the rampart is mostly obscured. Midway along each of the four sides of the camp is an entrance with an external traverse. The N entrance appears to have been blocked in a secondary phase; its traverse, which is reduced to a low bank 8.0 m long with only vague traces of an outer ditch, is not quite parallel to the line of the rampart. An outcrop of dolerite adjoins the W end. The S entrance is disturbed by what appear to be later drains. The traverse here is the best preserved of the four; measuring

Roman Camps in England

8.0 m long, its bank stands 0.5 m above the bottom of the ditch, which is 0.1 m deep. The E and W entrances are well preserved and seem to be inturned but this is probably the result of their continued use during reoccupation of the camp. The ditch to the N of the E entrance has been deepened, and the spoil deposited in a bank to the E. This was presumably carried out when the camp was reused. The E traverse bank is reduced and spread, with only possible slight traces of a ditch. The bank of the W traverse has been disturbed, perhaps by excavation, and the ditch is only partly visible.

The later, turf-covered remains within the camp are probably those of a farmstead, the date of which is unknown (cf RCHME 1970, 1–8, 44–53). In the NW corner are the footings of a bipartite rectangular building, possibly a house and attached byre, with traces of what may have been a stockyard adjoining the S side. There are the footings of a further building to the S of the stockyard, and the remnants of other buildings or enclosures are ranged along the S and W ramparts of the camp. Amorphous remains of stone-built structures and much disturbed ground occupy the NE sector.

When excavated in 1912 (Newbold 1913, 71–4) the presence of this former farmstead seems to have gone unnoticed. The rock here is very close to the surface and a trench just S of the W gateway of the camp revealed that the ditch was only about 0.6 m deep. In spite of this lack of

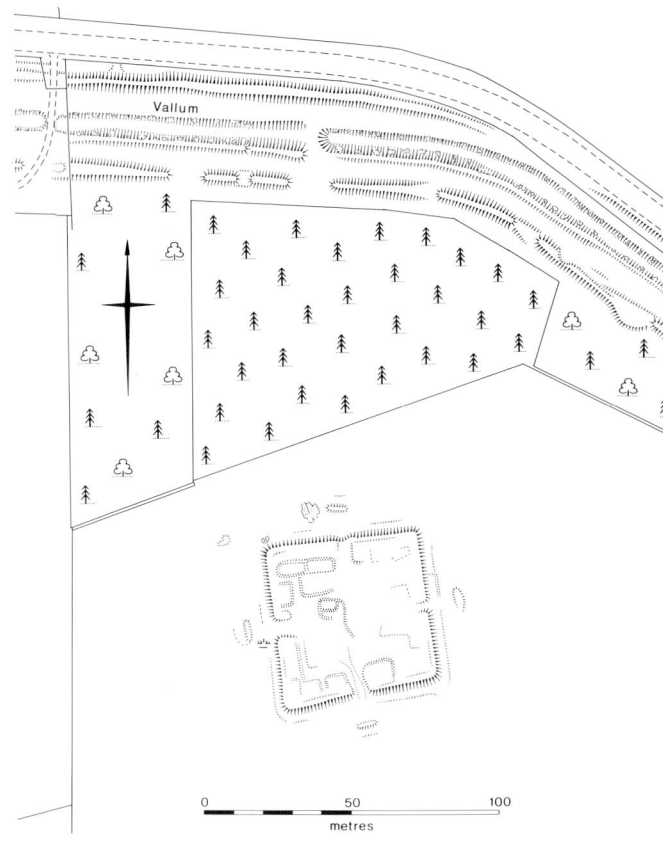

Figure 91 *Limestone Corner, Northumberland.*

Figure 92 *Limestone Corner, Northumberland, from the E. Hadrian's Wall and the Vallum lie to the N of the camp. The remains of the later farmstead are visible within the defences.* (4.2.71, CUCAP BEW 97)

depth, the excavators could not distinguish in the make-up of the rampart any of the turf that might have been expected to compensate for the shortage of material that must have resulted. The rampart was found to have been much spread, probably during the later occupation of the site.

In the interior, irregular flagged areas were found; they were numerous in the NE quarter but absent in the SW, and were presumably associated with the farmstead. Unusually, some Roman sherds were discovered, including some from cooking-pots and from a mortarium. Apart from some fragments which may be Black-Burnished ware (BB1) dating to the early to mid 2nd century, the pottery appears to belong to the late 3rd or early 4th century. The stratigraphical relationship of the pottery to the building of the camp is uncertain. The few sherds found in the rampart material are puzzling, but they could have been incorporated by animals or during the later occupation of the site.

About 10 m NW of the camp is a mound measuring 5.0 m by 4.0 m and 0.3 m high which contains some stone and has been disturbed on the W side. Its origin and purpose are uncertain.

NY 87 SE 14   Warden

Markham Cottage 1 and 2
Figs 89, 93 and 94

1: NY 70856609   2: NY 70896625

There are two camps at Markham Cottage: the larger and earlier camp 1 contains the smaller camp 2 within its N margin. The course of the Vallum lies 110 m to the N and the fort at Great Chesters (*Aesica*) is only 520 m to the NNW.

Camp 1 is situated astride a low E to W ridge between the gorge of the Haltwhistle Burn to the S and E and, on the N, the shallow valley of the stream that flows E from Peat Steel to cross the NW corner of the camp. The ridge shelves gently to the E, from 193 m above OD just S of Markham Cottage to about 179 m above OD in the NE and SE angles. On the crest of the ridge and immediately to the N of the Stanegate, which crosses the S part of the camp, the E end of one of the fort's cemeteries lies within the defences. Two certain and a third probable barrow are shown on the plan (b); at least two dozen others, of which about ten survive, were spread over a total distance of 400 m as far W as NY 70406594 (Wallis 1769, 11; NAR NY 76 NW 35 and 42).

The camp is the largest in the vicinity but it is in poor condition: severely eroded by former seasonal watercourses, especially on the W, it has also suffered from agriculture which has reduced stretches of the rampart and ditch on the E side to little more than prominent elements in a system of ridge-and-furrow. A modern field wall overlies a stretch of the N defences and the W rampart has been partly incorporated into a revetted hedge bank. Almost exactly rectangular on plan, the camp measures 460 m from N to S by 365 m transversely and encloses 16.8 ha (41.5 acres) within an earthen rampart and an external ditch. The defences are best preserved towards the N end of the E side where the bank stands 0.3 m high internally and the ditch is 0.3 m deep. The only entrance that can now be identified is at the medial point of the S side where a slight causeway is visible across the heavily silted ditch, all that can now be seen of the defences in this area. A low amorphous bank, 0.1 m high, which lies outside the line of the ditch here, is more likely to have been a traverse than an external *clavicula*.

Due to erosion and agricultural destruction the exact chronological relationship between camp 1 and the Stanegate cannot be demonstrated by fieldwork alone. However, their relative positions suggest that this large camp was constructed before the line of the road was established in the late 1st century AD. The camp is not likely to have continued in use thereafter. The presence of the cemetery, probably in use from the 2nd to the 4th century (cf Charlton and Mitcheson 1984, 19), implies a long life for this road; the modern lane and track preserves the line of a branch leading N to Great Chesters fort, avoiding the steeper slopes to the W (Horsley 1732, 150; *J Roman Stud* **42** (1952), 89). Camp 2 is almost certainly later than camp 1 but the interval between them is not known.

The NW corner of the camp 1 was formerly occupied by Wall, or Walltown, Mill. This was a watermill with the usual ancillary structures: two leats, the reservoir they served, with the site of the mill-wheel at its E end, the footings of one building and an adjacent walled enclosure — probably the miller's house and garden — are still visible. An incomplete female statue and an inscribed statue base were found in 1801 (Skinner 1978, 41–2; *RIB* 1731) when the miller was clearing one of the leats. Two tombstones (*RIB* 1742, 1747), most probably a third (*RIB* 1746) and 'an urn' (Horsley 1732, 230), were also found here, although their precise provenances are unknown. Dressed masonry and 'many foundations' had been dug up before 1840 on this low ridge to the N of the stream 'a little to the West' of Walltown Mill (Hodgson 1840, 203). None of these discoveries is likely to relate directly to camp 1, the NW corner of which thus seems to have lain very close to, or under, another of the cemeteries of Great Chesters fort.

The ground immediately to the NNE of the reservoir was cleared and graded in about 1980 and all evidence of the Roman defences was removed in this area. A small circular earthwork, 7.6 m in diameter overall, lies in the extreme NW corner of the camp. It consists of a low mound, no more than 0.1 m high, surrounded by the vestigial remains of a ditch only about 0.4 m wide. It overlies the position of the rampart and the comparatively recent ridge-and-furrow. Further ridge-and-furrow which predates the inclosure of Haltwhistle Common (Inclosure Award 1849: NRO QRA 33) is evident in the E half of the camp. Almost all traces of it have been destroyed in the modern arable field close to

Roman Camps in England

Figure 93 *Markham Cottage 1 and 2, Northumberland. Roman barrows are indicated by the letter 'b'.*

the SE angle. Perhaps broadly contemporary with this cultivation, or even earlier, is a bank, with a ditch on its NW side, which extends from close to the Haltwhistle Burn, in the NE, crosses the E and S defences of both camps and ends on the lip of a gully to the S of camp 1. Where it rides over the E side of the larger camp this bank is 0.4 m high and the ditch is 0.4 m deep, but elsewhere it has been reduced in places to a vestigial single scarp. There is no change of course apparent beside the Military Road (B6318), constructed in the 1750s, which the boundary probably predates.

Camp 2 is generally better preserved than camp 1. It occupies the gentle N-facing slope, under permanent pasture, at about 185 m above OD. Its S side lies on a false crest and its N defences appear to have been thrown up by reconstructing, or simply reusing, those of the larger camp 1. At its NE corner the ditch of camp 2 cuts through the remains of the rampart of camp 1 and the smaller camp is therefore undoubtedly later. Overall it measures 130 m from N to S by 106 m transversely, enclosing an area of 1.4 ha (3.4 acres) within a bank up to 0.3 m high internally and an external ditch now 0.3 m deep. Both bank and ditch survive in fairly good condition on the S and W sides, although the ditch has been scoured out by surface drainage in places. Fragmentary ridge-and-furrow within the camp has impinged upon parts of the S and E ramparts and the latter has disappeared entirely where it climbs over a rocky hillock. The N defences are cut by recent drains and partly overlain by a field wall, but elsewhere the outward-facing scarp of the rampart stands 0.7 m high. There is an entrance at the midpoint of the N side and at that of the S side. The former is a gap, 7.0 m wide, now occupied by a drainage channel. A field wall stands on the assumed position of a traverse of which there is no trace. The S entrance survives as a break in the rampart, 8 m wide, but the causeway across the ditch has been cut through and destroyed by a natural drainage channel. The traverse protecting this gate has also been damaged by surface water, although the remains of its bank still survive to a height of 0.3 m and its ditch is 0.2 m deep.

NY 76 NW 14 & 16   Haltwhistle

Figure 94 *Markham Cottage 1 and 2, Northumberland, from the NW. The smaller camp 2 is in the foreground, its interior covered with ridge-and-furrow cultivation. To the E, a portion of the E side of the very large camp 1 is clearly visible. The features to the W of camp 2 and on the N of the Haltwhistle Burn are the remains of Walltown Mill. (7.12.67, CUCAP ATV 46)*

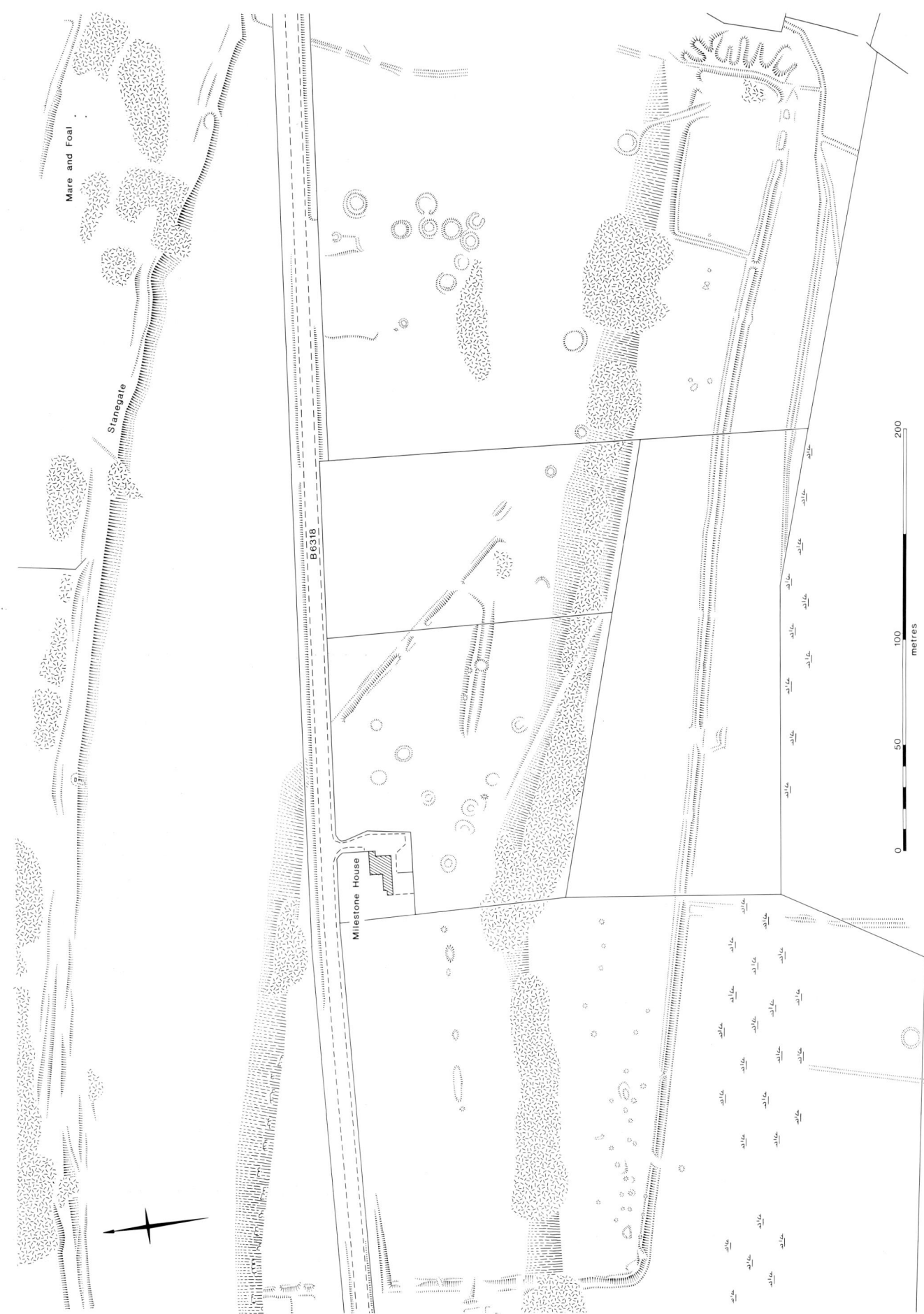

Milestone House *Fig 95*

NY 72186609

This camp, situated just above the 215 m above OD contour, occupies a saddle between a succession of N-facing limestone escarpments. The unusual layout of the camp, an irregular hexagon, has clearly been determined by these escarpments. The site is now in permanent pasture typified by bent-fescue grassland with areas of cotton-grass bog on the higher ground on the S and E limits of the camp.

The defences enclose an area of about 7 ha (17 acres) and are in various states of preservation, the most perfectly preserved being those in the westernmost fields, on both sides of the B6318 road. The W rampart, 180 m in length, runs N from the S crest of the saddle down a gentle gradient and across the modern road, before climbing the short dip slope of the next escarpment and ending on the lip of an almost vertical crag, 8 m high. Just S of the centre of this rampart is a gate with the disturbed remains of a traverse. Although disfigured by a more recent trackway, this traverse survives to a height of 0.6 m above the bottom of its ditch, which is 0.2 m deep. Several other breaks in this rampart have been caused by quarrying and by animals.

The long S side extends along the S-facing slope of the ridge, just below its crest. Measuring 575 m in overall length, it is better preserved in the W of the three fields. Here it consists of an external ditch, an earthen rampart, and what may be an internal drainage ditch similar to that found by excavation on camp 1 at Haltwhistle Burn (Gibson and Simpson 1909, 260). Another drain appears to cut across the outer side of the single gate on this side, linking the two ends of the ditch. This suggests that the drains are associated with the later use of the hill as represented by the ridge-and-furrow. The rampart here has an internal height of 0.5 m and stands 1.2 m above the bottom of the external ditch, which is itself 0.3 m deep.

Where the S rampart projects into the central and easternmost fields, it is much less well preserved, and in the central field at least appears to have been overlain by poorly developed ridge-and-furrow (not shown on plan) which has had the effect of flattening and broadening the defences. As in the W side, there is a gate near the central point of the rampart, now heavily disturbed; its traverse, 0.2 m high, has traces of an external ditch 0.2 m deep.

The E rampart is the shortest, apparently not much more than about 45 m in length; its ditch may have been recut at a later date to function as a drain. The short linear feature immediately to the N, though continuing the alignment of the defences, is a more recent field drain. Since the upcast here is on the E, rather than the W side of the ditch, this length of drain cannot be associated with the E defences of the camp.

The N side of the camp is most unusual. From the N end of the W rampart the natural crag seems to have been utilised as a defensive line, along which the provision of a rampart was superfluous. It is unlikely that any defences have been destroyed, for quarrying of the outcrop has only taken place farther to the W, outside the area of the camp.

The N face of the crag, at its steepest at its junction with the W rampart of the camp, gradually reduces in height and becomes less steep towards its E end. At the point where the modern road cuts the camp perimeter artificial defences were again necessary and a normal rampart and ditch were constructed obliquely across the saddle, towards the SE. This fragmentary section of rampart is only preserved for a length of a little more than 120 m. Outside its line are the slight remains of a traverse with a bank 0.1 m high and a ditch 0.2 m deep in what would have been the axial position, relative to the W gate and to the S defences. The SE section of this side has probably been lost through quarrying. Its exact course is difficult to determine, but rather than having extended along the foot of the natural scarp it may have again used the crest as a defence, linking with the N end of the E rampart without recourse to the construction of a formal rampart and ditch.

In the SE corner of the camp a later rectangular enclosure has been constructed, the internal dimensions of which are roughly 40 m from N to S by about 80 m transversely. This feature has a later trackway cut through its N perimeter. No definite entrance can be determined, but the most likely position for one may be on the S side near the SE corner of the camp, which has been heavily mutilated by trackways and perhaps by the recutting of the camp ditch.

One important feature of the camp is the fact that its position straddling a limestone escarpment, now much scarred by quarrying, reduces the area of flat usable ground within the interior by as much as one quarter. This factor must seriously have limited the number of men that could have been stationed in this comparatively large site. No interior features are visible; the small pits and upcast mounds on the crest of the ridge, close to the SW angle of the camp, are relatively recent quarries.

Over two dozen small, circular earthworks occur inside and outside the camp. Ranging in overall diameter from 4 m to 10 m, they usually consist of an annular or penannular bank of earth and stone about 0.3 m high, surrounded by an external ditch about 0.2 m deep. The main concentration of these features is a group of eleven centred 300 m ESE of Milestone House (NY 72506619), with a further fourteen scattered throughout the camp interior at the base of the much quarried limestone ridge. Two outliers occur to the S of the camp at NY 72146589 and NY 72216583. Although superficially similar to some prehistoric hut sites and burial cairns, and also to much later stack stands

Figure 95 *Milestone House, Northumberland. The stipple indicates areas of quarrying.*

(RCHME 1970, 54–60), these structures are the dismantled remains of simple limekilns, known locally as 'sow kilns' and used as recently as the beginning of the 20th century to produce lime for fertiliser (Jobey 1966). The examples at Milestone House would appear to be the group partly excavated by Hedley (1934, 307); comparable sow kilns, closely associated with a limestone outcrop, have been excavated on Wards Hill near Rothbury, Northumberland (NU 080968: Jobey 1966, 3; 1968, 46).

Immediately to the N of the camp lie the fragmentary remains of the Stanegate. This has been heavily disturbed by later hollow-ways and much robbed by quarrying, although its original course is still discernible. After crossing the Haltwhistle Burn at NY 71386603, it has followed the only practical route eastwards, at first along, and then just to the S of, the crest of the gentle ridge occupied by the 'Mare and Foal' standing stones, before attaining the higher ground to the W of Seatsides. There is no reason to think that the Stanegate swerves to avoid the camp (Bennett 1980, 160–1). However, the peculiar position chosen for the camp might suggest that the more habitable ground to the W, beside the Haltwhistle Burn, was already taken up by the fortlets and the camps there. The irregular shape of the defences probably indicates that this was a true marching camp, occupied for a minimal length of time.

NY 76 NW 21   Haltwhistle

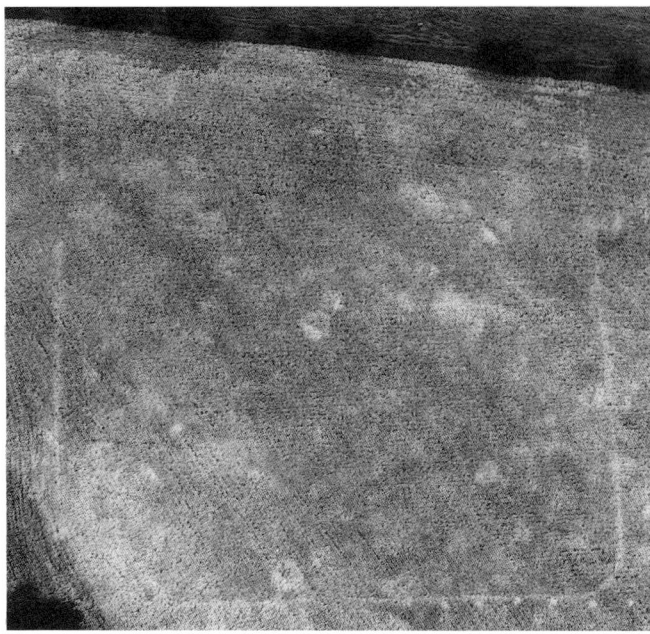

Figure 97 *Norham, Northumberland, from the SSE. (2.8.70, CUCAP BEE 83)*

Norham *Figs 96 and 97*

NT 88974542

The cropmarks of a small camp have been photographed from the air on the crest of the river terrace, on the S bank of the River Tweed, 70 m above the haughland at Bendibus Shiel (CUCAP BEE 82–3; St Joseph 1973, 215). Immediately to the W of the camp a shallow tributary valley provides added protection. There are good views downstream for at least 800 m, but upstream they are restricted by rising ground just W of the camp.

The camp measures only 70 m from E to W by about 80 m transversely and its ditch is broken by gates on three sides. There seems to have been a traverse outside each of the gates. A hint of a turn in the W ditch to form the NW angle suggests that the E and W gates may have been placed in an approximate 1:2 ratio along the N to S axis. The camp, therefore, faced N across the river, and its N defensive line, which is not visible, must have lain almost on the crest of the scarp, giving a probable area of 0.5 ha (1.2 acres).

Cropmarks cover much of the fields on either side of the camp. These consist of pit alignments, ring-ditches, unenclosed roundhouses of prehistoric type and, most prominently, an unusual circular ditched structure with opposed entrances, the SE one markedly inturned. One of the pit alignments seems to be partly contiguous with the S ditch of the camp but, by analogy with examples elsewhere, the two are not likely to be associated.

NT 84 NE 6   Norham

Figure 96 *Norham, Northumberland.*

North Yardhope *Figs 14 and 98*

NT 90890091

This camp lies in open heather moorland at about 275 m above OD and between two streams, the Longtae Burn to the N and an unnamed tributary to the S. Although it slopes gradually SE, the site provides the best expanse of comparatively level ground in the immediate vicinity. The views down the valley are extensive. The rather poor natural drainage of the boulder-clay subsoil has been improved by a system of modern land drains which have damaged the Roman defences. The camp has a roughly square ground plan, measuring about 137 m internally from NNE to SSW by about 144 m transversely and enclosing an area of 2.0 ha (4.9 acres). Only the N rampart has escaped disturbance from the land drains, although minor modern trackways have cut through the camp in the NW and NE corners. The N rampart also has the most complete surviving stretch of the associated ditch; this is 0.1 m deep, whilst the external face of the rampart still rises to a height of 0.6 m with an internal height of 0.1 m. On the W the ditch has been almost totally obliterated by a parallel land drain.

The camp faces E, down the valley, and has three gates, originally about 5 m wide and each defended by a traverse. On the S and E the mound of each traverse stands about 5 m forward of the line of the ditch. On the N, however, this distance is reduced to about 1 m, effectively making the gate no more than a postern, as a result of the proximity of the steep slope that falls 6.3 m to the Longtae Burn. This N traverse is the best preserved of the three: its mound still stands to a height of 0.6 m, although its ditch is now no more than a vegetation mark.

The identification of internal features has been hindered by the dense heather growth over most of the camp. However, just inside the S entrance a land drain has cut through the gate and exposed a concentration of small boulders and slabs. This stone spread does not occur to any equivalent degree in any of the other drains, and thus may represent a paved entrance designed to combat boggy conditions at this point and to maintain a dry thoroughfare. Just to the S of the camp lies the course of the Roman road linking High

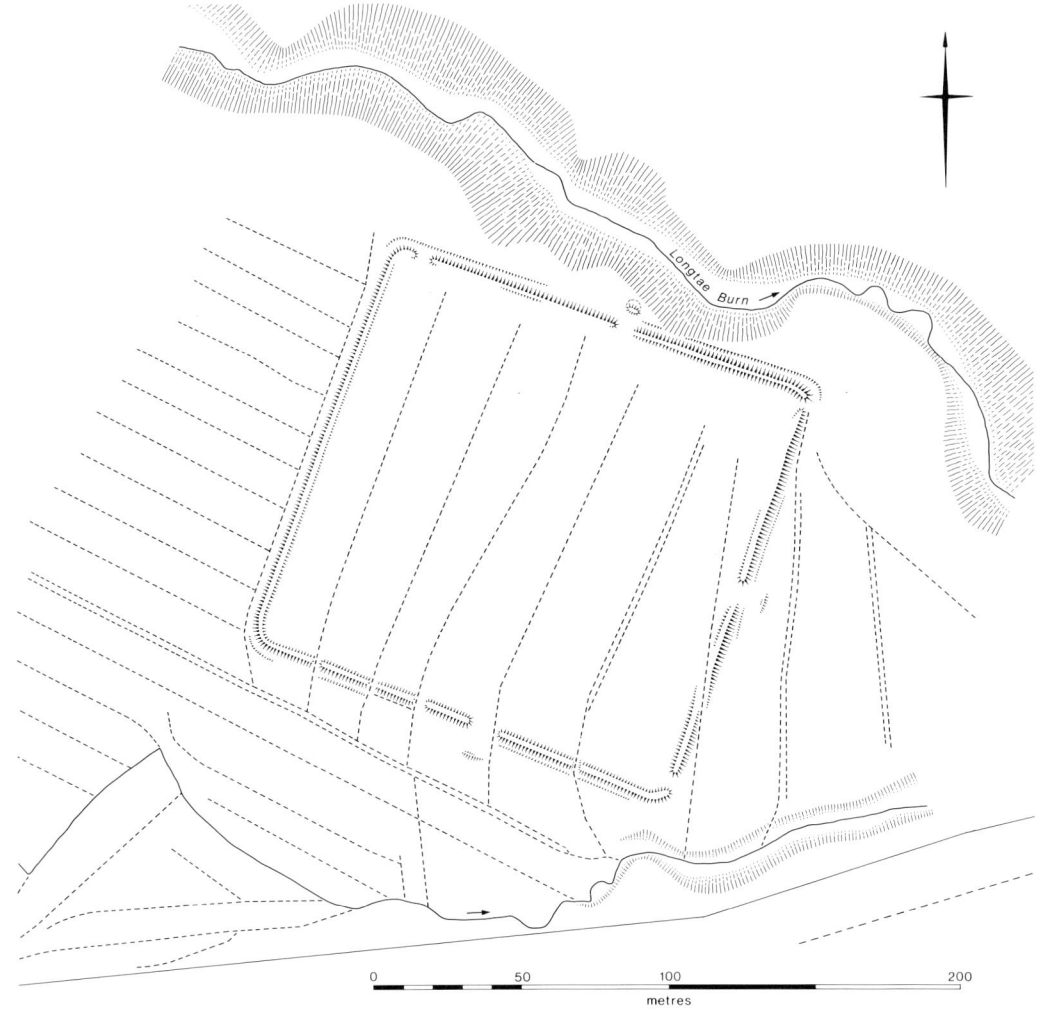

Figure 98 *North Yardhope, Northumberland.*

Rochester (*Bremenium*) on Dere Street with the Flavian fort at Low Learchild (?*Alauna*) on the Devil's Causeway (MacLauchlan 1864, 49; Richmond and Askew 1937, 47; Margary 1973, 482 (88)). This section of the road is now overgrown by a peat deposit roughly 0.4 m deep, although in several places modern trackways cut down to what appear to be fragments of the original road surface or its foundations.

NT 90 SW 14 Harbottle

Seatsides 1 *Fig 99*

NY 75136616

Seatsides Farm stands at about 245 m above OD on the E shoulder of a ridge which is aligned from E to W. The buildings occupy part of the W third of a camp which measures about 252 m from N to S by about 282 m transversely and encloses an area of about 6.7 ha (16.6 acres). The camp lies only 80 m to the S of Seatsides 2. The view to the W, up the ridge, is restricted to about 300 m but elsewhere the outlook is extensive, especially to Hadrian's Wall, 1.5 km to the N, and eastwards down the Stanegate towards the fort at Vindolanda. In this section of its course, the *agger* of the Roman road, 11 m wide and up to 0.9 m high, follows the crest of the ridge and passes through the camp. The camp may originally have been constructed before the road and seems to have had more than one period of occupation. The N and S sides each lie about 11 m below the crest of the ridge but are, nevertheless, parallel. The E and W sides may also have been parallel to one another but the NE and SW angles are slightly obtuse, thus forming a parallelogram.

The rampart is now spread to a width of about 6 m and stands up to 0.4 m high on the N and NW. An external ditch survives on the NW where it is still 0.5 m deep, but this is due largely to its incorporation into a later drainage system. On the E side, to the N of the modern road to the farm, there is a substantial field boundary bank, its E face revetted with drystone walling; this bank probably incorporates the rampart of the camp. A fragmentary outer ditch, partly overlain by the field bank, seems to have been kept open by natural scouring. To the S of the farm road, the rampart is poorly preserved, being no more than about 0.2 m high, but its general line is clear. Along the S side the defences have been severely reduced by ridge-and-furrow, which crosses them almost at right angles, and the bank is now only 0.3 m high at best. To the SW of the farm the rampart is crossed obliquely by this cultivation and is visible only as fragmentary but unusually high sections of the ridges.

The ground within the interior slopes gently to the N and to the S on either side of the ridge, which steadily declines in height towards the E. The S defences are set at the foot of the slope there and those on the N occupy a slight change of slope. There is little level ground, except along the crest of the ridge itself and inside the NE angle, but nowhere are the slopes steep enough to make the pitching of tents difficult.

Four gates are identifiable. On the NE and NW each is defended by a traverse, 0.3 m high, the W one retaining traces of its ditch. There are also the remains of a traverse outside the N gate but its mound is reduced to a single scarp, 0.3 m high, trimmed at either end by natural drainage channels. One of these channels runs obliquely through the gateway and appears to cut through the neck of an internal *clavicula*. This survives as a mound, 0.4 m in height. A similar *clavicula*, 0.3 m high, can be seen underlying the ridge-and-furrow on the S side. An everted external scarp on the W side of this S gate is probably the result of scouring down the furrow that runs through the gate. There is no evidence to suggest the presence of a double *clavicula* or of an external traverse here. The absence of any *clavicula* at the W and E gates could result from later land use but, equally, it may indicate that the presence of both types of defence at the N gate is due in this case to reuse and remodelling.

The S halves of the E and W sides are too poorly preserved for it to be certain that they did not possess gates in a mirror-image of their N portions. Nevertheless, the impression that the earthworks give is that the camp always faced E. The establishment of the Stanegate took place after this large camp had been constructed and abandoned, although the topography probably dictated that the road cut through central gates on the E and W. The provision of gates protected by simple traverses suggests that the N half of the camp was reoccupied, providing a defended area of about 3 ha (7.5 acres) immediately alongside the Stanegate. This postulated S side of a smaller camp would lie in the zone disturbed by the braided hollow-ways close to the fence and the revetted boundary bank that run E from the farm buildings. Its general line may even be represented by the field boundary itself which lies on the S skyline of the camp and which has a ploughing headland on its N side. Only excavation could substantiate this circumstantial evidence.

NY 76 NE 23 Henshaw

Seatsides 2 *Figs 100 and 101*

NY 75256647

This camp is situated at about 220 m above OD in improved pasture on a gently sloping shelf in the hillside on the S side of the Brackies Burn, 350 m S of the Vallum and 1.6 km W of Vindolanda. Beyond the N side of the camp, and especially in the NE, the ground drops away steeply to the burn. To the S the ground rises abruptly towards the summit

Figure 99 *Seatsides 1, Northumberland.*

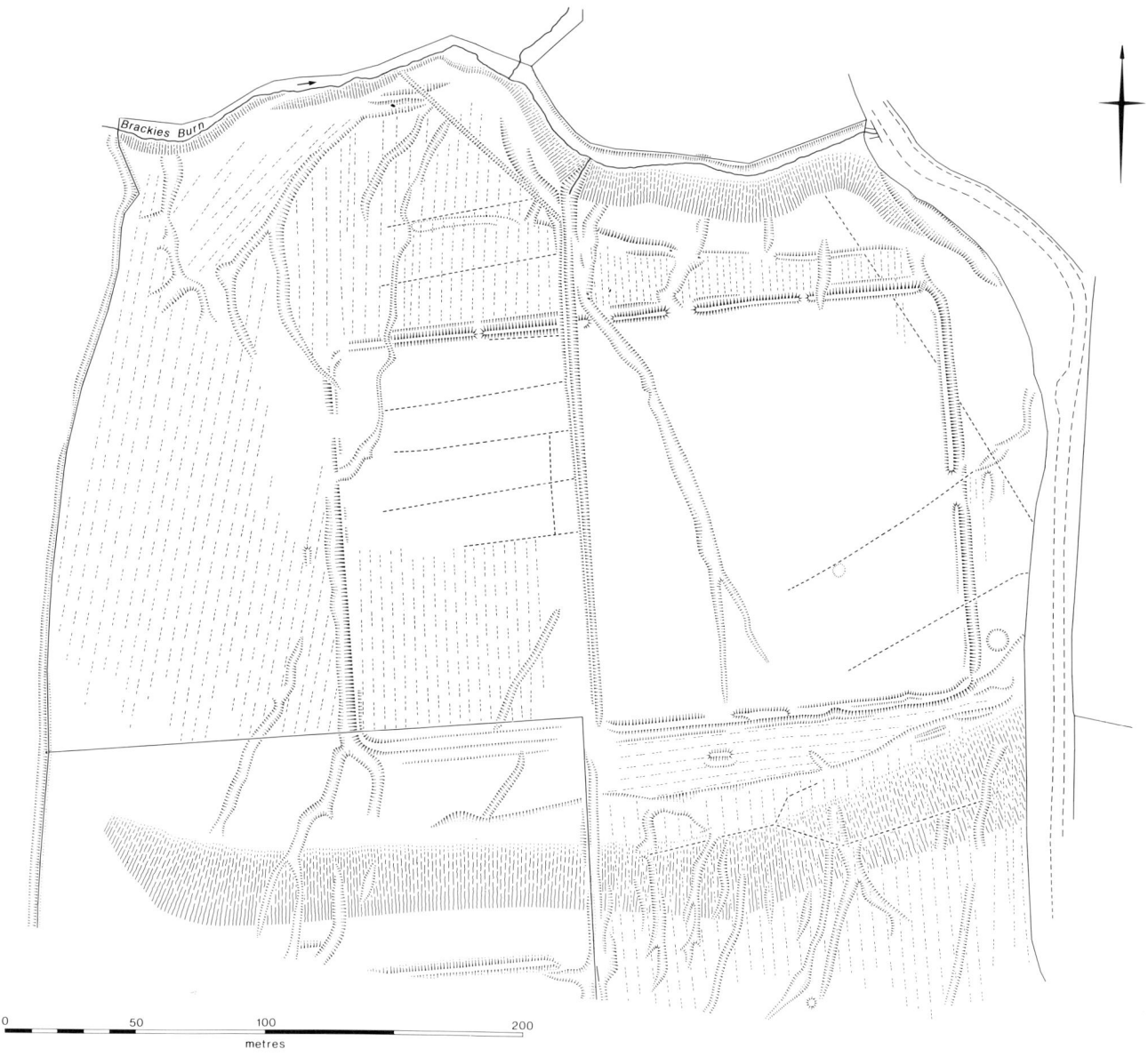

Figure 100 *Seatsides 2, Northumberland.*

occupied by Seatsides 1, the NE angle of which is only about 80 m away. Shallow former watercourses cross the hillside, all of which has been under ridge-and-furrow cultivation. To the W of the bank and ditch of the hedge line that almost bisects the camp, the earthworks are less well preserved.

The camp faces E. It measures 232 m from W to E by up to 149 m transversely and encloses an area of 3.4 ha (8.5 acres). Though abraded throughout its length, the rampart is generally well preserved, except along the W side where it stands no more than about 0.2 m high; elsewhere it averages 0.5 m in height above the bottom of its external ditch, which is 0.3 m deep. The internal scarp of the rampart is only 0.2 m high. Later drainage, both natural and artificial, has utilised the ditch of the camp, broadening it to a width of about 7 m on the W and cutting across the causeways of the gates on the E, W and S. The N gate is marked only by a gap in the rampart but a traverse survives at each of the other three gates. The W traverse is now barely discernible beneath ridge-and-furrow but those on the S and E each have a bank standing 0.4 m and 0.2 m high respectively. The ditch associated with the E traverse is 0.2 m deep.

Within the SE quadrant of the interior there is a small flat-topped mound, 6 m in diameter and 0.3 m in maximum height. Although cut tangentially by a modern drain it is unlikely to be earlier than the narrow ridge-and-furrow cultivation that overlies this half of the camp (CUCAP ATV 65). Outside the SE angle is a circular depression of

Figure 101 *Seatsides 2 and Twice Brewed, Northumberland, from the E. Seatsides 2 lies to the S (left) of the Brackies Burn. All of its interior and the land around it are covered by ridge-and-furrow cultivation. Twice Brewed camp is just visible to the N of the burn. (7.12.67, CUCAP ATV 67)*

unknown date and purpose. It measures 9 m in diameter and 0.4 m in maximum depth and has been levelled into the slope. There is no bank or any other trace of the material from its interior; a dip in the NE may be the remains of an entrance. Outside the N rampart and close to the crest of the slope above the Brackies Burn there is a boundary bank which is overlain by ridge-and-furrow. Aerial photographs (CUCAP ATV 59, 67) show it continuing for some distance to the W.

NY 76 NE 22   Henshaw

Silloans *Fig 102*

NT 82210068

The earthworks of a large camp were discovered from the air in 1937 (Richmond and St Joseph 1941) on the W bank of the Sills Burn, between Silloans Farm and a smaller unnamed stream that rises on the S slopes of Bellshiel Law. The camp lies on the broad summit of a gentle spur which extends from approximately the NW corner of the camp at about 255 m above OD, the highest point within the earthworks, to the centre of its S side which lies along a local crest. Another minor crest lies from N to S on the long axis of the camp, the line occupied by Dere Street. The two halves of the camp, on either side of the Roman road, are not, therefore, intervisible from one another; the N end of the E rampart is at the foot of the hillside and the SW angle had to be adapted in order to avoid the adjacent stream. There are good views from the S rampart down the valley to the S, and those to the E are to the watershed, 2 km away. However to the SW, NW and N, they are blocked at a distance of about 500 m by the outer flanks of Bellshiel Law.

The camp encloses an area of about 18.4 ha (45.4 acres). It occupies the last position up the valley of the Sills Burn that could accommodate a camp of this size. Although only 2 km from the fort at High Rochester (*Bremenium*), the camp seems to have faced N, along Dere Street and away from the fort, an option that may have been determined partly by the topography. Despite the awkward lie of the land, the NE, NW and SE corners of the camp are right angles, but at the site of the W gate the W defences were realigned a few degrees to the E. This may have resulted from an initial miscalculation in layout which, without the realignment, would have left the SW corner in the shallow bed of the stream that passes close to the camp at this point.

The defences are in varying states of preservation. The N rampart stands to an average height of 0.5 m but the ditch is now no more than 0.3 m deep and for some distance its former presence is marked only by a change in the vegetation.

Roman Camps in England

To the E of Dere Street the pasture within the interior of the camp has been improved. The internal scarp of the rampart has been almost levelled and the ditch is largely silted up. A small pocket of peat has built up immediately to the S of the E gate, masking the defences. This E side of the camp is best preserved to the S of the road to Holystone, where the outer and inner scarps of the rampart survive to heights of 1.0 m and 0.3 m respectively, and where the outer scarp of the ditch is 0.3 m high.

On the S side of the camp the earthworks are markedly different in character. The line chosen for them, ascending the gentle hillside, lies along a local crest line. To the E of Dere Street the Roman earthworks have been superseded by a later boundary bank 0.6 m high. The gully to the S is the result of the natural erosion of the Roman ditch to a depth of 0.7 m. There may be a vestige of the rampart, perhaps as much as 0.4 m high, surviving on the N lip of the gully and now represented as a berm between it and the boundary bank. At the point where it is crossed by Dere Street, this bank curves away to the NW, revealing the Roman defences once again. The rampart here stands up to 1.1 m high externally and 0.3 m high internally, and the ditch is up to 0.5 m deep. In addition to the realignment of the W side, the presence of the stream seems to have called for another minor revision of the SW corner. Although the other three rounded angles of the camp have relatively small radii, the surviving rampart here slices abruptly across the usual arc in an awkward fashion.

Along the S section of the W side the rampart is still well preserved, although the ditch has been utilised as a modern drain. Farther N, however, the rampart and the ditch fade out as the curving line of the boundary bank approaches from the SE. Thereafter, as far as the NW corner, this bank occupies the line of the Roman rampart and a drain has scoured out part of the earlier ditch. The resulting earthworks are sinuous and more irregular in their construction.

The modern road, following the line of Dere Street, crosses the N and S defences at their central point. The road changes direction slightly at the S crest but is realigned about 80 m outside the N rampart. This observation is directly contrary to the argument advanced by Richmond (Richmond and St Joseph 1941, 113). The chronological relationship between the road and the camp cannot be established without excavation, although gates presumably existed at these intersections. There was certainly a single gate in each of the E and W sides. A gap in the rampart survives on the E, guarded by an eroded bar-shaped traverse. Hillwash has reduced the inner scarp of the traverse and the outer scarp of the ditch to a height of 0.1 m but the outer scarp of the traverse stands 1.0 m high. The causeway for the W gate has been cut through for the drain associated with the boundary bank that overlies the rampart. The traverse, however, is well preserved, standing 0.4 m high internally and 0.8 m above the bottom of its ditch, which is 0.3 m deep.

A stretch of the N defences has been destroyed by a turning circle, and drains cut the E side of the camp. The curving boundary along the W side and around the SW angle is studded with a series of late 18th-century or early 19th-century boundary stones, marking the division between the infield land of Silloans and the Birdhope Craig estate to the W (NRO ZHE 14/1).

NT 80 SW 1   Rochester

Sills Burn North *Fig 103*

NT 82540006

This is the more northerly of two contrasting rectangular camps constructed to the E of Dere Street on the gently sloping ground above the narrow haughland of the Sills Burn, between the fort at High Rochester (*Bremenium*) and the camp at Silloans. The views from this site are not particularly extensive, stretching westwards only to the Bellshiel ridge, northwards to the S rampart of Silloans camp and eastwards up Harelaw Cleugh. Down the little valley of the Sills Burn the view is slightly better, for High Rochester and the crest above the haughland of the Rede are both visible. Although well preserved in part, the defences and the interior of the camp, have been overlain by ridge-and-furrow; this is not shown in detail on the plan but its general layout and extent is indicated by the modern drains laid in some of the furrows.

The defences are best preserved along the W side where the rampart stands 0.9 m high internally and 1.1 m above the bottom of the ditch, which is 0.4 m deep. The N side is overlain by a later earthen boundary bank which approaches the NW angle of the camp from the SW and extends across the gate. The ditch is less well preserved than on the W and has had a modern drain cut along its bottom; the material from this has been thrown up next to the rampart so as to create a slight ridge between the rampart and the outer scarp of the ditch. The position of the NE corner of the camp is now totally obscured by the earthworks of a building and some small enclosures, and by the angle of a much larger enclosure, all of medieval and post-medieval date. Well-developed ridge-and-furrow, reversed-S in plan, has obliterated any surface traces of the E side, except for a short length of rampart close to the NE corner. Although somewhat mutilated, this bank has acted as the headland for three cultivation ridges which run E towards the burn. The likely position of the ditch of the camp, connecting this fragment with the curving stub of the defences on the E end of the S

Figure 102 *Silloans, Northumberland. Modern drains are shown only where they intersect with the perimeter of the camp.*

Roman Camps in England

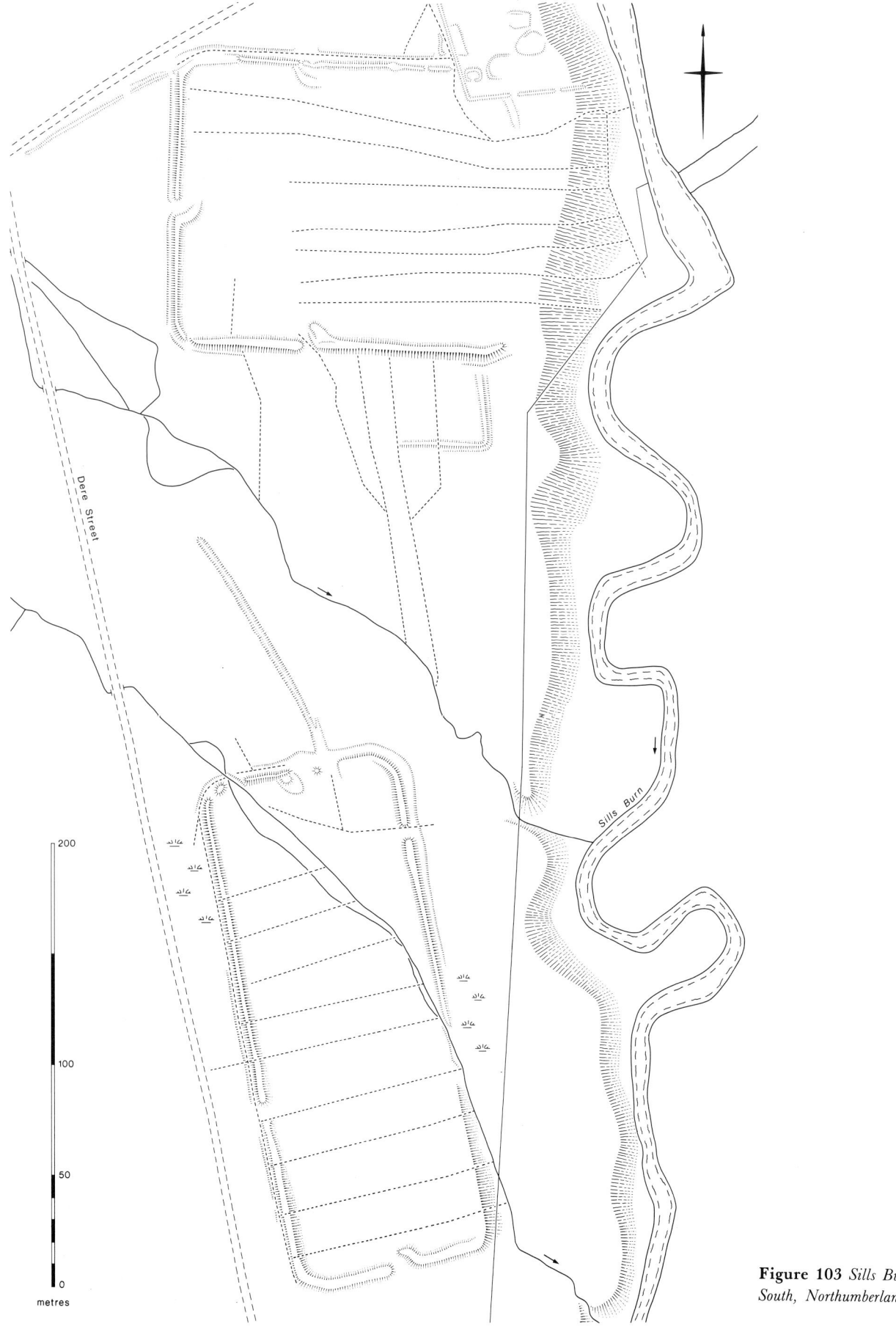

Figure 103 *Sills Burn North and South, Northumberland.*

side, is indicated as a darker line in the grass recorded from the air (CUCAP BD 7). This line would give the interior of the camp an area of approximately 1.9 ha (4.6 acres) and would set the rear rampart of the camp in a position that comfortably eliminates the dead ground that would otherwise have been created by the steeper slopes, 8 m high, down to the Sills Burn.

The S rampart has been much modified, as far W as the gate, by being reused as a cultivation ridge; its outer scarp remains 0.7 m high. The SW quarter of the camp, in the angle between the S and W gates, is occupied by ridge-and-furrow aligned N to S. In places this rides over the rampart, which is very low and spread, but does not seem seriously to have affected the ditch.

The camp faced W, towards Dere Street, as the arrangement of its three surviving gates demonstrates. These are defended by internal *claviculae*, now 0.3 m high; the S one has been incorporated into the end of an arable ridge and is cut off from the rampart by a furrow. The gateway has been worn down by traffic and subsequently damaged by a drain.

Outside the SE defences is a low angular earthwork, consisting of a bank no more than 0.2 m high, and an outer ditch; any W side has been obliterated and any junction with the camp has been cut through. The earthwork appears to precede the ridge-and-furrow cultivation and, although it could conceivably represent a small annexe to the camp, its date and function remain unknown.

NT 80 SW 2   Rochester

Sills Burn South *Fig 103*

NY 82519972

Only 170 m downstream from Sills Burn North, the space between Dere Street and the steep slopes on the W bank of the Sills Burn is reduced to less than 170 m. Despite this, the gently sloping ground here is occupied by another camp, its peculiar elongated design reflecting the constricted site. The camp measures approximately 230 m by 85 m and encloses an area of 1.8 ha (4.5 acres). It is cut diagonally by a small tributary into which a system of modern open drains flows. The position of these has been determined by the alignment of a block of ridge-and-furrow cultivation. Each drain is separated by four ridges (CUCAP BD 8; Richmond 1940, pl opp p 121).

The defences are best preserved close to the central point of the W side; here the rampart stands 1.0 m high and the ditch is 0.6 m deep. Ridge-and-furrow occupies the ground between the road and these defences, lying parallel to both. In the S part of this side, ploughing has ridden over the bank, leaving a swelling only 0.5 m high; on the short S side the bank was also incorporated into the ploughed land and is reduced to a height of 0.2 m internally, although it still stands 0.6 m high externally. No ditch is visible here on the surface, and the S end of the E side is little more than a scarp above the tributary. To the N, on the E of the tributary and outside the area of ploughing, the state of preservation improves, the bank being 0.7 m high and the ditch 0.2 m deep. A small plot of five short arable ridges, aligned N to S and bounded by drains in the extreme NE angle of the camp, has levelled part of the bank here.

Excavation in 1993, close to the NW angle, revealed that the inner and outer faces of the bank had been revetted with turf that had been removed from the course of the bank itself. The ditch was 1 m deep and had a shallow U-shaped profile (inf C Waddington).

A single gate is identifiable in the short N and S sides, each defended by an internal *clavicula*. The S *clavicula* has been overridden by the ploughing and is now no more than 0.2 m high; at 0.4 m, the N one is still much reduced in height, presumably on account of ploughing, but being outside the area of surviving ridge-and-furrow it is unclear how this has come about. Gaps in the defences at the points that divide the E and W sides in the ratio 1:2 probably indicate the former positions of gates. Any *claviculae*, however, have been destroyed by the drains or are masked by their upcast material. The indications are that the camp faced S, towards the fort at High Rochester (*Bremenium*). There is no evidence to support the suggestion (St Joseph 1935, 241) that there had once been a central rampart dividing the camp into two halves.

NY 89 NW 11   Rochester

Sunny Rigg 1 *Figs 104 and 105*

NY 69546564

This E-facing camp lies about 50 m to the S of and parallel to the Stanegate. It measures 80 m by 50 m and encloses an area of 0.4 ha (1.0 acres). The N defences occupy the broad crest of a ridge but in the camp itself the ground falls only very gently to the S. The site is in a slight saddle, 130 m ENE of Sunny Rigg, but the views along the Stanegate and N to Hadrian's Wall are extensive; only to the E, where the land rises a few metres to the site of Sunny Rigg 2, 230 m away, is the outlook at all restricted.

In 1966 the camp was still a well-defined earthwork, standing up to 0.5 m high (NAR NY 66 NE 15). By 1981, however, the rampart had been reduced to a height of 0.3 m externally; since then the site has been almost completely levelled by further cultivation. Its form was recorded by aerial photography from 1930 onwards (NMR AP NY 6965/2; Fig 105; CUCAP BAX 46, 60) and by the Ordnance Survey in 1955. A subsequent Ordnance Survey plan, made in 1966, was evidently less accurate. Each of the four gates was protected by a traverse. The N and S gates were offset in the

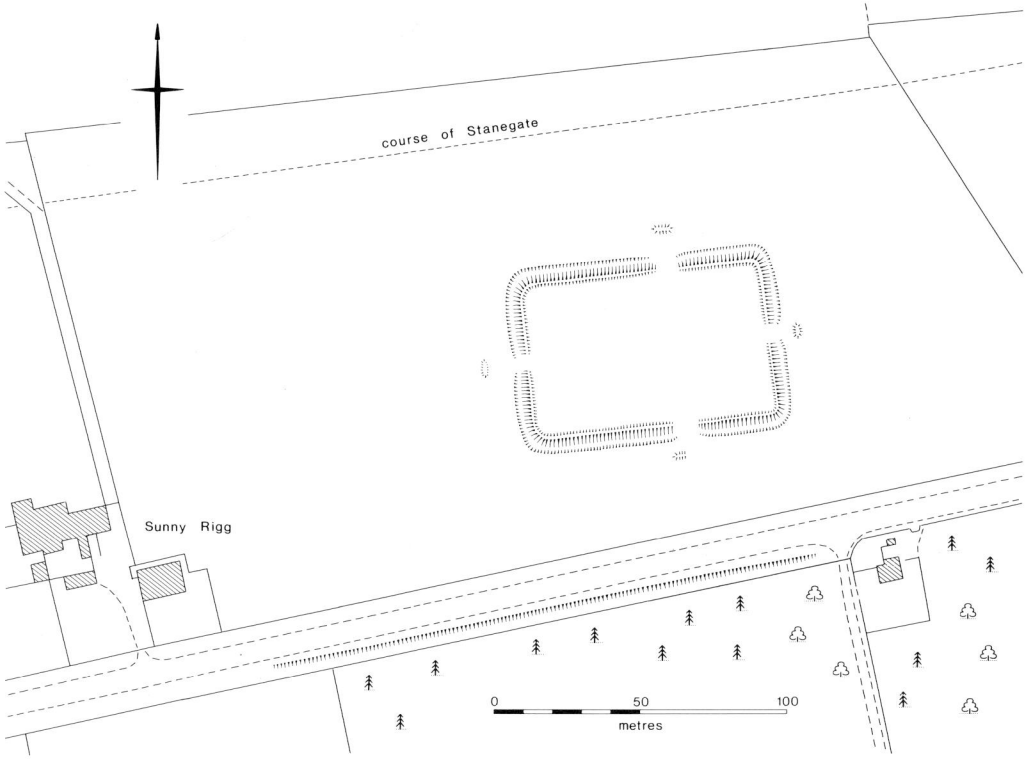

Figure 104 *Sunny Rigg 1, Northumberland. This drawing is based upon the survey made by G Geary for the Ordnance Survey in 1955. The camp is shown on published maps slightly too far to the E. This has been corrected here.*

Figure 105 *Sunny Rigg 1, Northumberland. A vertical photograph, with N to the top, taken in October 1930 by O G S Crawford. Since 1966 the remains of the camp have been almost completely levelled by cultivation.* (NMR AP NY 6965/2)

common proportion of 2:1 on the long axis; the S traverse had been mutilated by a shallow natural gully.

In 1981, during the construction of a new drainage scheme, a section was cut across the perimeter close to the NW corner. The rampart appeared to have been constructed largely of turf on an undisturbed old ground surface. The material required would have been greater than that which could have been provided from the ditch which was little more than a shallow external scoop (*Britannia* **13** (1982) 343; J Bennett pers comm).

NY 66 NE 15   Haltwhistle

Sunny Rigg 2 *Fig 106*

NY 69876571

The slight remains of this camp, which lies 460 m ENE of Sunny Rigg, were first identified from the air as an earthwork (St Joseph 1951, 55). These remains were almost entirely levelled by pasture improvements in about 1983. The camp is situated on the E end of a broad ridge with its N defences upon the crest. The ground falls gently away to the E. The Stanegate, here little more than a broad swelling, ran immediately to the N, but the precise layout of the camp seems to have been determined more by the natural topography than by the presence of the road, whatever their relative chronology.

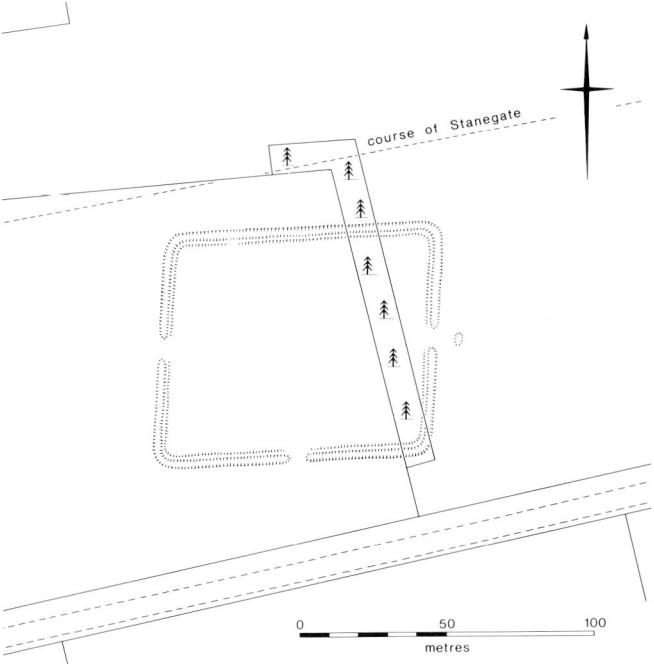

Figure 106 *Sunny Rigg 2, Northumberland. This drawing is based upon the survey made by J E Titmuss for the Ordnance Survey in 1951.*

A plan made by J E Titmuss for the Ordnance Survey in 1951 shows the camp as a parallelogram measuring about 86 m from E to W internally by about 70 m transversely and thus enclosing an area of approximately 0.6 ha (1.5 acres). Gates, the E one defended by a traverse, were identified at the central point of the E, W and S sides. Initial reconnaissance by RCHME in 1981 recorded the presence of a traverse mound about 7 m long, approximately 12 m outside the W gate and the possibility of a N gate, indicated by a causeway across the surviving ditch, with traces of its traverse mound, then on the very edge of the plantation. In addition, it seemed that the N and S gates were not placed in a central position but were offset to the E. No plan was made at the time and, in the absence of further evidence, the Ordnance Survey depiction of 1951 has been accepted as generally correct.

NY 66 NE 16   Haltwhistle

Sunny Rigg 3 *Fig 107*

NY 70056589

One of the smallest surviving camps, enclosing an area only 22 m square (0.1 acres), is situated on a broad, almost level, shelf in a N-facing hillside, 55 m N of the Stanegate. Almost immediately to the N the ground begins to fall away in a convex slope to the marshy ground drained by the burn flowing E from Peat Steel. To the S of the Stanegate the ground rises about 20 m to the ridge, 200 m away, along which the modern road runs. This site was not chosen for its natural strength for although the outlook to the E and N is generally good the view to the S is restricted by the near horizon and there is some dead ground on the N.

The rampart of the camp survives to a height of 0.2 m internally and stands 0.4 m above the bottom of the ditch, which is 0.2 m deep. There are only two entrances, on the E and on the S, both of which are guarded by a traverse. The bank of each is only 0.2 m high and the S one has been trimmed by a drain on its N side. The ditch of the E traverse is also visible although it is marked by little more than a change in the vegetation. There are no signs that the land has been cultivated but the camp has been damaged by modern drains.

NY 76 NW 17   Haltwhistle

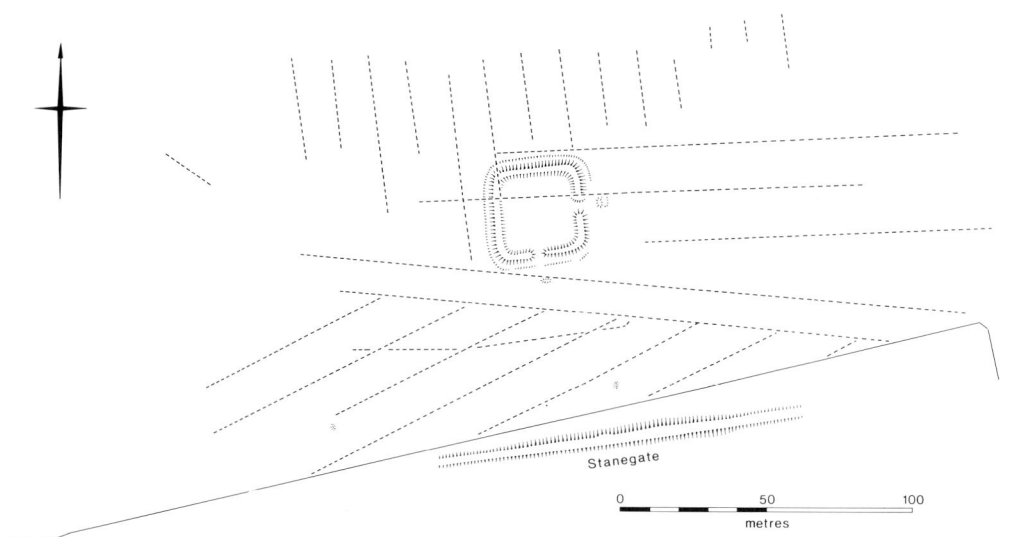

Figure 107 *Sunny Rigg 3, Northumberland.*

Swine Hill 1 and 2 (Four Laws)
Figs 8 and 108

1 and 2: NY 90458253

Camp 1 on Swine Hill lies 60 m W of Dere Street and 4 km SSE of the fort at Risingham (*Habitancum*). It was first recorded by MacLauchlan during his survey of the Roman road (1852a, 26; Richmond 1940, 118). The site chosen is a gently rounded knoll between the twin headwaters of the Broomhope Burn at 270 m above OD, overlooking the junction of Redesdale with North Tynedale. The ground falls away on all sides except the SE where the approach is level. A gully close to the NW angle of the camp, which must greatly have increased the defensive potential, rapidly decreases in depth until at the NE corner it is little more than a shallow fold in the ground.

The camp is almost square on plan, measuring about 168 m from E to W by 174 m transversely, and encloses an area of 2.4 ha (6.0 acres). It has three gates and evidently faced towards Dere Street. As a result of its location across a rounded summit the opposite sides of the camp are not intervisible. The N rampart ranges in height from 0.5 m to 0.9 m and its external ditch varies between 0.2 m and 0.4 m in depth. The E rampart stands, for the most part, up to 0.9 m high, although this is exaggerated by the natural slope to a maximum of 1.7 m at the NE angle; the ditch on this side is between 0.2 m and 0.4 m in depth. The S rampart is better preserved and achieves a maximum height of 1.1 m and the ditch here is up to 0.4 m deep. The W rampart, in contrast, is only 0.5 m high and its outer ditch must now be covered by a later bank. No provision for a gate seems to have been made on the W side, but on each of the other three sides there is a single gate guarded by an internal *clavicula*. These are exceptionally well preserved; the curving banks of the N and S examples stand to a height of 0.8 m, and that on the E still survives to a height of 0.7 m. At several places on the N, S and E ramparts the inner edge of the bank is interrupted by a small low bulge, conceivably representing a platform. These measure up to 2.5 m across and are up to 0.4 m high. Seven of them can be seen to the S of the gate on the E side, and others occur on the N and S sides. Without excavation, the significance of these remains unclear.

Within the NW angle is the very much smaller camp 2, which utilises in part the ramparts of its predecessor. It measures less than 60 m across internally, and encloses an area of only 0.3 ha (0.8 acres). The S and E defences of this

Figure 108 *Swine Hill 1 and 2, Northumberland.*

second camp are markedly less substantial than those of the first and are no more than 0.4 m high, being formed of upcast from a shallow external ditch now no more than 0.3 m deep. Two gates in the E side are defended by traverses; the S example is the better preserved, its mound standing 0.4 m high and its ditch being 0.2 m deep. There does not seem to have been a gate through any of the other three sides.

Close to the SE corner of this second camp are the slight earthworks of three timber houses of prehistoric type. A low bank, up to 0.2 m high, possibly a field boundary, extends from NW to SE across part of the interior of the smaller camp and fades out close to the westernmost of these buildings. Some poorly preserved plots of cord-rig cultivation, which may be contemporary with the buildings, can be made out within the larger camp and one portion appears to be cut by the SE angle of the smaller camp. These features, which would seem to be earlier than the camps, are so slight that it is unlikely that they would have interrupted the normal military arrangement of the interior.

In general, the earthworks are well preserved but trackways have cut through the NE corner of camp 1, taking advantage of the first point at which the gully on the N side can readily be crossed. Two banks, up to 0.6 m high, run parallel with the W side of this camp, the westerly one forming the parish boundary between Birtley and Corsenside. Two small circular depressions close to the E gate of camp 1, measuring 3 m in diameter and 1 m deep, are probably modern shell-holes.

NY 98 SW 6   Corsenside

Twice Brewed *Figs 101 and 109*

NY 75096675

The remains of this camp are situated at the E end of a spur at about 215 m above OD, 70 m S of the Vallum and 150 m N of Seatsides camp 2. The area, which is now improved pastureland showing faint traces of ridge-and-furrow oriented N to S, has been extensively ploughed. On the N and E good natural protection is provided by the steep slopes that drop away to a deep gully. This is occupied by a tributary of the Brackies Burn which itself runs E to W at the base of a gentle slope about 80 m S of the camp. This offers limited natural defences on this side, but there is no defence at all along the flat top of the spur to the W. For most of its course the rampart has been reduced to little more than a slight outer scarp, often barely visible. Because it is so mutilated along the N side it is now impossible to ascertain the exact size of the camp as a whole. Probably a parallelogram in plan, it must have measured about 145 m internally from E to W by about 100 m transversely, giving an area of about 1.4 ha (3.6 acres).

The turn of the NE corner is just discernible as a much reduced outward-facing scarp up to 0.2 m high. The rampart as a whole on the E side is about 5 m wide and mainly evident as an outer scarp nowhere more than 0.4 m high. It is slightly better preserved at the S end where there are faint traces of an outer ditch measuring 0.2 m in maximum depth. The centrally placed entrance, visible as a break about 6 m wide, has only the slightest remains of the inner scarp of a traverse about 6 m outside it.

The defences are best preserved at the SE corner where the outer scarp of the rampart survives to a height of 0.6 m. The S side is little more than an outward-facing scarp, up to 0.4 m high, with only a faint suggestion of an outer ditch. It is mutilated by several small breaks caused by later cultivation, by field drains that cross the camp diagonally, and by an old N to S fence line visible on aerial photographs (CUCAP ATV 60–6; RC 8 CP 181–2; RAF 106G UK 1392, 3275–7). The entrance, about 60 m from the SE corner, is only just discernible as a very slight break about 5 m wide with the remains of the S-facing scarp of a traverse about 12 m outside it.

The curve of the SW corner is still just evident. The removal of an E to W field wall to facilitate ploughing has greatly reduced the earthworks of the W side to a W-facing outer scarp measuring 0.2 m in maximum height; a slight suggestion of an outer ditch at the S end was too indeterminate to survey. There is now no trace of the entrance, which was close to the line of the former field wall; it was still visible in 1980, guarded by a traverse 12 m outside the line of the rampart.

At the NW corner and along the N side the presence of hollow-ways cutting across the area makes interpretation of the remains almost impossible. It may be significant that at a point opposite the S entrance a deep hollow-way descends the slope to cross the stream; however no direct evidence of a N gate or traverse survives. This hollow-way penetrated some 30 m southwards into the camp as far as a modern drystone wall crossing the camp from E to W, but otherwise the interior is featureless.

NY 76 NE 21   Henshaw

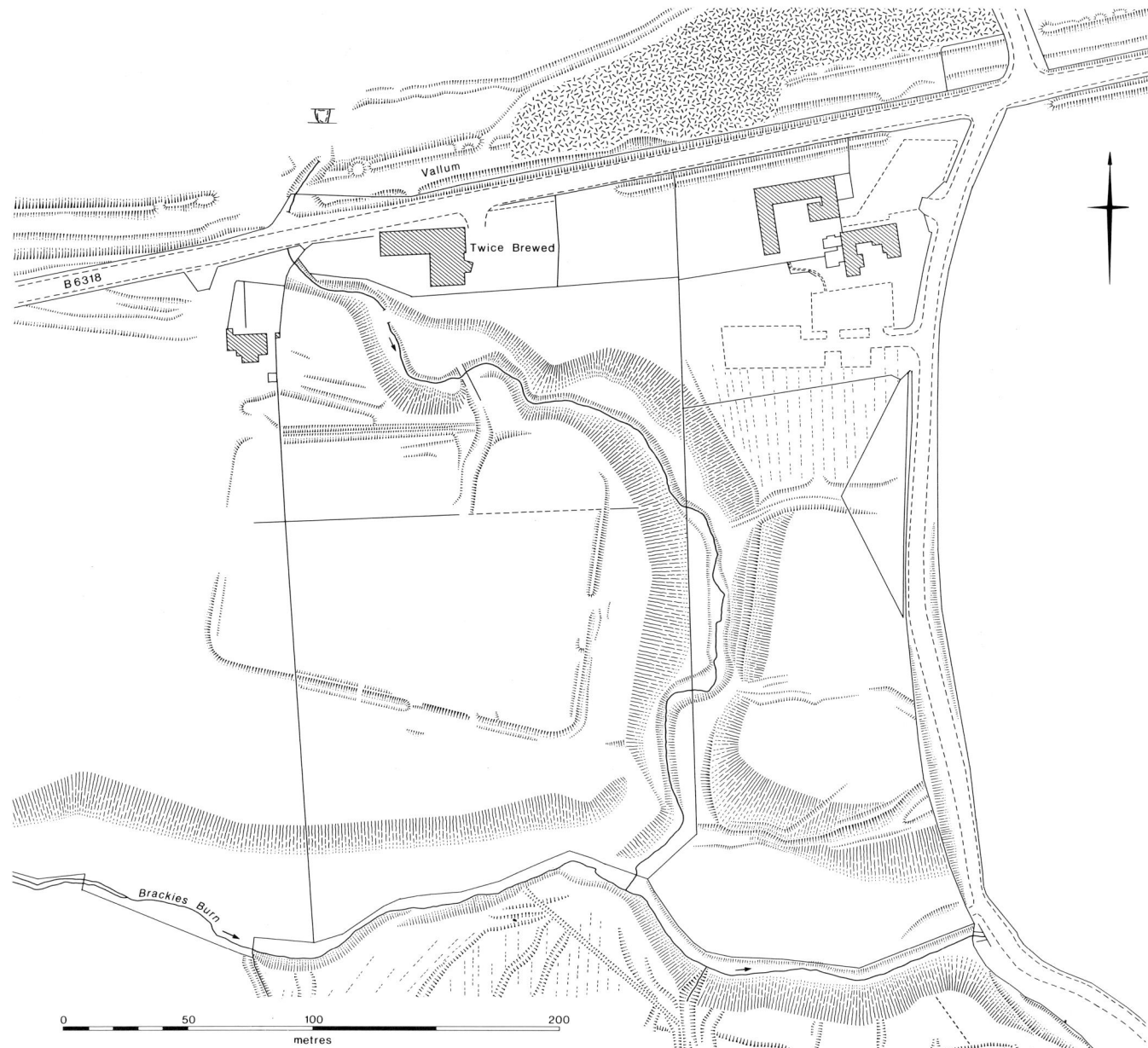

Figure 109 *Twice Brewed, Northumberland. The stipple indicates areas of quarrying.*

Walwick Fell *Fig 110*

NY 88677081

The much reduced remains of this camp are situated in the angle of the wall round Walwickfell Plantation, 300 m SW of Milecastle 29 on Hadrian's Wall, on a false crest of a hill at about 230 m above OD. This coniferous wood was described in 1912 as 'just planted' (Newbold 1913, 71) and is now partly felled. The site is much obscured by fallen trees but originally would have had extensive views from the E round to the SW as the ground drops away in gentle slopes through this arc.

The camp, consisting of a rampart and outer ditch with quite sharply rounded corners, measures 75 m square across the interior and encloses an area of 0.5 ha (1.4 acres). Where best preserved, at the S end of the NW side, the predominantly earthen rampart is 4 m wide and stands 0.7 m high above the interior. In the N half of the SE side the defences have been reduced to a single scarp; elsewhere, however, the ditch measures about 4 m wide and 0.4 m deep.

Four ill-defined breaks, each about 6 m long, mark the gates recorded by MacLauchlan (1858, 33). On the NW and SE sides the gates are positioned approximately at the

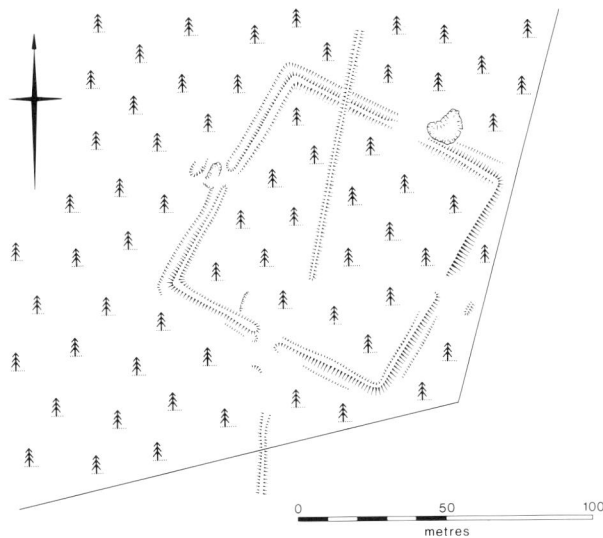

Figure 110 *Walwick Fell, Northumberland.*

central point. The SW gate, however, is offset about 2 m to the NW of centre. This seems to be mirrored on the opposite, NE, side where the breach in the rampart is offset to the SE. All but the NE gate retain slight traces of an accompanying traverse, though these have been almost obliterated by afforestation, felling and quarrying. The NE one has been destroyed altogether, probably by the felling of the old wood and the recent planting of conifers across this N corner of the camp.

The camp has been encroached upon by small stone quarries which scar much of the hill. It is also partly overlain by a boundary bank running NNE to SSW; this is probably associated with the later ridge-and-furrow on the slopes to the S which, in a much slighter and barely discernible condition, approach the SW side of the camp. The boundary bank runs across an enclosed native settlement (NAR NY 87 SE 18) lying about 150 m down the slope to the S.

NY 87 SE 13   Warden

West Woodburn Fig 111

NY 89578742

About 1.2 km NE of the fort at Risingham (*Habitancum*) in Redesdale, the earthworks of a camp survive in former arable land. The camp was constructed on the gentle SSE-facing slopes of a spur, around the foot of which the River Rede flows on the N, E and S. To the W the land is almost level for about 120 m but then rises to the shoulder traversed by Dere Street and to the summit of Corsenside Common. Visibility extends down Redesdale past Risingham, and southwards to the horizons on Stiddlehill and Chesterhope Commons. Some of the Lisles Burn valley can be seen but Darney Crag blocks sightlines to the E. To the E and N the Rede is in a very narrow valley but there are restricted views that stretch northwards to Cheviot itself.

The plan shows the state of the earthworks in 1982; only portions of the N, W and E sides survive. The area enclosed by the camp is, therefore, not known with certainty but there are some indications that it may have been about 11 ha (27 acres). The best-preserved section of the defences, measuring about 6.7 m across overall, is the W half of the N side. This is set on the crest of the hill, as little as 18 m from the lip of the steep slopes down to the Rede. The slopes create some dead ground on this side but most of the haugh-land can be seen from the camp. Here the bank survives to a height of 0.5 m internally; it is 0.7 m above the bottom of the ditch which seems to have been recut as a more modern drain, its scarp standing 0.4 m high. Some stone is visible in the make-up of the bank. The entrance is marked by a gap in the bank, a few metres to the W of the midpoint of this side. The mound of the traverse has been virtually levelled but the ditch is marked by a depression about 11 m long, the S scarp being 0.5 m high and the N one only 0.2 m high. The surviving fragment of the W side has been disturbed by tracks, and its scarps are nowhere more than 0.4 m high. There are traces of poorly developed narrow ridge-and-furrow in the field in which this part of the camp lies but the N defences seem to have marked the limit of agricultural activity even in recent times (NMR AP 541/A/442 3315–7).

In the field to the E, which contains the NE angle of the camp, ploughing has crossed the earthworks, spreading them to a width of 8.5 m. Much broken by trackways and natural scouring, the bank stands no more than 0.3 m high internally, and is 0.5 m above the bottom of the ditch which is 0.2 m deep. In the corner of the next field to the S there are the remains of a gate, marked only by a break in the bank and by the ditch of the traverse, the dimensions of which are almost exactly similar to those of the N example. When first surveyed in 1982 a shallow ditch containing a stone culvert could still be traced south-westwards from this gate for a distance of about 120 m. If this represented the line of the Roman ditch, as seems likely, then the E side of the camp would have been slightly realigned at the gate; this is not uncommon elsewhere although why it might have been thought necessary here is unclear. The field in which this ditch was recorded has subsequently been ploughed. Within it, in 1982, a single poorly preserved scarp could be traced, 75 m to the NW of Peel Cottage; before it was levelled by further cultivation, this scarp may have been the last surviving remains of the S side of the camp. Nothing can be seen in the improved pasture to the W of the lane, and in the field to the N the narrow ridge-and-furrow has obliterated all traces of the defences, apart from a slight hollow that seems to continue the line of the existing fragment of the W side for approximately 50 m.

NY 88 NE 24   Corsenside

Roman Camps in England

Figure 111 *West Woodburn, Northumberland.*

North Yorkshire

Bootham Stray *Fig 112*

1: SE 59875489   2: SE 59645485

The slight remains of two camps have been recorded about 2.5 km N of the fortress at York (*Eburacum*). If the reports of 18th-century antiquaries are accepted, a total of up to eight camps may once have existed in the general vicinity (Lukis 1887, 352, 380; Ramm 1953, 15–16). The surviving camps are situated on level, low-lying ground, at about 14 m above OD, and are cut by old hedges and deep drainage ditches; they have also been severely reduced by ploughing and mutilated by the construction of some outlying buildings and ancillary works of the former Second World War airfield to the W. The greater part of camp 1, containing the only sections of the defences that are now surveyable as earthworks, falls within Bootham Stray, a medieval common; camp 2 and the N portion of camp 1 lie within what were until the early 18th century 'half-year lands', that is ground that was arable for half the year and pasture for half (Ramm 1953, 15). This land use has led to the different levels of survival of the various elements of the earthworks.

The defences of camp 1 survive at best as a broad bank, 6 m to 7 m wide and up to 0.3 m high, although the average height is only 0.1 m. No trace of a ditch can be seen. Overall, the camp measures about 150 m from N to S by

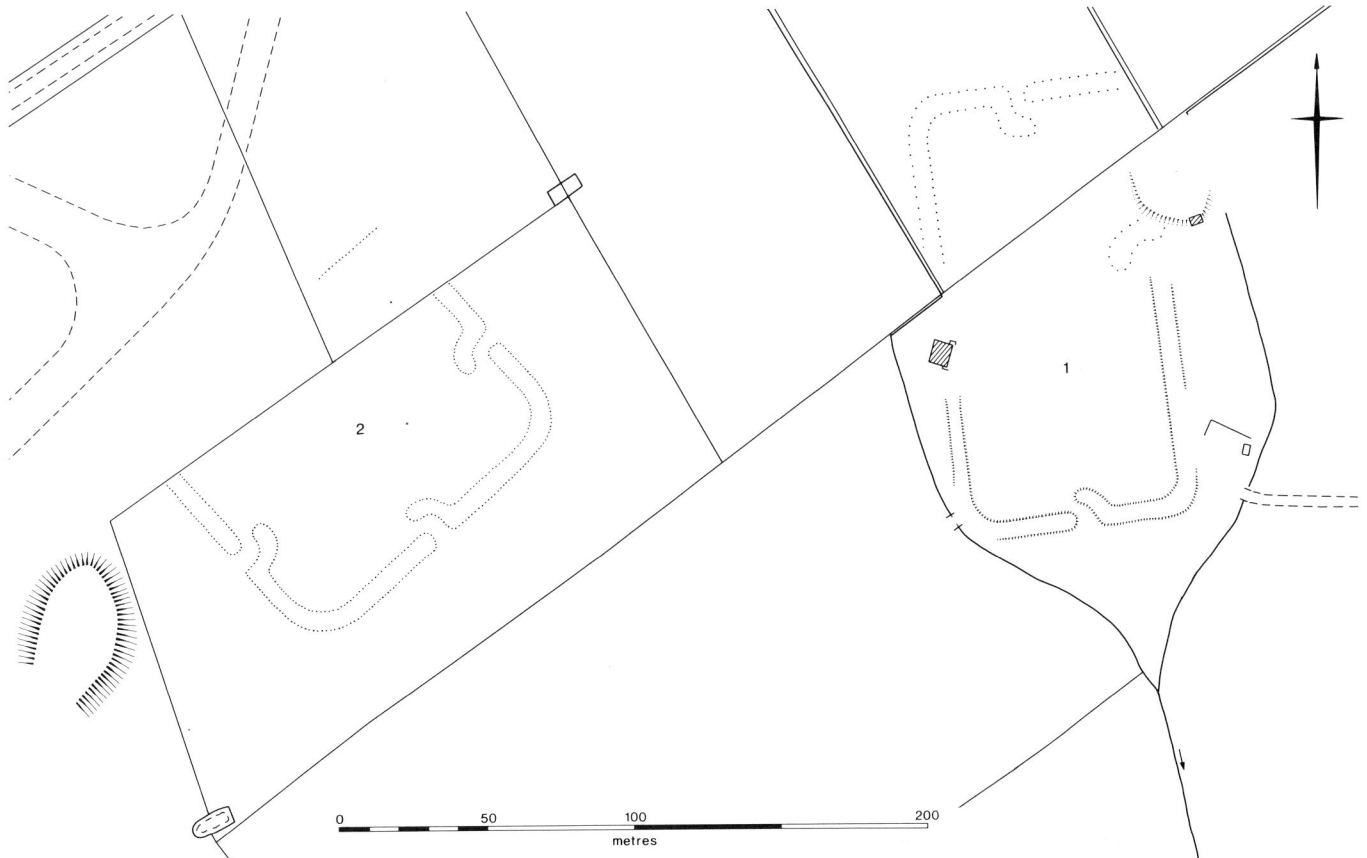

Figure 112 *Bootham Stray 1 and 2, North Yorkshire. The outlines of the N part of camp 1 are derived from aerial photographic evidence. Camp 2 was surveyed on the ground but as the scarps were too slight for depiction by conventional hachures the rampart is indicated by a dense dotted line.*

85 m transversely, enclosing an area of about 1 ha (2.4 acres). The earthworks of a gate survive on the S, with an internal *clavicula*, but aerial photographs (NMR AP SE 5954/1–2) suggest the former presence of similar gates on the E and N. A fourth gate may be postulated on the W. The E gate, the probable site of which has been disturbed in recent times (NMR AP F21 58/5515/38), seems to have been close to the centre of that side but the camp probably faced N. In 1952 a section was cut across the S defences to the E of the entrance (Ramm 1953, 19–20). The bank of heavy, stiff clay was found to have been 5.5 m wide; the V-shaped ditch, separated from the bank by a berm, 0.4 m wide, was about 1.3 m wide and 1.2 m deep.

Along the E side the bank has been worn down by a track running along its length. Near the SE angle the footings of a modern L-shaped building cross the line of the ditch and have encroached upon the bank (NMR AP F21 58/5515/38). Farther to the N, in the corner of the field, the line of the defences is covered by a spoil-heap. Regular ploughing has reduced the N defences to an almost imperceptible swelling. Aerial photographs (NMR AP SE 5954/1–2) show the N rampart as a soil mark, and in this form the inturned *clavicula* is clearly visible. Of the W defences, only the S section is traceable as an earthwork for about 50 m. To the N of this the course of the rampart is overlain by a brick building. The line of the bank enters the adjoining fields at the junction of three ditches; this would also be the likely position for the W gate but here no earthworks survive.

The earthworks of camp 2, which lies less than 200 m W of its neighbour, have been almost entirely levelled by ploughing and by mole-drains set at 4 m intervals. Faint indications survive, usually consisting of little more than the outer scarp of the bank; this has a maximum width of about 7 m and is no more than 0.1 m high. There is no trace of a ditch. Ground swellings and slight shadows on aerial photographs (NMR AP SE 5954/1–2) suggest that the gates on the NE, SW and SE were defended by internal *claviculae* (Ramm 1953, 18, 20). The same was also probably true of the NW side, the bank of which, probably mutilated during airfield construction, is marked only by a slight scarp, 30 m long, towards its W end. Internally, the camp thus seems to have measured about 107 m from NE to SW by about 81 m transversely and would thus have enclosed an area of 0.9 ha (2.1 acres).

1: SE 55 SE 19   2: SE 55 SE 66   Clifton Without

Breckenbrough *Fig 113*

SE 37618396

The cropmarks of the S angle of a camp were recorded in 1991 on the E side of Lower Swaledale, 1.2 km NE of the confluence of the Swale with the River Wiske, and about

Figure 113 *Breckenbrough, North Yorkshire. The field boundary which runs to the NW of the cropmarks of the camp has been removed.*

250 m S of Breckenbrough Castle Farm (NMR AP SE 3783/6–9). The camp occupies a slight hillock, at about 30 m above OD, in gently undulating terrain. The ground rises gently towards the NE part of the enclosure and there are good views in all directions. Although only 5 km to the E of Dere Street, the site is relatively isolated from other known military sites.

Only about 80 m of the SW side and approximately 200 m of the SE side are visible. The cropmark of the SE ditch is broken for 17 m, about 130 m from the angle; this is presumably a causeway for a gate, a suggestion strengthened by the fact that there is a slight change of alignment in the ditch at this point. Geological features obscure the cropmarks in the position where a traverse might be expected.

SE 38 SE 12   Newsham with Breckenborough

Catterick Bridge *Fig 114*

SE 23189910

A fragment of a possible camp has been recorded from the air immediately E of Catterick Racecourse (St Joseph 1955, 82; 1973, 214; CUCAP ACB 26). It lies at about 60 m above OD, on the relatively flat alluvial plain of the River Swale, near a point where the river bends southwards. Dere Street, the major Roman road from York to SE Scotland, passes about 350 m to the W, crossing the River Swale some 600 m WNW of the camp. The crossing-point was protected on the S bank by an early fort, which was later overlain by the town of Catterick (*Cataractonium*), and on the N bank, at Brompton-on-Swale, by a fortified bridge-head enclosure (P Wilson 1984).

The NE corner and parts of two sides of the camp are known from cropmarks (CUCAP RG 58). The E ditch is visible only as a discontinuous line, but it is unlikely to have been substantially longer than the 215 m so far recorded; it was probably not more than 230 m in length overall, as there are indications that the ditch is beginning to turn westwards to form the SE angle. There are no certain gates in this side; a cropmark of what could be a traverse might suggest an entrance, the causeway having perhaps been breached subsequently for drainage at this point. The N side extends to at least 160 m and there is a causeway for a gate, protected by a traverse, about 70 m W of the corner. Geophysical survey and excavation W of Leeming Lane, in the E part of the central reservation of Catterick Racecourse, found no evidence for the W side of the camp there (Central Excavation Unit, Catterick site 273; inf P Wilson). The area of the camp is thus unknown.

Immediately to the E of the modern A1 road and W of Dere Street, the cropmark of an E to W ditch with an entrance gap (at SE 22699875) has been claimed as a possible camp (NAR SE 29 NW 9; CUCAP AAB 21). It more probably relates to the land allotment, cemetery plots or ribbon development which excavation has shown to have spread S of Catterick town along the fringes of the Roman road (*Britannia* 16 (1985), 278; English Heritage 1986, 26, fig 2).

SE 29 NW 10   Catterick

Cawthorn *Figs 9, 115, 116, 117 and 118*

SE 78298996

A cluster of military earthworks, exceptionally well preserved, survives at 190 m above OD on the crest of the gentle S-facing dip slope that at this point forms the N rim of the Vale of Pickering. The steep N scarp, known as Cawthorn Banks and as Rawcliff Banks, falls 45 m to the diminutive Sutherland Beck which is dammed immediately to the NE to form Elleron Lake. The outlook to the N over Cropton Forest and Spaunton Moor extends for up to 7 km, and to the S, before the growth of the surrounding forest, most of the W half of the Vale of Pickering would have been in view. The site lies on either side of a small re-entrant valley which provides some access down Rawcliff Banks; this may have been a factor in the choice of location, although similar access could have been achieved no more than 1.5 km to the E or W.

The earthworks consist of four major elements. A camp, C, of unusual polygonal design, is partly overlain by a slightly later fort, D, which is probably datable to the late 1st century (NAR SE 79 SE 45; Jones 1975, 140–1). To the E of the camp are two structures which have often been classified as camps; on balance, however, the more westerly of the two is best regarded as a fort, A, which was subsequently provided with an annexe on its E side, thus forming a much larger defended area, B.

The earthworks were excavated between 1923 and 1929 (Simpson 1926; Richmond 1926; 1929; 1932). The identifying letters A–D usually ascribed to the earthworks are retained here, but most of the highly speculative functions and relationships put forward by Richmond have now been discarded. Certainly there seems to be no overriding reason to consider the sites as practice works. The few finds suggested that occupation may not have continued later than *c* AD 120.

The position chosen for the unusual camp C is almost level, sloping only very gently to the E and S. There is no evident topographical reason for its odd, coffin-shaped plan, which

Figure 114 *Catterick Bridge, North Yorkshire.*

Roman Camps in England

was probably determined by earlier phases of activity in the immediate vicinity which have not survived as earthworks.

The whole camp is very well preserved: internally it measures 260 m from N to S by a maximum of 95 m transversely, and encloses an area of 2.1 ha (5.2 acres). The defences consist of a bank which stands 0.8 m high internally and up to 1.2 m high above the bottom of a slightly ragged external ditch up to 0.8 m deep. The depth of the ditch is emphasised by the unusual provision of a broad, low counterscarp bank, about 3 m across and 0.3 m high. Richmond's excavations (1932, 40–2) revealed that the inner bank was made of turf (Fig 9); there was no berm between the bank and the ditch which was found to be about 1 m deep and which apparently had a narrow basal channel. The loose material upcast from the ditch formed the counterscarp bank.

On the short side that faces NE the defences are now fragmentary; short lengths of the inner bank survive but the ditch has been almost entirely levelled. The whole of this area seems to have been affected by quarrying. From his excavations, Richmond (1932, 40) suggested that the ditch

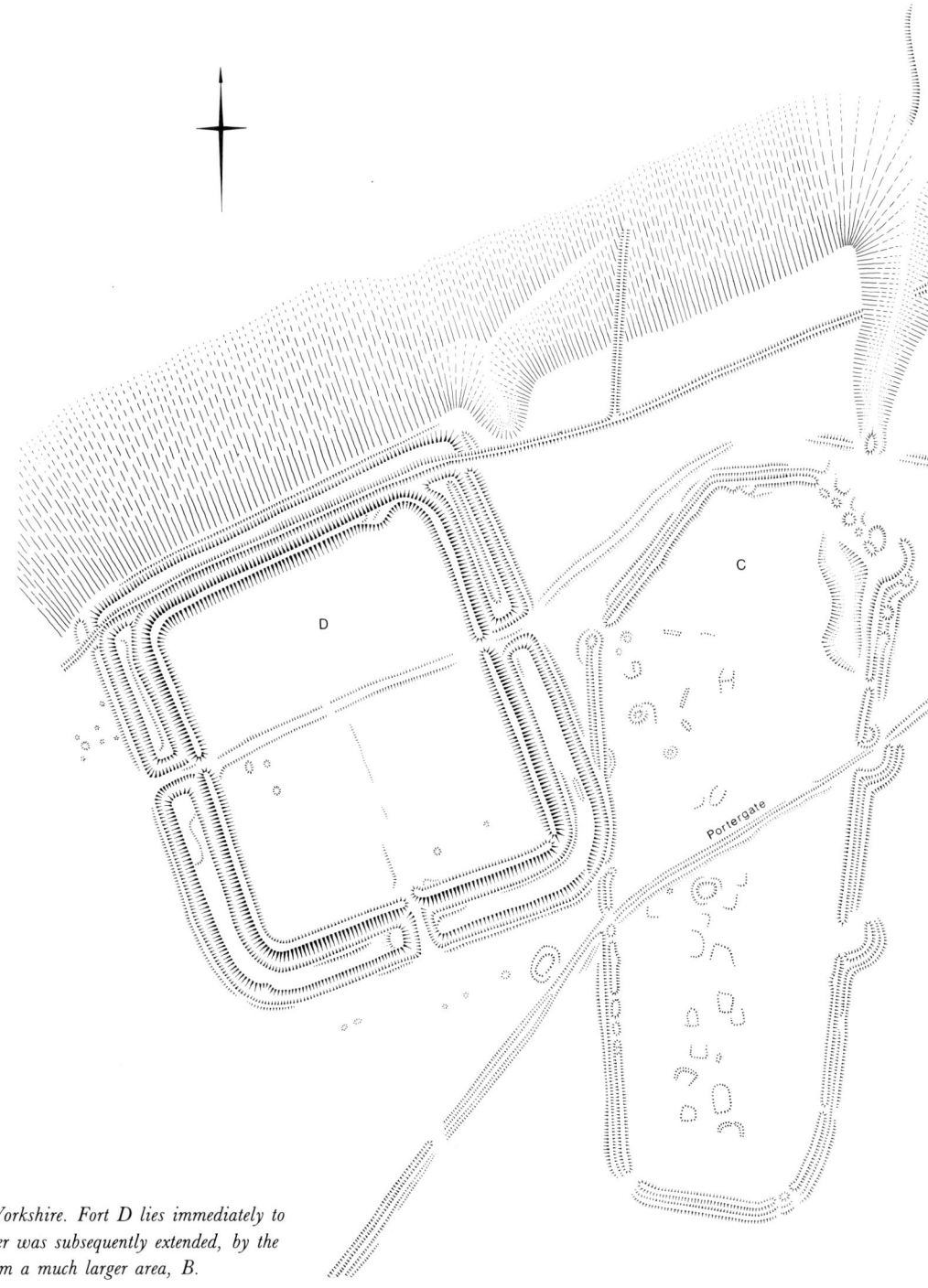

Figure 115 *Cawthorn C, North Yorkshire. Fort D lies immediately to the W and fort A to the E; the latter was subsequently extended, by the addition of an eastern annexe, to form a much larger area, B.*

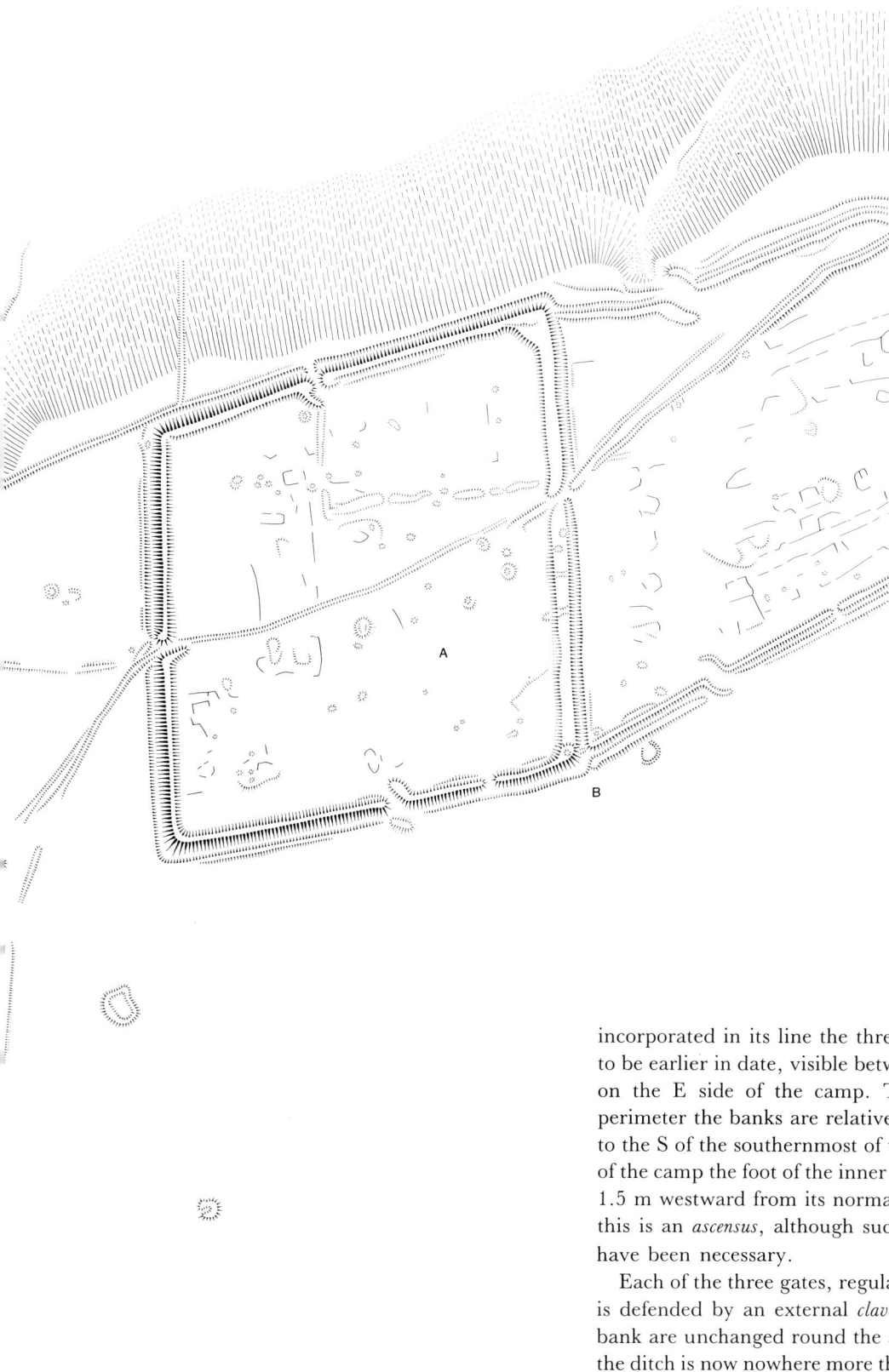

incorporated in its line the three pits, which he considered to be earlier in date, visible between the N and central gates on the E side of the camp. Throughout the rest of the perimeter the banks are relatively featureless, although just to the S of the southernmost of the three gates on the E side of the camp the foot of the inner side of the turf bank extends 1.5 m westward from its normal line. It is conceivable that this is an *ascensus*, although such a provision would hardly have been necessary.

Each of the three gates, regularly spaced along the E side, is defended by an external *clavicula*; the dimensions of the bank are unchanged round the arc of the *clavicula*, although the ditch is now nowhere more than 0.3 m deep. In each case the gap in the line of the turf bank is about 8.5 m wide; this is further restricted to about 5 m by the *clavicula* itself, which is an arc of more than forty-five degrees. The N gate is at the point where the defences are realigned sharply to the NW. It is possible that the gaps at the NW and SW angles also served as entrances, although there is no direct evidence for this. The interior of the camp was not investigated by Richmond, although he noted (1932, 40) that it contained pits and turf-built structures; these may be contemporary with the defences, although this has not been demonstrated. Most of the structures in the interior are subrectangular and are formed of banks no more than about 0.3 m high; apparently open-ended, some measure up to 6 m across overall but are now little more than 2 m across internally. These structures are visible only in a band up the centre of the camp and towards the NW angle. The interior is crossed by what appears to be a packhorse track, said to be the medieval Portergate; 3 m wide at the top but only 1 m wide at the base, it is cut down to a depth of 0.8 m.

Richmond's excavation (1932, 49) showed that the fort, D, immediately to the W, was constructed later than camp C, the SE angle of the former overlying the defences of the latter. This is surprising, for the fort occupies the better position, on a slight knoll on the crest of the escarpment. That being so, unless the visible earthworks of fort D had some form of predecessor in the same general position, thus restricting the choice of site available to the builders of camp C, it is unclear why the site of the camp was chosen at all. The postulated existence of a predecessor to the fort would go some way to explain why the NW angle of the camp is cut off in such an unusual way. Further, the dead ground to the N of the lip of the escarpment begins only 30 m from the N defences of camp C, an exceptional arrangement, whether or not the camp had serious defensive intent. The construction of fort D would not seriously have undermined the effectiveness of the defences of camp C, and thus its continuing occupation. The *agger* of a lightly metalled road (Richmond 1932, 21, 51), linking forts D and A, curves round the N side of camp C; if this road is of Roman date it may suggest that the camp remained in use at the same time as the forts were occupied. If fort and camp were contemporary in use, at least in part, the gap in the defences at the NW angle would have provided ready access to the camp. Further excavation is required to resolve these questions.

Only 75 m to the E of camp C are the impressive earthworks of another fort, A. Since internal and external *claviculae* survive at its gates, thus conforming broadly to the rules of contemporary castrametation, it has often been loosely described as a camp. However, it is markedly dissimilar from the other camps in England and it seems more

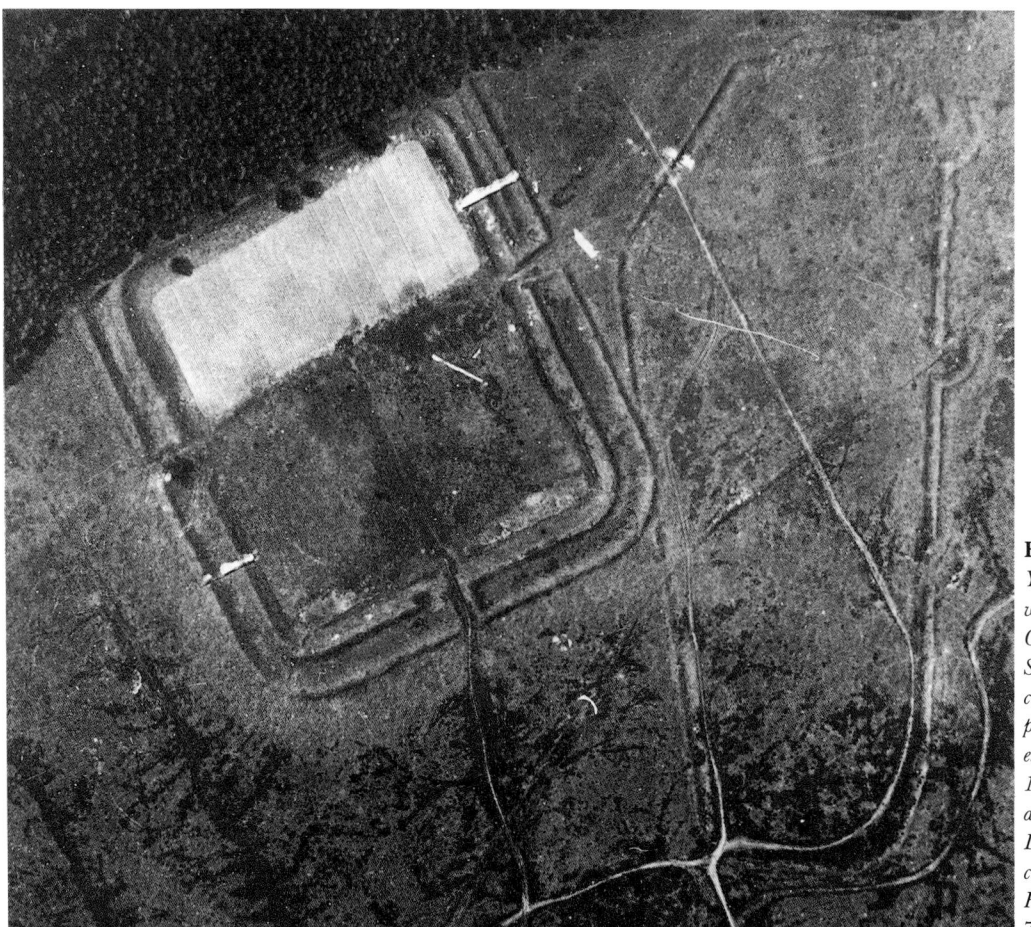

Figure 116 *Cawthorn C, North Yorkshire. Vertical photograph, with N to the top left, taken by O G S Crawford in 1925. The SE corner of the fort, D, clearly cuts the W side of the camp. The photograph was taken before the extensive woodland visible in Fig 117 grew up. The white gashes across the NE and SW sides of fort D are the trenches of the excavations carried out by I A Richmond and F G Simpson.* (NMR AP SE 7890/11)

Figure 117 *Cawthorn C, North Yorkshire, from the SE. The coffin-shaped camp C with its well-marked external* claviculae *is overlain by the SE corner of the later fort, D, and cut by the medieval trackway, Portergate. Part of fort A is just visible to the E. Since this photograph was taken the tree cover has been removed.* (5.11.68, CUCAP AWG 80)

reasonable to classify it as a fort to which, subsequently, an E annexe was attached. The scale and the method of construction of the defences seem to make this reclassification more appropriate. The interior of the fort and of its E annexe were still obscured by bracken, piles of timber and brash at the time of the survey by RCHME. No detailed description or analysis will be provided here (NAR SE 79 SE 45), but it is appropriate to underline the features that may illuminate the dividing line between the two monument types.

On its W side, on to which the three gates of camp C seem to face, the defences are 14 m across overall and consist of a rampart, an outer ditch, and a slight counterscarp bank only 0.2 m high. The rampart is 1.7 m high internally and 2.8 m above the bottom of the ditch which is 1.6 m deep. The position chosen, on the crest of the ridge, is similar to that of fort D. The true summit is just to the NW of the centre of the site and so most of the interior slopes gently to the S. Excavation revealed that the rampart consisted of material upcast from the ditch, with a thick capping of turf which, the excavator suggested, was added in the second phase when the annexe was constructed on the E. However, it is difficult to be sure quite what was revealed in the 1920s: the sections drawn (Richmond 1932, 25) do not correspond to the description in the text. At one stage or another there seems to have been extensive use of timber in the construction of the defences. There was a series of vertical posts on the lip of the ditch 10 ft (3.0 m) apart with, some 6 ft (1.8 m) farther back, a continuous trench for a palisade, cut into the upcast material. Between the gates on the S and E, deep holes for stout posts were found along the rear of the rampart, 1.8 m behind the palisade and 1.5 m apart. Such extensive use of timber makes it clear that this was a permanent or semi-permanent fort and not a camp.

Along the E side of the fort, the top of the rampart is markedly broader than elsewhere and its height has been reduced to 1.0 m internally and 1.0 m to 1.7 m externally. This change was presumably made when the annexe was added. The security provided by the ditch was not seriously compromised for it is still 1.0 m deep. It appears unlikely that the intention was to slight the defences on this side. This reinforces the impression that the additional defended area to the E was intended as an annexe to fort A and not to form one larger integrated entity (Richmond's B).

The annexe, much more like a camp in character, is laid out on an irregular subrectangular plan. This is especially marked on the N where the defences were set along the natural crest; they had to be realigned at the gate on that side in order to take account of a re-entrant valley which provides access down the escarpment. The bank stands up to 0.7 m high internally and was found to be constructed of turf; the ditch was 8 ft 9 in (2.7 m) wide and 3 ft 9 in (1.1 m) deep (Richmond 1932, 52). A counterscarp bank, now no more than 0.4 m high, was provided throughout. These defences are altogether slighter than those of the fort. The two gates, on the N and S, are protected by internal and external *claviculae* and are offset to the W, confirming that the internal layout was focused on fort A. No gate was provided in the rear, E, rampart.

The single gates in the W and S sides of fort A are each defended by internal and external *claviculae*, none of which was provided with a ditch; the N gate has an internal *clavicula* only. On the W, the gate has been damaged by the later hollow-way. In each case the internal *clavicula*, at only 0.6 m to 0.9 m in height, is appreciably lower than the adjacent ramparts. The report of the excavations (Richmond 1932, 22–30) confirms the impression that these *claviculae* were

Figure 118 *Cawthorn C, North Yorkshire. S entrance in E side, from S.* (6.6.93, NMR AA93/188)

additions to the defences. In the original design the ditch of the fort was 15 ft (4.6 m) wide and 7 ft (2.1 m) deep, and was driven across the line of the gateways. The latter, which were originally inturned and rectilinear, were defended by traverses on the E, W and S; the ditches of these were soon back-filled. The W example was unusual in that it was keyhole-shaped on plan, and it was suggested that this and the other traverses were never completed. No traverse was found at the N gate; either it had been eroded away or the steep natural slopes rendered such a provision superfluous. In a subsequent phase, when the *claviculae* replaced the traverses, only an internal *clavicula* was provided at the N gate. The excavations uncovered a single E gate, defended by a traverse, only about 40 m from the SE angle. No *clavicula* was subsequently provided here before the gate was demolished (Richmond 1932, 30, pls 7 and 20).

The E and W sides of the fort are parallel but the E defences are slightly longer than the other three sides. This plan, combined with the positions of the gates, must have affected the regularity of the internal arrangements. These were briefly studied by Richmond (1932, 29–30) who was of the opinion that only some of the many pits and ovens identified belonged to the first phase of occupation. Subsequently, at the time that the defences were extended to the E, turf structures were laid out which he interpreted as wind-breaks rather than the lower courses of buildings. These now stand up to 0.6 m high as banks up to 2.5 m broad; some of the areas enclosed appear to be as little as 2 m across internally. A single line, extending N to S within the fort as a discontinuous bank, suggests some regularity of planning. The layout of banks in the E annexe is rather clearer in places, especially in the SE corner. These were interpreted by the excavators as tented barracks. Despite this, there is insufficient clarity to define a conventional road-plan and it is not clear which way the fort originally faced. Some of the turf structures seem to be laid across internal lines of access to the N and S gates of the fort, and are thus not likely to be strictly contemporary. A mound close to the centre of the fort, now standing 0.9 m high and measuring about 9 m across, was identified by Richmond as the tribunal, a dais for the commanding officer. This was constructed by adding a turf platform to the N side of an earlier mound. The latter seems to have been a prehistoric barrow with a central pit which had been disturbed by earlier excavators (Richmond 1932, 61–3). Aerial photography by RCHME in 1993 revealed that the barrow was surrounded by a circular ditch more than 20 m in diameter. Further investigation is required, for the date, associations and functions of all the features within the fort and its annexe are unclear. Other structures, apparently not wholly dissimilar, survive outside the W and S sides of the defences.

A low bank, nowhere more than 0.5 m high, defines two sides of a subrectangular enclosure which takes in most of the NE corner of fort A. Its layout suggests that it may be later than the other internal features but this cannot be demonstrated without excavation. Its function is unknown.

SE 79 SE 45   Cawthorne

Malham *Figs 119 and 120*

SD 91456548

The remains of this isolated camp are situated on relatively dry rough grassland, on the W side of a fairly level saddle between High Stony Bank and Low Stony Bank, at about 385 m above OD. Although there are good views from the SW around to the W and N, it is not in a particularly strong defensive position. Overlooked by higher ground from the NE, and from the E where the crest of the saddle rises gently to about 400 m above OD, the site is also dominated by the elevated limestone pavement of Low Stony Bank, only about 140 m from the S edge of the camp. On the W the deep and narrow valley of the Gordale Beck offers some good natural protection, supplemented less effectively on the N by the shallow gully of an unnamed tributary.

Figure 119 *Malham, North Yorkshire.*

Roman Camps in England

The defences of the camp, which faces N, consist of a rampart with an outer ditch enclosing an area of nearly 8.1 ha (20 acres). There are four gates, each with an internal *clavicula*. The remains are in relatively good condition; such damage as there has been to the defences has resulted from the traffic along the green track of Mastiles Lane which almost bisects the camp immediately N of the E to W wall. Evidently there were problems with the original setting out of the camp which is not a perfect rectangle: the N side is 8 m shorter than the S, and the E side is 4 m longer than the W. The NE corner is a right angle but the E rampart veers outwards by up to 6 m at the SE corner, the angle of which is thus slightly acute. The E end of the S side also curves inwards off the general line of this side. These misalignments are probably due to the gently undulating topography. The four corners of the camp are not all intervisible, either from each other or from a central point.

The rampart is generally about 5.2 m in width, standing 0.2 m high internally and 0.5 m externally; where best preserved, on the N, the external scarp reaches a height of 0.8 m. The shallow ditch is less well defined but is generally about 3.2 m wide and 0.2 m deep. Little of it remains along the W side. There appear to be suggestions of part of an inner ditch, perhaps a quarry, towards the S end of the E side. As well as the breaks caused by farm tracks and by Mastiles Lane, the defences have been destroyed by subsidence, and the subsequent formation of a pond and marsh, in two places near the NE corner.

The N, S and E gates, each about 6 m wide, have well-preserved internal *claviculae*. The gate on the W side is less evident for the rampart here is on a W-facing slope and has been badly mutilated by Mastiles Lane. Nevertheless, its position is almost certainly marked at a point about 100 m S of the NW corner, directly opposite the E gate, by a break in the rampart about 6 m wide and by a slight scarp that runs diagonally into the interior.

Although the ground slopes gently from E to W, the NE angle of the camp lies in a slight hollow and the NW on a rise. The interior is mainly covered in tussock grass; this is shorter on the W side, but is rougher on the E where the ground is more undulating and pockmarked with solution hollows. Just to the N of the wall that runs along the S side

Figure 120 *Malham, North Yorkshire. Vertical photograph, with N to the top, taken 21.11.75. The deep narrow valley of the Gordale Beck lies to the W. The E half of the interior of the camp is marked by solution hollows.* (CUCAP RC 8 BE 167)

of Mastiles Lane, two linear 'ditches' are evidence of subterranean collapses in the limestone. To the W of these and 20 m N of the wall, is a large irregularly shaped stone with a central rectangular hole; this is the base of a medieval cross, one of a number marking the route of Mastiles Lane. The camp is also crossed, from the NE corner to just N of the W entrance, by the remains of a robbed boulder wall, partly double-faced at its E end. For much of its length it is only marked by an occasional large boulder protruding through the turf. Unfortunately it is broken where it meets the rampart on either side of the camp and it is not possible to ascertain its exact relationship to the Roman earthworks. Crossing the camp about 45 m parallel to the S of Mastiles Lane there are two narrow lines of disturbed turf which mark the positions of agricultural water-pipes laid in 1968 and 1976.

SD 96 NW 6   Malham

Wath *Fig 121*

SE 67477452

A camp of irregular, but almost square plan, enclosing about 4.9 ha (12.1 acres), was identified in 1976 on the N side of the Howardian Hills (St Joseph 1977, 130–1; CUCAP BZH 22). It lies on the level top of Diana Hill, on the edge of the limestone escarpment at a little over 80 m above OD; on its W side the ground falls steeply away to the Wath Beck. To the N the slope is less severe, and on the S side there is a relatively gentle gradient. There are good views in all directions, particularly northwards across the Vale of Pickering.

Almost the entire perimeter of the camp has been levelled by ploughing, the exception being its NW corner which lies within Wath Wood. There, a low scarp, up to 0.6 m high, may represent a residual rampart. Surmounted by small trees, the scarp probably once formed part of a hedge line beside a track (OS 1:2500 Yorkshire sheet CVI SW, 1892). Most of the remainder of the camp's perimeter is known, except for the SW corner and much of the adjacent part of the S side. The discontinuous line of the E ditch bows outwards markedly, so that the approximate dimensions are about 230 m from N to S by between 208 m and 217 m transversely. The apparent absence of any diagnostic features and the lack of definition of the rather fine cropmarks make it impossible to be sure which interruptions in the ditches should be accepted as gates. The N side, which occupies a false crest where the hill slope begins to steepen, appears to have had an entrance close to its central point. The position of a probable gate in the W ditch is to the S of centre and may be matched by another almost directly opposite. If so, the camp may have faced S.

SE 67 SE 25   Wath

Figure 121 *Wath, North Yorkshire.*

Nottinghamshire

Calverton 1 and 2 *Fig 122*

1: SK 61505084   2: SK 61505088

Two camps, one inside the other, have been recorded as cropmarks 200 m NE of Lodge Farm at about 60 m above OD, on the W side of the valley of the Dover Beck, a tributary of the River Trent (Riley 1983; Maxwell and Wilson 1987, 9; NMR AP SK 6150/20). They occupy the level crest of a low spur which projects south-eastwards and from which the ground falls away on all sides except the NW. There are good views, particularly to the SE along the valley of the Dover Beck, and to the WSW along a shallower unnamed valley towards the late Iron Age and possible Roman military site at Dorket Head, Arnold (NAR SK 54 NE 4). To the NW, however, the view is blocked by rising ground, itself now capped by the massive waste-heap from Calverton Mine.

The outer enclosure, camp 1, perhaps the earlier of the two, is incompletely known and is crossed by other cropmarks of unknown origin. Its NW corner is overlain by the modern road, and the damp low-lying ground of Oxton Bogs beside the Dover Beck obscures cropmark evidence on the NE side. The detailed topography of the camp's layout is unusual, for the E ends of the NW and SE defences cross the natural valley scarp; the NE ditch would have lain at the bottom of this slope. The camp measures just less than 280 m from NW to SE by at least 285 m transversely, giving

Figure 122 *Calverton 1 and 2, Nottinghamshire.*

a minimum area of about 8 ha (20 acres). It is not rectangular, for the SE side bows outwards, while the NW side bows slightly inwards. A faint gap at the centre of the SW side is probably a gate; another possible gap in the NW side is even less clear. A slight gap in the SE side, opposite the SE gate of camp 2, may be a further gate. The bowing in this SE side may support this interpretation, for a realignment at an entrance is not uncommon (NMR AP SKF 6150/17–20). If this gate is central, then the NE side of camp 1 would have been very close to the present course of the Dover Beck, providing a maximum area for the camp of about 10.5 ha (26 acres). No matching gap, however, is apparent at the equivalent point in the NW side, the only possible break in the cropmark being farther to the NE. No traverses are detectable for any of the entrances.

The perimeter of camp 2 is known in its entirety, enclosing an area of about 1.7 ha (4 acres). It has a broader ditch than that of camp 1 and its layout is distinctly irregular. Although the NE and SW sides, 150 m and 122 m long respectively, are parallel, the SE side, 115 m long, is not at right angles to them, but is parallel to the E half of the NW side. The NW side itself changes direction immediately W of its central gate, for no apparent topographical reason. The arrangement, however, still allows the SW gate to be in the centre of that side, and approximately in line with that in the SW side of camp 1, although its siting is not quite opposite its NE counterpart. A further irregularity is that the E corner has a very large radius in contrast to the N and S angles. Each entrance is guarded by a traverse, lying about 10 m outside the perimeter. The NE side of camp 2 lies on the edge of the valley scarp and its precise orientation seems likely to have been determined by this natural feature.

SK 65 SW 18   Calverton

Farnsfield Fig 123

SK 63855574

The cropmarks of a camp were discovered from the air in 1976, astride Longland Lane, 1 km SW of Farnsfield (Riley 1977, 191; NMR AP SK 6355/76/14, 6355/108). The camp occupies an almost level site on the summit of a broad ridge in gently undulating countryside at 66 m above OD. To the N and NW the ground falls gently away, and only to the S is the open aspect restricted by a ridge, less than half a kilometre away. There are no Roman roads in the immediate vicinity, but the vexillation fortress of Osmanthorpe lies about 4 km to the E.

The camp is not quite rectangular, measuring between about 206 m and 218 m from NE to SW, by about 182 m to 186 m transversely, and covering approximately 3.9 ha (9.6 acres). The NE and SW sides each have a central gate; any entrance on the NW perimeter would have been obliterated by Longland Lane. No traverses are visible. The highest part of the site coincides with the SW gate and, by analogy, the camp may therefore have faced NE; the N corner occupies a slight rise, a factor which may have conditioned the overall alignment of the camp.

In 1978 three trenches were cut across the NE side and the E corner (Swarbrick and Turner 1982). At the former (a on Fig 123), a gate about 5.7 m wide was located. At this point the V-shaped ditch had clearly defined rectangular terminals and was 2.8 m wide and 1.8 m deep; there was a cleaning slot 0.1 m wide at the bottom. The bank was set back 0.3 m from the lip of the ditch, and had an unusual base formed by filling a shallow trench, 2.2 m wide and about 0.2 m deep, with gravel. Vestigial fragments of turf from the bank itself, overlain by similar gravelly material, had spilled over the berm; at the rear, the base of the rampart was marked by a line of pebbles set at a steep angle. At the entrance, the bank extended just under 1 m beyond the end of the ditch, reducing the overall width of the gate to about 5.7 m. The excavation of the E corner (b on Fig 123) located the remains of turves, measuring on average 400 mm by 500 mm by 50 mm, which had slipped into the ditch from the adjacent bank. Pottery recovered from the ditches comprised a small number of sherds of both Romano-British and Iron Age types, none closely datable.

SK 65 NW 5   Farnsfield

Figure 123 *Farnsfield, Nottinghamshire. The letters 'a' and 'b' mark the sites of excavations in 1978.*

Gleadthorpe Plantation (Warsop)
Fig 124

SK 59487037

The cropmarks of a camp immediately W of Gleadthorpe Plantation were recognised on aerial photographs taken in 1979 (Riley 1980a, 58, 138–9, map 30; 1980b, 332–3, fig 10; NMR AP SK 5970/4). At just over 60 m above OD, it occupies the summit and slopes of an isolated hill on the N side of the valley of the River Meden. The N corner of the camp is a little to the N of the summit of the knoll, while the S corner is less than 55 m from the river and lies at the bottom of a marked scarp; some of the area enclosed may thus have been unsuitable for tents. The site commands extensive views W and E along the valley, and also to the S and N where the ground slopes away more gradually. No Roman road is known in the vicinity, but the camp at Farnsfield lies about 16 km to the S and is broadly similar in its size and proportions.

The camp is nearly rectangular, measuring about 162 m from NE to SW by 204 m transversely, and covers an area

Figure 124 *Gleadthorpe Plantation, Nottinghamshire.*

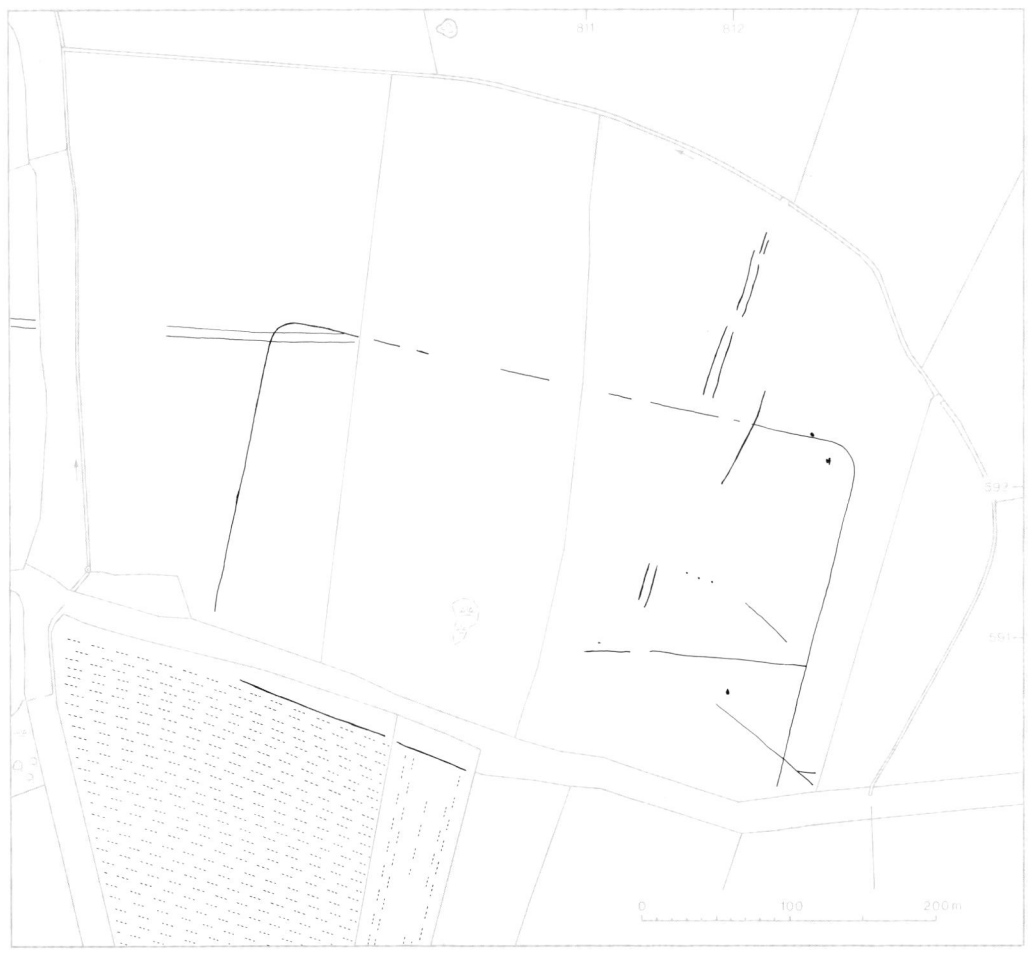

Figure 125 *Holme, Nottinghamshire.*

of about 3.3 ha (8.1 acres). No entrance can be identified with certainty although there is some evidence for one in the centre of the NE side. Some of the other interruptions in the cropmark of the ditch seem to be caused by the differential land use of the many small plots into which the field has been divided by the adjacent Ministry of Agriculture Experimental Husbandry Farm. No earthwork evidence for the E corner survives in Gleadthorpe Plantation itself, but the area has been disturbed by quarrying and tree-planting.

Other cropmarks in the vicinity comprise slight traces of a possible pre-Roman field system, part of which has been recorded in the same valley farther to the W (Riley 1980a, map 30).

SK 57 SE 15   Warsop

Holme *Fig 125*

SK 81055915

The cropmarks of the N part of a camp have been noted in the lowlands of the River Trent, a little over 500 m to the E of Holme (St Joseph 1961, 120; NMR AP SK 8159/20). It occupies level ground, at about 10 m above OD, between two tributaries of the Slough Dyke, a minor arm of the Trent. The position chosen may relate to a crossing of the river some 850 m to the W, near the present village. Although the site of the camp is only slightly elevated it nevertheless commands extensive views in all directions. The small Roman town of Brough (*Crococalana*), which probably had a military origin, lies 2.5 km to the ESE, on the Foss Way.

Only the N side of the camp, about 410 m long, and parts of the E and W sides are known and no gates can be identified with any certainty (NMR AP SK 8159/3–9; 8059/20). Although the W and N ditch lines are at right angles to one another, the NE angle is slightly acute, suggesting that the E ditch may have been deflected slightly westwards to avoid wetter ground. Whether or not the total area of the camp extended to the S of the modern road from Holme to Langford is uncertain. The crop indications on the extreme S end of the W side are ambiguous; on some aerial photographs they could be taken to indicate that the ditch turns eastwards to form the SW corner just N of the hedge line (NMR AP SK 8059/27), but cultivation marks make certainty impossible. The field to the S of the modern road is under permanent pasture and is covered with ridge-and-furrow. Irregularities in the alignment of the road and hedge line immediately to the S of the camp could perhaps relate to the former position of its S side, but this too is by no means conclusive. The defensive circuit N of the road would have enclosed at least 9.3 ha (23 acres). Double-ditched trackways of unknown date cross the E half of the site and cut the NW corner; their relationship to the camp is unknown.

SK 85 NW 33   Holme

Shropshire

Attingham Park *Figs 126 and 127*

SJ 55600975

In Attingham Park, ESE of the Hall, drought conditions have revealed the ditch line of a camp, a little over 200 m W of Norton camp 1 (CUCAP K 17 AM 72). The camp occupied the tip of a slight S-projecting spur some 50 m above OD, just E of the River Tern and about 600 m NE of its confluence with the River Severn. The site has good views up and down the Severn, including the sites of the camp at Cound Hall and the fortress and town of Wroxeter (*Viroconium*). The outlook towards the E and NE is restricted to some extent by undulating ground which rises gradually to the E.

The parch marks have revealed the NE angle, about 330 m of a N side and 290 m of an E side. The angle between them is slightly obtuse and a number of breaks in the ditch are apparent, but none can definitely be identified as an entrance. Interpretation is hindered by the marks of medieval ridge-and-furrow and other undated features over the whole site. The construction of modern military camps and other installations associated with the former Uckington airfield has also caused considerable disturbance.

The orientation of the camp is approximately determined by the falling ground on its E, W and S sides. The S part of the E ditch coincides with the lip of the shallow NNE to SSW valley which forms the E edge of Attingham Park, but the N end of its line lies back from the scarp. The ground beyond the N defences is level. What line was followed by the W side of the camp cannot even be guessed at from the topography. Any W side conforming to the orientation of the rest of the camp would have lain awkwardly across the gentle natural slope forming the S end of the spur. The interior of the camp, as far as this can be established, occupies fairly level ground which rises slightly to the N suggesting that its outlook to the S was of paramount importance. Its overall position was clearly topographically superior to that of the nearby camp, Norton 1.

SJ 50 NE 87   Wroxeter

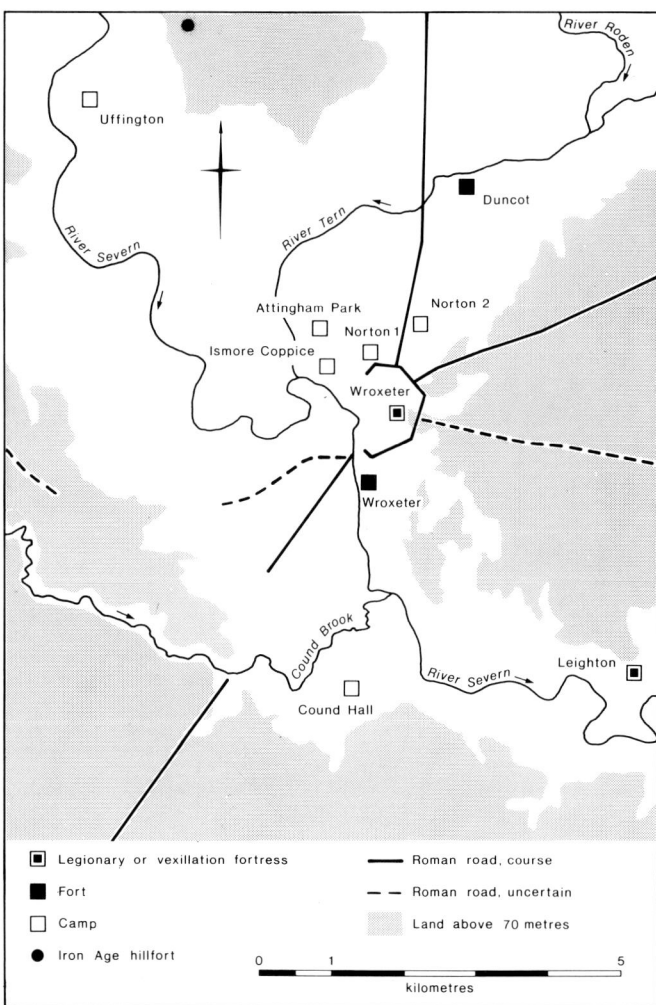

Figure 126 *Camps and other military sites in the vicinity of Wroxeter, Shropshire.*

Bromfield *Figs 51, 128 and 129*

SO 48337741

The existence of a camp immediately N of the village of Bromfield has long been known from aerial reconnaissance (St Joseph 1953, 85). It occupies the SW side of a gravel spur, at about 94 m above OD, between the Rivers Corve and Teme, and just over 600 m N of the confluence of the

Figure 127 *Attingham Park and Ismore Coppice, Shropshire.*

latter with the River Onny. Though somewhat isolated, the camp is less than 8 km E of the major N to S road that led S from the legionary fortress at Wroxeter (*Viroconium*), via the Church Stretton Gap. The probable extension of the course of a more minor S to N Roman road from Weston under Penyard (*Ariconium*) (Margary 1973, 331 (613); Houghton 1966), passes close to the N corner of the camp.

The ditch of the camp is clearly visible on aerial photographs (CUCAP BYS 39; Fig 129), but is slowly being destroyed by sand and gravel quarrying. Since the mid 1960s this has removed a central portion of the SW side, the entire NW defences, including the W and N corners, and part of the NE side. Much of the SW side, however, was observed during quarrying in 1968 (Stanford 1970a). The position of the S angle is occupied by a cricket pitch. The sub-rectangular outline of the camp measures about 330 m from ENE to WSW by about 260 m transversely, and encloses an area of approximately 8.5 ha (21.2 acres). Two gates have been recorded from the air, one central to the NE side, and the other on the NW side offset towards the WSW in an approximate 2:3 ratio. A third entrance, on the SW side, set slightly SE of centre, was indicated by the butt-end of a ditch (a on Fig 128), apparently the SE side of a gate, noted during soil stripping in 1968 (Stanford 1970a). Unfortunately it was destroyed by the quarry before its precise position and character could be recorded. No indication of any certain traverse ditches has been observed, not even in the exceptional drought conditions of 1989, when the cropmarks of the NE side, NE entrance, and part of the SE side were clearly visible, even from ground level.

Excavation and salvage observation in the face of the advancing quarry have taken place on a number of occasions from 1956 onwards and have supplied some unusually diverse information (Houghton 1966; Stanford 1970a; CBA Group 8 *West Midlands Archaeol* **26** (1983), 87; Stanford 1985, 4; Watson 1988; Hughes 1992). On the SW and on the NW, and on the NE side (c on Fig 128), the ditch, up to 0.5 m deep and up to 1 m wide, varied in profile from V to U-shaped. It showed little evidence of weathering or silting; there was some iron staining in the bottom, suggestive of deliberate back-filling (Stanford 1970a; Watson 1988). In a section excavated in 1983 (b on Fig 128) the bottom of the ditch contained burnt stakes *in situ* and iron slag in the back-filling (CBA Group 8 *West Midlands Archaeol* **26** (1983), 87).

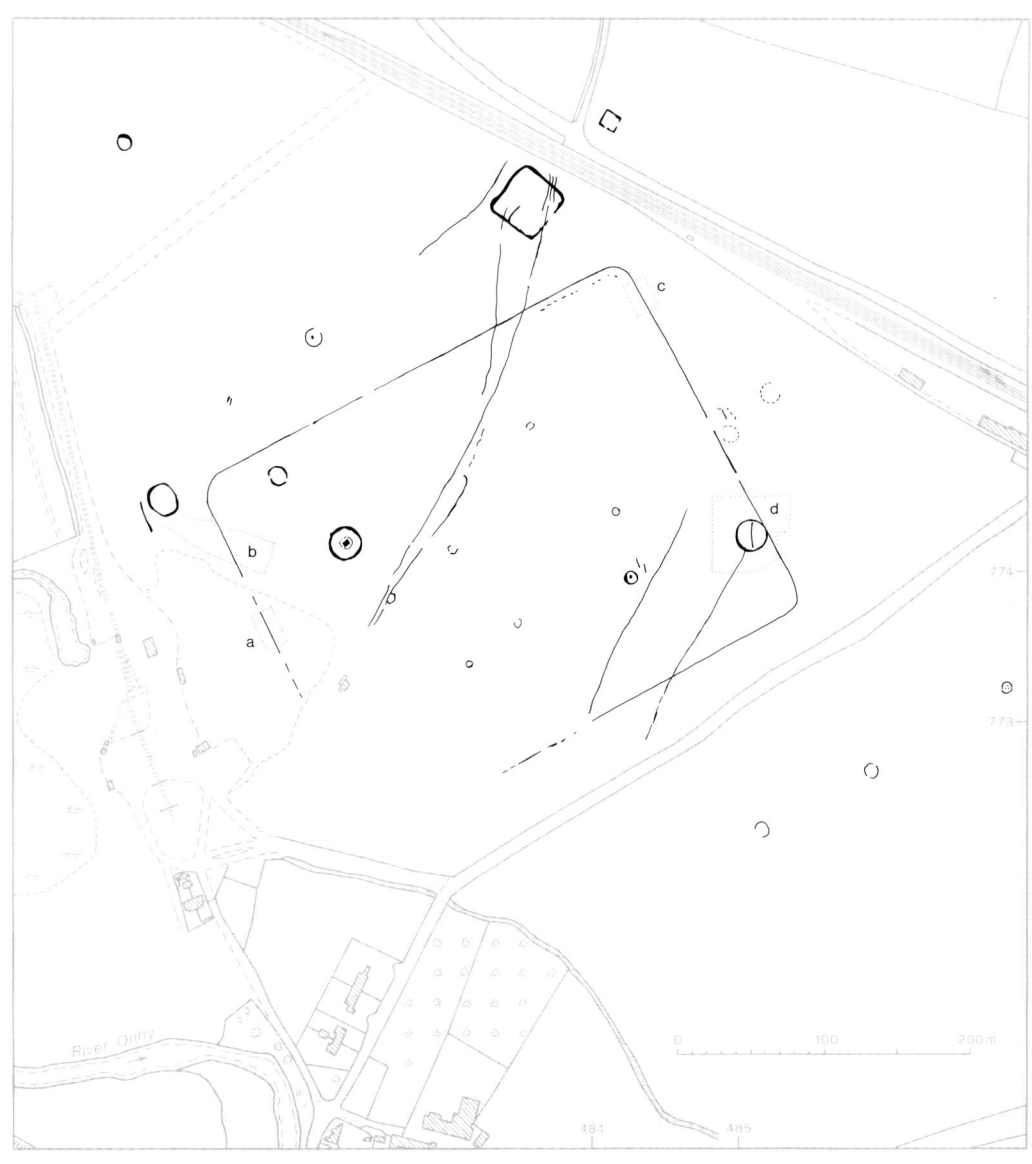

Figure 128 *Bromfield, Shropshire. The broken line across the SW side of the camp marks the extent of quarrying in the late 1960s. The interrupted line within it indicates the line of the camp ditch noted during the quarrying. The letters 'a' to 'd' indicate the location of excavations carried out between 1956 and 1991.*

Figure 129 *Bromfield, Shropshire, from the E. The photograph shows a relatively early stage of the quarrying, before it had destroyed most of the NW half of the camp. The ring-ditches are the remains of prehistoric barrows which formed part of an extensive Bronze Age cemetery.* (1.7.76, CUCAP BYS 39)

A line of pits, apparently immediately inside the rampart, is visible close to the N angle (CUCAP BYS 38–40), but no datable material was found in those examined during salvage work.

In 1991, area excavation of a 47 m length of the NE side (d on Fig 128), S of the gate, showed the ditch of the camp to have been of a remarkably regular character, its section being the shape of an inverted bell (Hughes 1992, 6–7, 9–10). Evidence of decayed turf in the primary silt suggested that part of the rampart had been deliberately pushed back into the bottom of the ditch soon after abandonment, though the upper part of the ditch-fill indicated that, thereafter, the earthworks had been left to erode and silt naturally. Fragments of iron slag were probably derived from small-scale iron-working. Four small ovens were located (Hughes 1992, fig 5, pls 11–13), three apparently cut into the base of the rampart; these implied a rampart width of approximately 3 m to 3.5 m. Their stratigraphy, representing several firing episodes, may indicate that the camp was not merely an overnight halting place, but that it had served as a temporary base to which troops returned repeatedly during the campaigning season.

Within and around the camp are the remains of barrows, represented on aerial photographs by ring-ditches, which formed part of a more extensive cemetery, mainly Bronze Age in date, some of which, together with Neolithic and Iron Age features, has been excavated (Stanford 1982; Jones 1993). At least two of the four barrows inside the camp, three of which have now been excavated (Leach 1989; Hughes 1992), may have survived to some significant height at the time that the camp was occupied, and this would have affected its internal dispositions. The NE side of the camp, of which the ditch exactly cuts the ring-ditch of a barrow, was probably deliberately aligned on it, so that the barrow mound could have been incorporated into its rampart. A well-defined roughly square ditched enclosure just to the N of the camp (CUCAP BYS 36–8) was found on excavation to be an Iron Age site of relatively short-lived occupation; much later, an Anglo-Saxon/early Christian graveyard was laid out within its confines (Stanford 1985, 4–7; 1991, 113–15).

SO 47 NE 8   Bromfield

Brompton 1 and 2 *Fig 130*

1: SO 24969343   2: SO 24969334

On the border with Wales, and crossed by the line of Offa's Dyke, the cropmarks of at least two camps have been recorded around Brompton Hall (St Joseph 1969, 119–20; 1973, 235–6, fig 19; CUCAP BNK 52–3). The valleys of the Caebitra and the Camlad provide good access eastwards towards the main military route through the Church Stretton Gap, and northwards and westwards to the Severn valley. The camps themselves occupy the level summit of a slight E-facing spur, at about 42 m above OD, from which the land drops on the S to the Caebitra. They are overlooked from the W and NW, but have excellent views eastwards, to the confluence of the Caebitra and Camlad near Church Stoke and ESE down the Camlad valley. Barely 150 m to the WSW lies the fort of Pentrehyling, (*Archaeology in Wales* **28** (1988), 66; Allen 1990) and the large fort of Forden Gaer is only about 6.5 km to the NW. It has been suggested that the modern B4385 road, which crosses the sites of the camps from SE to NW, may follow the approximate line of a branch Roman road from Bishopsmoat to Forden Gaer (Houghton 1962, 240; NAR RRX 28g); it clearly would have postdated the camps.

The smaller camp, 2, seems to have been rectangular but the N angles of camp 1 are obtuse. Neither camp is known in its entirety, for no cropmarks have been recorded for most of their E and S sides. On topographical grounds, the S sides, which may have coincided, are unlikely to have been more than about 5 m to 10 m to the S of the modern A489 road. This occupies a break in the slope, close to the lip of the valley scarp, which falls gently to the flood plain of the Caebitra. On this basis, the dimensions of camp 1 may have been in the region of 375 m to 400 m from E to W by about 390 m transversely; camp 2 seems to have measured some 230 m from E to W by about 225 m transversely. The areas enclosed are unlikely to have exceeded about 15.5 ha (38 acres) and 5.2 ha (13 acres) respectively.

No gates can be identified positively in either camp, although the almost central gap in the N ditch of camp 1, immediately W of Offa's Dyke, may be one. Excavation, in advance of road widening, at the point where the S end of the W side of the larger camp meets the modern road, showed that the camp ditch had a shallow V-shaped profile, varying between 0.5 m and 0.8 m in depth and between 0.5 m and 1.8 m in width with some evidence of silting in the bottom (Cane and Allen 1989, 3). The ditch had later been cut by the substantial N side-ditch of a Roman road which has been recorded from the air as two parallel cropmarks aligned on the E gate of the fort at Pentrehyling. About 33 m to the W of the W ditch of camp 1, and parallel to it, was a small V-shaped ditch, also predating the ditch of the Roman road. It has been interpreted as the possible ditch of another camp, although it could perhaps relate to an annexe. In another trench, immediately to the S of the A489, the W ditch of camp 2 had survived to a depth of 1.3 m and was over 1 m wide (Jones, A E 1991, 4, figs 5 and 6). It is not clear how much farther S the camp extended (CBA Group 8 *West Midlands Archaeol* **33** (1990), 60–1).

The N side of camp 1 lies on a slight N-facing slope, with no particular topographical advantage. The E half of the N defences of this camp seems to have determined the line of the subsequent field boundary, although there is no elevation to the hedgerow; an apparent kink in the line of Offa's Dyke, where it overlies the perimeter of the camp, may not be an original feature but is probably the result of differential erosion at a point used by farm vehicles to cross the dyke.

The interiors of the camps slope very gently to the E. A noteworthy feature in the NW quadrant of camp 1 is the large barrow, known locally as The Rossett (NAR SO 29 SW 3). Its mound, contained within three concentric ditches, is now subcircular and has apparently been disturbed in its S half; it is gradually being levelled by ploughing, but still survives to a height of 1.2 m. If, as is likely, the barrow predates the camp, its presence will have interfered with the standard arrangements of the internal layout of the camp.

It has been suggested that another camp existed (St Joseph 1973, 235–6, fig 19). This suggestion is based on the cropmarks of a ditch that ran from E to W across the N third of camp 1, with an interruption and change of direction at the barrow; no diagnostic features have been recorded and, as yet, there is no evidence to suggest that this ditch belonged to a camp. The origins of a short length of curving ditch to the NW of the NE corner of camp 2 at SO 25009348, and another crossing the S part of the W side of camp 1 are not known.

The fort, just E of Pentrehyling, is known from aerial reconnaissance, geophysical prospection, and excavations conducted between 1978 and 1990 (Allen 1990; Jones, A E 1991, 4–12, figs 7–10). It too, sits on the edge of the valley scarp, but at a very slightly higher elevation than the camps. There were at least two phases of occupation, both of late 1st or early 2nd-century date. The first apparently comprised a timber fort of normal military character, with an annexe attached to part of the S side. The second phase, overriding the layout of earlier buildings, but respecting at least part of the defensive bank, was characterised by industrial activities. Limited excavation indicated the existence of a substantial *vicus* to the N, E and SE of the fort; pits and furnaces associated with industrial processes extended beside the Roman road at least as far as the S part of the W ditch of camp 1. The fort and *vicus* were probably abandoned in the 2nd century, but there is evidence for small-scale reoccupation in the late 3rd to early 4th century.

SO 29 SW 7   Brompton and Rhiston

Figure 130 *Brompton 1 and 2, Shropshire. The information relating to the fort to the SW depicted on this plan is derived from geophysical work and from excavation as well as from aerial photographs.*

Figure 131 *Burlington 1 and 2, Shropshire. The letter 'a' marks the position of the excavation across the ditch.*

Burlington 1 and 2 *Figs 131 and 132*

1: SJ 77901064   2: SJ 77981078

Two camps, one inside the other, occupy a low, slightly undulating spur, at about 98 m above OD, on the S side of Watling Street, 12 km to the W of the military complex at Water Eaton (St Joseph 1969, 105; 1973, 233–4; CUCAP BBX 46–8). Immediately to the NE, Burlington Pool feeds a tributary of the River Worfe which flows in a shallow valley to the E of the camps. There are good views up and down the valley but the W flank of the camps is overlooked by a ridge of high ground including Lizard Hill, less than 1 km to the SW.

The larger camp, 1, measuring about 460 m from ENE to WSW by about 340 m transversely, covers an area of about 15.5 ha (38.6 acres). The cropmarks of its ditch are not particularly well defined, especially in the W corner, where the ground is rather undulating. The N corner appears to have been destroyed by shallow quarrying. The perimeter has a regular plan, with parallel opposing sides, and one reasonably clear gate, marked simply by a gap in the ditch close to the centre of the NE side. There appears to be a comparable break at the equivalent point on the SW side; a curving mark just inside it could conceivably represent an internal *clavicula*, but the cropmarks in that part of the camp are faint and discontinuous.

The relationship of the camp to the Roman road is unclear, since the orientation of the defences has been dictated by the topography. The SE defences and part of those on the SW side have been positioned just below the top of the slopes there, while the NE side coincides with a local crest, now

Figure 132 *Burlington 1 and 2, Shropshire, from the SW. Only camp 2, set within the N angle of camp 1, is visible. Frost fractures and the lines of drains and former field boundaries obscure much of the remains. The modern road to the N of the camp follows the line of Watling Street.* (23.7.70, CUCAP BDX 26)

accentuated by ploughing and shallow quarrying, at a point where the valley side begins to fall away more steeply. This scarp probably determined the overall alignment of the camp.

Camp 2, measuring on average about 200 m from WNW to ENE by about 130 m transversely, occupies an area of only about 2.5 ha (6.4 acres), and lies in the N angle of the larger camp. Its position and the better definition of its cropmarks may suggest that it is the later of the two. The proximity to the point where Watling Street crosses the stream seems to have been the major consideration in its siting within the other camp, since most of its SE and SW sides lie within a local dip. It is less regular than the larger camp, its SE and SW sides being out of alignment with the other two; the S angle is therefore obtuse, an irregularity perhaps caused by a slight scarp at this point. The radius of its S corner seems to be slightly smaller than those of camp 1, but the W corner is so shallow as to be almost straight.

Economy of effort would have been served by not taking a longer curving line for the ditch when cutting through the rampart of the older camp. Interruptions in the ditch of camp 2 occur at the centre of the SE side and at approximately the centre of the SW side, but there is no sign of any gate on the NE, nor any certain entrance on the NW, the side closest to Watling Street. No traverses are evident.

A section cut across the NW defences of both camps, at a point (a on Fig 131) approximately 90 m SW of the N angle, revealed a V-shaped ditch about 1.5 m wide and 0.7 m deep (St Joseph 1973, 233–4).

Other cropmarks include frost fractures and the lines of drains and former field boundaries, together with a gully immediately to the S of Watling Street and parallel to it, which may represent the side ditch of the Roman road.

SJ 71 SE 14   Shifnal

Cound Hall *Figs 126 and 133*

SJ 56180504

The line of a ditch of part of a probable camp has been observed from the air in arable just over 200 m SE of Cound Hall (NMR AP SJ 5605/7–10). It occupies an excellent position on a pronounced NW to SE spur at 55 m above OD, between the Coundmoor Brook to the W, the Cound Brook to the N and, nearly 1 km away, the River Severn to the E. The position chosen gives good long-distance views northwards up the Severn valley to Wroxeter and beyond, but to the SE the ground rises towards Harnage.

The aerial photographs show a single rounded E corner, approximately a right angle, and about 80 m of the NE side and 210 m of the SE side of the camp. There is no certain evidence for an entrance; the apparent gap in the SE ditch coincides with a change in soil type and may not necessarily be archaeological in origin. The interior is more or less level and its N part presumably lies within the surviving parkland of the early 18th-century Cound Hall. Several hollows within the park, apparently natural, may have influenced the position of the camp's perimeter. If so, a marked hollow S of the Hall may indicate a maximum length of about 180 m for the NE side. There are no topographical features to suggest a probable line for the SW side. The NE ditch of the camp, which is cut by a later field boundary, may have been roughly aligned on the small valley immediately to the SE of the Hall.

SJ 50 NE 64   Cound

Figure 133 *Cound Hall, Shropshire.*

Ismore Coppice *Figs 126 and 127*

SJ 55670933

The NE angle of a possible camp lies in an area of miscellaneous cropmarks and traces of former ridge-and-furrow immediately NE of Ismore Coppice, beside the B4380 from Wroxeter to Atcham (CUCAP BYO 78). It occupies level ground, only about 250 m S of the camp in Attingham Park and probably less than 300 m W of Norton camp 1, and is overlooked by both. Its siting, at about 46 m above OD, is not very prominent but, like the camp in Attingham Park, it commands good views along the Severn. The outlook to the N and E is completely obscured by higher ground.

Only the NE corner, about 40 m of the N side and barely 30 m of the E side of the camp are traceable on the aerial photographs. No earthworks are evident in the interior of Ismore Coppice, since the ground has been extensively disturbed by a modern military camp, now disused, associated with the old Uckington airfield. If the classification is accurate, the E side of the Roman camp must have been aligned on a shallow NNE to SSW valley, now marked by a wide dark cropmark and by the course of a drain within Ismore Coppice. To the S, this feature merges with the pronounced W to E scarp above the Severn. On topographical grounds, therefore, the N to S dimension of the camp is unlikely to have exceeded about 210 m.

SJ 50 NE 105   Wroxeter

Norton 1 and 2 *Figs 126 and 134*

1: SJ 56210950   2: SJ 57140989

Two camps have been recognised within an exceptionally dense series of cropmarks immediately to the N of the Roman town of Wroxeter (*Viroconium*).

The outline of a camp, 1, can be distinguished immediately N of the main defences of the Roman town, and less than 600 m N of the Nero-Flavian legionary fortress which preceded it (St Joseph 1973, 234; CUCAP BXW 5). The site occupies fairly level ground, some 200 m W of Norton Farm, at 55 m above OD. It commands good views on most sides, except to the E, where undulating but gradually rising ground restricts sight-lines. To the S lies the valley of the Bell Brook, while just to the W is a shallow SSW to NNE valley. To the N the ground towards the valley of the River Tern, almost 2 km away, is fairly level.

The NE angle of this camp, much of its N side, and most of its E side are clearly defined, lying at right angles to one another (CUCAP K 17 Y 42). A straight ditch, 130 m long, parallel to the N side and about 300 m S of it, seems to have been part of the S defences (CUCAP CJN 41). Another ditch alignment, lying at an obtuse angle to the postulated S side, is likely to have formed the S portion of the W side (CUCAP BOF 8; NMR AP SK 5609/79). The reason for this irregularity is not apparent on the ground. The probable site of the NW corner may, however, have been determined by the topography, since it appears to have coincided with the lip of the gentle W-facing valley scarp that borders Attingham Park, thus maximising the outlook in that direction.

If these interpretations are correct, camp 1 would have enclosed an area of almost 13 ha (32 acres). One possible entrance can be identified, approximately in the centre of the E side. The course of the modern A5, which runs W to E, also appears to pass through the W side at or close to its centre, and may well have made use of a gate through the earthworks there. The extensive medieval ridge-and-furrow over the site appears to have contributed to the interruption of the cropmark of the ditch in the central sector of the N side of the camp. The SE corner of the camp and a portion of the S side may have been obliterated by the construction of the N defensive circuit of the Roman town or further masked by the subsequent use of its counterscarp bank as a headland for the ridge-and-furrow. These defences are unlikely to have been constructed until at least the second quarter of the 2nd century AD, and possibly later (Baker 1970; Barker 1985; Webster 1988, and 1989, 206).

Within the interior of camp 1 a curved angle, which might have formed the NE corner of another camp, is traceable (a on Fig 134), and a ditch line continues westwards from it for almost 150 m (CUCAP BXW 8–9). North-east of camp 1, another ditched angle is discernible (at b), but its origin remains uncertain (CUCAP BXW 6, 15).

Cropmarks which may perhaps be interpreted as part of another camp, 2, have been recorded 400 m NE of Norton crossroads and about 700 m ENE of camp 1 (Webster 1966, 34–5, fig 3; CUCAP VD 56–63). The site, positioned at about 60 m above OD, is level but elevated, and like that of camp 1 has good views in most directions, although these are somewhat restricted to the E.

The cropmarks include a well-defined rounded corner that seems to constitute the right-angled S corner of a camp. However, only 50 m to the W of this angle the cropmarks of the ditch stop abruptly as its line converges with a plough furrow; another ditch, set back about 13 m to the N, is of a markedly different character and does not appear to be associated. The perfectly straight E side seems to have been about 320 m long; the rounded NE angle is of approximately the same radius as the SE one but the ditch extending to the W makes a more acute angle than might be expected. The identification of these cropmarks as those of a camp must remain in question. A section cut through the E side in 1957 uncovered a ditch with a slot in the bottom, but no dating evidence was found (*West Midlands Archaeological News Sheet* **2**, 1959 (1969), 7).

Another rounded angle occurs within the Norton cropmarks and SW of camp 2 (c on Fig 134). On present evidence, it does not appear to relate to any other part of a supposed perimeter of a camp.

1: SJ 50 NE 15   2: SJ 50 NE 13   Wroxeter

Figure 134 *Norton 1 (left) and 2 (right), Shropshire. Some of the ditched trackways and fields apparently preceded the construction of the defensive circuit of the Roman town of Wroxeter; the relationship with camp 1 is uncertain. Most of these features were overridden by medieval ridge-and-furrow; the counterscarp bank of the town defences became a headland, masking the cropmark evidence immediately adjacent. The complexities of the interior of Wroxeter town and its multi-period defences have not been transcribed in detail. (See Baker 1970; Barker 1985, fig 80; Wilson 1984b; Webster 1989, fig 16.4.)*

Figure 135 *Quatt, Shropshire.*

Quatt *Fig 135*

SO 73818898

A small camp, defined by the fine cropmarks of a narrow ditch, was recorded in 1979, immediately to the W of Lodge Farm, and almost 2 km NW of Quatt (Maxwell and Wilson 1987, 9; CUCAP CJG 70–3). It occupies the flat top of a steep-sided gravel spur, at 58 m above OD, above the E bank of the River Severn and commands excellent views up and down the valley.

The camp is very regular in outline, measuring approximately 140 m NNW to SSE by 95 m transversely, and covers an area of about 1.3 ha (3.3 acres). Apart from the rounded angles, no diagnostic features are apparent. A single break in the ditch of the N side seems to be slightly offset from the centre. A gap may have existed in the centre of the S side, but the cropmarks appear too faint for certainty and are confused by geomorphological features.

To the NE of the site some rectilinear enclosures, apparently of more than one phase, have been recorded as cropmarks (NAR SO 78 NW 6). Their relationship to the camp is unknown; on morphological grounds they may be Iron Age or Romano-British.

SO 78 NW 17   Quatt Malvern

Stretford Bridge 1 and 2 *Figs 51 and 136*

1: SO 42908410
2 (Craven Arms): SO 43008369

Two camps have been discovered to the S of Stretford Bridge in a strategic position, close to the confluence of the River Onny and the Byne Brook (NMR AP SO 4284/12; CUCAP WP 75–6). They are just to the S of the fort at Stretford Bridge, on the W side of the valley of the Onny, and command good views along the valleys of the Onny and the Byne. The western Watling Street, the main Roman road linking Wroxeter (*Virocónium*) and Leintwardine (*Bravonium*), which cuts obliquely across camp 1 and passes immediately adjacent to camp 2, crossed the Onny near this point. The camp at Upper Affcot lies only 2.5 km to the NE.

Camp 1 (St Joseph 1965, 85), the larger of the two, occupies a slight spur of uneven ground at about 125 m above OD. The cropmarks reveal the complete W side, about 375 m long, two approximate right angles, and at least 360 m of the S side. The total extent of the camp cannot, therefore, be determined, but it is unlikely to have been less than about 13 ha (33 acres). The land on which it lies has been arable for several decades; the fields to the E, which contain slight indications of ridge-and-furrow, are in permanent pasture and have produced no cropmarks. No gate

Figure 136 *Stretford Bridge 1 and 2, Shropshire, with the fort to the N.*

Shropshire

has been identified with certainty but the gap at the W end of the S side is not likely to represent an original entrance. The position of the camp, astride Watling Street, presumably indicates that it predates the construction of the road. The hedge line which crosses the W side kinks markedly near the SW corner, suggesting that the defences of the camp may still have been upstanding when the field boundary was first laid out.

The camp does not have strong natural defences and, indeed, does not utilise the broken topography to best advantage. Internally the ground slopes eastwards, with the highest point midway along the W side, perhaps suggesting that the camp faced E. The N and S defences occupy comparatively weak terrain, the N side lying within a small valley now marked by a modern drain; the entire S perimeter, and particularly the SW angle, are also sited on lower ground. The topography is not helpful in suggesting a location for the missing E rampart and ditch.

Within the defences of the camp, immediately E of the railway, stands a mutilated flat-topped mound, 1 m high (SO 43048406; NAR SO 48 SW 5). It is undated but may be a prehistoric barrow. If it predates the camp, its relatively central position within the defences would have interfered with the standard internal arrangements. The cropmarks of an oval single-ditched enclosure, perhaps a prehistoric ceremonial monument, are visible in the NW part of the camp; its internal features may be more regular than depicted here (cf Whimster 1989, 36–7).

Just to the SE of the postulated barrow, on a level terrace immediately E of Watling Street, are the cropmarks of two parallel ditches about 140 m apart; these have been suggested as the N and S sides of another possible camp (St Joseph 1973, 235). The ditches, however, are not oriented on the same axis as Watling Street, and more evidence is needed before the existence of a camp can be proved.

Camp 2 lies a little over 100 m to the S of camp 1 (St Joseph 1961, 125). It occupies a level terrace, at just under 125 m above OD and less than 40 m to the E of Watling Street. Only the W part of the rectangular camp is known from cropmarks, that to the E being masked by the railway and by permanent pasture. It comprises a complete W side, about 125 m long, with a gap, possibly an entrance, about 8 m S of the central point. The N and S sides are fragmentary, with no certain gates, but they indicate a W to E dimension of at least 105 m, giving a total area for the camp of not less than 1.3 ha (3.2 acres).

Although no traces of earthworks can be discerned on the ground, the SW corner and the W part of the S side of the camp appear to coincide with an L-shaped natural rise up to 0.4 m high, immediately to the E of which the ground falls slightly. This feature almost certainly determined the position of the camp's defences, for no other detailed topographical considerations appear to have influenced its siting.

1: SO 48 SW 2   2: SO 48 SW 14   Wistanstow

Figure 137 *Uffington, Shropshire.*

Uffington *Figs 126 and 137*

SJ 52431283

Drought conditions in 1975 revealed the cropmarks of a camp, apparently of more than one period, underlying a well-developed system of medieval and later ridge-and-furrow (St Joseph 1977, 145; CUCAP BUH 64–9). The cropmarks of five former field boundaries, now destroyed but shown on the 1954 OS 6-inch map (SJ 51 SW), meet close to the centre of the site. Two ponds also formerly existed within the defended area, but these too are almost completely filled in. The site is a fairly level alluvial terrace at about 50 m above OD, within a wide meander on the E bank of the River Severn. The fortress, forts and camps in the vicinity of Wroxeter lie about 6 km to the SW.

The camp appears to have had two phases, the later apparently involving a reduction or extension of its area. The overall shape is not precisely rectangular, but at its greater extent may have been determined largely by the local topography. The long NW side, not quite at right angles to the SW and NE sides, sits back from the riverine scarp, the NE end of its ditch falling just S of a gentle summit. The short sides, which are parallel, occur close to natural crests, the SW side coinciding with the lip of the slope down to the flood plain of the Severn. The SE side follows the edge of a slight hollow but the cropmarks here are very poorly defined, probably because of a lack of geological uniformity. It appears that the extreme SW angle was slightly acute and if so, there must have been at least one change of direction in the defences on this side. Interpretation is complicated by the probable presence of two phases of defences, by the uneven geology and by the distorting effect of the ridge-and-furrow. The area enclosed was at some point altered, from about 18 ha (44.5 acres) to about 16.3 ha (40.0 acres), or vice versa, the length of the NE to SW axis varying by about 50 m. Without excavation the exact sequence can be no more than speculation. The position of any entrance is also uncertain. Although there are a number of breaks visible in the cropmarks of the ditches, none can be unambiguously identified as a gate. The well-marked gaps in the NE side are extremely broad and are set off-centre; it is likely, nevertheless, that there was a gate somewhere in this area and that the camps probably faced NE.

SJ 51 SW 42   Uffington

Upper Affcot *Figs 51 and 138*

SO 44338640

Cropmarks of part of a camp have been observed from the air immediately S of the hamlet of Upper Affcot (St Joseph 1961, 125; Houghton 1966, 188; CUCAP ADQ 34). The camp is situated on a spur at about 142 m above OD, to the W of the Quinny Brook, 750 m NW of its confluence with the Byne Brook, and only 2 km above the point at which it flows into the River Onny. The position affords commanding views to the S and particularly to the W. The Roman road from Gloucester (*Glevum*) to Wroxeter (*Viroconium*), via the Church Stretton Gap, passes just over 1 km to the W. A minor Roman road from Weston under Penyard and Gloucester, using the Gap, was apparently located by

Roman Camps in England

Figure 138 *Upper Affcot, Shropshire.*

excavation about 350 m to the SE of the camp (Houghton 1966, 188) and may have passed close to its E side. This reinforces the impression that the camp faced E.

Parts of two sides and the S angle, which is just less than a right angle, are visible as cropmarks; this is not enough to provide any firm estimate of the size of the camp, although it is possible that parts of the W and N sides are perpetuated by modern field boundaries. Immediately to the N of the hamlet, a boundary running WNW to ESE on both sides of the modern road (SO 44178661 to 44458652) is almost precisely parallel with the known S side of the camp. No significant earthworks survive on this line, but the lane leading E changes alignment at the point where, on this hypothesis, it should have crossed the defences of the camp. No cropmarks have been recorded to the N of this postulated NE angle, even in the most favourable crop conditions. In 1976 a watching brief, which was conducted in this NE corner during the construction of an extension to a chicken hatchery, failed to locate any signs of the camp ditch (CBA Group 8 *West Midlands Archaeol News Sheet* **19** (1976), 44). However it is clear from earlier aerial photographs (CUCAP WP 81; ACA 45–6; NMR AP SO 4486/12) that the area had already been disturbed.

The topography suggests that the W side of the camp may be masked by the modern boundary which lies on a natural crest to the W of the hamlet (SO 44218654 to 44178644).

The camp would thus have measured about 300 m by 200 m, an area of 6.0 ha (14.8 acres).

In 1957 two sections were cut across the camp ditch. It was found to be about 0.7 m deep and about 1.8 m wide, with a pronounced slot at the bottom; the single sherd recovered from it was not closely datable (NAR SO 48 NW 6).

SO 48 NW 6   Wistanstow

Whittington *Fig 139*

SJ 35053033

A camp of unusual and irregular layout at Perry Farm, Whittington, a little over 5 km E of Oswestry, has been recorded by aerial photography from 1969 onwards (Baker 1972, 30–1; St Joseph 1973, 236; NMR AP SJ 3530/37/10/74–81). It sits on a low rise, at just over 85 m above OD, on the NE side of the valley of the River Perry, a tributary of the Severn. The vexillation fortress at Rhyn Park lies 8 km to the NW.

The camp measures about 460 m from E to W by about 330 m transversely and encloses an area of about 15.3 ha (38.0 acres). There is poorly drained ground on its E, W, and S sides, but its elevation, though relatively slight, nevertheless provides good all-round visibility, particularly to the S and E. Almost all of the perimeter has been recorded, apart from the S part of the W side which is overlain by Perry Farm, and the W part of the N side. In contrast to the familiar rounded shape of the NW and SE corners, the NE angle is rather sharp and obtuse. The E side of the camp changes direction about 15 m N of the midpoint. Here a narrow break in the line of the ditch most probably marks an entrance, the only one tentatively identified. Just to the N of this, a sudden offset in the ditch may represent the point where a SW to NE drain crosses it, though the precise reason for this effect is unclear.

Figure 139 *Whittington, Shropshire. The letters 'a' and 'b' mark the sites of excavations in 1972.*

The layout of the camp makes careful use of local topographical details and its unusual shape is undoubtedly a corollary of this. The N, S and E defences and part of the W side all occupy the crests of the rise, from which the ground falls away quite sharply by between 1.4 m and 6 m to what must once have been marshland. Only the N part of the W ditch lies slightly back from the edge of a natural scarp. The change in alignment of the E side at the gate and the obtuse angle of the NE corner relate to a pronounced local hollow, at least 1.4 m deep, immediately E of the NE angle. It seems likely that when the camp was planned, the E side to the S of the gate was laid out approximately parallel to the W side. However, the presence of the hollow meant that the position of the NE angle had to be set back farther to the W than intended in order to avoid it. In 1972 trenches were cut across the N and W sides of the camp (a and b on Fig 139) near the NW corner and to the W of Berghill Lane (Day 1978). A V-shaped ditch about 1.4 m wide and 0.8 m deep was recorded on the N perimeter, but later activity, perhaps the recutting of the ditch as a drain, had distorted the profile of the W defences. No information was obtained about the adjacent rampart, as the areas excavated were insufficiently large.

The effect of the original earthworks of the camp upon the later landscape is apparent only along the N side, where the lane to Keeper's Cottage evidently ran along the rampart for about 150 m. Just over 120 m to the N of the camp is the strongly defined cropmark of a rectilinear ditched enclosure, probably an Iron Age or Romano-British settlement, with at least one other less clearly delineated compound, and perhaps a field system, attached. Some of the less distinct and more random cropmarks over the whole area, including that occupied by the camp, may be of natural origin.

SJ 33 SE 5   Whittington

Somerset

Norton Fitzwarren *Fig 140*

ST 18132596

Less than 1.5 km W of Norton Fitzwarren, in undulating country, some cropmarks of what seems to have been a small isolated camp were noted in 1990 (NMR AP ST 1825/1–2). The camp lies on a W to E spur, between the valleys of the River Tone to the S and the Norton Brook to the N, on level ground between two slight knolls at about 30 m above OD. There are excellent views to the S, across the Tone, and reasonably good visibility over more broken terrain to the N, WNW, and NNE. To the E, however, the camp is overlooked by higher ground. No Roman roads are known in this area but, just over 9 km to the W, a Roman fort has been recorded at Wiveliscombe (NAR ST 09 NE 2).

The cropmarks are fragmentary but seem to define an approximately rectangular shape measuring about 94 m from NE to SW by about 68 m transversely, with three broadly rounded corners; it encloses an area of about 0.6 ha (1.6 acres). There is a faint hint of an entrance with an internal *clavicula* in the centre of the SE side. The corres-

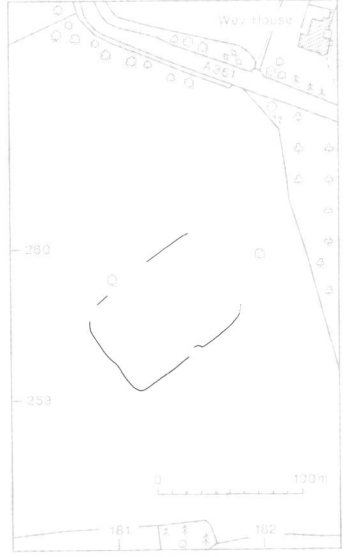

Figure 140 *Norton Fitzwarren, Somerset.*

ponding position on the NW side is obscured on the photographs by the shadow of a tree, but the SW end of the NE segment of the ditch stops abruptly, as if for a gate. No interruption is detectable in the cropmark of the SW side.

ST 12 NE 29   Norton Fitzwarren

Staffordshire

Greensforge 1, 2, 3, 4 and 5
Figs 141, 142 and 143

1: SO 86378851   2: SO 86338852
3: SO 86538904   4: SO 85788800
5: SO 85658850

This complex of forts and camps just SW of Wolverhampton lies on and immediately W of a level S-projecting tongue of land at 65 m above OD, between the small marshy valley of the Smestow Brook on the W and the broad shallow valley of the Dawley Brook on the E. The site lies at what seems to have been a nodal point in the Roman road system of the area (Webster 1981b, 79–80), some 23 km S of Watling Street, at an important crossing-place of the Smestow, 550 m N of its confluence with the Dawley.

The greater part of the plateau between the streams is occupied by two double-ditched forts (St Joseph 1966; Frere and St Joseph 1983, 96–9). That on the S, fort A, about 1.6 ha in area, and with outworks to the N and E (D Wilson 1984, 51–2, 55), takes up the prime naturally defended position and is therefore probably the earlier. Its N counterpart, fort B, which was almost exactly the same size, possessed an annexe and outwork, and was probably later in date (Frere and St Joseph 1983, 96–9). From the very limited excavations undertaken, it seems that both may have been established within the Claudio-Neronian period (CBA Group 8 *West Midlands Archaeol News Sheet* **11** (1968), 13; Webster 1981b, 82).

Between the two forts, the overlapping cropmarks of what may have been two camps, 1 and 2, have been recorded (CUCAP ABR 32, 36; BUI 4). Both appear to precede the S ditch of the annexe or outwork of fort B, for the ditches of all three are coincident for a short stretch. Their relative chronologies are, however, unknown. The E and W ditches of the camps are crossed by a substantial angled ditch, which may have originally cut off the S end of the spur. This angled ditch has been interpreted as an extra outwork for fort A (D Wilson 1984, 55), but its context has yet to be established by excavation.

The larger of the two postulated camps, 1, is represented only by its NE side and a short length of the SE side (CUCAP BUI 9; ABR 32). The NNE ditch seems to change direction at a central causeway. The smaller possible camp, 2, is defined by the cropmark of a ditch within the NW part of camp 1 (CUCAP ABR 38; BUI 4). Though a modern road truncates its SW angle, it probably comprised an area of about 0.4 ha (1.0 acres). No gates are recorded on the aerial photographs, so the exact classification of this enclosure must remain in doubt. The position of the N side of both camps may have been conditioned by a slight gully immediately to their N, which opens into the valley of the Smestow Brook. There has been considerable plough erosion on the plateau in the past few centuries, and this feature was probably more pronounced in the Roman period.

About 320 m NE of fort B is what appears to be the curved W angle of another camp, 3. As recorded (St Joseph 1973, 233; CUCAP BDX 81, 84), the short stretch of the SW side runs almost parallel to a pit alignment that extends farther to the NW and also continues on the far side of the Dawley Brook to the SE. The aerial photographs also suggest that a ditch running roughly parallel to the pit alignment meets the ditch of the suggested camp at its angle (SO 86468904), apparently deliberately respecting it and therefore probably postdating it. The interior of the presumed camp and its two sides are crossed obliquely by the Roman road leading NNE to Water Eaton, visible in the crop as a pair of thinly delineated ditches.

Camps 4 and 5, also discovered during aerial reconnaissance (St Joseph 1973, 233), occupy broken ground W of the main complex; their slightly higher position on the W edge of the Smestow valley would have allowed them considerable tactical advantage. Both probably faced E.

Camp 4 lies less than 400 m WSW of fort A at about 75 m above OD, on a low irregular WSW to ENE saddle which may have conditioned its general siting. Cropmarks (CUCAP BDX 69) have revealed most of its subrectangular perimeter, but as yet evidence is lacking for its W side and its SW angle; a slight curve at the W end of the N side suggests that the overall dimensions were approximately 140 m N to S by about 235 m transversely, giving an area of about 3.3 ha (8.1 acres). No certain entrances can be identified, but they could coincide with one or more of several substantial interruptions in the cropmark of the perimeter ditch. The precise position of the N ditch was probably dictated by the presence of a hollow, just to the N

Figure 141 *Greensforge 4 and 5, Staffordshire. The possible E ditch of camp 5 is marked by the letter 'a'.*

Roman Camps in England

Figure 142 *Greensforge 1, 2 and 3, Staffordshire. Camp 2 seems to have reused the NW angle of camp 1, between forts A and B.*

Figure 143 *Greensforge, Staffordshire, from the NE. The SE third of fort B, together with its annexe, occupies the lower part of the photograph. Above its S corner is the outline of the E half of camp 2. The NW side and part of the SE side of camp 1 lie beside it to the SE. (12.7.75, CUCAP BUI 9)*

of the camp; the ground falls away in all directions, giving good views southwards along the valley of the Spittle Brook and down the Smestow Brook towards its confluence with the River Stour.

Camp 5, also visible as a cropmark in arable fields, is the largest of the group (CUCAP BDX 60). It lies less than 190 m N of camp 4 and is separated from it by the hollow already mentioned; it is situated on a pronounced W to E ridge which falls slightly to the E, but for the most part this is higher than the terrain occupied by camp 4. The layout of camp 5 was evidently rectangular. The E side has not been positively identified, and may have been obscured by activity connected with a probable civil settlement associated with the forts to the E (Webster 1981a). The cropmarks, however, do not confirm this. Its position on the E side of the camp could be indicated by a length of N to S ditch (a on Fig 141). If this possible line is accepted, the camp would have measured approximately 315 m N to S by 420 m E to W, enclosing an area of 13.2 ha (32.7 acres). The cropmark of the perimeter ditch is generally rather thin and no certain gates have been identified among the many interruptions in the S and E sides. Of all the establishments at Greensforge, it is camp 5 which utilises the local topography to best advantage. The most important factor in its detailed siting was the alignment of its W side, which occupies a local high point at about 90 m above OD. This gives commanding views W, S and N, with the camp at Swindon clearly in sight some 2 km to the N.

1:	SO 88 NE 1	Kinver
2:	SO 88 NE 1	Kinver
3:	SO 88 NE 15	Kinver
4:	SO 88 NE 13	Kinver
5:	SO 88 NE 14	Kinver and Swindon

Swindon *Fig 144*

SO 85569040

On the SE-facing slopes of a slight spur, above the W bank of the Smestow Brook and 500 m W of Swindon village, part of the defensive ditch of a camp has been revealed by aerial photography (St Joseph 1969, 104–5; 1973, 233; CUCAP ATG 38; BU 1). The camp apparently occupied a strong position on a fairly level shelf at 85 m above OD, on the edge of steep scarps which fall some 20 m north-eastwards to the valley floor. The N aspect affords impressive views up the valley of the Smestow Brook towards Wombourne and beyond, but also to the NW towards Smestow Gate, and to the E and S as far as Greensforge. Only to the W is the view obscured by a narrow N to S ridge about 1 km away, which rises to about 130 m above OD. In terms of military dispositions the camp is not isolated: the complex of forts and camps at Greensforge lies only 2 km to the SSE, and the Roman road that strikes N and NW from Droitwich (*Salinae*), via Greensforge, to Wroxeter (*Viroconium*) or to Redhill near Oakengates (Margary 1973, 295 (192)) passes only 180 m W of the SW corner of the camp.

The defensive circuit is not completely known, but the area within the ditch seems to measure about 480 m from WNW to ESE by about 320 m transversely, a ratio of 3:2, enclosing approximately 15 ha (38 acres). The perimeter is not exactly rectangular, the S and N angles being slightly acute. Moreover, the single gate in the centre of the NW side — the only one positively identified so far — is marked by a change in the alignment of the ditch, which bows outwards at the entrance gap, a feature evident in a number of other camps. The S part of the camp has been damaged by the construction of a pipeline just to the S of Whitehouse Lane (CUCAP AYA 49); this almost certainly accounts for the break in the SE side. In the 1960s, a section of the SE ditch,

Figure 144 *Swindon, Staffordshire.*

V-shaped and less than 0.9 m deep, was exposed in a roadside cutting (St Joseph 1969, 104), but this is now completely obscured by vegetation.

The precise orientation of the camp appears to have been influenced less by the course of the nearby Roman road, which may be of later construction, than by the local topography. The NE side is approximately parallel to the crest of the steep slopes above Swindon.

SO 89 SE 17   Swindon

Wall 1 and 2 *Fig 145*

1: SK 09040663   2: SK 09900640

A complex of military establishments, including two camps, a sequence of forts and a probable vexillation fortress, together with the later small fortified settlement or posting-station of *Letocetum*, has been recorded in the vicinity of the present village of Wall. The sites lie along Watling Street, the major Roman road from London to the legionary fortress of Wroxeter (*Viroconium*). The junction with Ryknield Street, a nodal point in the Roman road system of the region, lay only 0.5 km ESE of the present village (Margary 1973, 286 (18b), 291 (1h)).

Immediately N of Watling Street and less than 740 m W of the W corner of the fort, cropmarks have revealed the existence of camp 1 (St Joseph 1961, 123; CUCAP BEG 75). It lies on an E-facing valley side, at the point where the incline decreases a little to form a slight but gently sloping shelf. An unnamed stream in the bottom of a broad valley separates the camp from the main military complex around Wall village. There are good views SE, S and SW, but the outlook to the NE is blocked by rising ground. The NW quadrant of camp 1 is missing and the layout is not rectangular, the three visible corners being slightly acute (CUCAP BEG 73–8). The area enclosed comprises about 2.5 ha (6 acres). The S ditch, about 182 m long, and the E ditch, about 152 m long, are each interrupted, almost at their central points, for a gate; the same was probably also true of the W side. In no case, however, is any traverse evident. On topographical grounds, the camp appears to have faced E, its highest, W, side lying at the foot of steeper terrain to the W. The cropmarks of the ditch of the camp are relatively narrow, and are somewhat obscured by the marks of former field boundaries and ridge-and-furrow.

A small rectangular ditched enclosure, perhaps associated with the Roman road and adjacent to its N side, appears to overlie the SE corner of the camp (NAR SK 00 SE 12); their relative chronology cannot be determined without excavation. An extensive area W of the forts and N of the Roman road is known to have contained cemeteries (NAR SK 00 NE 4), and it is possible that this enclosure, and a very small square cropmark with a possible central pit visible in the NE corner of the camp, may represent burials. South of the A5 a dark rectangular feature is probably a medieval moated site. The traces of 'a much larger camp', in the SW quadrant of which this camp was said to lie (St Joseph 1973, 233), are not convincing as a camp and their function is unknown.

About 80 m to the S of Watling Street, the cropmarks of the rounded but slightly acute NW angle of what seems to be another camp, 2, are visible immediately SW of the defences of *Letocetum* (St Joseph 1973, 233). The N side of the camp appears to be cut through by these late perimeter ditches (CUCAP BDX 15–17) and the W side is overlain by the embankment of the Wall bypass, the present A5 road. The cropmark of a ditch, parallel to the town defences, also crosses the corner of the camp. The camp itself sits on the SSW-facing side of a small valley and its S extremity is likely to stop short of the flood plain, at least 100 m from the stream. The topography, however, does not even hint at a possible location for the E side. The camp commands extensive views to the S, and to the E along Watling Street, but is overlooked from the W and also from the N by the spur on which the village of Wall stands.

Topographically, each camp would have been quite satisfactory as an isolated unit. Nevertheless, the proximity of both to a sequence of forts (Gould 1964, 1967; Round 1970), which would have overlooked them, could suggest a relationship between the various establishments.

1: SK 00 NE 9   2: SK 00 NE 16   Wall

Water Eaton (Kinvaston or Stretton Mill) 1, 2; 3, 4 and 5 *Figs 146 and 147*

1: SJ 90371133   2: SJ 90381112
3: SJ 89821112   4: SJ 89951113
5: SJ 90001120

A large group of military installations, comprising a vexillation fortress, two forts and a number of camps, lies in the vicinity of Water Eaton and Stretton Mill (St Joseph 1965, 76–7), near the point where Watling Street, the early Roman road from London to the legionary fortress of Wroxeter (*Viroconium*), crosses the River Penk (Margary 1973, 291–2, (1h)). This strategic location developed into a nodal point in the Roman road system from which roads left Watling Street for Chester, Wroxeter, Greensforge, and perhaps Metchley. In the later Roman period a small defended settlement, probably a posting-station, called *Pennocrucium*, was laid out astride Watling Street.

The camps lie on either side of the Penk Valley, N of Watling Street. For the most part, the valley sides are quite gentle, but they are broken in places by steeper natural scarps. These have been exploited to good effect by the positioning of the various military installations which are all intervisible. Virtually all the features have been levelled by

Roman Camps in England

ploughing and most are covered with the marks of former ridge-and-furrow.

Camp 1 occupies a level terrace on the SE side of the valley, in the angle between the River Penk and an unnamed tributary flowing NW (NMR AP SJ 9011/44; CUCAP ADR 4; ADQ 90; BQW 67–8). Significant height differences over a relatively small area, as well as geological irregularities, have caused difficulties in plotting and have blurred the clarity of the cropmarks. However, the camp appears to be almost rectangular, though slightly narrower in its SW half, with broadly rounded corners. It measures approximately 162 m from NE to SW, by between about 92 m and 97 m transversely, and encloses an area of about 1.5 ha (3.8 acres). No certain entrances can be discerned, but a modern drain, which passes through the approximate centre of the NW and SE sides, may have utilised, and thereby obscured, original entrances at these points. Any central gate on the NE side is hidden by a profusion of cropmarks there. The N half of the NW side lies on the edge of a slight scarp, and is aligned approximately with it; this perhaps determined the overall axis of the camp, although the S part of this ditch awkwardly straddles the slope.

The camp has good views along the valley, but is totally overlooked from the E, SE and W; its only topographical advantage are the scarps down to the watercourses on the N and W. In all, its less than satisfactory position suggests that it may not have been a primary feature within the Roman landscape. Its position, only about 240 m WSW of the Kinvaston vexillation fortress (Webster 1955), may indicate a relationship between the two.

Staffordshire

Figure 145 *Wall 1 and 2, Staffordshire. The probable line of the W and N ditches of the posting station of* Letocetum *and the reconstructed defences of a sequence of superimposed forts are based on excavated evidence (after Gould 1964 and Round 1970).*

Camp 2 lies just over 50 m S of camp 1, on the same river terrace (St Joseph 1973, 133). Only the N angle and parts of two sides are known (CUCAP: BEG 80, 85, 90; CBC 65, 69; BQW 68, 70). The NW ditch is at least 200 m in length and is markedly realigned on either side of the pronounced entrance causeway. Evidence for a traverse protecting this gate gap is lacking. On the NE, the ditch of the camp is likely to have extended to approximately 175 m to take in a pronounced crest. The extra height at this point would have afforded good views up and down the Penk Valley, as well as to the E and W along Watling Street. The SE defensive line would therefore have lain W of Water Eaton Lane near the scarp edge. The topography is not particularly helpful in suggesting a possible position for the SW side, but the SE to NW lane linking Water Eaton Lane and Water Eaton itself occupies a slight natural hollow, which may have lain immediately outside and parallel to the defensive line. If these parameters are even approximate to the original extent of the camp, its total area would have been in the region of 3.3 ha (8 acres).

Three other cropmarks, each consisting of a right angle with a rounded corner, have been recorded on the W side of the Penk Valley and to the NE of the small fort at Stretton Mill. The most westerly example, camp 3, intersects with the defences of the fort there (CUCAP ADR 5–6; NMR AP 8911/1–2), and, if it is indeed a portion of a camp, as seems likely, it will have presumably preceded them. It is situated on the N edge of a slightly raised area, most of which is occupied by the fort. Much of the NE and part of the putative SE quadrant have been destroyed by quarrying; the

Roman Camps in England

Figure 146 *Water Eaton 1, 2, 3, 4 and 5, Staffordshire, with the vexillation fortress to the NE, the settlement of* Pennocrucium *to the S, and two forts.*

Staffordshire

Roman Camps in England

Figure 147 *Water Eaton 1, Staffordshire, from the SW. In addition to the perimeter of the camp, the photograph shows traces of ridge-and-furrow cultivation, a former hedge line and ditches of unknown date. (30.6.75, CUCAP BTM 40)*

former NE side is unlikely to have been more than 90 m in length as there is a 2 m drop in the natural valley scarp here. This topographical feature was clearly also respected by the SE side of the fort annexe. The fort and its annexe, and the later ridge-and-furrow, would mask the SW side of such a camp. It could perhaps have utilised the same crest line as the SW defences of the fort, although that would have resulted in somewhat elongated proportions. The site commands good views to the S along the Penk Valley, and to the NE towards Cannock Chase, and, though the outlook is restricted or very poor to the W and E, there seem to be reasonable grounds for accepting it as a probable camp.

The cropmarks of the possible camps 4 and 5 (NMR AP SJ 9911/1) lie NE of camp 3, on a shelf about 3 m to 4 m above the flood plain of the river. They occupy a relatively weak position, markedly inferior to that of camp 3. They are completely overlooked by higher ground to the W but command good views towards the NE. Neither is likely to have extended E of the valley scarp. For this reason camp 4, comprising parts of a NE and NW side and a N angle, would have been proportionately very narrow in its NW to SE dimension; quarrying and part of a former leat have destroyed the SW segment. Similarly camp 5, represented by a SSW corner and by fragments of the W and S sides, would also have been disproportionately narrow from E to W. The unsatisfactory position of these possible camps suggests that they would not have been designed to stand alone.

Within the whole Water Eaton complex none of the camps occupies a position as good as those utilised by the two forts and the vexillation fortress. The presumption must be that, with the possible exception of camp 3, each of them was dependent upon one of the permanent establishments.

1: SJ 91 SW 27   Penkridge
2: SJ 91 SW 37   Penkridge
3: SJ 81 SE 22   Stretton Mill
4: SJ 81 SE 23   Stretton Mill
5: SJ 81 SE 24   Stretton Mill

Addenda

Middlewich, Cheshire

SJ 70216696

On the W side of King Street, to the N of Middlewich (*Salinae*) and just to the S of the crossing of the River Dane, geophysical survey and sample excavation in 1993 revealed a camp, almost square in plan, which enclosed an area of approximately 1.2 ha (3.2 acres). In the E and W sides there was a gate, marked by a causeway across the ditch at the central point; on the N and S the gates were offset to the E towards the Roman road. The excavators suggested the possible presence of a timber building within the interior. (Information from Gifford and Partners.)

SJ 76 NW 21   Middlewich

Mindrum, Northumberland

NT 84133311

Air photography by Tim Gates in 1994 revealed the cropmarks of part of the perimeter of a camp on low ground to the NW of the Bowmont Water, at 85 m above OD. The cropmarks define four sides of an irregular polygon measuring about 500 m from NE to SW by at least 240 m transversely. One gate, defended by a traverse, is identifiable in the centre of the short N side.

NT 83 SW 51   Carham

Red House, Northumberland

NY 96816526

The cropmarks of a camp, which measured approximately 130 m from E to W by 75 m transversely and which enclosed an area of 1.0 ha (2.4 acres), were recorded from the air by Tim Gates in 1994. Its position and the comparative clarity of the cropmarks suggest that the E third of the camp overlies a NW portion of the Agricolan vexillation fortress at Red House (NY 96 NE 37; Hanson *et al* 1979). Two gates are visible, at the central point of the E and W sides, each defended by a traverse.

NY 96 NE 48   Sandhoe

Asthall, Oxfordshire

SP 28401080

On the S side of Akeman Street, about 1 km SW of the crossing of the Windrush, the cropmarks of a camp were identified and photographed from the air by the RCHME in 1994. Aligned on the road, the camp is almost square, measuring 98 m from NW to SE by 86 m transversely, an area of 0.8 ha (2.1 acres). Immediately to the SW are the cropmarks of an enclosure, possibly of Iron Age date.

SP 21 SE 121   Asthall

References

Allan, T M and Richardson, G G S 1978. 'The lost Roman Road from Hutton Moor to the Vale of Keswick'. *Archaeol Newsbulletin* CBA Regional Group 3, 2 ser **6** (Dec 1978), 13–15

1980. 'The lost Roman road from Hutton Moor to the Vale of Keswick'. *Archaeol Newsbulletin* CBA Regional Group 3, 2 ser **11** (Sept 1980), 10–12

Allen, J 1990. *The Roman fort at Pentrehyling, Shropshire. Summary of excavation and survey 1978–90*. Privately issued typescript

Annis, R G forthcoming. 'Bowes Moor', in Vyner, B E (ed) *The Stainmore Pass. An Archaeological and Palaeo-environmental Survey of Bowes Moor*

Austen, P S 1977. 'Haltwhistle Common, Northumberland'. *Archaeol Newsbulletin* CBA Regional Group 3, 2 ser **1** (April 1977), 6

1991. *Bewcastle and Old Penrith*. Cumberland Westmorland Antiq Archaeol Soc Res Ser 6. Kendal

Baker, A 1970. 'Viroconium: a study of the defences from aerial reconnaissance'. *Trans Shropshire Archaeol Soc* **58** (1965–8), 197–219

1972. 'Aerial reconnaissance over Viroconium and military sites in the area in 1969'. *Trans Shropshire Archaeol Soc* **59** (1969–74), 24–31

Barker, P 1985. 'Aspects of the topography of Wroxeter (Viroconium Cornoviorum)', in Grew, F and Hobley, B *Roman Urban Topography in Britain and the Western Empire*, CBA Res Rep 59, 109–17

Bellhouse, R L 1954. 'The Roman road from Old Penrith to Keswick, and beyond'. *Trans Cumberland Westmorland Antiq Archaeol Soc* 2 ser **54**, 17–27

1956. 'The Roman temporary camps near Troutbeck'. *Trans Cumberland Westmorland Antiq Archaeol Soc* 2 ser **56**, 28–36

Bennett, J 1980. '"Temporary" camps along Hadrian's Wall', in Hanson, W S and Keppie, L J F (eds) *Roman Frontier Studies 1979*, Papers presented to the 12th International Congress of Roman Frontier Studies. Brit Archaeol Rep Int Ser 71, 151–72. Oxford

Bishop, M C and Freeman, P W M 1993. 'Recent work at Osmanthorpe, Nottinghamshire'. *Britannia* **24**, 159–89

Bosanquet, R C 1925. 'The Makendon camps'. *Hist Berwickshire Natur Club* **25** (1923–5), 59–69

Bowman, A K and Thomas, J D 1991. 'A military strength report from Vindolanda'. *J Roman Stud* **81**, 62–73

Breeze, D J and Dobson, B 1985. 'Roman military deployment in North England'. *Britannia* **16**, 1–19

Campbell, D B 1984. '*Ballistaria* in first to mid-third century Britain: a reappraisal'. *Britannia* **15**, 75–84

Cane, J and Allen, J 1989. *The Archaeological Evaluation of a Cropmark Complex at Brompton, Shropshire*. Birmingham Univ Fld Archaeol Unit and Central Marches Archaeol Res Group

Charlesworth, D 1974. 'Temporary camp and fort, Troutbeck'. *Archaeol Newsbulletin* CBA Regional Group 3, **6** (Jan 1974), 7

Charlton, B and Mitcheson, M 1984. 'The Roman cemetery at Petty Knowes, Rochester, Northumberland'. *Archaeol Aeliana* 5 ser **12**, 1–31

Collingwood, R G 1930. *The Archaeology of Roman Britain*. London

Collingwood, W G 1927. 'Rey-Cross'. *Trans Cumberland Westmorland Antiq Archaeol Soc* 2 ser **27**, 1–10

Cunliffe, B W (ed) 1968. *Fifth Report on the Excavations of the Roman Fort at Richborough, Kent*. Oxford

Daniels, C M 1978. *Handbook to the Roman Wall*. (J Collingwood Bruce, 13th edn.) Newcastle upon Tyne

Daniels, C M and Jones, G D B 1969. 'The Roman camps on Llandrindod Common'. *Archaeol Cambrensis* **118**, 124–34

Davies, R W 1989. *Service in the Roman Army*. Edinburgh

Day, W 1978. 'Temporary Roman camp at Perry Farm, Whittington'. *Trans Shropshire Archaeol Soc* **59** (1969–74), 280–1

Edwards, D E 1976. 'The air photographs collection of the Norfolk Archaeological Unit'. *East Anglian Archaeol* **2**, 251–69

1978. 'The air photographs collection of the Norfolk Archaeological Unit: Third Report'. *East Anglian Archaeol* **8**, 87–105

English Heritage 1986. *Preservation by Record: the Work of the Central Excavation Unit 1975–85*. London

Farrar, R A H 1980. 'Roman signal-stations over Stainmore and beyond', in Hanson, W S and Keppie, L J F (eds) *Roman Frontier Studies 1979*, Papers presented to the 12th International Congress of Roman Frontier Studies. Brit Archaeol Rep Int Ser **71**, 211–31. Oxford

Frere, S S 1987. 'Brandon Camp, Herefordshire'. *Britannia* **18**, 49–92. Cambridge

Frere, S S and St Joseph J K S 1983. *Roman Britain from the Air*. Cambridge

Gibson, J P and Simpson, F G 1909. 'The Roman fort on the Stanegate at Haltwhistle Burn'. *Archaeol Aeliana* 3 ser **5**, 213–85

Gould, J 1964. 'Excavations at Wall (Staffordshire), 1961–3, on the site of the early Roman forts and of the late Roman defences'. *Trans Lichfield South Staffordshire Archaeol Hist Soc* **5** (1963–4), 1–50

—— 1967. 'Excavations at Wall, Staffs, 1964–66, on the site of the Roman forts'. *Trans Lichfield South Staffordshire Archaeol Hist Soc* **8** (1966–7), 1–40

Griffith, F M 1984. 'Roman military sites in Devon: some recent discoveries'. *Proc Devon Archaeol Soc* **42**, 11–32

Hanson, W S 1978. 'Roman campaigns north of the Forth-Clyde isthmus: the evidence of the temporary camps'. *Proc Soc Antiq Scotl* **109** (1977–8), 140–50

Hanson, W S, Daniels, C M, Dore, J N and Gillam, J P G 1979. 'The Agricolan supply-base at Red House, Corbridge'. *Archaeol Aeliana* 5 ser **7**, 1–97

Hartley, B R 1972. 'The Roman occupations of Scotland: the evidence of the samian ware'. *Britannia* **3**, 1–55

Hedley, W P 1934. 'Notes on hut circles, sow kilns and coins'. *Proc Soc Antiq Newcastle* 4 ser **6** (1933–4), 307–8

Henderson, A A R and Keppie, L J F 1987. 'Titulus or titulum?' *Britannia* **18**, 281–4

Higham, N and Jones, B 1985. *The Carvetii*. Gloucester

Hodgson, J 1840. *History of Northumberland* pt ii, vol iii. Newcastle

Horsley, J 1732. *Britannia Romana*. London

Houghton, A W J 1962. 'The Roman road from Greensforge through the Central Welsh March'. *Trans Shropshire Archaeol Soc* **56** (1957–60), 233–43

—— 1966. 'A Roman road from Ashton, North Herefordshire to Marshbrook, Salop'. *Trans Shropshire Archaeol Soc* **57** (1961–4), 185–90.

Hughes, E G 1992. *Excavations at Bromfield, Shropshire 1991: an Interim Report*. Birmingham Univ Fld Archaeol Unit Rep 193

Hutchinson, W 1776. *An Excursion to the Lakes in Westmoreland and Cumberland; with a Tour Through Part of the Northern Counties in the Years 1773 and 1774*. London

Hyginus. *De munitionibus castrorum*. Lenoir, M (ed) 1979: Pseudo-Hygin, *Des fortifications du camp*. Paris

Jobey, G 1966. 'A note on "sow" kilns'. *J Univ Newcastle Agr Soc* **20**, 2–3

—— 1968. 'Excavations of cairns at Chatton Sandyford, Northumberland'. *Archaeol Aeliana* 4 ser **46**, 5–50

—— 1978. 'Burnswark Hill, Dumfriesshire'. *Trans Dumfries Galloway Natur Hist Antiq Soc* 3 ser **53** (1977–8), 57–104

Jones, A E 1991. 'Prehistoric and Roman features', in Jones, A E, Sterenberg, S, Richardson, S and Ferris, I M *Brompton, Shropshire, Excavations 1990: Site Narratives and Post-Excavation Research Design*. Birmingham Univ Fld Archaeol Unit Rep 155, 1–12

Jones, G D B 1976. *Hadrian's Wall from the Air*. Manchester

—— 1991. 'The emergence of the Tyne-Solway frontier', in Maxfield, V A and Dobson, M J (eds) *Roman Frontier Studies 1989. Proceedings of the XVth International Congress of Roman Frontier Studies*. Exeter

—— 1992. 'Old Police House Camp, Bowness-on-Solway'. *Britannia* **23**, 230–1

Jones, G D B and Maude, K 1985. *Solway Frontier 1984*. Duplicated typescript compilation

Jones, L 1993. *Bromfield Barrow Survey 1993*. Birmingham Univ Fld Archaeol Unit Rep 29

Jones, M J 1975. *Roman Fort-defences to AD 117*. Brit Archaeol Rep Brit Ser 21. Oxford (reprinted 1977)

Josephus. *Bellum Judaicum*

Leach, P 1989. *Bromfield: The Excavation of Ring Ditch B8, 1989. An Interim Report*. Birmingham Univ Fld Archaeol Unit.

Lenoir, M 1977. 'Lager mit Claviculae'. *Mélanges de l'école Française de Rome (Antiquités)* **89**, 697–722

—— 1979. *see* Hyginus

Lepper F and Frere, S S 1988. *Trajan's Column*. Gloucester

Livy. *Periochiae*

Lukis, W C (ed) 1887. *The Family Memoirs of the Rev William Stukeley MD, and of William Stukeley, Roger and Samuel Gale, etc Vol III*. Surtees Soc **80** (1885)

Lysons, D and Lysons, S 1816. *Magna Britannia, Vol 4, Cumberland*. London

MacDonald, G 1916. 'The Roman camps at Raedykes and Glenmailen'. *Proc Soc Antiq Scotl* **50** (1915–16), 317–59

—— 1917. 'General William Roy and his "Military Antiquities of the Romans in North Britain"'. *Archaeologia* **68** (1916–17), 161–228

MacLauchlan, H 1849. 'On the Roman roads, camps and other earthworks between the Tees and the Swale'. *Archaeol J* **6**, 213–25, 335–51

—— 1852a. *Memoir written during a Survey of the Watling Street from the Tees to the Scotch Border in 1850 and 1851*. London

—— 1852b. *The Watling Street . . . from the River Swale to the Scotch Border . . . from the Original Surveys*. Folio volume of plans and surveys, privately printed for the Duke of Northumberland

—— 1857. *The Roman Wall. And illustrations of the principal vestiges of Roman occupation in the North of England. Consisting of plans of the military works, the stations, camps, ancient ways, and other remains of the earlier periods, in the Northern Counties*. Atlas volume. London

—— 1858. *Memoir written during a survey of the Roman Wall through the Counties of Northumberland and Cumberland, in the years 1852–1854*. London

—— 1864. *Memoir written during a survey of the Eastern branch of the Watling Street in the County of Northumberland*. Atlas volume. London

Margary, I D 1973. *Roman Roads in Britain*, 3rd edn. London

Maxwell, G S 1981. 'Agricola's campaigns: the evidence of the temporary camps', in Kenworthy, J (ed) *Agricola's Campaigns in Scotland* (*Scott Archaeol Forum* **12**), 25–54. Edinburgh

—— 1982. 'Roman temporary camps at Inchtuthil: an examination of the aerial photographic evidence'. *Scott Archaeol Rev* **1**, 105–13

—— 1989. *The Romans in Scotland*. Edinburgh

Maxwell, G S and Wilson, D R 1987. 'Air reconnaissance in Roman Britain 1977–84'. *Britannia* **18**, 1–48

Milner, N P 1993. *see* Vegetius

Newbold, P 1913. 'Excavations on the Roman Wall at Limestone Bank'. *Archaeol Aeliana* 3 ser **9**, 54–74

Pitts, L F and St Joseph, J K 1985. *Inchtuthil*. Britannia Monogr Ser 6. London

Poulter, A 1982. 'Old Penrith: Excavations 1977 and 1979'. *Trans Cumberland Westmorland Antiq Archaeol Soc* **82**, 51–65

Ramm, H G 1953. 'Roman camps on Bootham Stray, York'. *Trans Yorkshire Philosophical Soc* (1952), 15–20

RIB. Collingwood, R G and Wright, R P 1965. *The Roman Inscriptions of Britain, 1: Inscriptions on Stone*. Oxford

Richmond, I A 1926. 'The Roman camps at Cawthorn, near Pickering'. *Yorkshire Archaeol J* **28** (1925–6), 332–9, 421–6

1929. 'The Roman camps at Cawthorn, near Pickering'. *Yorkshire Archaeol J* **29** (1927–9), 90–6, 225–31, 327–31

1932. 'The four Roman camps at Cawthorn, in the North Riding of Yorkshire'. *Archaeol J* **89**, 17–78

1940. 'The Romans in Redesdale', in Hope Dodds, M (ed) *History of Northumberland* vol 15, 63–154. Newcastle

1951. 'Exploratory trenching at the Roman fort of Cappuck, Roxburghshire, in 1949'. *Proc Soc Antiq Scotl* **85** (1950–1), 138–45

Richmond, I A and Askew, G 1937. 'The Roman road from High Rochester (Bremenium) to Bridge of Aln'. *Proc Soc Antiq Newcastle* 4 ser **8** (1937–8), 44–52

Richmond, I A and Hodgson, K S 1936. 'The Roman temporary camp at Watchcross'. *Trans Cumberland Westmorland Antiq Archaeol Soc* 2 ser **36**, 170–2

Richmond, I A and Keeney, G S 1937. 'The Roman works at Chew Green, Coquetdalehead'. *Archaeol Aeliana* 4 ser **14**, 129–50

Richmond, I A and McIntyre, J 1934. 'The Roman camps at Rey Cross and Crackenthorpe'. *Trans Cumberland Westmorland Antiq Archaeol Soc* 2 ser **34**, 50–61

Richmond, I A and St Joseph, K 1941. 'A Roman camp at Silloans, High Rochester'. *Proc Soc Antiq Newcastle* 4 ser **9** (1939–41), 110–13

Ridpath, G 1810. *The Border History of England and Scotland*. London

Riley, D N 1977. 'Roman defended sites at Kirmington, S Humberside and Farnsfield, Notts, recently found from the air'. *Britannia* **8**, 189–92

1980a. *Early Landscape from the Air. Studies of Crop Marks in South Yorkshire and North Nottinghamshire*. Sheffield

1980b. 'Two new Roman military stations in Mid-Nottinghamshire'. *Britannia* **11**, 330–5

1983. 'Temporary camps at Calverton, Notts'. *Britannia* **14**, 270–1

Robinson, P forthcoming. 'Rey Cross', in Vyner, B E (ed) *The Stainmore Pass. An Archaeological and Palaeo-environmental Survey of Bowes Moor*

Round, A A 1970. 'Excavations at Wall, Staffordshire, 1966–67, on the site of the Roman forts' (Wall Excavation Report No. 9). *Trans Lichfield South Staffordshire Archaeol Hist Soc* **11** (1969–70), 7–31

Roy, W 1793. *The Military Antiquities of the Romans in North Britain*. Society of Antiquaries of London. London

RCAHMS 1956. Royal Commission on the Ancient and Historical Monuments of Scotland, *An Inventory of the Ancient and Historical Monuments of Roxburghshire*. Edinburgh

1957. *An Inventory of the Ancient and Historical Monuments of Selkirkshire*. Edinburgh

1978. *Lanarkshire: An Inventory of the Prehistoric and Roman Monuments*. Edinburgh

RCHME 1970. Royal Commission on the Historical Monuments of England, *Shielings and Bastles*. London

St Joseph, J K S 1935. 'Roman camps near High Rochester from the air'. *Proc Soc Antiq Newcastle* 4 ser **6** (1933–4), 238–43

1951. 'Air reconnaissance of North Britain'. *J Roman Stud* **41**, 52–65

1953. 'Air reconnaissance of Southern Britain'. *J Roman Stud* **43**, 81–97

1955. 'Air reconnaissance in Britain 1951–5'. *J Roman Stud* **45**, 82–91

1958. 'Air reconnaissance in Britain 1955–7'. *J Roman Stud* **48**, 86–101

1961. 'Air reconnaissance in Britain, 1958–60'. *J Roman Stud* **51**, 119–35

1965. 'Air reconnaissance in Britain, 1961–64'. *J Roman Stud* **55**, 74–89

1966. 'Air reconnaissance: recent results, 8'. *Antiquity* **40**, 300–4

1969. 'Air reconnaissance in Britain, 1965–68'. *J Roman Stud* **59**, 104–28

1973. 'Air reconnaissance in Britain, 1969–72'. *J Roman Stud* **63**, 214–46

1977. 'Air reconnaissance in Roman Britain, 1973–76'. *J Roman Stud* **67**, 125–61

Sallust. *Jugurtha*

Selkirk, R 1980. 'Aerial archaeological survey: possible Roman and Romano-British sites in northern England'. *Archaeol Newsbulletin* CBA Regional Group 3, 2 ser **12** (Dec 1980), 16–17

Silvester, R J 1978. 'Cropmark sites at North Tawton and Alverdiscott'. *Proc Devon Archaeol Soc* **36**, 249–54

Simpson, F G 1926. 'The Roman camps at Cawthorn, near Pickering'. *Yorkshire Archaeol J* **28** (1925–6), 25–33

Skinner, J 1978. *Hadrian's Wall in 1801*. (Coombs, H and P, eds) Bath

Smith, A H 1928. *The Place-names of the North Riding of Yorkshire*. English Place-name Society V. Cambridge

Stanford, S C 1970a. 'The Roman marching camp at Bromfield (Salop)'. *Trans Shropshire Archaeol Soc* **58** (1965–8), 195–6

1970b. 'The Roman forts at Leintwardine and Buckton'. *Trans Woolhope Natur Fld Club* **39** (2) (1968), 222–326

1982. 'Bromfield, Shropshire — Neolithic, Beaker and Bronze Age sites, 1966–79'. *Proc Prehist Soc* **48**, 279–320

1985. 'Bromfield excavations — from Neolithic to Saxon times'. *Trans Shropshire Archaeol Soc* **64** (1983–4), 1–7

1991. *The Welsh Marches*. 2nd edn, privately printed. Leinthall Starkes

Steer, K A and Feachem, R W 1954. 'The Roman fort and temporary camp at Oakwood, Selkirkshire'. *Proc Soc Antiq Scotl* **86** (1951–2), 81–105

Swarbrick, C J and Turner, J 1982. 'Excavations at Farnsfield Roman Camp, Nottinghamshire'. *Trans Thoroton Soc of Notts* (1982), 108–10

Todd, M 1981. *The Roman Town at Ancaster, Lincolnshire: The Excavations of 1955–71*. Nottingham

van Driel-Murray, C 1990. 'New light on old tents'. *J Roman Military Equipment Stud* **1**, 109–37

Vegetius. *Epitoma rei militaris*. Milner, N P (ed and trans) 1993: Vegetius, *Epitome of Military Science*. Liverpool

Wallis, J 1769. *The Natural History and Antiquities of Northumberland*, II. London

Watson, M D 1988 (unpubl). *Investigations at Bromfield, 1988*. Summary in Shropshire County Council Archaeological Records.

Webster, G 1955. 'Further excavations at the Roman fort, Kinvaston, Staffordshire'. *Trans Birmingham Archaeol Soc* **73**, 100–8

1966. 'Fort and town in Early Roman Britain', in Wacher, J S (ed) *The Civitas Capitals of Roman Britain*, 31–45. Leicester

1981a. 'Further light on the Roman site at Greensforge'. *Trans Birmingham Warwickshire Archaeol Soc* **91**, 126–32

1981b. *Rome against Caratacus*. London

1988. 'Wroxeter (*Viroconium*)', in Webster, G (ed) *Fortress into City*, 120–44. London

1989. '*Viroconium* from the air', in Kennedy, D I (ed) *Into the Sun: Essays in Air Photography in Archaeology in Honour of Derrick Riley*, 200–7. Sheffield

Welfare, A T 1986. 'The Greenlee Lough (Northumberland) palimpsest: an interim report on the 1985 season'. *Northern Archaeol* **7**, pt 2, 35–7

Whimster, R 1989. *The Emerging Past*. London

Wilson, D R 1984a. 'Defensive outworks of Roman forts in Britain'. *Britannia* **15**, 51–61

1984b. 'The plan of Viroconium Cornoviorum'. *Antiquity* **58**, 117–20

Wilson, P R 1984. 'Recent work at Catterick', in Wilson, P R, Jones, R F J and Evans, D M (eds) *Settlement and Society in the Roman North*, 75–82. Leeds

Index

Page references in **bold** indicate illustrations and tables

aerial photography 3, 6, 21
Agricola, period of 25, 111, 181
agriculture
    and camp survivals 3, 6
    cord-rig cultivation **14**, 104, 107, **108**, 110, 131
    effects of 38, 42, 43, 51, 80, 94, 95, 113, **128**, 135, 136, 170
    enclosures 36
    field systems 10, 149, 168
    lack of cultivation 84
    medieval 26
    and medieval common land 135
    modern drainage systems 26–7, **27**
    and modern ploughing 18
    pastoral 3, 135
    post-Roman enclosures 33–4
    traces of former 103
    water-pipes 145
    see also cropmarks; ridge-and-furrow cultivation
airfields
    Bootham Stray 135, 136
    Uckington 150, 158
Alcester 64
Alverdiscott *see* Higher Kingdon
Ancaster (Lincolnshire) 5, **67**, 67
    fort 67
Anglo-Saxon burials 153
Anglo-Scottish wars 26
Annandale 31, 36
annexes
    additions of 17
    Bagraw (Northumberland) 74
    Brompton (Shropshire) 154
    Chew Green 86, **89**, 89
    Greensforge (Staffordshire) 170, **173**
    Moss Side (Cumbria) 41
    see also Cawthorn
aqueduct: Great Chesters fort 85
Arnold (Nottinghamshire) 146
ascensus 20, 80, 81, 83, 100, 139
Ashmolean Museum, Oxford 88
Asthall (Oxfordshire) 181
Atcham 158
Attingham Park (Shropshire) 5, 150, **151**, 158, 159
Aylsham (Norfolk) 70

Bagraw (Northumberland) 5, 15, 17, 72–4, **73**
Baker, Arnold 6
Baldersdale 58
'*ballistaria*' 88

banks
    and camp size/design 10
    construction 1, 3, 17
    of earth and stone 75, 77, 80, 133
    and gates 19, 20
    of turf **18**, 57, 79, 80, 127, 138, 139, 140, 147
    and turf/clay 45
    see also claviculae; ramparts; traverses
Barrockside (Cumbria) 5, **30**, 30–1
    asymmetry of 16
    and camp orientation 14
    gates 19
barrows
    Birdhope (Northumberland) 25
    Knockcross (Cumbria) 40
    prehistoric 10, 22, 142, **153**, 153, 164
    Roman 25, 79, 113, **114**
    The Rossett (Brompton) 154
    round 66
    see also burials
The Barton (Devon) 54, 56
basketwork 22, 38
Bean Burn (Northumberland) 10, **74**
    camp 1   5, 74
    camp 2   5, 24, 75
Beaumont (Cumbria) 5, 27, **31**, 31
    labour camp 24
Bell Brook, valley of (Shropshire) 159
Bellshiel Law (Northumberland) 75, 123, 125
Bellshiel (Northumberland) 5, 75–7, **76**
    camp design 10
    claviculae/traverses 20, 21
    coal-pits 27
    defences 15, 17
    later use of site 27
    and prehistoric remains 10, 22
Bendibus Shiel (Northumberland) 118
berms 17, 38, 45, 58, 89, 104, 107, 125, 136, 138, 147
Birdhope Craig (Northumberland) 125
Birdhope (Northumberland) 77–9, **78**
    clavicula 20
    coal-pits 27
    dating 25
    later use of site 27
    camp 1   5, 22, **23**, 77, 79
    camp 2   5, 14, 17, 22, **23**, 79
    camp 3   5, 22, **23**, 79
Birtley parish (Northumberland) 131
Bishopsmoat (Shropshire) 154
Blakehope (Northumberland) 92
    fort 72
Blencathra (Cumbria) 45
bog/marshland 8, 22, 129

and gates 20
and siting of camps 8
peat 41, 95
Malham 144
Plumpton Head 43
Rey Cross 58
Smestow Brook (Staffordshire) 170
Whittington 168
Boomby Lane (Cumbria) 5, 31–2, **32**
    gates 18, 19
    labour camp 24
    site reuse 23
    topography 8, 16
    camp 1   31–2
    camp 2   31, 32
Bootham Stray (North Yorkshire) 5, **135**, 135–6
    camp orientation 14
    clavicula 20
    multiple camps 10, 24
    camp 1 **135**, 135–6
    camp 2 **135**, 135, 136
boundaries, field
    and camp defences 27
    Ancaster 67
    Bagraw 72
    Beaumont 31
    Bellshiel 75
    Brampton Bryan 63
    Breckenbrough **136**
    Brompton 154
    Buckton Park 64
    Burlington **157**, 157
    Cawfields 83
    Cound Hall 158
    Farnley 96
    Fell End 101
    Glenwhelt Leazes 103
    Golden Fleece 38
    Higher Kingdon 54
    Horstead 71
    Lees Hall 111
    Moss Side 41
    Plumpton Head 44
    Rey Cross 60
    Seatsides 120
    Silloans 125
    Stretford Bridge 164
    Troutbeck 48
    Uffington 164
    Upper Affcot 166
    Walford 66
Bowes (*Lavatris*): fort 57, 59, 60
Bowes Moor (County Durham) 5, **57**, 57, 60
    construction of defences 17
    as labour camp 24

Bowmont Water (Northumberland) 181
Bowness-on-Solway (*Maia*): fort 40
Brackenrigg 1 and 2 (Cumbria) 5, 32–4, **33**
   defences 18
   samian pottery 25
   site reuse 22
Brackies Burn (Northumberland) 120, **123**, 123, 131
Brampton Bryan (Hereford and Worcester) 5, **61**, 61–3, 65
   camp size 11
   gates 19
   later use of site 26
Brandon Brook, valley of (Hereford and Worcester) 64
Brandon Camp (Hereford and Worcester): Iron Age 65
Brathay Centre 46
Breckenbrough (North Yorkshire) 5, **136**, 136
Briggle Beck (Cumbria) 41
Bromfield (Shropshire) 5, 150–3, **152**, **153**
   defences 17–18
   gates 19
   ovens 22
   and prehistoric remains 10, 22
Brompton (Shropshire)
   and camp size/design 10–11
   defences 18
   prehistoric remains 10, 22
   proximity of fort 10, 154
   site reuse 22
   camp 1   5, 9, 25, 154, **155**
   camp 2   5, 154, **155**
Brompton-on-Swale (North Yorkshire) 137
Bronze Age: burials **153**, 153
Broomhope Burn (Northumberland) 130
Brough (*Crococalana*): Roman town (Nottinghamshire) 149
Brough under Stainmore (*Verteris*): fort 51, 57, 59, 60
Brougham (Cumbria) 5, **34**, 34, 51
   Brocavum (fort) 34, 41, 44
   and camp surveying 15–16
   later use of site 27
   use of higher ground 8
Brown Dikes (Northumberland) 5, 79–80, **80**
   camp design 10
   and camp surveying 15
   early discovery 1
   later use of site 23, 26
Brown Moor (Northumberland) 79
Brownhart Law 85, 90
Buckton (Hereford and Worcester): fort 10, **63**, 63, 64, 65
Buckton Park (Hereford and Worcester) 5, **63**, 63–4
   and camp surveying 15
   as labour camp 24
   use of higher ground 8
buildings
   remains of 112
   of timber 19, 24, 64, 90, 131, 181
   of turf 110, 142
   see also stone
Bure valley (Norfolk) 70
Burgh-by-Sands (*Aballava*): fort 31

burials
   Anglo-Saxon/early Christian 153
   Birdhope (Northumberland) 25
   Bronze Age **153**, 153
   Brougham (Cumbria) **34**, 34
   cairns 117
   Catterick 137
   Great Chesters (*Aesica*) 113
   Petty Knowes cemetery 79
   Roman **78**, 79, 113
   Wall (Staffordshire) 175
   see also barrows
Burlington (Shropshire) **156**, 156–7, **157**
   camp surveying 15
   defences 18
   site reuse 22
   camp 1   5, 9, 156, **157**, 157
   camp 2   5, **157**, 157
Burnhead Crag (Northumberland) 107, 110
Burnhead (Northumberland) 5, 80–1, **81**, 107
   camp design 10
   camp orientation 11, 14
   dating 25
   function 24
   and gate defence 20
   later use of site 27
   use of higher ground 7
Burnswark (Annandale and Eskdale) 36
Buzzard Hill (County Durham) 57
Byne Brook (Shropshire) 162, 165

Caebitra, valley of 154
cairns, prehistoric 10, 22, 75, **76**, 117
Calverton (Nottinghamshire) 5, 8, **146**, 146–7
   site reuse 22
   atypical features 15
   camp 1   146–7
   camp 2   146, 147
Camlad, valley of 154
camps
   asymmetrical 51, 95
   atypical plans 15
   choice of site 6–10
   classification 1–2, 24
   design and construction 1, 2–3, 10–11, **11**, **12–13**, 14–17
   distribution 3, **4–7**, 6, 11, **62**
   and forts 1, 22, 24
   function 2, 23–4
   internal structures 21–2
   in later landscape 26–7
   orientation 7, 11, **12–13**, 14
   proportions and size 10–11, **11**
   reuse of 22–3
   surveying 7, 15–16
   see also dating; defences; gates; labour camps; marching camps; practice camps; topography *and* individual camps
Cannock Chase (Staffordshire) 180
Cappuck (Roxburgh) 88
Carham (Northumberland) 5, 24, 26, **82**, 82
Carleton (Cumbria) 8, 38
Carlisle 15, 41
   airport 51
   Luguvalium 30, 36, 38, 39, 40, 43, 51, 57, 107

Carvoran (*Magnis*): fort 100, 101, 103, 104
Castle Douglas: Glenlochar (Stewartry) 41
castles, medieval 3
castrametation, science of 24
Catterick Bridge (North Yorkshire) 5, 136–7, **137**
Catterick (*Cataractonium*): town 137
Catterick Racecourse 136, 137
Caw Burn (Northumberland) 82, 85
Cawfields (Northumberland) 5, **82**, 82–3, **83**, 107
   camp orientation 11
   dating 25
   function 24
   gates 19, 20
   traverse 20
Cawfields Quarry (Northumberland) **108**, **109**
Cawthorn (North Yorkshire) 1, 3, 25, 137–42
   camp (C) 5, 137–40, **138–9**, **140**, **141**, 141, **142**
   claviculae 20, **141**
   defences 17, **18**, 18
   function 24
   gates 19
   internal structures 22
   later use of site 26
   siting of 8
   unusual features 16
   fort (A) 24, 88, 137, **138–9**, 140–2, **141**
      annexe (B) 137, **138–9**, 141, 142; *claviculae* 20; timberwork 24
   claviculae/traverses 21
   fort (D) 10, 137, **138–9**, **140**, 140, **141**, 141
cemeteries *see* burials
Chapel Rigg (Northumberland) 5, 83–4, **84**
   claviculae/traverses **21**, 21
   dating 25
   function 24
   gates 19
   topography 8, 16
Cheshire 175, 181
Chester 175
Chesterhope (Northumberland) 133
Chesters Pike (Northumberland) 5, 8, 24, **85**, 85
Cheviot Hills (Northumberland) 16, 21, 133
Chew Green (Northumberland) ii, 85–90, **89**, 97
   choice of site 1, 7
   site reuse 22, 23
   camp I 5, 23, 85–6, **87**, 88, **89**, 89
      camp design 10
      clavicula 20
      construction 17
      later use of site 26
      site of gate 19
   II ('fortlet') 88, 89
   camp III 5, 23, 85, 86, **87**, 88, **89**, 89
      and adjacent road 9
      camp design 10
      defences 17, 21
      later use of site 27
   IV (fort) **ii**, 10, 21, 24, 85, 86, **87**, 88, **89**, 89
   V (fortlet) 26, 85, 86, **87**, 88–9, **89**, 90

Church Stoke (Shropshire) 154
Church Stretton Gap (Shropshire) 151, 154, 165
civil engineering 6, 23–4
classification 1–2, 24
Claudio-Neronian period 170
claviculae 19, 20
   and camp chronology 21
   Bean Burn 2 75
   Bellshiel 77
   Birdhope **23**, 77, 79
   Bootham Stray 136
   Brackenrigg 33
   Burlington 156
   Cawthorn 25, 139, 140, **141**, 141–2
   Chapel Rigg **21**, 84
   Chew Green 86, 88, 89
   Dargues 94
   Featherwood West 100
   Glenwhelt Leazes 103, 104
   Greenlee Lough 104
   Haltwhistle Burn 110
   Lees Hall 111
   Malham 144
   Markham Cottage 113
   Newton on Trent 69
   Norton Fitzwarren 169
   Seatsides 120
   Sills Burn 127
   Swine Hill **16**, 130
   Troutbeck 44, 45, 48, 49, 50
clay
   in banks 45
   and defences 136
   and ramparts 38, 104
Clun, River 61, 63, 64
coal
   coal-pits 27, 75, **76**, 77, **78**, 79
   colliery tramway **101**, 103
Cocklakes Ridge (Cumbria) 32
Coesike (Northumberland) 10, 24, **90**, 90–1, **91**
   Coesike East 5, 90, 91
   Coesike West
      gate omitted 19
      site reuse 22
      camp 1 5, 90–1
      camp 2 5, 90, 91
construction/design 1, 2–3, 10–11, **11**, **12–13**, 14–17
cooking-pots 25, 88, 113
Coquet, River 85
Coquetdale 97
Corbridge
   fort (*Coria*) 96, 107
   Red House 25, 96, 181
Corsenside (Northumberland)
   Common 133
   parish 131
Corve, River 150
Cottonshope Burn (Northumberland) 16, 97
Cound Hall (Shropshire) 5, **158**, 158
Coundmoor Brook (Shropshire) 158
Crackenthorpe (Cumbria) 5, 34–6, **35**
   and adjacent road 9
   early survey of 1
   gates 18, 19
   later ploughing 27

   natural features at 22
   stream crossing 8
   topography 16
   traverse 20
Crawford, O G S **128**, **140**
Crooks (Northumberland) 5, 8, 19, **92**, 92
cropmarks
   and chronology 10
   and site identification 1, 3, 6, 24, 27
   camp layout 10
   evidence for defences 17
   gates 19, 20, 21
   site changes/reuse 23
   Ancaster 67
   Barrockside **30**, 30
   Beaumont 31
   Boomby Lane 31, 32
   Brackenrigg 32, 33, 34
   Brampton Bryan 61, 63
   Breckenbrough **136**, 136
   Brompton 154
   Brougham 34
   Buckton Park 64
   Burlington 156, 157
   Calverton 146, 147
   Carham 82
   Catterick 137
   Crackenthorpe 36
   East Learmouth 96
   Farnley 96
   Farnsfield 147
   Galley Gill 38
   Gleadthorpe Plantation 148, 149
   Greensforge 170, 173
   Higher Kingdon **53**, 53, **54**, 54
   Holme 149
   Horstead 70, 71
   Ismore Coppice 158
   Kirkby Thore 39
   Knockcross 40
   Knowe Farm 40
   Langwathby Moor 41
   Mindrum 181
   Moss Side 41
   Newton on Trent 69
   Norham 118
   North Tawton 54, 56
   Norton 159, **160–1**
   Norton Fitzwarren 169
   Nowtler Hill **2**
   Plumpton Head **19**, 43, 44
   Quatt 162
   Red House 181
   Stretford Bridge 162, 164
   Uffington 164
   Upper Affcot 165, 166
   Walford 65, 66
   Wall 175
   Warcop 51
   Watchclose 51
   Water Eaton 176, 177
   Wath 145
   Whittington 168
Cropton Forest (North Yorkshire) 137
Cumbria 5, 30–52
   see also individual camps

Dane, River 181
Dargues farm (Northumberland) 93, 94

Dargues (Northumberland) 5, 20, 92–5, **93**, **94**
   and adjacent road 9, 14
   camp design 10
   camp orientation 14
   gates 19
   use of steep ground 8
Darney Crag (Northumberland) 133
dating 21, 22, 24–6
   Birdhope 79
   Cawthorn 140, 142
   Chew Green 88, 89, 90
   Haltwhistle Burn 107
   Lees Hall 111
   Moss Side 42
   radiocarbon: Galley Gill 38
   Silloans 125
Dawley Brook (Staffordshire) 170
de Bathe Cross (Devon) 54
dead ground 7, 8
   Bowes Moor 57
   Brougham 34
   Crooks 92
   Featherwood West 97
   Sills Burn North 127
   Sunny Rigg 129
   Troutbeck 49
   West Woodburn 133
Deep Dale 58
defences
   and camp design/planning 9, 10, 15
   construction 17–18
   frontier 25
   gates 20–1
   later use of 26–7
   permanent and temporary 24
   ploughing 27
   practice camps 24
   topography 7–8, 16–17
   Bellshiel 75
   Birdhope 77
   Bootham Stray 135–6
   Bromfield 153
   Brompton 154
   Buckton Park 64
   Cawthorn **18**, 138–40, 141–2
   Chew Green 86, 88–9
   Coesike 90–1
   Crackenthorpe 36
   Fell End 100, 102–3
   Glenwhelt Leazes 103–4
   Haltwhistle Burn 107, 110
   Lees Hall 110–11
   Malham 143, 144
   Milestone House 117
   Newton on Trent **68**, 69
   North Yardhope 119
   Plumpton Head 44
   Rey Cross 57–9, 60
   Silloans 123, 125
   Sills Burn 125, 127
   Stretford Bridge 164
   Swine Hill 130
   Troutbeck 48–9, 50
   Twice Brewed 131
   Willowford 52
   Wroxeter (*Viroconium*) 159, **160–1**
   see also banks; ditches; gates; outworks

Dere Street 14, 20, 25
　camp survivals along 6
　influence on camp design 16
　at Bagraw 72
　at Bellshiel 75
　at Birdhope 77, 79
　at Breckenbrough/Catterick 136, 137
　at Cappuck (Roxburgh) 88
　at Chew Green 85, 86, 88, **89**, 89, 90
　at Dargues 93, 95
　at Farnley 96
　at Featherwood East/West 97, 100
　at High Rochester 120
　at Sandforth Moor 60
　at Silloans 123, 125
　at Sills Burn camps 125, 127
　at Swine Hill **16**, 130
　at West Woodburn 133
Derwent Water (Cumbria) 45
design *see* construction
Devil's Causeway 120
Devon 5, 6, 25, 53–6
　see also Higher Kingdon; North Tawton
Diana Hill (North Yorkshire) 145
distribution, of camps 3, **4–7**, 6, 11, **62**
ditches 17, 18, 24
　camp size 10
　claviculae 20
　construction 1, 17
　defences 16, 17
　drainage systems 26–7
　gates 19
　survival of 3
　Bootham Stray 135
　Brackenrigg 33
　Bromfield 152, 153
　Brompton 9
　Burnhead 80, 81
　Cawthorn **18**
　Coesike 91
　Crooks 92
　Dargues 94, 95
　Featherwood West 100
　Fell End 100–1
　Galley Gill 38
　Higher Kingdon **53–4**, 53, 54
　Kirkby Thore 39
　Malham 145
　Milestone House 117
　Nowtler Hill 43
　Plumpton Head **19**
　Rey Cross 58
　Seatsides 120, 122
　Troutbeck 45
　see also traverses
Dorket Head, Arnold (Nottinghamshire) 146
Dover Beck, valley of 146, 147
drainage 54, 65, 86
　lack of 8, 77, 84
　modern 34, 38, 41, 50, 51, 52, 79, **92**, 92, 97, **98–9**, 100, 107, **124**, 125, 127, 128, 129, 136, 164
　natural 66
　and natural erosion 38
　and site damage 19, 111, 119
　see also ditches
Droitwich 64
　Salinae 174

drought 67, 70, 150, 152, 164
drystone walls 80, 120, 131
Dunham on Trent 67
Dunstan Plantation (Northumberland) 82
Durham, County 5, 6, 57–60
　see also Bowes Moor; Rey Cross; Sandforth Moor

Eamont, River and valley 34, 41
earth
　in banks 1, 75, 80
　for defences 17
East Learmouth (Northumberland) 5, 15, **95**, 95–6
Eden, River 31, 39, 44
　and valley 8, 15, 34, 41, 43, 51, 57
Elleron Lake (North Yorkshire) 137
enclosures
　Brougham **34**, 34
　effect on earthworks 36
　fortified bridge-head 137
　of fortlet size 56
　Iron Age 71, 181
　medieval 86, 125
　native settlement 133
　post-Roman **33**, 33–4
　prehistoric **53**, 164
　for stock 90
Ermine Street 67
Eskdale 31, 36
Ettrick and Lauderdale: Oakwood 17, 45
Exeter 54

Farnley 1, 2 and 3 (Northumberland) 5, 9, 14, **96**, 96
Farnley Grange (Northumberland) 96
Farnsfield (Nottinghamshire) 5, **147**, 147, 148
　defences 17, 18
　site of gate 19
Featherwood East (Northumberland) 5, 97, **98**
　camp layout 15
　and camp orientation 14
　dating 25
　gates 19
　later industrial use 27
　traverse 20
Featherwood West (Northumberland) 5, 97, **99**, 100
　and adjacent road 9
　camp design 10, 16
　and camp orientation 14
　classification 24
　dating 25
　and internal layout 22
　traverse 20
Fell End (Northumberland) 5, **26**, 100–3, **101**
　and adjacent road 9
　atypical features 15
　and camp reuse 23
　defences 15, 17
　effect of higher ground 8, 22
　gates 19
　later use of site 27
　as pre-Roman site 10
　and water supply 8
Fieldhead (Cumbria) 45

Firestone Sill (stone) 102
firewood, need for 7
Flavian period
　camp construction/use 17, 25, 38
　Lees Hall 111
　Low Learchild (fort) 120
　Moss Side 41
　Norton (fortress) 159
　Oakwood (Ettrick and Lauderdale) 45
　pottery 38, 88
　Rey Cross 60
　supply base 96
flooding
　avoidance of 7
　flood plains
　　River Petteril 43
　　River Tweed 8
Forden Gaer (fort) 154
forest *see* woodland
fortlets
　Haltwhistle Burn 107, **108**, **109**, 111, 118
　Throp (Northumberland) 92
　see also under Chew Green
fortresses
　and proximity of camps 10
　at Norton 159
　see also vexillation fortresses; Wroxeter; York
forts
　and camps 1, 3, 9, 10, 22, 24
　and outworks 111
　gates of 20
　ramparts of 58
　Ancaster 67
　Blakehope 72
　Bowes (*Lavatris*) 57, 59, 60
　Bowness-on-Solway (*Maia*) 40
　Brompton 10, 154
　Brough under Stainmore (*Verteris*) 51, 57, 59, 60
　Brougham (*Brocavum*) 34, 41, 44
　Buckton 10, **63**, 63, 64, 65
　Burgh-by-Sands (*Aballava*) 31
　Carvoran (*Magnis*) 100, 101, 103, 104
　Corbridge (*Coria*) 96, 107
　Forden Gaer 154
　Great Chesters (*Aesica*) 25, 80, 85, 113
　High Rochester (*Bremenium*) 25, 72, 75, 77, 79, 97, 119–20, 123, 125, 127
　Housesteads (*Vercovicium*) 104
　Kirkby Thore (*Bravoniacum*) 34, 39
　Leintwardine (*Bravonium*) 61, 65
　Low Learchild (?*Alauna*) 120
　Newstead 88
　North Tawton 10, 54, **55**, 56
　Old Penrith (*Voreda*) 30, 36, **37**, 38, 40, 43, 44
　Pentrehyling 9, 25, 154
　Piercebridge 60
　Risingham (*Habitancum*) 130, 133
　Shurnock 64
　Stretford Bridge (Shropshire) 9, 10, 162, **163**
　Stretton Mill (Staffordshire) 25, 175, 177, **178**
　Troutbeck 44, **45**, 45, **48**, **49**, 50
　Vindolanda 11, 106, 120
　Water Eaton 10, 175, 177, **178–9**, 180
　Wiveliscombe 169

see also Cawthorn; Chew Green;
   Greensforge; Wall 1 and 2
   (Staffordshire); Wroxeter
Foss Way 149
Foulplay Head (Northumberland) 16, 97
Four Laws see Swine Hill
Frettenham (Norfolk) 71

Galley Gill (Cumbria) 5, 36–8, **37**, 40
   and access to water 8
   defences 17, 18
   later usage of site 26
   pits and post–holes 22
   pottery 25
   site of gate 19
Gammaton Moor (Devon) 53
Garret Shiels (Northumberland) 92–3
gates 18–20
   and internal layout 22
   and later roads 26
   dating 21, 25
   defences 20–1
   identification of 27
   positioning 7, 15, 22
   'Stracathro-type' 20
   types 20, 24
   and camp orientation 14
   and camp reuse 23
   Chapel Rigg 83, 84
   Chew Green 89
   Featherwood West 100
   Glenwhelt Leazes 104
   Lees Hall 111
   North Tawton 54
   Rey Cross 58, 60
   Seatsides 120, 122
   Sills Burn North 127
   Troutbeck 45
   Walford 65–6
   see also claviculae, traverses
Gates, Tim 181
Gaylock Sike (Cumbria) 36
Geary, G: survey **128**
Gleadthorpe Plantation (Nottinghamshire)
   5, **148**, 148–9
Glenderamackin, River 45
Glenlochar, Castle Douglas (Stewartry) 41
Glenwhelt Leazes (Northumberland) 5,
   102, **103**, 103–4
   and camp orientation 14
   claviculae/traverses 20, 21
   dating 25
   earlier trackway 10
Gloucester (Glevum) 165
Golden Fleece (Cumbria) 5, **38**, 38
   and camp orientation 14
   gates 19
   use of higher ground 8
Gordale Beck, valley of 143, **144**
grain 22, 38
grassland 80, 100, 117, 143, 144
Great Chesters (Aesica): fort 25, 80, 85, 113
Greathill Beck (Cumbria) 31
Greenlee Lough (Northumberland) 5, **14**,
   104, **105**
   and camp orientation 14
   clavicula 20
   defences 17, 18
   as pre-Roman site 10

Greensforge (Staffordshire) 5, 170–3, 174,
   175
   annexe 170, **173**
   camp 1 170, **172**, **173**
   camp 2 170, **172**, **173**
   camp 3 9, 170, **172**
   camp 4 170, **171**, 173
   camp 5 7, 170, **171**, 173
   forts 9, 10, 170, **172**, **173**, 173
Greta, River 57
   and valley 8, **9**, 58
Grey Havens (Knockcross, Cumbria) 40
Greystone (boulder) 52
Grindon Hill (Northumberland) 5, **106**,
   106
   camp surveying 15
   function 24
Grindon School (Northumberland) 5, **106**,
   106–7
   camp design 10
   function 24
Grinsdale Common (Cumbria) **2**
Grinsdale village (Cumbria) 42
gromae 15

Hadrian, Emperor 25
Hadrian's Wall
   and labour camps 23–4
   and pastoral farming 3
   camps adjacent 3, **5–7**, 6, 7, 8, 10, 14, 26
   military activity around 25
   study of 1
   at Boomby Lane 31, 32
   at Brackenrigg 32
   at Brown Dikes 79
   at Burnhead 80, **81**
   at Chapel Rigg 83
   at Coesike 90, 91
   at Crooks 92
   at Fell End 100
   at Haltwhistle Burn 107, **108**, 110
   at Knockcross 40
   at Lees Hall 111
   at Limestone Corner 111, **112**
   at Nowtler Hill 43
   at Seatsides 120
   at Sunny Rigg 127
   at Watchclose 51
   at Willowford 51
   Milecastles
      29   132
      42   **83**, **109**
      61   41
      71   31
   Turret 48b 51
Haltwhistle Burn (Northumberland) 5,
   107–10, **108**, **109**, 113, **115**, 115
   camp orientation 11
   labour camps 24
   as pre-Roman site 10
   fortlet 107, **108**, **109**, 111, 118
   camp 1   117
      and camp orientation 14
      construction of defences 17
      gates 19
      later use of site 26
      traverse 20
   camp 2
      camp design 10

external ditch 17
site reuse 23
traverse 21
camp 3   107, 109, 110
   site reuse 23
camp 4   110
   dating 25
   function 24
   gates 18
Haltwhistle Common (Northumberland)
   111, 113
Haltwhistle Golf Course **103**, 103, 104
Harelaw Cleugh (Northumberland) 125
Harnage (Shropshire) 158
headquarters, camp 14, 21, 111
hedgerows
   and defences 27
   Boomby Lane 32
   Bootham Stray 135
   Brompton 154
   Crackenthorpe 36
   Glenwhelt Leazes 103
   Holme 149
   Horstead 70
   Markham Cottage 113
   Nowtler Hill 43
   Seatsides 122
   Stretford Bridge 164
   Walford 66
   Water Eaton **180**
   Wath 145
Hereford and Worcester 5, 61–6, **62**
   see also individual camps
High Rochester (Bremenium): fort 25, 72,
   75, 77, 79, 97, 119–20, 123, 125, 127
High Stony Bank (North Yorkshire) 143
Higher Kingdon (Devon) 5, **53–4**, 53–4
   camp layout 15
   use of higher ground 8
hillforts
   sites of 7
   Brandon Camp (Iron Age) 65
   Greenlee Lough 104, **105**
Hodgson, John 42
Holme (Nottinghamshire) 5, **148**, 149
   and river crossing 8
   topography 16
Holystone (Northumberland) 125
Horsley, John 1, 27, 51, 80
Horstead (Norfolk) 5, **70**, 70–1
   cropmarks 10
   gates 18
   later use 26, 27
Housesteads (Vercovicium): fort 104
Howardian Hills (North Yorkshire) 145
Hyginus Gromaticus 8, 20, 22
   De munitionibus castrorum 2
   camp surveying 15
   and traverses 20–1
   and use of claviculae 21

industry
   iron–working 152, 153
   ironstone mining 107
   and site use 27, 75, 154
   see also coal
Inkberrow see Shurnock
Iron Age
   enclosures 71, 181

hillfort: Brandon Camp 65
   pottery 147
   sites 146, 153, 162, 168
iron-working 152, 153
ironstone mining, 19th century 107
Irthing, River 51
Ismore Coppice (Shropshire) 5, **151**, 158

Jenkins Burn (Northumberland) 104
Jewish revolt (AD 66–70) 2
Josephus: on Jewish revolt 2
Jugurthine wars (Numidia) 2

Keswick (Cumbria) 44
Kinvaston (Staffordshire)
   vexillation fortress 10, 175, 176, **179**
   see also Water Eaton
Kirkby Thore 1, 2 and 3 (Cumbria) 5, **39**, 39
   and access to water 8
   Bravoniacum (fort) 34, 39
   camp orientation 11
   and camp surveying 15
   choice of site 10
   site reuse 22
Knockcross (Cumbria) 5, 32, **40**, 40
   and camp orientation 14
   use of steep ground 8
Knowe Farm (Cumbria) 5, 36, **37**, **40**, 40–1
Kyloe Knowe (Northumberland) 97

labour camps 2, 23–4, 64
Langford (Nottinghamshire) 149
Langwathby Moor (Cumbria) 5, **41**, 41
latrines 22
leather: tents 1
Leeming Lane (North Yorkshire) 137
Lees Hall (Northumberland) 5, **110**, 110–11
   access to water 8, 22
   camp design 10
   and camp orientation 14
   and camp reuse 23
   clavicula 20
   defences 19, 24, 25
   topography 7, 16, 17
Leintwardine (*Bravonium*) 162
   fort 61, 65
Letocetum (Wall): posting-station 175, **177**
Liddesdale 31
limekilns 27, 81, 118
limestone 104, 117, 118, 145
   quarrying 27, 58, 81
   ridge 67
Limestone Corner (Northumberland) 5, 111–13, **112**
   and camp surveying 15
   dating 25
   ditch 17
   gate defence 20
   later usage of site 26, 112
   pottery 25
Lincolnshire 5, 67–9
   see also Ancaster; Newton on Trent
Lisles Burn valley (Northumberland) 133
Lizard Hill (Shropshire) 156
Llandrindod (Wales): function of camps 24
Loan Edge (Northumberland) 97
Lofshaw Hill (Cumbria) 44, 48, 49

Long Marton (Cumbria) 36
Longland Lane (Nottinghamshire) 147
Longtae Burn (Northumberland) 119
Low Hesket (Cumbria) 30
Low Learchild (?*Alauna*): fort 120
Low Stony Bank (North Yorkshire) 143
Lower Swaledale 136
Lowther, River 34
lynchets 50, 111
Lysons, Daniel 42, 43
   and Samuel 1
   Magna Britannia (1816) **2**

MacLauchlan, Henry: surveys 1, **94**, 95, 130
Malham (North Yorkshire) 5, **143**, 143–5, **144**
   and camp orientation 14
   clavicula 20
   siting of 8
Manchester University 46
March Sike (Northumberland) 85, 86
marching camps 2, 118
Markham Cottage (Northumberland) 5, **109**, 113–15, **114**, **115**
   camp orientation 11
   site reuse 22, 27
   camp 1 27, 113, 115
      and adjacent road 9
      dating 25
   camp 2 113, 115
      use of higher ground 7
marshland see bog
Mastiles Lane (North Yorkshire) 144–5
mattocks 17
Meden, River 148
medieval period
   agriculture 26, 135
   castles 3
   enclosures 86, 125
   occupation 88, 125
   Portergate (road) 140, **141**
   Scots army 26, 82
Metchley 175
Middlewich (*Salinae*) 181
Milecastles see Hadrian's Wall
Milestone House (Northumberland) 5, 81, 102, **116**, 117–18
   and camp orientation 14
   later industrial use 27
   temporary nature of 24
   topography 8, 16–17, 22
military use
   medieval: of camps 26, 82
   modern
      of camps 158
      effects 97, 100
      Redesdale Camp (Northumberland) **23**, 77
      and trenches 75, **76**, 77
   see also airfields
Mindrum (Northumberland) 181
mole-drains **92**, 92, 136
mortarium 25, 88, 113
Moss Side (Cumbria) 5, 41–2, **42**, 51
   camp layout 17
   gates 18
   site reuse 23

Naddles Beck (Cumbria) 45

Naddles Crag (Cumbria) 49
Neolithic sites 153
Nero, Emperor, period of 159, 170
Newstead (Tweeddale) 88
Newton Cliff (Lincolnshire) 67
Newton on Trent 1 and 2 (Lincolnshire) 5, 24, 67–9, **68**
   clavicula 20
   vexillation fortress 10, 67, **68**, 69
Norfolk 5, 6, 25, 70–1
   see also Horstead
Norham (Northumberland) 5, **118**, 118
   and camp orientation 14
   gates 19
   use of steep ground 8
Norman chapel (Chew Green) 26, 90
North Tawton (Devon) 5, 24, 54–6, **55**
   camp 1 54, 56
   fort 10, 54, **55**, 56
North Yardhope (Northumberland) 5, **119**, 119–20
   camp design 10
   and camp orientation 14
   gates 19
   later agriculture **27**, 27
   traverse 21
North Yorkshire 5, 6, 135–45
   see also individual camps
Northumberland 5, 6, 72–134, 181
   see also individual camps
Norton Brook (Somerset) 169
Norton Fitzwarren (Somerset) 5, **169**, 169
   clavicula 20
Norton (Shropshire)
   camp 1 5, 26, 150, 158, 159, **160**
   camp 2 5, 159, **161**
Nottinghamshire 5, 146–9
   see also individual camps
Nowtler Hill (Cumbria) **2**, **42**, 42–3
   camp 1 5, 42–3
   camp 2 5, 18, 43

Oakwood (Ettrick and Lauderdale) 17, 45
observation post (Second World War) 69
Offa's Dyke 154
Old Penrith (*Voreda*): fort 30, 36, **37**, 38, 40, 43, 44
Old Police House see Knockcross
Onny, River 151, 162, 165
Osmanthorpe (Nottinghamshire): vexillation fortress 147
Oswestry (Shropshire) 166
Oundle School 46
outworks
   Greensforge (Staffordshire) 170
   Lees Hall 110, 111
ovens: Bromfield (Shropshire) 22
Oxford: Ashmolean Museum 88
Oxfordshire 6, 25, 181
Oxton Bogs (Nottinghamshire) 146

peat
   bogs 41, 58, 95
   growth of 3, 77, 79, 86, 88, 94, 100, 120
   layer of 57, 104
   masking defences 27, 125
Peat Steel (Northumberland) 113, 129
Peatsteel Crags (Northumberland) 103
Peel Cottage (West Woodburn) 133

Pember's Ditch (Hereford and Worcester) 64
Penk, River 175, 176
Penk Valley 175, 177, 180
Pennines 57
Pennocrucium (near Water Eaton): posting-station 175, **179**
Pentrehyling (fort) 9, 25, 154
Perry Farm, Whittington (Shropshire) 166, 167
Perry, River 166
Petteril, River 36, 40, 41
   and valley 30–1, 38, 43
Petty Knowes cemetery (Northumberland) 79
Piercebridge (fort) 60
Plumpton Head (Cumbria) 5, **19**, 43–4, **44**
   asymmetry of 43
   gates 19
   and internal layout 22
   later use of site 27
   topography 16
   traverse 20
Poltross Burn (Northumberland) 92
Portergate (medieval road) 140, **141**
posting-stations
   Letocetum (Wall) 175, **177**
   Pennocrucium (Water Eaton) 175, **179**
pottery
   4th century 22, 23, 58, 60
   19th century 58
   Black-Burnished Ware (BB1) 113
   coarse wares 88
   cooking-pots 25, 88, 113
   Dragendorff (33) 88
   Flavian period 88
   Flavian/Trajanic 38
   Galley Gill 25
   Limestone Corner 25
   mortarium 25, 88, 113
   Rey Cross 25, 58, 60
   Romano-British/Iron Age 147
   samian ware 25, 33, 88
Powburgh Beck valley (Cumbria) 31
Powis Cottage (Cumbria) 36
practice camps 2, 11, 23, 24, 84, 137
praetentura 95
prehistoric sites
   barrows 10, 22, 142, **153**, 153, 164
   cairns 10, 22, 75, **76**, 117
   and camp construction 10
   Cawthorn 142
   cord-rig cultivation 107, **108**, 110
   Greenlee Lough 104
   Higher Kingdon **53**, 54
   Milestone House 117
   Norham 118
   ring-ditches **153**, 153
   roundhouses 118
   standing stones 118
   stone circle **59**
   Swine Hill 131

quarrying
   limestone 27, 58, 81
   Ancaster 67
   Bromfield 151–2, **152**, 153
   Burlington 156, 157
   Burnhead 81

Cawfields **83**, **108**, **109**
Cawthorn 138
Featherwood East 97
Fell End **26**, 100, **101**, 101–2, 103
Gleadthorpe Plantation 149
Haltwhistle Burn 107
Malham 144
Milestone House **116**, 117, 118
Rey Cross **9**, 58, **59**, 60
Troutbeck 49, 50
Twice Brewed **132**
Walford 65
Walwick Fell 133
Water Eaton 177, 180
Quatt (Shropshire) 5, **162**, 162
Quinny Brook (Shropshire) 165

radiocarbon dating: Galley Gill 38
ramparts
   Bagraw 72
   Brown Dikes 79–80
   of clay 38, 104
   Coesike 90–1
   construction of 17
   Featherwood West 97
   of forts 58
   Galley Gill 38
   and gates 19, 20
   positioning of 16
   of practice camps 24
   stakes in 18
   and topography 7, 8, 16
   and traverses 20
   of turf 38, 86, 88, 104, 107, 128, 141
Rawcliff Banks (North Yorkshire) 137
Red House (Northumberland) 25, 96, 181
Rede, River 75, 77, 79, 125, 133
   and valley 72, 92
Redesdale Camp (Northumberland) **23**, 77
Redesdale (Northumberland) 10, 72, 77, 97, 130, 133
Redhill (near Oakengates) 174
Rey Cross (County Durham) 5, **9**, 57–60, **59**
   and adjacent road 9, 25
   camp design 10
   defences 8, 17, 20, 24, 36, 57–9, 60
   early survey of 1
   internal layout 22
   later industrial use 27
   pottery 25, 58, 60
   as pre-Roman site 10
   site reuse 22, 23
   topography 16
   traverse 20
Rhyn Park (vexillation fortress) 166
Richborough (Kent): early discovery 3
Richmond, I A 59, 86, 88, 137, 138–9, **140**, 140, 141, 142
ridge-and-furrow cultivation
   Attingham 150
   Bean Burn 74, 75
   Beaumont 27, 31
   Bellshiel 75, **76**, 77
   Burnhead 81
   Cawfields 82, **83**, 83
   Chesters Pike 85
   Coesike 91
   Dargues 94
   Fell End **26**, 101

Glenwhelt Leazes 103, 104
Greenlee Lough **14**, 104
Grindon Hill/School 106
Holme 149
Ismore Coppice 158
Knockcross 40
Lees Hall 111
Markham Cottage 27, **109**, 113, **115**, 115
Milestone House 117
Norton 159, **160–1**
Sandforth Moor 60
Seatsides 120, 122, **123**, 123
Sills Burn 125, 127
Stretford Bridge 162
Troutbeck 27, 48, 50
Twice Brewed 131
Uffington 27, 164
Wall (Staffordshire) 175
Walwick Fell 133
Water Eaton 176, **180**, 180
West Woodburn 133
Willowford 52
Ridlees (Northumberland) 97
Riley, Derrick 6
ring-ditches 54, 118
   prehistoric **153**, 153
Risingham (*Habitancum*): fort 130, 133
river-crossings 8, 9
roads
   Berghill Lane, Whittington 168
   Longland Lane (Nottinghamshire) 147
   Mastiles Lane (North Yorkshire) 144–5
   Military Road (B6318) 115
   Portergate (medieval) 140, **141**
   post-Roman 26
   Salt Way 64
   Whitehouse Lane, Swindon (Staffordshire) 174
   modern 19, 63, 75, 80–1, 97, 101, 103, 107, 146, 166
     A1 (North Yorkshire) 137
     A5 (Shropshire/Staffordshire) 159, 175
     A66 **9**, 36, 45, **49**, **57**, 57, 58, **59**
     A68 (Northumberland) 93, 95
     A489 (Shropshire) 154
     A695 (Northumberland) 96
     A696 (Northumberland) 72
     A3072 (Devon) 54
     B1354 (Norfolk) 70
     B4380 (Shropshire) 158
     B4385 (Shropshire) 154
     B4530 (Hereford and Worcester) 65–6
     B6275 (County Durham) 60
     B6318 (Northumberland) 90, 115, 117
   see also Roman roads
Roman roads 44, 119–20, 130, 151, 154, 165–6, 170, 174, 175, 181
   across Stainmore Pass 51
   and adjacent camps 36, 39, 40, 41, 43, 46, 48, **49**, 50
   at Crackenthorpe 34, 36
   and Barrockside 30
   and camp planning/construction 9, 10, 14, 16, 18, 22, 23, 25
   County Durham **57**, 57, 58, 60
   cropmarks alongside 6
   Devon 54, **55**
   Foss Way 149

Hereford and Worcester 64
internal camp 19, 22, 60
and line of A66 **57**, 57, 58
near Golden Fleece (Cumbria) 38
Rey Cross 60
Ryknield Street 175
see also Dere Street; Ermine Street; Stanegate; Watling Street
Romano-British period
  pottery 147
  settlement 162, 168
Rome: Trajan's Column 2
The Rossett (Brompton): barrow 154
Rothbury (Northumberland) 118
roundhouses, prehistoric 118
Roxburghshire (Scotland): Cappuck 88
Roy, William 27, 36, 58, 90
  as early surveyor 1
  Military Antiquities of the Romans in North Britain **ii**
rubbish pits 22
rubble
  and camp defence 44
  and ramparts 38
  use in banks 1
Ryknield Street 175

Sallust: on Jugurthine wars (Numidia) 2
Salt Way 64
Sandford see Warcop
Sandforth Moor (County Durham) 5, **60**, 60
sandstone 102, 104
Scandinavia: names 60
Scotland 31, 36, 41
  border of 85
  dating comparison in 25
  and Dere Street 6, 88, 136
  Ettrick and Lauderdale 17, 45
  medieval army of 26, 82
  Roman road to 57
  Roy's discoveries in 1
  'Stracathro-type' gateways 20
Scott, Walter: *The Antiquary* 1
Seatsides (Northumberland) 74, 118
  camp 1   5, 120, **121**, 122
    and adjacent road 9
    camp layout 15
    and camp orientation 14
    claviculae/traverses 21
    gates 19
    site reuse 23, 27
    use of higher ground 8
  camp 2   5, 120, **122**, 122–3, **123**, 131
    camp design 10
    and camp orientation 14
Settlingstones Burn (Northumberland) 106
Severn, River 23, 150, 158, 162, 164, 166
  valley 154
sheepfolds 104
shielings 26, 80, 104, **105**
Shropshire 5, 6, **62**, 150–68
  see also individual camps
Shurnock (Hereford and Worcester) 5, 8, **64**, 64–5
siegework 24
signal stations **57**, 57, 60, 90
Silloans (Northumberland) 5, 97, 123–5, **124**

and adjacent road 9, 25
camp design 10
camp size 11
and camp surveying 15
later use of site 27
topography 16
traverse 20
Sills Burn camps (Northumberland)
  and access to water 8
  clavicula 20
  North 5, 125–7, **126**
    and adjacent road 9
    camp layout 17
    and camp orientation 14
    gates 27
  South 5, **126**, 127
    and adjacent road 9, 25
    and camp orientation 14
    construction of defences 17
    gates 19
    proximity of road 14
    stream at 8, 22
Sills Burn (stream) 75, 77, 123
Simpson, F G **140**
Skiddaw (Cumbria) 45
Slough Dyke (Nottinghamshire) 149
Smestow Brook (Staffordshire) 170, 173, 174
Solway Firth 32, 40
Somerset 5, 25, 169
  see also Norton Fitzwarren
Southhope Burn (Northumberland) 97
'sow kilns' 27, 118
Spaunton Moor (North Yorkshire) 137
Spittle Brook, valley of (Staffordshire) 173
Staffordshire 5, 6, 170–80
  see also individual camps
Stainmore Pass 8, 10, 15, 22, 36, 51, 57
stakes
  evidence for 17
  in ramparts 18
  stake-holes 22
standing stones, 'Mare and Foal' 118
Stanegate
  Chapel Rigg 83
  Crooks 92
  Fell End 8, **26**, 100, 101
  Glenwhelt Leazes **103**, 103, 104
  Grindon Hill **106**, 106
  Haltwhistle Burn 107, **109**
  Lees Hall 25, 111
  Markham Cottage 25, 113
  Milestone House 118
  Moss Side 41
  Seatsides 120
  Sunny Rigg 127, 128, 129
  Watchclose 51
Steadfolds see Watchclose
Steel Rigg (Northumberland) 111
Stiddlehill (Northumberland) 133
stone
  in banks 58, 75, 77, 80, 133
  and boundaries 60, 75, 125
  circles 10, **59**, 60
  and defences 38, 44, 64
  drystone walls 80, 120, 131
  for earthworks 17
  Firestone Sill 102
  and gates 19–20

Greystone 52
  remains 95, 112, 113
  sandstone 102, 104
  standing stones 118
  see also quarrying
stores, camp 21, 22
Stour, River 173
'Stracathro-type' gateways 20
Stretford Bridge (Shropshire) 10, 162, **163**, 164
  camp 1   5, 9, 10, 162, 164
  camp 2   5, 162, 164
  fort 9, 10, 162, **163**
Stretton Mill (Staffordshire)
  fort 25, 175, 177, **178**
  see also Water Eaton
Sunny Rigg (Northumberland)
  water supply 8
  camp 1   5, 127–8, **128**
    design 10
    and orientation 14
    construction of defences 17
  camp 2   5, 127, 128–9, **129**
  camp 3   5, **129**, 129
    and camp surveying 15
    function 24
    gates 18
surveying, of camps 7, 15–16
Sutherland Beck (North Yorkshire) 137
Swale, River 136
Swindon (Staffordshire) 5, 173, **174**, 174–5
  atypical features 15
  camp design 10
  defences 18
Swine Hill (Northumberland)
  as pre-Roman site 10
  camp surveying 15
  claviculae/traverses 20, 21
  site reuse 22, 27
  use of steep ground 8
  camp 1   5, 14, **16**, **130**, 130, 131
  camp 2   5, **16**, **130**, 130–1

Tate, Robert 86
Taw, River 54, 56
Teesdale 57
Teme, River 61, 63, 64, 150–1
  valley 65
tents 1
  as barracks 21–2, 142
  erection of 10, 16, 36, 120, 148
  and practice camps 24
  tent-lines 19
Tern, River 150
  and valley 159
Thames Valley: lack of camps 6
Thirlmoor (Northumberland) 77
Thirlwall Common (Northumberland) 92
Throp (Northumberland): fortlet 92
timber
  buildings 19, 24, 64, 90, 131, 181
  burnt 88
  defences 141
Tipalt Burn (Northumberland) 83, 103, 104
Titmuss, J E: survey **129**, 129
titulum see traverses
Tone, River 169
tools: for constructing earthworks 17

topography 16–17, 26
   camp construction 3
   camp gates 19
   camp planning 15
   camp position 22
   choice of site 7–8, 9, 10, 26
   and gates 18
   military use of 27
Torridge valley (Devon) 53
towers, timber 19
Trajanic period 38
Trajan's Column (Rome) 2
traverses
   and camp chronology 21
   and defence 19, 20–1
   lack of (Farnley) 96
   Bagraw 72
   Barrockside 31
   Bean Burn 74
   Beaumont 31
   Bellshiel 77
   Birdhope 79
   Boomby Lane 31
   Brackenrigg 32
   Brampton Bryan 63
   Breckenbrough 136
   Brougham **34**, 34
   Brown Dikes 80
   Burlington 157
   Burnhead 80–1
   Calverton 147
   Carham 82
   Catterick 137
   Cawfields **83**, 83
   Cawthorn 25, 142
   Chapel Rigg **21**, 84
   Chesters Pike 85
   Chew Green 86, 88, 89
   Coesike 91
   Crackenthorpe 36
   Crooks **92**, 92
   East Learmouth 95
   Farnsfield 147
   Featherwood East 97
   Featherwood West 100
   Fell End 100–1
   Glenwhelt Leazes 103, 104
   Golden Fleece 38
   Grindon Hill 106
   Grindon School 107
   Haltwhistle Burn 107, 109, 110
   Kirkby Thore 39
   Knockcross 40
   Knowe Farm 41
   Langwathby Moor 41
   Limestone Corner 111–12
   Markham Cottage 113, 115
   Milestone House 117
   Mindrum 181
   Moss Side 41
   Norham 118
   North Yardhope 119
   Nowtler Hill 43
   Plumpton Head **19**, 43
   Red House 181
   Rey Cross **9**, 58
   Seatsides 120, 122
   Silloans 125
   Sunny Rigg 127–8, 129
   Swine Hill 131
   Troutbeck 27
   Twice Brewed 131
   Wall 175
   Walwick Fell 133
   Warcop 51
   Watchclose 51
   Water Eaton 177
   West Woodburn 133
   Willowford 51, 52
Trent, River 8, 67, 146, 149
Trout Beck (Cumbria) 36, 45
Troutbeck (Cumbria) 5, 44–50, **45**
   claviculae 44
   camp 1 45–6, **46**, 49
      and adjacent road 9
      claviculae 20
      construction of defences 17
      site of gate 19
   camp 2 45, 46, **47**, 48–50
      and adjacent road 9
      and camp orientation 14
      claviculae 20, 48, 49, 50
      dating 25
      defences 15, 17, 48–9, 50
      gates 18
      later ridge-and-furrow ploughing 27
      later site usage 26–7
      topography 16
   camp 3 **48**, **49**, 50
      claviculae 20, 50
      dating 25
      defences 17
   fort 44, **45**, 45, **48**, **49**, 50
trysting–place: Chew Green 26, 90
Tungrians, First Cohort of 11
turf
   and banks 1, 3, 45, 57, 79, 80, 127, 138, 139, 140, 147
   and camp remains 112, 113
   and Chew Green defences 86, 88
   and *claviculae* 20
   in defences **18**, 153
   for earthworks 17
   ramparts of 38, 86, 88, 104, 107, 128, 141
   structures 110, 142
   and traverses 20
   walls 52, 145
turnpikes 36
Turret 48b (Cumbria), 51
tutulus see traverses
Tweed, River 8, 95, 118
Tweeddale 82, 88
Twice Brewed (Northumberland) 5, **123**, 131, **132**
   later use of site 26
   site of gate 19
Tyne, River 96
   South Tyne valley 111
Tynedale 90
   North Tynedale 77, 111, 130

Uckington (Shropshire): former airfield 150, 158
Uffington (Shropshire) 5, 164, **165**
   camp size 11
   later agriculture 27
   site changes 23

Upper Affcot (Shropshire) 5, 162, 165–6, **166**
   defences 18
   later use of site 27

Vale House 57
Vale of Pickering (North Yorkshire) 137, 145
Vale of York: lack of camps 6
Vallum
   Boomby Lane 31
   Cawfields **83**
   Coesike 90
   Glenwhelt Leazes **103**, 103
   Grindon School 106
   Haltwhistle Burn 107, **109**, 110
   Limestone Corner 111, **112**
   Markham Cottage 113
   Moss Side 41
   Nowtler Hill 43
   Seatsides 120
   Twice Brewed 131
vegetation 80, 119
   and camp construction 3
   Chapel Rigg 84
   Dargues 94
   see also grassland; hedgerows; woodland
Vegetius
   Epitoma Rei Militaris 2
   on camp construction 3, 22, 25
   and camp defence 18
   camp design 10
   and earthworks 17
vexillation fortresses
   temporary nature of 2
   Kinvaston (Water Eaton, Staffordshire) 10, 175, 176, **179**
   Newton on Trent 10, 67, **68**, 69
   Osmanthorpe (Nottinghamshire) 147
   Red House (Corbridge) 25, 96, 181
   Rhyn Park 166
   Wall (Staffordshire) 175
vicus
   at Brompton 154
   at Galley Gill (Cumbria) 38
Vindolanda (Northumberland) 11, 106, 120

Walford (Hereford and Worcester) 5, **65**, 65–6
   defences 15
   gates 18, 19
   later use of site 27
   topography 16
Wall 1 and 2 (Staffordshire) 5, 175, **176–7**
   forts 10, 175, **176–7**
Wall (Walltown) Mill (Northumberland) 113, **115**
Walltown (Northumberland) 111
Walwick Fell (Northumberland) 5, 132–3, **133**
   camp design 10
   and camp surveying 15
Warcop (Cumbria) 5, 15–16, **50**, 50–1
Wardoughan 92
Wards Hill, Rothbury (Northumberland) 118
Warsop *see* Gleadthorpe Plantation
The Wash 67

watch-posts **57**, 57, 90
Watchclose (Cumbria) 5, 41, **51**, 51, 80
   and camp planning 15
   early discovery 1
   gate omitted 19
   survival of site 27
Watchcross *see* Watchclose
water, access to 7, 8, 10, 14
Water Eaton (Staffordshire) 5, 156, 170, 175–80, **178–9**
   camp 1   176, 177, **180**
   camp 2   177
   camp 3   25, 177, 180
   camp 4   8, 180
   camp 5   8, 180
   forts 10, 175, 177, **178–9**, 180
   vexillation fortress 10, 175, 176, **179**
watermills 113
Wath Beck (North Yorkshire) 145
Wath (North Yorkshire) 5, 8, **145**, 145
Watling Street 156, **157**, 157, 162, 164, 170, 175, 177
wattle and daub 88
weather: factor in camp construction 3

West Woodburn (Northumberland) 5, 15, 17, 133, **134**
Weston under Penyard (*Ariconium*) 151, 165
Whin Sill (Northumberland) 103
White Moss (Cumbria) 41
Whitehouse Lane, Swindon (Staffordshire) 174
Whittington (Shropshire) 5, 166–8, **167**
   and camp surveying 15
   defences 8, 15, 18
   later use of site 26
   topography 16
Willowford (Cumbria) 5, 51–2, **52**
   and camp planning 15
   gate omitted 19
   later use of site 27
   use of higher ground 7
Windrush, the 181
Winshields (Northumberland) 111
Wiske, River 136
Wiveliscombe (Somerset): fort 169
Wolverhampton 170
Wombourne (Staffordshire) 174

woodland/forestry
   need to avoid 7
   Cawfields 83
   Cawthorn 137, **140**, **141**
   Cropton Forest (North Yorkshire) 137
   Dunstan Plantation (Northumberland) 82
   Gleadthorpe Plantation (Nottinghamshire) **148**, 148–9
   Horstead 71
   Walwick Fell 132–3, **133**
   Wath Wood (North Yorkshire) 145
Worfe, River 156
writing-tablets 11
Wroxeter (*Viroconium*) 159, **160–1**, 162, 165, 174
   fortress and town 25, 150, 151, 175
   modern town 158
   and proximity of fort 10
   sites in area of 24, **150**, 164

York (*Eburacum*) 39, 41, 43, 51, 57, 136
   and Dere Street 6
   fortress 10, 24, 135